THE WRITER'S PERSPECTIVE

Theme for English B

The instructor said,

> Go home and write
> a page tonight.
> And let that page come out of you—
> Then, it will be true.

I wonder if it's that simple?
I am twenty-two, colored, born in Winston-Salem.
I went to school there, then Durham, then here
to this college on the hill above Harlem.
I am the only colored student in my class.

The steps from the hill lead down into Harlem,
through a park, then I cross St. Nicholas,
Eighth Avenue, Seventh, and I come to the Y,
the Harlem Branch Y, where I take the elevator
up to my room, sit down, and write this page:

It's not easy to know what is true for you or me
at twenty-two, my age. But I guess I'm what
I feel and see and hear, Harlem, I hear you:
hear you, hear me—we two—you, me, talk on this page.
(I hear New York, too.) Me—who?

Well, I like to eat, sleep, drink, and be in love.
I like to work, read, learn, and understand life.
I like a pipe for a Christmas present,
or records—Bessie, bop, or Bach.
I guess being colored doesn't make me *not* like
the same things other folks like who are other races.
So will my page be colored that I write?
Being me, it will not be white.
But it will be
a part of you, instructor.
You are white—
yet a part of me, as I am a part of you.
That's American.
Sometimes perhaps you don't want to be a part of me.
Nor do I often want to be a part of you.
But we are, that's true!
As I learn from you,
I guess you learn from me—
although you're older—and white—
and somewhat more free.

This is my page for English B.

Langston Hughes
(1902–1967)

"Theme for English B" by Langston Hughes from *Montage of a Dream Deferred*, Henry Holt, 1951. Copyright © 1951 by Langston Hughes, renewed 1979 by George Houston Bass. Reprinted by permission of Harold Ober Associates Incorporated.

THE WRITER'S PERSPECTIVE
Voices from American Cultures

Maria Cecilia Freeman

University of California, Santa Cruz

PRENTICE HALL
Englewood Cliffs, New Jersey 07632

Library of Congress Cataloging-in-Publication Data

The Writer's Perspective: voices from American cultures/|compiled
by| Maria Cecilia Freeman.
   p.   cm.
  Includes index.
  ISBN 0-13-948308-X
   1. College readers. 2. English language—Rhetoric. 3. Ethnic
groups—United States—Problems, exercises, etc. 4. Ethnology—
United States—Problems, exercises, etc. 5. Culture—Problems,
exercises, etc. I. Freeman, Maria Cecilia, (date)
PE1417.W667 1994
808'.0427—dc20   93-3518
                                        CIP

© 1994 by Prentice-Hall, Inc.
A Simon & Schuster Company
Englewood Cliffs, New Jersey 07632

Acquistions Editor: Alison Reeves
Editorial Assistant: Kara Hado
Copy Editor: Nikki Herbst
Cover: Illustration by Seymour Chwast
Cover Design: Design Solutions
Prepress Buyer: Herb Klein
Manufacturing Buyer: Bob Anderson

Printed in the United States of America
10 9 8 7 6 5 4 3 2 1

ISBN   0-13-948308-X

Prentice-Hall International (UK) Limited, *London*
Prentice-Hall of Australia Pty. Limited, *Sydney*
Prentice-Hall Canada Inc., *Toronto*
Prentice-Hall Hispanoamericana, S.A., *Mexico*
Prentice-Hall of India Private Limited, *New Delhi*
Prentice-Hall of Japan, Inc., *Tokyo*
Simon & Schuster Asia Pte. Ltd., *Singapore*
Editora Prentice-Hall do Brasil, Ltda., *Rio de Janeiro*

This book is dedicated to my parents.

Contents

_____ II   IDENTITY AND COMMUNITY

_____ **III**   OTHER GENERATIONS AND
           TRADITIONS

_____ **IV**   A SENSE OF TIME AND PLACE

_____ V   WRITING AND SOCIAL CHANGE

_____ TOPICS FOR WRITING

_____ AUTHOR AND TITLE INDEX

Rhetorical Table of Contents

I PERSONAL WRITING

The essays in this group are narrative and descriptive, intended primarily to share a perspective on experience or reflect upon a matter of personal significance.

II EXPOSITORY WRITING

While the essays in this group draw upon the writers' experiences, they function primarily to inform and to explain the authors' points of view; they are more critical and analytical than purely personal essays.

III   PERSUASIVE WRITING

Most of the essays in this group are not formal arguments, yet their main purpose is to persuade the reader of the writers' opinions on sensitive or controversial issues, and in some cases to bring about action.

IV   SHORT FICTION

This group includes short stories and excerpts from novels. Although they are closely based on the authors' experience, they are presented as fiction.

Preface

This book is a collection of essays and short fiction by outstanding writers representing various cultures of modern American (U.S.) society. Two intersecting themes run through the book. First, many of the selections are about writing, directly or indirectly. Readers will see that people like themselves become writers, for reasons that they will recognize. Second, the selections in the book illuminate the diversity of American culture and social experience, by letting readers share the perspectives of writers from a range of different American cultures.

These two themes are naturally connected. The writers included in this book write for many reasons, but often it is to establish or confirm identity, to recognize the richness of tradition, to preserve heritage, to chronicle change and loss, to illuminate conflicts, and to fight injustice from a perspective of race, culture, gender, or social class. They talk about these issues when they talk about their writing. By the same token, we can be readers of literature and students of writing at the same time.

The authors included in this collection have made important contributions to modern American literature, and their writing will stand the test of time. Some are already recognized; others have just recently begun to attract the attention they deserve. Familiarity with their work will enhance any reader's sense of our culture and our literature.

These writers' lives span most of the twentieth century, and their writing is influenced by the historical events and social concerns that have shaped their lives. In their writing they draw upon family and cultural heritage, oral traditions, places they know, and political circumstance. They write for different reasons and with different styles, but they all underscore the validity of personal and collective experience as a basis for writing; and because their experience is so diverse, their writing communicates a sense of the diversity of perspectives in the multinational society we live in. "The world is here," says Ishmael Reed.

Many of the selections in this book have not been anthologized before; here is a fresh opportunity to become acquainted with a range of our literature that has so far been available only through small presses and journals. The readings include both stories and essays. Many, in fact, straddle the line between the two, blurring the distinction between fiction and nonfiction. Some are long; some are short. Some are easy and fun to read, while others are more challenging and reflective. Many will spark recognition; some will arouse sympathy, and some might even be troubling.

The readings are organized in five topical sections, developing the themes of the book. Section I, "On Being a Writer," and Section V, "Writing and Social Change," are linked in title and concept, forming a framework for the three middle sections. The readings in Section I reveal some of the ways writers approach their writing—what motivates them, how they got started, what is important to them as writers. The ideas expressed in this section are illustrated in later passages throughout the book. The readings in Section II explore concepts of personal and collective identity, as they are shaped by national origin, ethnicity, gender, social class, and common experience within a community. In Section III the readings treat relationships with older generations—parents, ancestors, and elders of the community. They also reveal the significance of stories passed down as lessons or as part of a community's oral tradition. The readings in Section IV evoke a sense of time and place; writers convey their perspectives on the history of a place, the natural environment, social change and loss, or just the quality of everyday life in a particular time and place. Section V turns to the ways writing contributes to social change. Essays in this section address the topic directly and encourage readers to do the same; fiction selections illustrate other ways writers address social and political issues through their writing. Many of the writers in the book are represented in more than one section, to reflect their perspectives on different topics.

Because it is useful to have a bit of knowledge about an author's life as background for reading his or her work, the introductory section "About the Authors" provides a brief biographical sketch for each writer whose work is represented in the book. In each case there is mention of other work; the anthology will be a success if it leads readers to acquaint themselves further with the writing of some of these authors.

At the end of each reading is a set of comments and questions entitled "Response." Most of the questions are not ones that can be answered at a glance; they are intended to lead the reader back to a close examination of the text and in so doing to enhance understanding and clarify the author's purpose. Many invite interpretation of the author's words and intent, and have no right answer. Others elicit an association or opinion from the reader's experience and other reading. The questions are designed not to check comprehension, but to guide analysis and interpretation. They might serve as the basis for discussion, group work, or short writing in or outside of class.

At the end of the book are a number of suggested topics for longer writing. Some topics invite the student to use a reading passage as a prompt for a personal essay, exploring subject matter related to the content of the reading. Other topics call for some sort of analysis of the reading and a critical response based upon experience and observation. Many of these topics tie together more than one reading and suggest comparisons or synthesis of ideas. Still other topics invite students to do some research into the historical, social, or political context in which an author wrote.

There are many connections to be drawn among the readings in this book, beyond the organizing themes and suggested topics. The book can be used in a variety of ways according to the purpose and plan of a class. It lends itself to a syllabus organized thematically, as well as to a syllabus that moves from personal to expository and argumentative writing. The contents can also be considered author by author, and, when appropriate, they can be studied in terms of ethnic and regional representation or historical development. The Instructor's Manual for this book suggests different options for organizing the material in a course and suggests class activities related to using the text.

Returning to New York in 1959 after a number of years living in Paris, James Baldwin wrote, "That the tensions of American life, as well as the possibilities, are tremendous is certainly not even a question. . . .The time has come, God knows, for us to examine ourselves, but we can only do this if we are willing to free ourselves of the myth of America and try to find out what is really happening here." I hope that any reader of this book will find that it adds to her or his sense of what is really happening here, that it stimulates questions and leads to further reading. Even more important, I hope the book will lead readers to recognize themselves as participants in both the tensions and the possibilities and maybe to write about it.

I welcome the opportunity to thank those who contributed, directly and indirectly, to this project. I am truly indebted to my friends and colleagues at the University of California for their encouragement, advice, and good ideas. In particular I want to thank June McKay, Susan Rosa, and Helen Fragiadakis for their consistent support and substantive contributions. I thank Don Larkin for helping me in every way to complete this book. I thank Tom, Sim, and Melina for their good influence and cooperation. I thank two writers, Christopher Russell and Cristina Freeman Bryan, for their suggestions and helpful discussions about writers and writing. I thank David Sweet for invaluable editorial assistance. I thank Alison Reeves, Kara Hado, and Judy Winthrop at Prentice-Hall. I thank Thomas Recchio, University of Connecticut, Phillip Sipiora, University of South Florida, and Ann Merill, Emory University for their reviews of the manuscript and their helpful comments. I thank my students at U.C. Santa Cruz and U.C. Berkeley for all their stimulating ideas and good insights. Last and first, I thank the writers whose work I have had the privilege of reading and assembling in this collection.

Maria Cecilia Freeman

About the Authors:
Biographical Notes

RUDOLFO A. ANAYA (1937–   ), a native New Mexican, is a writer of poetry and fiction. He is a professor of English at the University of New Mexico and has lectured at a number of other universities in the United States and in Mexico. Anaya's writing has won many honors. He is best known for his award-winning novel, *Bless Me, Ultima* (1972), followed by *Heart of Aztlan* (1976) and *Tortuga* (1979). His novels portray life in rural New Mexico and the importance of myth and tradition in the Chicano culture. He has also edited anthologies of contemporary Chicano fiction and essays, including *Voces: An Anthology of Nuevo Mexicano Writers* (1987) and *Tierra: Contemporary Fiction of New Mexico* (1989).

The New World Man
from *Bless Me, Ultima*

GLORIA E. ANZALDUA (1946–   ) is a Chicana lesbian-feminist writer of poetry, fiction, and nonfiction. She was born in Raymondville, Texas, into a family that had lived in the lower Rio Grande Valley for generations. With Cherríe Moraga she coedited *This Bridge Called My Back: Writings by Radical Women of Color* (1981), which won the 1986 Before Columbus Foundation American Book Award. Anzaldua writes with a strong sense of "the dilemma of the mixed breed," acknowledging ties to indigenous, Mexican, and white cultures at once and recognizing the conflicts among them. Her book *Borderlands/La Frontera* (1987) deals with life on the Texas/Mexico border where she was raised, but more broadly with the "border-lands" between cultures, languages, classes, and sexes.

Lifeline

Speaking in Tongues: A Letter to Third World Women Writers

JAMES BALDWIN (1924–1987), one of the foremost writers in American literature, authored numerous novels, short stories, essays, and plays during his long writing career. Baldwin was born and educated in New York. In 1944 he met Richard Wright, who encouraged him and helped him obtain financial support for his writing. In 1948, Baldwin went to Paris. Living in Europe helped him come to terms with both his racial identity and his bisexuality; this led to a period of great creativity. Some of his best-known novels are *Go Tell It on the Mountain* (1953), *Giovanni's Room* (1956), and *Another Country* (1962). *Going to Meet the Man* (1965) is a collection of his short stories. *Notes of a Native Son* (1955), *Nobody Knows My Name* (1961), *The Fire Next Time* (1963), *No Name in the Street* (1972), and *The Evidence of Things Not Seen* (1985) are books of essays. Baldwin also wrote dramas, including *The Amen Corner* (1955) and *Blues for Mister Charlie* (1964), both of which were produced on Broadway. His work exposes the painful personal and social reality of being black in America and offers a bitter but sensitive analysis of race relations in this country. In his writing he was concerned with the psychological damage of racism not only to its victims but to white society as well. Baldwin's painful experience of both racism and homophobia in the United States drove him to live in France during much of his later life, but he did not consider himself an expatriate.

Autobiographical Notes

The Discovery of What It Means to Be an American

Fifth Avenue, Uptown: A Letter from Harlem

A Talk to Teachers

TONI CADE BAMBARA (1939–   ) was born in New York City and educated there and in Europe. She has taught English and African-American Studies at a number of colleges and universities. She is a writer of fiction as well as award-winning screenplays. She also contributes to numerous journals and has edited anthologies of literature by African Americans. Her short stories are published in two collections, *Gorilla, My Love* (1972) and *The Sea Birds Are Still Alive* (1977). Her novel *The Salt Eaters* (1980) won the American Book Award in 1981. Bambara's stories are noted for their portrayals of life in African American neighborhoods of big cities as well as small southern towns.

The Lesson

JIM BARNES (1933–   ) is a poet and writer of stories and essays. Of Choctaw and Welsh ancestry, Barnes was born and raised in "Choctaw country" in eastern Oklahoma. He teaches comparative literature at Northeast Missouri State University and edits *Chariton Review*. Barnes writes with a strong sense of the natural environment. He has said, "I often choose places that have all the signs of having once been full of life but that are now neither full of life nor lifeless. This in-betweenness is important in my work." His books of poetry include *This Crazy Land* (1980), *The Fish on Poteau Mountain* (1980), and *The American Book of the Dead* (1982). His writing has also appeared in numerous anthologies and journals. In addition, Barnes has won awards for his English translation of poetry from the German.

On Native Ground

RAYMOND BARRIO (1921–   ) was born in New Jersey but has lived in California most of his life. He is not only a writer but an artist as well; he has taught art in colleges, and his work has been exhibited widely. Most of his extensive publications are books and essays on art and literature. He writes fiction and poetry as well. He is best known for his novel *The Plum Plum Pickers* (1969), about Chicano migrant workers in California and about the economic system that exploits them. This book, which Barrio published himself in 1969, became known as an "underground classic"; it was published in a second edition in 1984 and is now recognized as a classic in Chicano literary history.

from *The Plum Plum Pickers*

FRANK CHIN (1940–   ), born in Berkeley, California, is a native of the West Coast from Seattle to Los Angeles. Before he became a professional writer and university lecturer, he worked on the Western Pacific and Southern Pacific railroads as a clerk and brakeman. He is an outspoken, controversial writer of essays, novels, and short stories. "All my writing . . . is Chinaman backtalk," he says. His two plays *The Chickencoop Chinaman* and *The Year of the Dragon* were published together in 1981 and produced in New York. He has called himself "a Chinaman Playwright in search of an Asian American theater that stands for the real." Chin has won awards for both his fiction and playwriting. He is one of the editors of two antholo- gies of Asian-American literature, *Aiiieeeee!* (1974) and *The Big Aiiieeeee!* (1991). In 1988 a collection of his short stories was pub- lished, *The Chinaman Pacific and Frisco R.R. Co.* His first novel, *Donald Duk*, appeared in 1990.

Railroad Standard Time

SANDRA CISNEROS (1954–   ), writer of poetry and short sto- ries, was born in Chicago to a Mexican father and Mexican-Ameri- can mother. She spent her childhood moving often between Chicago and Mexico City, countering her sense of isolation by reading and introspective journal-writing. The stories in her book *The House on Mango Street* (1984) depict the life of the poor neighborhoods in Chi- cago where she grew up; the book won the American Book Award in 1985. Cisneros has also published several volumes of poetry, in- cluding *My Wicked, Wicked Ways* (1987). As an adult she has adopted San Antonio, Texas, as her home, and that is the setting for her second book of stories, *Woman Hollering Creek* (1991). In her writing her particular concern is the lives and unrealized strength of working-class Latina women.

Ghosts and Voices: Writing from Obsession
from *The House on Mango Street*
Notes to a Young(er) Writer

ELIZABETH COOK-LYNN (1930–   ) is a member of the Crow Creek Sioux tribe, born in Fort Thompson, South Dakota, and raised on the reservation. She is a writer of poetry, short stories, and liter- ary criticism, and she has published a novel, *From the River's Edge* (1991). Her book *Then Badger Said This* (1977) is a collection of poetry, narratives, and tribal stories. The stories collected in *The Power of Horses* (1990) focus on the culture of the Dakotapi of the Upper Plains. She lives in eastern Washington, where she is an As- sociate Professor Emeritus of Native American Studies at Eastern Washington University, and she edits *Wicazo Sa Review*, a journal concerned with Native American education. "Writing is an essen- tial act of survival for contemporary American Indians," says Cook- Lynn. "I'm interested in cultural, historical, political survival of In- dian Nations, and that's why I write and teach."

You May Consider Speaking About Your Art
The Power of Horses

JOAN DIDION (1934–   ) was born and grew up in Sacramento, in a family descended from pioneers that had come to California as part of the nineteenth-century westward migration. After graduating from the University of California at Berkeley, she lived for eight years in New York City, where she worked for *Vogue* magazine. Since her return to California she has lived in Los Angeles. She has written four novels: *Run River* (1963), *Play It as It Lays* (1970), *A Book of Common Prayer* (1977), and *Democracy* (1984). Her essays are collected in two volumes, *Slouching Towards Bethlehem* (1968) and *The White Album* (1979). She published a book of journalistic nonfiction, *Salvador*, in 1983. She also writes screenplays and contributes stories, essays, and reviews to national magazines. Didion's prose is noted for its finely crafted sentences, precise detail, and visual imagery. Her novels and essays often depict a fragmented popular culture in which "things fall apart"; in her writing, she says, she forces herself to "come to terms with disorder."

Why I Write
Notes from a Native Daughter

ROLANDO HINOJOSA (1929–   ) was born in Mercedes, Texas, in the lower Rio Grande Valley that is the site of his fiction. His family had strong roots on both sides of the Texas-Mexico border. Hinojosa has been a professor of Chicano Studies and English in universities in Minnesota and Texas, and he writes fiction in both Spanish and English. His writing has won numerous awards, including the prestigious international literary prize Premio Casa de las Americas, which was awarded for *Klail City y sus alrededores* (1976), the second in his "Klail City Death Trip" series of six novels portraying Chicano life in a fictitious Texas border town. After he completed that series with *Rites and Witnesses* in 1982, he published *Partners in Crime* (1985) and *Becky and Her Friends* (1990). He says, "My goal is to set down in fiction the history of the Lower Rio Grande Valley."

The Sense of Place

BELL HOOKS is the pen name of Gloria Watkins (1952–   ). She grew up in Kentucky, until she left home to attend Stanford University and went on to teach at Yale. She took the pen name "bell hooks" (which she spells without capital letters) from her great-grandmother, "a strong woman, a woman who spoke her mind." She says, "Claiming this name was a way to link my voice to an ancestral legacy of woman speaking—of woman power." Hooks writes on issues of gender, race, and class in a particularly humane and sensitive voice. She is the author of several nonfiction books including *Ain't I a Woman: Black Women and Feminism* (1981), *Feminist Theory from Margin to Center* (1984), *Talking Back: Thinking Feminist, Thinking Black* (1989), and *Yearning: Race, Gender, and Cultural Politics* (1990). In the introduction to *Talking Back* she says that the importance of talking back is not just personal, but "a real race and class issue."

Talking Back
Keeping Close to Home

MAXINE HONG KINGSTON (1940–   ) was born in Stockton, California, shortly after her parents emigrated from China. In her book *Woman Warrior: Memoirs of a Girlhood Among Ghosts* (1976), she draws on her experience of struggling to reconcile the values of two cultures, blending autobiography with fiction and legend passed on to her by her mother's "talk-story." Her second book, *China Men* (1980), is a fictionalized historical account of Chinese men in America, drawing on histories of men in Kingston's family and community. Both books won national literary awards. Kingston says she writes in the "peasant talk-story Cantonese tradition" and tries to connect traditional myth with modern reality in her writing. Her first novel, about a young Chinese-American writer in San Francisco during the 1960s, is *Tripmaster Monkey*, published in 1989.

No Name Woman

AUDRE LORDE (1934–1992) was an award-winning poet, essayist, and fiction writer, as well as a professor of English at Hunter College, City University of New York. She was born in New York, the child of immigrant parents who had come from Grenada in the 1920s. She wrote about growing up in Harlem and Greenwich Village in her "biomythography" *Zami: A New Spelling of My Name* (1982). Of her writing, Lorde has said, "I have a duty to speak the truth as I see it." Her nine volumes of poetry deal with topics from love and parenting to passionate anger at the injustices of racism and sexism. Her essays and speeches, dealing with a range of social concerns from a black lesbian feminist perspective, have been published in *The Cancer Journals* (1980), *Sister Outsider* (1984), and *Burst of Light* (1988).

from *Zami: A New Spelling of My Name*
The Transformation of Silence into Language and Action

PAULE MARSHALL (1929–   ) was born and grew up in Brooklyn. She still lives and writes in New York City, and she lectures on creative writing and Black literature in colleges and universities. Marshall's West Indian parents came to New York from Barbados, and she was raised in "Bajan Brooklyn," the Barbadian community depicted in her semiautobiographical first novel, *Brown Girl, Brownstones* (1959). Her other novels include *The Chosen Place, The Timeless People* (1969) and *Praisesong for the Widow* (1983), which won the American Book Award. She has also published two books of stories and novellas, *Soul Clap Hands and Sing* (1961) and *Reena and Other Stories* (1983).

From the Poets in the Kitchen

N. SCOTT MOMADAY (1934–   ) was born in Oklahoma. His father was a member of the Kiowa tribe, and Momaday was raised among Kiowas first, then among the Jemez Indians on reservations in New Mexico where his parents were schoolteachers. He is Regent's Professor of English at the University of Arizona. His poetry and fiction have earned many awards, including the Pulitzer Prize awarded for his novel *House Made of Dawn* (1968). His book *The Way to Rainy Mountain* (1969) is a collection of Kiowa folk tales. In *The Names: A Memoir* (1976) Momaday combines autobiography with tribal myth, history, and imagination. His most recent novel is *The Ancient Child* (1989). His work reflects his deep respect for the oral tradition and a keen sense that the storyteller is giving continuity to the voice of past and future generations.

from *The Names*

TOSHIO MORI (1910–1980) was a fiction writer, best known for his book *Yokohama, California* (1949), which depicts life in the Japanese-American community of Oakland and San Leandro, California, where Mori lived most of his life. Mori's stories have sometimes been called "koans," after the paradoxical sayings presented to students of Zen; such stories encourage intuitive understanding rather than reliance on rational explanations. Mori's stories often reflect the view that ordinary individuals have the power to transcend, through small actions, the confines of their worldly condition—including public opposition or indifference. During World War II Mori's family was sent to Topaz Relocation Center in Utah, where Mori continued to write stories that portray the quiet dignity of ordinary individuals. In Topaz he served as editor of *Trek*, the camp magazine. A collection of his work is published under the title *The Chauvinist and Other Stories* (1979).

Confessions of an Unknown Writer
The Long Journey and the Short Ride
Tomorrow Is Coming, Children

JOHN OKADA (1923–1971) was born in Seattle, Washington, served in the U.S. Army during World War II, then worked as a librarian and writer until his death at age 47. He left only one published novel, *No-No Boy*. Originally published by Charles Tuttle of Tokyo in 1957, the book remained obscure during Okada's lifetime. Okada wrote a second novel, about the experiences of Issei (first-generation Japanese-American) immigrants, but the manuscript was destroyed with all of his other papers after his death. Several young Asian-American writers, including Frank Chin, subsequently rediscovered *No-No Boy* and arranged for its republication in 1976. It has since been widely recognized as an important literary work and document of Asian-American history.

from *No-No Boy*

SIMON J. ORTIZ (1941–   ) was born and raised in Acoma Pueblo in New Mexico. He has taught at various colleges and universities in the West but still considers Acoma Pueblo his home. He has written more than a dozen books of poetry, essays, and fiction, including *Going for the Rain* (1976), *A Good Journey* (1977), and *From Sand Creek* (1981), all poetry collections, and *Fightin'* (1983), a collection of short stories. His most recent book is *Woven Stone: A 3-in-1 Volume of Poetry and Prose* (1991). Ortiz has also edited an anthology, *Earth Power Coming: Short Fiction in Native American Literature* (1983), and contributed to numerous other anthologies. Ortiz's writing consistently reflects his concern with the continuity of Native American culture, as well as all people's relationship to the land. He says, "If the survival and quality of the life of Indian peoples is not assured, then no one else's life is, because those same economic, social, and political forces which destroy them will surely destroy others."

The Language We Know
The Panther Waits

CYNTHIA OZICK (1928–   ), a writer of novels, short stories, and essays, was born in New York and grew up in the Bronx; she continues to live and write in New York. Her writing often draws on her family's ties to its Russian and Jewish heritage. She has won numerous literary prizes for fiction. Her short fiction books include *The Pagan Rabbi and Other Stories* (1971), *Bloodshed and Three Novellas* (1976), *Levitation* (1982), and *The Shawl: A Story and Novella* (1989). Her novels are *The Cannibal Galaxy* (1983) and *The Messiah of Stockholm* (1987). She has also published two books of essays, *Art and Ardor* (1983) and *Metaphor and Memory* (1988), and she writes regularly for *The New York Times Book Review*. Her writing is noted for its meticulously crafted sentences and its range of styles.

The Seam of the Snail
A Drugstore in Winter

ISHMAEL REED (1938–   ) is an award-winning writer of novels, poetry, plays, and nonfiction. He was born in Chattanooga, Tennessee, but grew up in working-class neighborhoods of Buffalo, New York. He has taught at Harvard, Yale, Dartmouth, and the University of California at Berkeley. He is one of the founders of the Before Columbus Foundation, which promotes multiethnic literatures. Reed never shrinks from controversy; he once wrote that "as a black male writer, sometimes you have to be strident to get your point across, to get somebody to pay attention." His writing reliably attacks racism and other forms of social injustice. Reed's essays, collected in *Writin' Is Fightin'* (1988) and *Shrovetide in Old New Orleans* (1989), have earned him a reputation for unorthodox, sometimes combative, and often controversial social commentary. His recent novels include *The Last Days of Louisiana Red* (1989) and *Mumbo Jumbo* (1989).

Boxing on Paper
America: The Multinational Society

PHILIP ROTH (1933–   ) has published fifteen books of fiction during a writing career that spans more than thirty years. Much of his writing draws on his years of growing up in the Jewish immigrant community of Newark, New Jersey. His collection of short stories *Goodbye, Columbus* (1959) won the National Book Award for Fiction. Some of his novels are *Portnoy's Complaint* (1969), *The Ghost Writer* (1979), *The Anatomy Lesson* (1983), and *The Counterlife* (1986). He commented on his own development as a writer in *Reading Myself and Others* (1975) and *The Facts: A Novelist's Autobiography* (1988). Roth has taught and been writer-in-residence at several universities including Princeton and the University of Pennsylvania.

My Baseball Years

R. A. SASAKI (1952–   ), or Ruth Sasaki, grew up in San Francisco, the granddaughter of Japanese immigrants. Her short stories often deal with relationships between family members of different generations; while they illuminate the experience of life in the Japanese-American community, they touch on the ties between generations in any American community. Her stories appear in various anthologies and are collected in the book *The Loom and Other Stories* (1991).

The Loom
American Fish

LESLIE MARMON SILKO (1948–   ) grew up at the Laguna Pueblo Reservation in New Mexico and now lives on a ranch outside Tucson, Arizona, where she teaches English at the University of Arizona. Silko attributes her sensibilities as a storyteller and writer to her life in the Laguna community. She is best known for her first novel, *Ceremony* (1977). Her other publications include *Laguna Woman* (1974), a book of poetry, and *Storyteller* (1981), a collection of poems and stories that combine personal experience and oral tradition. Silko won the Pushcart Prize for poetry in 1977. Her poems, stories, and articles have appeared in many anthologies and journals.

Yellow Woman

GARY SOTO (1952–   ) comes from Fresno, California, and much of his writing is based on his experience of growing up there. Soto has received national recognition and numerous awards for his poetry, of which he has published several volumes. He has also written several books of autobiographical essays: *Living Up the Street* (1985), which won the American Book Award, *Small Faces* (1986), *Lesser Evils* (1988), and *Baseball in April* (1991). In words that apply equally well to his poetry and his prose, Soto has said, "I like to think of my poems as a 'working life,' by which I mean that my poems are about commonplace, everyday things. . . . The poems keep alive the small moments which add up to a large moment: life itself." Soto teaches

Chicano Studies and English at the University of California, Berkeley.

> Like Mexicans
> Looking for Work
> One Last Time

PIRI THOMAS (1928–   ) grew up in the Puerto Rican community in Harlem, New York City. When he was 22, he was sent to prison for attempted armed robbery. He served six years, during which time he began to write. After his release in 1956 he worked in drug rehabilitation centers in New York and Puerto Rico, while he continued writing. His autobiographical *Seven Long Times* (1974) looks back at his years of drug addiction and prison. He has published three other books of autobiographical stories: *Down These Mean Streets* (1967), *Savior, Savior Hold My Hand* (1972), and *The View from El Barrio* (1978). Thomas's stories range from frankly violent and sexually explicit scenarios to pensive reflections on life in Spanish Harlem.

> from *Seven Long Times*
> All-Around Man

KURT VONNEGUT, JR. (1922–   ) is, according to the title page of his novel *Slaughterhouse Five* (1969), "a fourth-generation German-American now living in easy circumstances on Cape Cod and smoking too much." Born in Indianapolis, Indiana, he studied anthropology and worked as a journalist before he began writing novels. He is the author of more than a dozen novels, many of them best-sellers, beginning with *Player Piano* (1952) and including *Cat's Cradle* (1963), *Mother Night* (1967), *Slaughterhouse Five* (1969), *Breakfast of Champions* (1973), *Deadeye Dick* (1982), and *Bluebeard* (1987). He published a collection of short stories in *Welcome to the Monkey House* (1970). He is also a popular essayist; his nonfiction writing is collected in *Wampeters, Foma and Granfalloons* (1974), and *Palm Sunday* (1981). He continues to contribute fiction and essays to popular magazines.

> How to Write with Style

RICHARD WRIGHT (1908–1960) lived in rural Mississippi and Memphis, Tennessee, until, at the age of nineteen, he moved to Chicago and from there to New York City. Largely self-educated, Wright had an abiding concern with uncovering the social roots of racism; this concern led him to political activism and motivated his writing. His first book, *Uncle Tom's Children* (1938), was a collection of short stories. In 1940 his novel *Native Son* was published and immediately became a best-seller, the first novel by an African American to achieve such popular and critical recognition. Wright's autobiography—both a traumatic personal narrative and searing social criticism—was published as two separate books, *Black Boy* (1945) and *American Hunger* (1977). After the publication of *Black Boy*, Wright moved to Paris, where he became an active supporter of African movements for national independence. In France Wright wrote more nonfiction, and novels such as *The Outsider* (1953), which expressed his sense of alienation and rootlessness. He lived as an expatriate in France until he died at the age of 52.

from *Black Boy*
from *American Hunger*

HISAYE YAMAMOTO (1921–   ) has been writing short stories, essays, and journalism since her early youth. Her work won national acclaim during the years following World War II and was included in several annual collections of *Best American Short Stories* (edited by Martha Foley). Her stories draw upon the people, places, and experiences of her own life. They often reveal the pressures and restrictions in the lives of Issei, that is, first-generation Japanese-American immigrants, especially women. The daughter of Japanese immigrants, Yamamoto was born in Redondo Beach, California. She and her family were interned in Poston, Arizona, during the war. She later lived in Massachusetts and New York before returning to southern California. Her work has been published in a large number of journals in the United States and Japan. A collection of her fiction spanning forty years was published in 1988 as *Seventeen Syllables and Other Stories*.

Seventeen Syllables

I
ON BEING A WRITER

Autobiographical Notes

James Baldwin

Baldwin wrote the following essay as an introduction to his book Notes of a Native Son, *first published in 1955. Only the beginning and end of the essay are autobiographical in a conventional sense; in the body of the essay Baldwin explores his social responsibility as a writer and connects his writing with his need to establish a sense of his own identity as an African American.*

I was born in Harlem thirty-one years ago. I began plotting novels at about the time I learned to read. The story of my childhood is the usual bleak fantasy, and we can dismiss it with the restrained observation that I certainly would not consider living it again. In those days my mother was given to the exasperating and mysterious habit of having babies. As they were born, I took them over with one hand and held a book with the other. The children probably suffered, though they have since been kind enough to deny it, and in this way I read *Uncle Tom's Cabin* and *A Tale of Two Cities* over and over and over again; in this way, in fact, I read just about everything I could get my hands on—except the Bible, probably because it was the only book I was encouraged to read. I must also confess that I wrote—a great deal—and my first professional triumph, in any

case, the first effort of mine to be seen in print, occurred at the age
of twelve or thereabouts, when a short story I had written about the
Spanish revolution won some sort of prize in an extremely short-
lived church newspaper. I remember the story was censored by the
lady editor, though I don't remember why, and I was outraged.

Also wrote plays, and songs, for one of which I received a letter
of congratulations from Mayor La Guardia, and poetry, about which
the less said, the better. My mother was delighted by all these goings-
on, but my father wasn't; he wanted me to be a preacher. When I
was fourteen I became a preacher, and when I was seventeen I
stopped. Very shortly thereafter I left home. For God knows how
long I struggled with the world of commerce and industry—I guess
they would say they struggled with *me*—and when I was about
twenty-one I had enough done of a novel to get a Saxton Fellowship.
When I was twenty-two the fellowship was over, the novel turned
out to be unsalable, and I started waiting on tables in a Village restaurant and writing book reviews—mostly, as it turned out, about
the Negro problem, concerning which the color of my skin made me
automatically an expert. Did another book, in company with pho-
tographer Theodore Pelatowski, about the store-front churches in
Harlem. This book met exactly the same fate as my first—fellowship, but no sale. (It was a Rosenwald Fellowship.) By the time I was
twenty-four I had decided to stop reviewing books about the Negro
problem—which, by this time, was only slightly less horrible in print
than it was in life—and I packed my bags and went to France, where
I finished, God knows how, *Go Tell It on the Mountain*.

Any writer, I suppose, feels that the world into which he was
born is nothing less than a conspiracy against the cultivation of his
talent—which attitude certainly has a great deal to support it. On
the other hand, it is only because the world looks on his talent with
such a frightening indifference that the artist is compelled to make
his talent important. So that any writer, looking back over even so
short a span of time as I am here forced to assess, finds that the
things which hurt him and the things which helped him cannot be
divorced from each other; he could be helped in a certain way only
because he was hurt in a certain way; and his help is simply to be
enabled to move from one conundrum to the next—one is tempted
to say that he moves from one disaster to the next. When one begins
looking for influences one finds them by the score. I haven't thought
much about my own, not enough anyway; I hazard that the King
James Bible, the rhetoric of the store-front church, something ironic
and violent and perpetually understated in Negro speech—and
something of Dickens' love for bravura—have something to do with
me today; but I wouldn't stake my life on it. Likewise, innumerable

people have helped me in many ways; but finally, I suppose, the most difficult (and most rewarding) thing in my life has been the fact that I was born a Negro and was forced, therefore, to effect some kind of truce with this reality. (Truce, by the way, is the best one can hope for.)

One of the difficulties about being a Negro writer (and this is not special pleading, since I don't mean to suggest that he has it worse than anybody else) is that the Negro problem is written about so widely. The bookshelves groan under the weight of information, and everyone therefore considers himself informed. And this information, furthermore, operates usually (generally, popularly) to reinforce traditional attitudes. Of traditional attitudes there are only two—For or Against—and I, personally, find it difficult to say which attitude has caused me the most pain. I am speaking as a writer; from a social point of view I am perfectly aware that the change from ill-will to good-will, however motivated, however imperfect, however expressed, is better than no change at all.

But it is part of the business of the writer—as I see it—to ex-   5
amine attitudes, to go beneath the surface, to tap the source. From this point of view the Negro problem is nearly inaccessible. It is not only written about so widely; it is written about so badly. It is quite possible to say that the price a Negro pays for becoming articulate is to find himself, at length, with nothing to be articulate about. ("You taught me language," says Caliban to Prospero, "and my profit on't is I know how to curse.") Consider: the tremendous social activity that this problem generates imposes on whites and Negroes alike the necessity of looking forward, of working to bring about a better day. This is fine, it keeps the waters troubled; it is all, indeed, that has made possible the Negro's progress. Nevertheless, social affairs are not generally speaking the writer's prime concern, whether they ought to be or not; it is absolutely necessary that he establish between himself and these affairs a distance which will allow, at least, for clarity, so that before he can look forward in any meaningful sense, he must first be allowed to take a long look back. In the context of the Negro problem neither whites nor blacks, for excellent reasons of their own, have the faintest desire to look back; but I think that the past is all that makes the present coherent, and further, that the past will remain horrible for exactly as long as we refuse to assess it honestly.

I know, in any case, that the most crucial time in my own development came when I was forced to recognize that I was a kind of bastard of the West; when I followed the line of my past I did not find myself in Europe but in Africa. And this meant that in some subtle way, in a really profound way, I brought to Shakespeare, Bach,

Rembrandt, to the stones of Paris, to the cathedral at Chartres, and to the Empire State Building, a special attitude. These were not really my creations, they did not contain my history; I might search in them in vain forever for any reflection of myself. I was an interloper; this was not my heritage. At the same time I had no other heritage which I could possibly hope to use—I had certainly been unfitted for the jungle or the tribe. I would have to appropriate these white centuries, I would have to make them mine—I would have to accept my special attitude, my special place in this scheme—otherwise I would have no place in *any* scheme. What was the most difficult was the fact that I was forced to admit something I had always hidden from myself, which the American Negro has had to hide from himself as the price of his public progress; that I hated and feared white people. This did not mean that I loved black people; on the contrary, I despised them, possibly because they failed to produce Rembrandt. In effect, I hated and feared the world. And this meant, not only that I thus gave the world an altogether murderous power over me, but also that in such a self-destroying limbo I could never hope to write.

One writes out of one thing only—one's own experience. Everything depends on how relentlessly one forces from this experience the last drop, sweet or bitter, it can possibly give. This is the only real concern of the artist, to recreate out of the disorder of life that order which is art. The difficulty then, for me, of being a Negro writer was the fact that I was, in effect, prohibited from examining my own experience too closely by the tremendous demands and the very real dangers of my social situation.

I don't think the dilemma outlined above is uncommon. I do think, since writers work in the disastrously explicit medium of language, that it goes a little way towards explaining why, out of the enormous resources of Negro speech and life, and despite the example of Negro music, prose written by Negroes has been generally speaking so pallid and so harsh. I have not written about being a Negro at such length because I expect that to be my only subject, but only because it was the gate I had to unlock before I could hope to write about anything else. I don't think that the Negro problem in America can be even discussed coherently without bearing in mind its context; its context being the history, traditions, customs, the moral assumptions and preoccupations of the country; in short, the general social fabric. Appearances to the contrary, no one in America escapes its effects and everyone in America bears some responsibility for it. I believe this the more firmly because it is the overwhelming tendency to speak of this problem as though it were a thing apart. But in the work of Faulkner, in the general attitude

and certain specific passages in Robert Penn Warren, and, most significantly, in the advent of Ralph Ellison, one sees the beginnings—
at least—of a more genuinely penetrating search. Mr. Ellison, by the
way, is the first Negro novelist I have ever read to utilize in language, and brilliantly, some of the ambiguity and irony of Negro life.

About my interests: I don't know if I have any, unless the mor-
bid desire to own a sixteen-millimeter camera and make experimen-
tal movies can be so classified. Otherwise, I love to eat and drink—
it's my melancholy conviction that I've scarcely ever had enough to
eat (this is because it's *impossible* to eat enough if you're worried
about the next meal)—and I love to argue with people who do not
disagree with me too profoundly, and I love to laugh. I do *not* like
bohemia, or bohemians, I do not like people whose principal aim is
pleasure, and I do not like people who are *earnest* about anything. I
don't like people who like me because I'm a Negro; neither do I like
people who find in the same accident grounds for contempt. I love
America more than any other country in the world, and, exactly for
this reason, I insist on the right to criticize her perpetually. I think
all theories are suspect, that the finest principles may have to be
modified, or may even be pulverized by the demands of life, and that
one must find, therefore, one's own moral center and move through
the world hoping that this center will guide one aright. I consider
that I have many responsibilities, but none greater than this: to last,
as Hemingway says, and get my work done.

I want to be an honest man and a good writer.   10

Response ————————————————————————————

1. Baldwin observes that for a writer, "the things which hurt him
    and the things which helped him cannot be divorced from each
    other; he could be helped in a certain way only because he was
    hurt in a certain way" (paragraph 3). How did this paradox hold
    true in Baldwin's experience? Although Baldwin, writing in
    1955, used only masculine pronoun forms, the passage can be
    taken to refer to both men and women. Are there ways in which
    Baldwin's statement has been true for you?
2. What does Baldwin take to be a writer's responsibility? In par-
    agraph 5 Baldwin asserts that "before [the writer] can look for-
    ward in any meaningful sense, he must first be allowed to take
    a long look back." Explain why he saw this as essential for any
    writer and particularly for himself.
3. Baldwin called himself "a kind of bastard of the West" (para-

graph 6). Based on this paragraph, how can his phrase be interpreted?

4. Baldwin talks about "the gate [he] had to unlock before [he]
could hope to write about anything else" (paragraph 8). What
do you think he was referring to? Why did he have to do this?

5. In his conclusion Baldwin says, "I want to be an honest man
and a good writer." Explain why, for him, these two ideas go
together. What kind of a man does Baldwin reveal himself to
be in this essay?

Ghosts and Voices:
Writing from Obsession

Sandra Cisneros

*This essay was originally delivered as a lecture at
Indiana University in November 1986. In it Cisneros
looks back at her development as a writer and gives
some insight into what motivates her work.*

I like to think one of the circumstances that led me to my
writing is the fact I was born an only daughter in a family of six
sons—two older, four younger. There was a sister, born next in se-
quence after me, but she died when she and I were both so young I
hardly remember her, except as an image in a few blurred photographs.

The six brothers soon paired themselves off. The oldest with
the second-oldest, the brother beneath me with the one beneath him
and the youngest two were twins, genetically as well as socially
bound. These three sets of men had their own conspiracies and al-
legiances, leaving me odd-woman-out forever.

My parents would be hard-pressed to recall my childhood as
lonely, crowded as the nine of us were in cramped apartments where
there were children sleeping on the living room couch and fold-out
Lazy Boy, and on beds set up in the middle room, where the only
place with any privacy was the bathroom. A second- or third-floor
flat, but invariably the top floor because "noise travelled down," or

Sandra Cisneros, "Ghosts and Voices: Writing from Obsession," *The Americas
Review* 6:1 (1989). University of Houston, Arte Publico Press. Reprinted by permission of the publisher of *The Americas Review*—University of Houston.

so we naively believed, convinced us it was wiser to be the producer of noise rather than its victim.

To make matters worse, we were constantly moving back and forth between Chicago and Mexico City due to my father's compulsive "homesickness." Every couple of years we would have to pack all our things, store the furniture I don't know where, pile into the station wagon, and head south to Mexico. It was usually a stay of a few months, always at the grandparents' house on La Fortuna, número 12. That famous house, the only constant in the series of traumatic upheavals we experienced as children, and, no doubt for a stubborn period of time, my father's only legitimate "home" as well.

5   In retrospect, my solitary childhood proved important. Had my sister lived or had we stayed in one neighborhood long enough for a friendship to be established, I might not have needed to bury myself in books the way I did. I remember, I especially liked reading about "the olden times" because the past seemed more interesting than my dull present.

But in school we were also required to take books out of our class library. Since our school was poor, so were the choices. As a result I read a lot of books I might not have read otherwise; the lives of saints, or very stodgy editions of children's stories published in the 1890's—usually didactic, Horatio Alger-type tales which I enjoyed all the same because of the curious English.

About this time I began hearing a voice in my head, a narrator—just like the ones in the books—chronicling the ordinary events that made up my life: "I want you to go to the store and get me a loaf of bread and a gallon of milk. Bring back all the change and don't let them gyp you like they did last time." In my head my narrator would add: . . . *she said in a voice that was neither reproachful nor tender. Thus clutching the coins in her pocket, our hero was off under a sky so blue and a wind so sweet she wondered it didn't make her dizzy.* This is how I glamorized my days living in the third-floor flats and shabby neighborhoods where the best friend I was always waiting for never materialized.

One of the most important books in my childhood (and still a favorite now) was Virginia Lee Burton's *The Little House*, a picture book that tells the story of a house on a country hill whose owner promises never to sell her "for gold or silver" and predicts his great, great grandchildren will live in her.

Stable and secure in the country, the little house is happy witnessing the changes of seasons and generations, although curious about the distant lights of the big city. The sun and changing moons across the top of the page as well as the alterations in the landscape and dress fashion, make us aware time is passing. Finally, the city that has been growing ever larger, catches up with the little house, until she finds she is no longer in the country but eventually surrounded by tall buildings and noisy traffic. The inhabitants move away, and the little house, no longer able to see the stars at night, grows sad; her roof sags and the doorstep droops; the windows that serve as eyes, one on either side of the door, are broken. Fortunately, the great-granddaughter of the man who built the house rescues her in one of the best moments in the book. Traffic is halted on the busy boulevard for the little house to be wheeled away to the country and settled on a hill just like the one it originally sat on, happy and once again loved.

Wasn't *The Little House*, the house I dreamed of, a house where one family lived and grew old and didn't move away? One house, one spot. I read and reread that book, sometimes taking the book out of the library seven times in a row. Once my brother and I even schemed to keep it. If we lied and told the librarian we'd lost it, we would simply be fined the price of the book, and then it would be ours forever without the anxiety of the rubber-stamped due date. That was the plan, a good one, but never executed—good, guilty Catholics that we were. (I didn't know books could be legitimately purchased somewhere until years later. For a long time I believed they were so valuable as to only be dispensed to institutions and libraries, the only place I'd seen them.)

The Little House was my own dream. And I was to dream myself over again in several books, to re-invent my world according to my own vision. I dreamed our family as the fairy-tale victims of an evil curse, the cause of our temporary hard times. "Just for a spell," we were told, and in my head my narrator interpreted, "Just a spell."

"Don't play with those kids," my mama and papa warned. "Don't hang around with that kind. We didn't raise you to talk like that. That's how *gente baja* behave. Low class." As if it didn't have anything to do with us.

I dreamed myself the sister in the "Six Swans" fairy tale. She too was an only daughter in a family of six sons. The brothers had been changed into swans by an evil spell only the sister could break. Was it no coincidence my family name translated "keeper of swans?" I dreamed myself Andersen's "Ugly Duckling." Ridiculous, ugly, perenially the new kids. But one day the spell would wear off. I kept telling myself. "Temporary."

There were other books that spoke to me. Hugh Lofting's *Doctor Dolittle* series. Imagine being able to talk to animals. Didn't it seem as if they were the only ones who understood you anyway. And *The Island of the Blue Dolphins*, the survival story of a lonely girl who inhabits a one-citizen island. *Hittie: Her First 100 Years*, a century account of a wooden doll who is whisked through different homes and owners but perseveres. And *Alice in Wonderland* and *Through the Looking Glass* for the wonderful way of transforming the everyday into the fantastic.

15   As a young writer in college I was aware I had to find my voice, but how was I to know it would be the voice I used at home, the one I acquired as a result of one English-speaking mother and one Spanish-speaking father. My mother's English was learned in the Mexican/Italian neighborhood she grew up in on Chicago's near south side, an English learned from playmates and school, since her own parents spoke Spanish exclusively. My father, on the other hand, spoke to us in a Spanish of grandmothers and children, a language embroidered with the diminutive. To give you an example:

> *My mother:* "Good lucky I raised you kids right so you wouldn't hang around with the punks and floozies on the corner and wind up no good to nobody."
>
> *My father:* (translated more or less from the Spanish): "Eat a little bit more, my heaven, before leaving the table and fill your tum-tum up good."

These two voices at odds with each other—my mother's punch-you-in-the-nose English and my father's powdered-sugar Spanish—curiously are the voices that surface in my writing. What I'm specially aware of lately is how the Spanish syntax and word choice occurs in my work even though I write in English.

It's ironic I had to leave home to discover the voice I had all along, but isn't that how it always goes. As a poor person growing up in a society where the class norm was superimposed on a t.v. screen, I couldn't understand why our home wasn't all green lawn and white wood like the ones in "Leave It to Beaver" or "Father Knows Best." Poverty then became the ghost and in an attempt to escape the ghost, I rejected what was at hand and emulated the voices of the poets I admired in books: big, male voices like James Wright and Richard Hugo and Theodore Roethke, all wrong for me.

It wasn't until Iowa and the Writers' Workshop that I began writing in the voice I now write in, and, perhaps if it hadn't been for Iowa I wouldn't have made the conscious decision to write this way. It seems crazy, but until Iowa I had never felt my home, family, and neighborhood unique or worthy of writing about. I took for granted the homes around me, the women sitting at their windows, the strange speech of my neighbors, the extraordinary lives of my family and relatives which was nothing like the family in "Father Knows Best." I only knew that for the first time in my life I felt "other." What could I write about that my classmates, cultivated in the finest schools in the country like hothouse orchids, could not? My second-rate imitations of mainstream voices wouldn't do. And imitating my classmates wouldn't work either. That was their voice, not mine. What could I write about that they couldn't? What did I know that they didn't?

During a seminar titled "On Memory and the Imagination" when the class was heatedly discussing Gustav Bachelard's *Poetics of Space* and the metaphor of a house—*a house, a house*, it hit me. What did I know except third-floor flats. Surely my classmates knew nothing about that. That's precisely what I chose to write: about third-floor flats, and fear of rats, and drunk husbands sending rocks through windows, anything as far from the poetic as possible. And this is when I discovered the voice I'd been suppressing all along without realizing it.

Recently, talking with fellow writer and friend Norma Alar-   20
cón, we agreed there's no luxury or leisure in our lives for us to write of landscapes and sunsets and tulips in a vase. Instead of writing by inspiration, it seems we write by obsession, of that which is most violently tugging at our psyche.

If I were asked what it is I write about, I would have to say I write about those ghosts inside that haunt me, that will not let me sleep, of that which even memory does not like to mention. Sometimes it seems I am writing the same story, the same poem, over and over. I found it curious that Cherríe Moraga's new book is titled *Giving up the Ghost*. Aren't we constantly attempting to give up the ghost, to put it to sleep once and for all each time we pick up the pen?

Perhaps later there will be time to write by inspiration. In the meantime, in my writing as well as in that of other Chicanas and other women, there is the necessary phase of dealing with those ghosts and voices most urgently haunting us, day by day.

Response

1. How did Cisneros' family circumstances help lead her to writing?

2. In this essay Cisneros uses the term "voice" in several different ways. Find phrases containing the term "voice" and compare the different senses in which she uses it. What is Cisneros' main point about "voice"?

3. Cisneros says that not until she left her home, family, and neighborhood to go to the University of Iowa did she realize the uniqueness of her own experience, the richness of daily life

that she had taken for granted. What do you think she means when she says, "for the first time in my life I felt 'other'" (paragraph 18)? Do you think it is necessary to leave home, physically and/or culturally, to achieve this feeling?

4. How do you interpret the notion of "ghosts" that haunt Cisneros and motivate her writing? Cisneros identifies herself with "other Chicanas and other women" with "no luxury or leisure in our lives," who write from "obsession" rather than from "inspiration." Why, in her view, is this the case?

5. To what extent do you think Cisneros and Kurt Vonnegut, Jr. ("How to Write with Style") would agree about what makes writing good?

6. Comparing herself to her classmates at Iowa, Cisneros asked: "What could I write about that they couldn't? What did I know that they didn't?" Ask these questions of yourself. What are some aspects of ordinary life you may have taken for granted, that may never have seemed "worthy of writing about" but that you know so well that you could, in fact, write about them?

You May Consider Speaking About Your Art

Elizabeth Cook-Lynn

In this essay Cook-Lynn discusses the responsibility of being a writer, and in particular a Dakotah writer. The essay first appeared in a collection of autobiographical statements by Native American writers, I Tell You Now *(1987).*

Ever since I learned to read, I have wanted to be a writer.

I was born in the Government Hospital at Fort Thompson, South Dakota, in 1930, and when I was a "child of prairie hawks" (*Seek the House of Relatives*), I lived out on the Crow Creek (a tributary of the James and the Missouri) in what anthropologists like to call "an extended family." And I loved to read.

Reading, if it is not too obvious to say so, precedes writing, though I teach college students today who are examples of an apparently opposing point of view. They have read nothing.

On the contrary, I read everything: the Sears catalog, *Faust*, Dick and Jane, *Tarzan of the Apes*, *The Scarlet Letter*, the First Letter to the Corinthians, *David Copperfield*, "The Ancient Mariner," Dick Tracy, "Very Like a Whale," *Paradise Lost*, *True Confessions*, and much more. I went to whatever libraries were available as often as I went anywhere.

Elizabeth Cook-Lynn, "You May Consider Speaking About Your Art," in *I Tell You Now: Autobiographical Essays by Native American Writers*, ed. by Brian Swann and Arnold Krupat. Lincoln, Nebraska: University of Nebraska Press, 1987. Copyright © 1987 by the University of Nebraska Press. Reprinted with permission from the University of Nebraska Press.

But I read nothing about the Dakotapi. Much later I took a history course at South Dakota State College called "The Westward Movement," and there was not one mention of Indian Nations! I keep the text for that course on my own library shelf as a marvelous example of scholarly ineptitude and/or racism.

5   Wanting to write comes out of that deprivation, though, for we eventually have to ask, what happens to a reasonably intelligent child who sees him- or herself excluded from a world which is created and recreated with the obvious intent to declare him or her *persona non grata*? Silence is the first reaction. Then there comes the development of a mistrust of that world. And, eventually, anger.

That anger is what started me writing. Writing, for me, then, is an act of defiance born of the need to survive. I am me. I exist. I am a Dakotah. I write. It is the quintessential act of optimism born of frustration. It is an act of courage, I think. And, in the end, as Simon Ortiz says, it is an act that defies oppression.

In those early days, even though I had a need to write—that is, survive—I lived in a world in which the need to write was not primary. The need "to tell," however, was. And so I listened and heard about a world that existed in the flesh and in the imagination, too, and in the hearts and minds of real people. In those days I thought the world was made up of "Siouxs" and "Wasichus."

It is this dichotomous nature of the real world and the literary world and, yes, the present world that accounts for the work I do. It is the reason I call myself a Dakotah poet, however hesitantly I accept the label, however unclear the responsibilities that come with that label.

The best way to begin a philosophical discussion concerning the nature and substance of the work of a contemporary Dakotah poet is to admit, oddly enough, to a certain kind of timidity and lack of confidence and to conclude by saying that I do not speak for my people.

10   First of all, one must be timid because there is the consideration that poets have a tendency to think too much of themselves. It is quite possible that we poets think we are more significant, more important than we are; that the events we choose to signal as important for one reason or another are, after all, something else; that the statements and interpretations we have given to these events are mistaken and/or irrelevant.

Second, the idea that poets can speak for others, the idea that we can speak for the dispossessed, the weak, the voiceless, is indeed one of the great burdens of contemporary American Indian poets today, for it is widely believed that we "speak for our tribes." The frank truth is that I don't know very many poets who say, "I speak for my people." It is not only unwise; it is probably impossible, and it is very surely arrogant, for *We Are Self-Appointed* and the self-appointedness of what we do indicates that the responsibility is ours and ours alone.

Therein lies another dichotomy: I claim to be a Dakotah poet by disclaiming that I speak for my people.

I am not greatly surprised that this dichotomy does not exist for the "real" poets of our tribes, the men and women who sit at the drum and sing the old songs and create new ones. That is an entirely different matter, for it remains communal. Thus, when I hear the poetry of the Crown Butte Singers, the Porcupine Travelers, and the Wahpekute Singers, I have every confidence that they speak in our own language for the tribes, Oyate.

"A Poet's Lament: Concerning the Massacre of American Indians at Wounded Knee" is a good example to use to discuss and illustrate the problems that I see involved in the matter of responsibility for a poet like me, one who writes English, using contemporary forms.

This poem describes what was and is a very public event. Yet 15 as a self-appointed poet I bring my own perceptions into this tribal event even as I am aware of the public nature of the event and the history that surrounds it. The private histories which do not rely upon the written word, research, and text are a part of that perception.

All things considered, they said,
Crow Dog should be removed.
With Sitting Bull dead
It was easier said.

And so the sadly shrouded songs of poets,
Ash-yellowed, crisp with age
arise from drums to mark in fours
three times the sacred ways
that prayers are listened for; an infant girl stares
past the night, her beaded cap of buckskin brightens
Stars and Stripes that pierce
her mother's breast; Hokshina, innocent
as snow birds, tells of Ate's blood as red as plumes
that later decorate the posts of death.

"Avenge the slaughtered saints," beg mad-eyed
poets everywhere as if the bloody Piemontese are real
and really care for liberty of creed; the blind
who lead the blind will consecrate the Deed, indeed!

All things considered, they said,
Crow Dog should be removed.
With Sitting Bull dead
It was easier said.

In this specific case I mean to suggest that it is the responsibility of a poet like me to "consecrate" history and event, survival and joy and sorrow, the significance of ancestors and the unborn; and I use one of the most infamous crimes in all of human history, which took place against a people who did not deserve to be butchered, to make that responsibility concrete. Only recently has the mainstream of American society been confronted with the monstrous nature of this historical act and others like it, but Indians have always known it.

The ceremony I describe in the second stanza really did occur, I'm told; the people and the warriors gathered within hours after the dreadful killing, and they swept into the grounds and guarded their dead, placing twelve red-draped markers at the perimeters of the site. I don't know if this is "true." I wasn't a witness. I have not read any account of it. Surely, though, in the memories of the people, this ceremony took place in order to consecrate the event. And the poem that I write in English and in contemporary form, and the songs that continue to rise from drums in Dakota and in traditional forms a century later, recreate that consecration. That is what I mean to hold on to when I talk of responsibility in the creative process.

It is no accident that I refer to the number "twelve" to record this event in sacred terms, for that number figures prominently in sacred ritual. It is no accident that I begin and end with the names of Sitting Bull and Crow Dog, both religious leaders of the people, because I mean to deliberately place this event which is usually described in military terms into the religious context to which it speaks.

Ceremony, in literary terms, can be said to be that body of creative expression which accounts for the continued survival and development of a people, a nation. In this instance, it relies upon ancient symbols which are utilized spontaneously in a communal effort to speak with the givers of prayers, to recall the knowledge about life and death that has its origins in mythology and imagination.

20   The people who gathered to perform this ceremony a hundred years ago did so at risk of their lives. It was then and remains now an important commitment to nationhood and culture. They imagined the grief of the Unktechies who arose from the water, hundreds, perhaps thousands of years ago, to give the people a religion and then went deep into the Earth to listen for the sounds of our drums, songs, poetry, and prayers. The people wept and sang of their own grief and sorrow.

Years ago when I was twenty and I first started sending out my poems, an editor wrote on an acceptance letter a question that has haunted me for the rest of my so-called career as a poet. She asked, "WHY is Native American poetry so incredibly sad?"

Now I recognize it as a tactless question asked out of astounding ignorance. It reflects the general American attitude that American Indians should have been happy to have been robbed of their lands and murdered. I am no longer intimidated, as I once was, by that question, and I make no excuses for the sorrow I feel in my heart concerning recent history. I do not apologize for returning to those historical themes, for that is part of the ceremonial aspect of being a Dakotah poet.

Attending to ceremonial matters as a writer does not mean, however, that I am not writing about myself. Quite the opposite is true. There is a self-absorption in my work which is inherent in my survival as a person, and my identity as a Dakotah. This self-absorption has always been a part of tradition, I think, for Dakotahs, in spite of the pervasive articulation in recent times of the idea that the Indian "self" was somehow unimportant; that Indians have been absorbed in the contemplation of the natural world, readily giving themselves up to it, mastered by it philosophically as well as physically; that submission to environment dominates American Indian life and belief.

This overstatement has been handy for the perpetuation of the longed-for nineteenth-century idea concerning the ultimate and expected disappearance of Natives and Native America from this continent. It is convenient to suggest from this imagined obsession with the natural world that the American Indian would become an artifact, too unreal and obsolete for survival in the modern world. The Indian's "journey," then, as a race of people, would be concluded.

The function of contemporary American poetry is to disavow   25
that false notion.

One of what I consider my best poems is entitled, "Journey," and it is an attempt to express that disavowal:

I. DREAM

        Wet, sickly
smells of cattle yard silage fill the prairie air
far beyond the timber; the nightmare only just
begun, a blackened cloud moves past the sun
to dim the river's glare, a malady of modern times.
        We prayed
to the giver of prayers and traveled to the spirit
mounds we thought were forever; awake, we feared that
hollow trees no longer hid the venerable ones we were taught
to believe in.

II. MEMORY

Dancers with cane whistles,
the prairie's wise and knowing kinsmen
They trimmed their deer skins
in red down feathers,
made drum sticks from the gray grouse,
metaphorically speaking, and knocked on doors
which faced the East.
Dancers with cane whistles,
born under the sign of hollow stems,
after earth and air and fire and water
you conjure faith to clear the day.
Stunningly, blessedly you pierce the sky
with sound so clear each winged creature soars.

In my mind Grandmothers, those old partisans of faith
who long for shrill and glowing rituals of the past,
recall the times they went on long communal
buffalo hunts; because of this they tell the
lithe and lissome daughters:
> look for men who know the sacred ways
> look for men who wear the white-striped quill
> look for dancers with cane whistles
> and seek the house of relatives to stay the night.

III. SACRISTANS

This journey through another world, beyond bad dreams
beyond the memories of a murdered generation,
cartographed in captivity by bare survivors
makes sacristans of us all.

The old ones go our bail, we oblate preachers of our tribes.
Be careful, they say, don't hock the beads of
kinship agonies; the moire-effect of unfamiliar hymns
upon our own, a change in pitch or shrillness of the voice
transforms the ways of song to words of poetry or prose
and makes distinctions
no one recognizes.
Surrounded and absorbed, we tread like Etruscans
on the edge of useless law; we pray
to the giver of prayer, we give the cane whistle
in ceremony, we swing the heavy silver chain
of incense burners. Migration makes
new citizens of Rome.

The journey theme is pervasive in contemporary Native American poetry. The oral traditions from which these expressions emerge indicate a self-absorption essential to our lives. They follow the traditions of native literatures which express as a foremost consideration the survival of the individual, thus the tribe, thus the species, a journey of continuing life and human expectancy.

The final responsibility of a writer like me, and an essential reason to move on from "wanting to be a writer" to actually writing, is to commit something to paper in the modern world which supports this inexhaustible legacy left us by our ancestors. Grey Cohoe, the Navajo poet and artist, once said to a group of Native American students we were working with: "Have confidence in what you know."

That is difficult when we ordinarily see ourselves omitted from the pages of written histories, but not impossible.

Response

1. What "deprivation" motivated Cook-Lynn to write? In what sense does she see writing as "an act of defiance"?
2. Cook-Lynn identifies herself as a Dakotah poet but says, "I do not speak for my people" (paragraph 10). How can this paradox be understood? Why does she reject the notion that a poet can speak for others?
3. Cook-Lynn attaches significance to the fact that she writes in English and uses contemporary forms; this, she suggests, imposes on her a special "responsibility in the creative process." How does she see her role as different from that of traditional tribal singers?
4. As a Dakotah writer Cook-Lynn takes it as her responsibility to "'consecrate' history and event." How does she try to carry out this duty in her writing? What do you think she means by "the ceremonial aspect of being a Dakotah poet"?
5. According to Cook-Lynn, what is the significance of the journey theme in her own poem and in other contemporary Native American writing?
6. Cook-Lynn observes at the end of her essay that it is difficult to "have confidence in what you know" when your own heritage is overlooked by written histories. What other circumstances might make it difficult for a person to follow Grey Cohoe's advice?

Why I Write

Joan Didion

This essay, published in 1976 in The New York
Times Book Review, *derives from a talk Didion gave
to the faculty at the University of California at
Berkeley. In the opening lines she draws a parallel
between her work and that of George Orwell, a
critical observer of society in his own time. In her
essay Didion explains how she writes to gain access
to the thoughts and feelings in her own mind.*

Of course I stole the title for this talk from George Orwell. One
reason I stole it was that I like the sound of the words: *Why I Write.*
There you have three short unambiguous words that share a sound,
and the sound they share is this:

I
I
I

In many ways writing is the act of saying *I*, of imposing oneself
upon other people, of saying *listen to me, see it my way, change
your mind.* It's an aggressive, even a hostile act. You can disguise
its aggressiveness all you want with veils of subordinate clauses and

qualifiers and tentative subjectives, with ellipses and evasions—with the whole manner of intimating rather than claiming, of alluding rather than stating—but there's no getting around the fact that setting words on paper is the tactic of a secret bully, an invasion, an imposition of the writer's sensibility on the reader's most private space.

I stole the title not only because the words sounded right but because they seemed to sum up, in a no-nonsense way, all I have to tell you. Like many writers I have only this one "subject," this one "area": the act of writing. I can bring you no reports from any other front. I may have other interests: I am "interested," for example, in marine biology, but I don't flatter myself that you would come out to hear me talk about it. I am not a scholar. I am not in the least an intellectual, which is not to say that when I hear the word "intellectual" I reach for my gun, but only to say that I do not think in abstracts. During the years when I was an undergraduate at Berkeley I tried, with a kind of hopeless late-adolescent energy, to buy some temporary visa into the world of ideas, to forge for myself a mind that could deal with the abstract.

In short I tried to think. I failed. My attention veered inexorably back to the specific, to the tangible, to what was generally considered, by everyone I knew then and for that matter have known since, the peripheral. I would try to contemplate the Hegelian dialectic and would find myself concentrating instead on a flowering pear tree outside my window and the particular way the petal fell on my floor. I would try to read linguistic theory and would find myself wondering instead if the lights were on in the bevatron up the hill. When I say that I was wondering if the lights were on in the bevatron you might immediately suspect, if you deal in ideas at all, that I was registering the bevatron as a political symbol, thinking in shorthand about the military–industrial complex and its role in the university community, but you would be wrong. I was only wondering if the lights were on in the bevatron, and how they looked. A physical fact.

I had trouble graduating from Berkeley, not because of this inability to deal with ideas—I was majoring in English, and I could locate the house-and-garden imagery in *The Portrait of a Lady* as well as the next person, "imagery" being by definition the kind of specific that got my attention—but simply because I had neglected to take a course in Milton. For reasons which now sound baroque I needed a degree by the end of the summer, and the English department finally agreed, if I would come down from Sacramento every Friday and talk about the cosmology of *Paradise Lost*, to certify me proficient in Milton. I did this. Some Fridays I took the Greyhound

5

bus, other Fridays I caught the Southern Pacific's City of San Francisco on the last leg of its transcontinental trip. I can no longer tell you whether Milton put the sun or the earth at the center of his universe in *Paradise Lost*, the central question of at least one century and a topic about which I wrote 10,000 words that summer, but I can still recall the exact rancidity of the butter in the City of San Francisco's dining car, and the way the tinted windows on the Greyhound bus cast the oil refineries around Carquinez Straits into a grayed and obscurely sinister light. In short my attention was always on the periphery, on what I would see and taste and touch, on the butter, and the Greyhound bus. During those years I was traveling on what I knew to be a very shaky passport, forged papers: I knew that I was no legitimate resident in any world of ideas. I knew I couldn't think. All I knew then was what I couldn't do. All I knew then was what I wasn't, and it took me some years to discover what I was.

Which was a writer.

By which I mean not a "good" writer or a "bad" writer but simply a writer, a person whose most absorbed and passionate hours are spent arranging words on pieces of paper. Had my credentials been in order I would never have become a writer. Had I been blessed with even limited access to my own mind there would have been no reason to write. I write entirely to find out what I'm thinking, what I'm looking at, what I see and what it means. What I want and what I fear. Why did the oil refineries around Carquinez Straits seem sinister to me in the summer of 1956? Why have the night lights in the bevatron burned in my mind for twenty years? *What is going on in these pictures in my mind?*

When I talk about pictures in my mind I am talking, quite specifically, about images that shimmer around the edges. There used to be an illustration in every elementary psychology book showing a cat drawing by a patient in varying stages of schizophrenia. This cat had a shimmer around it. You could see the molecular structure breaking down at the very edges of the cat: the cat became the background and the background the cat, everything interacting, exchanging ions. People on hallucinogens describe the same perception of objects. I'm not a schizophrenic, nor do I take hallucinogens, but certain images do shimmer for me. Look hard enough, and you can't miss the shimmer. It's there. You can't think too much about these pictures that shimmer. You just lie low and let them develop. You stay quiet. You don't talk to many people and you keep your nervous system from shorting out and you try to locate the cat in the shimmer, the grammar in the picture.

Just as I meant "shimmer" literally I mean "grammar" liter-

ally. Grammar is a piano I play by ear, since I seem to have been out
of school the year the rules were mentioned. All I know about grammar is its infinite power. To shift the structure of a sentence alters
the meaning of the sentence, as definitely and inflexibly as the position of a camera alters the meaning of the object photographed.
Many people know about camera angles now, but not so many know
about sentences. The arrangement of the words matters, and the
arrangement you want can be found in the picture in your mind.
The picture dictates the arrangement. The picture dictates whether
this will be a sentence with or without clauses, a sentence that ends
hard or a dying-fall sentence, long or short, active or passive. The
picture tells you how to arrange the words and the arrangement of
the words tells you, or tells me, what's going on in the picture. *Nota
bene:*

It tells you. 10
You don't tell it.

Let me show you what I mean by pictures in the mind. I began
Play It as It Lays just as I have begun each of my novels, with no
notion of "character" or "plot" or even "incident." I had only two
pictures in my mind, more about which later, and a technical intention, which was to write a novel so elliptical and fast that it would
be over before you noticed it, a novel so fast that it would scarcely
exist on the page at all. About the pictures: the first was of white
space. Empty space. This was clearly the picture that dictated the
narrative intention of the book—a book in which anything that happened would happen off the page, a "white" book to which the reader
would have to bring his or her own bad dreams—and yet this picture
told me no "story," suggested no situation. The second picture did.
This second picture was of something actually witnessed. A young
woman with long hair and a short white halter dress walks through
the casino at the Riviera in Las Vegas at one in the morning. She
crosses the casino alone and picks up a house telephone. I watch her
because I have heard her paged, and recognize her name: she is a
minor actress I see around Los Angeles from time to time, in places
like Jax and once in a gynecologist's office in the Beverly Hills Clinic
but have never met. I know nothing about her. Who is paging her?
Why is she here to be paged? How exactly did she come to this? It
was precisely this moment in Las Vegas that made *Play It as It Lays*
begin to tell itself to me, but the moment appears in the novel only
obliquely, in a chapter which begins:

> *Maria made a list of things she would never do. She would never:
> walk through the Sands or Caesar's alone after midnight. She would
> never: ball at a party, do S-M unless she wanted to, borrow furs from
> Abe Lipsey, deal. She would never: carry a Yorkshire in Beverly Hills.*

That is the beginning of the chapter and that is also the end of the chapter, which may suggest what I meant by "white space."

I recall having a number of pictures in my mind when I began the novel I just finished, *A Book of Common Prayer*. As a matter of fact one of these pictures was of that bevatron I mentioned, although I would be hard put to tell you a story in which nuclear energy figured. Another was a newspaper photograph of a hijacked 707 burning on the desert in the Middle East. Another was the night view from a room in which I once spent a week with paratyphoid, a hotel room on the Colombian coast. My husband and I seemed to be on the Colombian coast representing the United States of America at a film festival (I recall invoking the name "Jack Valenti" a lot, as if its reiteration could make me well), and it was a bad place to have fever, not only because my indisposition offended our hosts but because every night in this hotel the generator failed. The lights went out. The elevator stopped. My husband would go to the event of the evening and make excuses for me and I would stay alone in this hotel room, in the dark. I remember standing at the window trying to call Bogotá (the telephone seemed to work on the same principle as the generator) and watching the night wind come up and wondering what I was doing eleven degrees off the equator with a fever of 103. The view from that window definitely figures in *A Book of Common Prayer*, as does the burning 707, and yet none of these pictures told me the story I needed.

15   The picture that did, the picture that shimmered and made these other images coalesce, was the Panama airport at 6 A.M. I was in this airport only once, on a plane to Bogotá that stopped for an hour to refuel, but the way it looked that morning remained superimposed on everything I saw until the day I finished *A Book of Common Prayer*. I lived in that airport for several years. I can still feel the hot air when I step off the plane, can see the heat already rising off the tarmac at 6 A.M. I can feel my skirt damp and wrinkled on my legs. I can feel the asphalt stick to my sandals. I remember the big tail of a Pan American plane floating motionless down at the end of the tarmac. I remember the sound of a slot machine in the waiting room. I could tell you that I remember a particular woman in the airport, an American woman, a *norteamericana*, a thin *norteamericana* about 40 who wore a big square emerald in lieu of a wedding ring, but there was no such woman there.

I put this woman in the airport later. I made this woman up, just as I later made up a country to put the airport in, and a family to run the country. This woman in the airport is neither catching a plane nor meeting one. She is ordering tea in the airport coffee shop.

In fact she is not simply "ordering" tea but insisting that the water be boiled, in front of her, for twenty minutes. Why is this woman in this airport? Why is she going nowhere, where has she been? Where did she get that big emerald? What derangement, or disassociation, makes her believe that her will to see the water boiled can possibly prevail?

> *She had been going to one airport or another for four months, one could see it, looking at the visas on her passport. All those airports where Charlotte Douglas's passport had been stamped would have looked alike. Sometimes the sign on the tower would say "Bienvenidos" and sometimes the sign on the tower would say "Bienvenue," some places were wet and hot and others dry and hot, but at each of these airports the pastel concrete walls would rust and stain and the swamp off the runway would be littered with the fuselages of cannibalized Fairchild F-227's and the water would need boiling.*
>   "*I knew why Charlotte went to the airport even if Victor did not.*
>   "*I knew about airports.*"

These lines appear about halfway through *A Book of Common Prayer*, but I wrote them during the second week I worked on the book, long before I had any idea where Charlotte Douglas had been or why she went to airports. Until I wrote these lines I had no character called "Victor" in mind: the necessity for mentioning a name, and the name "Victor," occurred to me as I wrote the sentence. *I knew why Charlotte went to the airport* sounded incomplete. *I knew why Charlotte went to the airport even if Victor did not* carried a little more narrative drive. Most important of all, until I wrote these lines I did not know who "I" was, who was telling the story. I had intended until that moment that the "I" be no more than the voice of the author, a 19th-century omniscient narrator. But there it was:

>   "*I knew why Charlotte went to the airport even if Victor did not.*
>   "*I knew about airports.*"

This "I" was the voice of no author in my house. This "I" was someone who not only knew why Charlotte went to the airport but also knew someone called "Victor." Who was Victor? Who was this narrator? Why was this narrator telling me this story? Let me tell you one thing about why writers write: had I known the answer to any of these questions I would never have needed to write a novel.

Response

1. In recalling her college days Didion underscores her preoccupation with physical details of experience. How is this reflected in her writing—and illustrated, for example, in paragraphs 5 and 15?

2. How do the "shimmering images" in Didion's mind relate to arrangements of words on a page? Examine the metaphor Didion presents when she says "grammar is a piano I play by ear, since I seem to have been out of school the year the rules were mentioned" (paragraph 9). What is the difference between playing by ear and following rules? Can instruction be of any value?

3. Through examples Didion tells us about her process of writing. She suggests that her stories, unplanned, create themselves as the details of real life merge with elements of fiction—that she, the narrator, discovers the story as it is written. How does this description reflect her reasons for writing as expressed in paragraph 7 and implied in the last sentence of the essay? Do you believe that writing can work this way?

4. Didion opens and closes this essay with the notion of "I." She portrays herself as a writer concerned solely with the act of writing and with herself as a topic: "I write entirely to find out what I'm thinking, what I'm looking at, what I see and what it means" (paragraph 7). At the end of the essay she generalizes her motivation to other writers. To what extent do you think other writers in this section would share Didion's view that "writing is the act of saying 'I', . . . an imposition of the writer's sensibility on the reader's most private space"?

Talking Back
bell hooks

This is the title essay of hooks's 1989 book Talking
Back. *In the introduction to that book she explains,
"It has been a political struggle for me to hold on to
the belief that there is much which we—black
people—must speak about, much that is private that
must be openly shared, if we are to heal our wounds
(hurts caused by domination and exploitation and
oppression), if we are to recover and realize
ourselves."*

In the world of the southern black community I grew up in,
"back talk" and "talking back" meant speaking as an equal to an
authority figure. It meant daring to disagree and sometimes it just
meant having an opinion. In the "old school," children were meant
to be seen and not heard. My great-grandparents, grandparents, and
parents were all from the old school. To make yourself heard if you
were a child was to invite punishment, the back-hand lick, the slap
across the face that would catch you unaware, or the feel of switches
stinging your arms and legs.

To speak then when one was not spoken to was a courageous
act—an act of risk and daring. And yet it was hard not to speak in
warm rooms where heated discussions began at the crack of dawn,
women's voices filling the air, giving orders, making threats, fuss-

bell hooks, "Talking Back," in *Talking Back: Thinking Feminist, Thinking
Black*. Boston: South End Press, 1989. Reprinted with permission from the publisher.

ing. Black men may have excelled in the art of poetic preaching in the male-dominated church, but in the church of the home, where the everyday rules of how to live and how to act were established, it was black women who preached. There, black women spoke in a language so rich, so poetic, that it felt to me like being shut off from life, smothered to death if one were not allowed to participate.

It was in that world of woman talk (the men were often silent, often absent) that was born in me the craving to speak, to have a voice, and not just any voice but one that could be identified as belonging to me. To make my voice, I had to speak, to hear myself talk—and talk I did—darting in and out of grown folks' conversations and dialogues, answering questions that were not directed at me, endlessly asking questions, making speeches. Needless to say, the punishments for these acts of speech seemed endless. They were intended to silence me—the child—and more particularly the girl child. Had I been a boy, they might have encouraged me to speak believing that I might someday be called to preach. There was no "calling" for talking girls, no legitimized rewarded speech. The punishments I received for "talking back" were intended to suppress all possibility that I would create my own speech. That speech was to be suppressed so that the "right speech of womanhood" would emerge.

Within feminist circles, silence is often seen as the sexist "right speech of womanhood"—the sign of woman's submission to patriarchal authority. This emphasis on woman's silence may be an accurate remembering of what has taken place in the households of women from WASP backgrounds in the United States, but in black communities (and diverse ethnic communities), women have not been silent. Their voices can be heard. Certainly for black women, our struggle has not been to emerge from silence into speech but to change the nature and direction of our speech, to make a speech that compels listeners, one that is heard.

5   Our speech, "the right speech of womanhood," was often the soliloquy, the talking into thin air, the talking to ears that do not hear you—the talk that is simply not listened to. Unlike the black male preacher whose speech was to be heard, who was to be listened to, whose words were to be remembered, the voices of black women—giving orders, making threats, fussing—could be tuned out, could become a kind of background music, audible but not acknowledged as significant speech. Dialogue—the sharing of speech and recognition—took place not between mother and child or mother and male authority figure but among black women. I can remember watching fascinated as our mother talked with her mother, sisters, and women friends. The intimacy and intensity of their speech—

the satisfaction they received from talking to one another, the plea-sure, the joy. It was in this world of woman speech, loud talk, angry words, women with tongues quick and sharp, tender sweet tongues, touching our world with their words, that I made speech my birthright—and the right to voice, to authorship, a privilege I would not be denied. It was in that world and because of it that I came to dream of writing, to write.

Writing was a way to capture speech, to hold onto it, keep it close. And so I wrote down bits and pieces of conversations, confess-ing in cheap diaries that soon fell apart from too much handling, expressing the intensity of my sorrow, the anguish of speech—for I was always saying the wrong thing, asking the wrong questions. I could not confine my speech to the necessary corners and concerns of life. I hid these writings under my bed, in pillow stuffings, among faded underwear. When my sisters found and read them, they ridi-culed and mocked me—poking fun. I felt violated, ashamed, as if the secret parts of my self had been exposed, brought into the open, and hung like newly clean laundry, out in the air for everyone to see. The fear of exposure, the fear that one's deepest emotions and inner-most thoughts will be dismissed as mere nonsense, felt by so many young girls keeping diaries, holding and hiding speech, seems to me now one of the barriers that women have always needed and still need to destroy so that we are no longer pushed into secrecy or si-lence.

Despite my feelings of violation, of exposure, I continued to speak and write, choosing my hiding places well, learning to destroy work when no safe place could be found. I was never taught absolute silence, I was taught that it was important to speak but to talk a talk that was in itself a silence. Taught to speak and yet beware of the betrayal of too much heard speech, I experienced intense confusion and deep anxiety in my efforts to speak and write. Reciting poems at Sunday afternoon church service might be rewarded. Writing a poem (when one's time could be "better" spent sweeping, ironing, learning to cook) was luxurious activity, indulged in at the expense of others. Questioning authority, raising issues that were not deemed appropriate subjects brought pain, punishments—like telling mama I wanted to die before her because I could not live without her—that was crazy talk, crazy speech, the kind that would lead you to end up in a mental institution. "Little girl," I would be told, "if you don't stop all this crazy talk and crazy acting you are going to end up right out there at Western State."

Madness, not just physical abuse, was the punishment for too much talk if you were female. Yet even as this fear of madness haunted me, hanging over my writing like a monstrous shadow, I could not stop the words, making thought, writing speech. For this terrible madness which I feared, which I was sure was the destiny of daring women born to intense speech (after all, the authorities emphasized this point daily), was not as threatening as imposed silence, as suppressed speech.

Safety and sanity were to be sacrificed if I was to experience defiant speech. Though I risked them both, deep-seated fears and anxieties characterized my childhood days. I would speak but I would not ride a bike, play hardball, or hold the gray kitten. Writing about the ways we are traumatized in our growing-up years, psychoanalyst Alice Miller makes the point in *For Your Own Good* that it is not clear why childhood wounds become for some folk an opportunity to grow, to move forward rather than backward in the process of self-realization. Certainly, when I reflect on the trials of my growing-up years, the many punishments, I can see now that in resistance I learned to be vigilant in the nourishment of my spirit, to be tough, to courageously protect that spirit from forces that would break it.

10   While punishing me, my parents often spoke about the necessity of breaking my spirit. Now when I ponder the silences, the voices that are not heard, the voices of those wounded and/or oppressed individuals who do not speak or write, I contemplate the acts of persecution, torture—the terrorism that breaks spirits, that makes creativity impossible. I write these words to bear witness to the primacy of resistance struggle in any situation of domination (even within family life); to the strength and power that emerges from sustained resistance and the profound conviction that these forces can be healing, can protect us from dehumanization and despair.

These early trials, wherein I learned to stand my ground, to keep my spirit intact, came vividly to mind after I published *Ain't I A Woman* and the book was sharply and harshly criticized. While I had expected a climate of critical dialogue, I was not expecting a critical avalanche that had the power in its intensity to crush the spirit, to push one into silence. Since that time, I have heard stories about black women, about women of color, who write and publish (even when the work is quite successful) having nervous breakdowns, being made mad because they cannot bear the harsh responses of family, friends, and unknown critics, or becoming silent, unproductive. Surely, the absence of a humane critical response has tremendous impact on the writer from any oppressed, colonized group who endeavors to speak. For us, true speaking is not solely an expression of creative power; it is an act of resistance, a political gesture that challenges politics of domination that would render us nameless and voiceless. As such, it is a courageous act—as such, it represents a threat. To those who wield oppressive power, that which is threatening must necessarily be wiped out, annihilated, silenced.

Recently, efforts by black women writers to call attention to our work serve to highlight both our presence and absence. Whenever I peruse women's bookstores, I am struck not by the rapidly growing body of feminist writing by black women, but by the paucity of available published material. Those of us who write and are published remain few in number. The context of silence is varied and multi-dimensional. Most obvious are the ways racism, sexism, and class exploitation act to suppress and silence. Less obvious are the inner struggles, the efforts made to gain the necessary confidence to write, to re-write, to fully develop craft and skill—and the extent to which such efforts fail.

Although I have wanted writing to be my life-work since childhood, it has been difficult for me to claim "writer" as part of that which identifies and shapes my everyday reality. Even after publishing books, I would often speak of wanting to be a writer as though these works did not exist. And though I would be told, "you are a writer," I was not yet ready to fully affirm this truth. Part of myself was still held captive by domineering forces of history, of familial life that had charted a map of silence, of right speech. I had not completely let go of the fear of saying the wrong thing, of being punished. Somewhere in the deep recesses of my mind, I believed I could avoid both responsibility and punishment if I did not declare myself a writer.

One of the many reasons I chose to write using the pseudonym bell hooks, a family name (mother to Sarah Oldham, grandmother to Rosa Bell Oldham, great-grandmother to me), was to construct a writer-identity that would challenge and subdue all impulses leading me away from speech into silence. I was a young girl buying bubble gum at the corner store when I first really heard the full name bell hooks. I had just "talked back" to a grown person. Even now I can recall the surprised look, the mocking tones that informed me I must be kin to bell hooks—a sharp-tongued woman, a woman who spoke her mind, a woman who was not afraid to talk back. I claimed this legacy of defiance, of will, of courage, affirming my link to female ancestors who were bold and daring in their speech. Unlike my bold and daring mother and grandmother, who were not supportive of talking back, even though they were assertive and powerful in their speech, bell hooks as I discovered, claimed, and invented her was my ally, my support.

That initial act of talking back outside the home was empowering. It was the first of many acts of defiant speech that would make it possible for me to emerge as an independent thinker and writer.

15

In retrospect, "talking back" became for me a rite of initiation, testing my courage, strengthening my commitment, preparing me for the days ahead—the days when writing, rejection notices, periods of silence, publication, ongoing development seem impossible but necessary.

Moving from silence into speech is for the oppressed, the colonized, the exploited, and those who stand and struggle side by side a gesture of defiance that heals, that makes new life and new growth possible. It is that act of speech, of "talking back," that is no mere gesture of empty words, that is the expression of our movement from object to subject—the liberated voice.

Response

1. According to hooks, what kind of talk was approved and tolerated in childhood? What was considered inappropriate—a threat to "safety and sanity"? Hooks portrays her role as a writer by analogy to her childhood experience. Examine her analogy: What is the significance of writing for her, given her particular experience? What does she consider "true speaking," and why is it courageous? What circumstances can serve to suppress and silence writers?

2. To what extent do you think the "fear of exposure" and "fear of saying the wrong thing" (paragraph 6) are, as hooks suggests, problems particular to the experience of girls and women? Explain your opinion.

3. In what ways could hooks's essay be seen as an illustration of James Baldwin's observation that "the things which hurt [one] most and the things which helped [one] most cannot be divorced from each other" ("Autobiographical Notes")?

4. What attitudes about speech did you experience growing up? How do you think this experience affects your present behavior? How much of your own speech or writing would fit hooks's idea of "talking back"?

5. Hooks, like Paule Marshall in "The Poets in the Kitchen" (Section III), recognizes the richness of the "world of woman talk" that was part of her childhood. How does hooks value and respond to that experience? Compare hooks' response with Marshall's.

6. In "The Transformation of Silence into Language and Action" (Section V), Audre Lorde also writes about speaking out. Compare the two women's views about the pressures to remain silent.

Confessions of an Unknown Writer
Toshio Mori

Mori wrote this essay in 1936, about a period in his life when he was working long hours every day in his family's nursery, then writing every night until 2 A.M. In it he both laments his lack of outward success and celebrates his inner capability. The essay is included in The Chauvinist and Other Stories *(1979).*

"GO AND BUY a coat and a hat," I told her. "You're going to a wedding and your coat is five years old and that hat is old style." My mother was going to a wedding in the city and yesterday she wished she had something new to wear to the affair. I was in her room with a batch of old magazines I had bought in the city. Nickel apiece for *Story, Harper, New Yorker, Atlantic Monthly, Fiction Parade, Scribner's,* and *Writer's Digest.* I wanted her to go in new clothes so she would feel good, so she would feel she belonged to the age, the year, the feminine fashion of the day. I wanted her to feel good when she joined her friends at the party.

"Everything's a bargain now," I said. "Twenty dollars will do. Buy it tomorrow."

"No," she said. "I don't want it. It isn't your wedding. My clothes will do."

"Oh, go ahead and buy it," I said.

Toshio Mori, "Confessions of an Unknown Writer," in *The Chauvinist, and Other Stories.* Asian American Studies Center, Los Angeles: U.C.L.A., 1979. Reprinted with permission.

5   "I don't want it," she said. "I don't want a new coat. Just get
your story in some magazine and I'll feel better."

I sat on the bed and leafed *The Atlantic*. I wanted very much
to appear in a magazine and hadn't got in. I had grown old and was
a half-writer and a half-nurseryman. This was no place to feel bad
but after having six stories returned from the magazines that afternoon I felt rotten. I wanted to talk of the future but I couldn't. Sometimes if you're a writer it's fun to talk of the future. It's very nice to
see something that'll be you in the future if the luck's with you. But
something's been wrong with me lately: I was a dead-beat. I didn't
want her to know how I was feeling but she knew how I was feeling
these days, and it made it all the worse.

I sat there in her room holding the magazines and thinking of
names and dates. Dreiser wrote his *Sister Carrie* at twenty-eight;
Thomas Wolfe began at twenty-eight; Dostoyevsky at twenty-five;
Saroyan at twenty-four; Hemingway in the early twenties. It wasn't
just the desperation from lack of time. It wasn't just the literary side
of the matter. It was everything. It was time I was thinking of myself
as a solitary man in the world: the man alone like everyone else,
matured and immatured. The man alone as a writer, and the man
alone as a means of living. I couldn't be a writer and I was one.

When you are young everything is simple outside of yourself.
When you get a little older you begin to see everything is not simple
including yourself. And when you are about to die and about to be
death itself, everything becomes simple again. We know the cycle
of life. We have scientifically searched the individual cases over and
over so today we know how the human beings act and react, and
why. We know the law and order. We paint things up these days but
we know it's the old stuff. The meaning of work today is same as
the meaning of work before Christ. To get to the point: one writer
writes and another writer follows and writes. When you think of it
seriously it's curious. After the millions of writers through the ages
get through with expression what has the latest writer got that
wasn't expressed before unless it's after-death mystery? A tailor tailors and another tailor follows suit and tailors. It's simple: practical
use. A scientist experiments and another scientist adds, and that's
understandable: progress. You might say a writer follows the millions of writers for moral, spiritual, and material progress and let it
go at that. That's a generous tag and sometimes it turns out comical.
You might say writers bob up every minute or so because of the
imperfect world. And you might add that there will always be writers on earth because you know man's world will never be perfect. I
won't argue with anybody about this opinion because I am a little
older and know everything is not so simple, including myself the
writer.

If you are a Japanese or have Japanese friends who talk you will understand the situation a young man is in when the friendly men and women of the older generation come around to you and talk about marriage. They begin mentioning names of the girls and describing their personalities. This probably won't happen to the boys who go out early and pick a girl and marry her. It won't happen to the veterans of love affairs because they are left alone, and justly so on account of their abilities. It will happen to men who are shy and respectable and to men who are still unattached at a respectable age and have had no luck. Well, this particular friend comes in every once in a while and starts rattling off the girls' names to me.

"Why don't you marry?" he keeps asking me. There are several   10
others but I won't mention them.

"I don't want to marry just now," I tell this friend of mine.

"Why?" he comes right back, and I must tell him the truth to make him go away and shut up.

"I want to write," I tell him. This is an unreasonable and inadequate answer but it was all I could get out of myself.

"You can marry and write at the same time," my particular friend says. "They mix well. Why wait for a better spring?"

I couldn't answer this one because I haven't had experience in   15
that line. Anyhow I shook my head vigorously and said, "I want to write." I didn't say it lamely. I was very sure of myself, and I don't know why. I stood him off very well. "Yes," I admitted, "you can marry and write. You can marry if you have money to set up a home."

But what struggling writer has time enough to write and have money enough to set up a new home for a bride? You either write and get in a little money and marry or you marry and become acclimated with everything, including money, and then write. It's an angle, one way or the other. You have no money and you have no girl or you have no money and you have a girl. But in either case you are to write, and also live.

Sometimes I kick myself inwardly for being a fool. My friends who came out of the school in the same year or later have become substantial citizens in their community. George Matsuo has a good-sized bank account and is single. What has a guy like that got to worry about unless he has crazy ideas? Tadashi Nozato is a good salaried salesman plus bonus and commission. Averages two hundred a month or more, owns a home, and has a beautiful wife. Tommy Doi is a hustling grocer. Has a wife and three kids, three smooth-running stores, and owns a Buick. Shigeo Kawashima now a big-shot in an important company. Good old Tack Toyama, now Doctor Toyama, physician-surgeon. I could go on for pages but I must eventually return to myself.

In the middle of drilling a hole in my abscessed tooth I confided to my dentist that I was secretly writing. He wasn't a bit surprised when I confessed. He is an artist of dentistry because he makes you forget he is fixing your teeth, and when you hear him talking you are admitting to yourself that a dentist has been working all the time. His fingers are sensitive to the touch. They detect the feel of a nerve center when a drill is working so you can enjoy a conversation with him. We were talking about the structure and the resistance and the decay of not only the teeth but life itself. He looked at me, when I said I was writing, as if I were a young tooth or a young cypress. He didn't know what sort of writing I was doing but his smile of "Ah, good for you," made me forget bad writing and the blue days. "Take fifty years," he told me. "Take a lifetime." He had married late and accomplishments came late. When he was young he had a hell of a time. "I once had to go around to the white dentists and solicit for dental plate work," he said. "I had opened an office on Twelfth and Broadway and no customers came for months. The plate work paid the rent and a sign on my door and I was fortunate to eat." First it was the problem of an abscessed tooth; then it was the resistance and decay of life; and now it was writing we talk about.

I am sitting in my mother's room thinking of the roll of my short life. If I were to die tonight I would leave nothing behind. With death I would be forever erased; with life I would be forever divorced. If I were to find myself alive tomorrow morning at eight I would still be a half-writer and a half-nurseryman. I would put every ounce of my body behind my words, thinking of death. Tomorrow I would be death seeking life. This is the comical history of my thoughts. This is endless because I am alive. This is comical because I am dead serious. And I would add that my history is like a thousand nights and days: the dots and dashes of a brief light in a smoky city.

20 "Don't you want to go to the wedding?" I asked mother. It was a foolish question. She was inside the closet taking down her garments and looking them over.

"Yes, I'm going," she said. Then I heard clearly "The Wedding March" on a church organ. I visioned the scene of a toast and dreamed the passing of wedding night. Not far off I heard the drums and bugle calls; the armies marching; and the diplomats rejoicing, sweating, and crying. What do I want to say to the world? Over in the next house a woman has a cancer on the breast and has eleven days to go. A florist is picking his nose for want of business. My barber who has been through the mill spits on love (love in marriage) for the benefit of men customers. Guy Lombardo's sweet lingering music coming out of the men's shack which was once a henhouse.

What do I want out of life and what do I want to say? The pussywillows bend with the wind; the magazines go to press without a genius; a writer crosses the ocean in search of material for a book. The letter writer using mannerism. A postcard is for the world to see, and it costs only a cent and a half. Ah, what shall I say? The magnificence of a traffic roar and the grandeur of a stinking city. The lovely silence of death and the lovely silence of life: irresistible, and irritable.

Do you know what capabilities man has? Sit down some day and leisurely think it over. It is a fine story. I am sitting here quietly and I know I have many capabilities. I speak of it because I am sure of myself and know I am not bragging. It is a time like this (sure of myself and know I am not bragging) when I like to sit before a clean white sheet and put my story down. It is this: sometimes I am capable of murder; sometimes I can love; or I am a fanatic or the suppressed or a dreamer or the listless or a coward or any other traits of a being. It is this capability of man which is so natural to occur that I am taking myself as the story and firmly believe its worth. I believe in this capability of man; thus, a saint is no different from a dissipator; a prophet no wiser than a disbeliever; a capitalist and a laborer are pals; a diplomat and a soldier are brothers; a Marian Anderson and an inarticulate are singing the same tune; a producer and a consumer are the union; a citizen and an alien make the flag of man, and; thus, an unpublished and an immortal are writers from the same heart. I believe in man and also disbelieve, and there is no harm. It is temporary as all are fleeting and of decay; and there is no end to it in the ages to come. It is necessary that I should add one climax to this little world of mine: the approach of man to the world (and to himself which is the seed) which makes or breaks the tip of his arrow.

I am back in my little room writing the end of this piece and thinking about myself, the writer. I am settled back and comfortable. I do not need to hurry. My head is clearer and I am returning consciously to the glare of a clean white paper before me. I become smaller and the size of the blank white sheet grows bigger. I become panicky and then dull. The silence of my room which is usually very dear to me begins to irritate me. All I have is myself, I think, and to commune with a clean sheet of paper is the costliest time of my life. I have no place to go, and I have nobody waiting for me. I am a fool, I am a big fool, I think to myself. I am wasting my life on nothing and, like a fool, will continue wasting it forever.

For something to do I rush up to the mirror and look at my face. The biggest little sap, the biggest little sap, I keep saying to myself. What have I done in the past, and what shall be my future? I look at my old face and become sad. I think of my mother and her patience, and her belief in me. This is terrible. This is tragedy. I put the mirror down and look at the familiar objects. My old desk with scattered papers, the old magazines, second-hand books, an old typewriter, and the bare yellow walls. I walk up and down the little room until I become exhausted. Dimly I hear the train whistle, and the trains roar by. It is three in the morning, I think to myself. I sit down in the only seat I have in the room before my typewriter. Then, as I sit for minutes or perhaps hours, it becomes natural for me to sit before the typewriter and face the challenge of a white paper and life. Only then, I realize, I will sit and write even if I should become a fool. I will go on writing for life no matter that may happen for a few mad hours or days, that being a fool will not stop one from becoming what nature had intended him to be.

Response

1. What seems to be Mori's attitude toward worldly success, in terms of recognition and money?
2. How is Mori's friend the dentist an artist? What do Mori the writer and his dentist have in common?
3. In this essay Mori frequently juxtaposes opposites. In paragraph 7, for example, he says "I couldn't be a writer and I was one." Examine paragraphs 19 through 22, which present a number of paradoxical notions. What do they indicate about Mori's view of human endeavors, including his own?
4. In paragraph 8 Mori raises the question of why writers write. He observes with a touch of irony, "We know the cycle of life. We have scientifically searched the individual cases over and over so today we know how the human beings act and react, and why." His examples then lead him to the more truthful statement that "everything is not so simple, including myself the writer." He suggests that the answer is not a matter for rational explanation. What, then, is the role of the writer in his view, and what motivates him to keep writing?
5. Some critics have observed oddities in Mori's grammar. In the introduction to Mori's book *The Chauvinist*, Hisaye Yamamoto (whose stories also are represented in this volume) says, "I think Toshio, just as I, was trying to use the very best English of which he was capable, and we have both run aground on occasion. Probably this was because we both spent the prekindergarten years speaking only Japanese." How would you evaluate the effectiveness of Mori's writing style?

The Language We Know

Simon J. Ortiz

This essay appears in I Tell You Now *(1987), a collection of autobiographical essays by Native American writers. In it Ortiz discusses how the language and traditions of the Acoma people influence his writing.*

I don't remember a world without language. From the time of my earliest childhood, there was language. Always language, and imagination, speculation, utters of sound. Words, beginnings of words. What would I be without language? My existence has been determined by language, not only the spoken but the unspoken, the language of speech and the language of motion. I can't remember a world without memory. Memory, immediate and far away in the past, something in the sinew, blood, ageless cell. Although I don't recall the exact moment I spoke or tried to speak, I know the feeling of something tugging at the core of the mind, something unutterable uttered into existence. It is language that brings us into being in order to know life.

My childhood was the oral tradition of the Acoma Pueblo people—Aaquumeh hano—which included my immediate family of three

Simon J. Ortiz, "The Language We Know," in *I Tell You Now: Autobiographical Essays by Native American Writers*, edited by Brian Swann and Arnold Krupat, Lincoln, Nebraska: University of Nebraska Press, 1987. Copyright © 1987 by the University of Nebraska Press. Reprinted by permission of University of Nebraska Press.

older sisters, two younger sisters, two younger brothers, and my mother and father. My world was our world of the Aaquumeh in McCartys, one of the two villages descended from the ageless mother pueblo of Acoma. My world was our Eagle clan-people among other clans. I grew up in Deetziyamah, which is the Aaquumeh name for McCartys, which is posted at the exit off the present interstate highway in western New Mexico. I grew up within a people who farmed small garden plots and fields, who were mostly poor and not well schooled in the American system's education. The language I spoke was that of a struggling people who held ferociously to a heritage, culture, language, and land despite the odds posed them by the forces surrounding them since 1540 A.D., the advent of Euro-American colonization. When I began school in 1948 at the BIA (Bureau of Indian Affairs) day school in our village, I was armed with the basic ABC's and the phrases "Good morning, Miss Oleman" and "May I please be excused to go to the bathroom," but it was an older language that was my fundamental strength.

In my childhood, the language we all spoke was Acoma, and it was a struggle to maintain it against the outright threats of corporal punishment, ostracism, and the invocation that it would impede our progress towards Americanization. Children in school were punished and looked upon with disdain if they did not speak and learn English quickly and smoothly, and so I learned it. It has occurred to me that I learned English simply because I was forced to, as so many other Indian children were. But I know, also, there was another reason, and this was that I loved language, the sound, meaning, and magic of language. Language opened up vistas of the world around me, and it allowed me to discover knowledge that would not be possible for me to know without the use of language. Later, when I began to experiment with and explore language in poetry and fiction, I allowed that a portion of that impetus was because I had come to know English through forceful acculturation. Nevertheless, the underlying force was the beauty and poetic power of language in its many forms that instilled in me the desire to become a user of language as a writer, singer, and storyteller. Significantly, it was the Acoma language, which I don't use enough of today, that inspired me to become a writer. The concepts, values, and philosophy contained in my original language and the struggle it has faced have determined my life and vision as a writer.

In Deetziyamah, I discovered the world of the Acoma land and people firsthand through my parents, sisters and brothers, and my own perceptions, voiced through all that encompasses the oral tradition, which is ageless for any culture. It is a small village, even smaller years ago, and like other Indian communities it is wealthy with its knowledge of daily event, history, and social system, all that make up a people who have a many-dimensioned heritage. Our family lived in a two-room home (built by my grandfather some years after he and my grandmother moved with their daughters from Old Acoma), which my father added rooms to later. I remember my father's work at enlarging our home for our growing family. He was a skilled stoneworker, like many other men of an older Pueblo generation who worked with sandstone and mud mortar to build their homes and pueblos. It takes time, persistence, patience, and the belief that the walls that come to stand will do so for a long, long time, perhaps even forever. I like to think that by helping to mix mud and carry stone for my father and other elders I managed to bring that influence into my consciousness as a writer.

Both my mother and my father were good storytellers and sing-   5
ers (as my mother is to this day—my father died in 1978), and for their generation, which was born soon after the turn of the century, they were relatively educated in the American system. Catholic missionaries had taken both of them as children to a parochial boarding school far from Acoma, and they imparted their discipline for study and quest for education to us children when we started school. But it was their indigenous sense of gaining knowledge that was most meaningful to me. Acquiring knowledge about life was above all the most important item; it was a value that one had to have in order to be fulfilled personally and on behalf of his community. And this they insisted upon imparting through the oral tradition as they told their children about our native history and our community and culture and our "stories." These stories were common knowledge of act, event, and behavior in a close-knit pueblo. It was knowledge about how one was to make a living through work that benefited his family and everyone else.

Because we were a subsistence farming people, or at least tried to be, I learned to plant, hoe weeds, irrigate and cultivate corn, chili, pumpkins, beans. Through counsel and advice I came to know that the rain which provided water was a blessing, gift, and symbol and that it was the land which provided for our lives. It was the stories and songs which provided the knowledge that I was woven into the intricate web that was my Acoma life. In our garden and our corn-fields I learned about the seasons, growth cycles of cultivated plants, what one had to think and feel about the land; and at home I became aware of how we must care for each other: all of this was encompassed in an intricate relationship which had to be maintained in order that life continue. After supper on many occasions my father would bring out his drum and sing as we, the children, danced to themes about the rain, hunting, land, and people. It was all that is contained within the language of oral tradition that made me explicitly aware of a yet unarticulated urge to write, to tell what I had learned and was learning and what it all meant to me.

My grandfather was old already when I came to know him. I was only one of his many grandchildren, but I would go with him to get wood for our households, to the garden to chop weeds, and to his sheep camp to help care for his sheep. I don't remember his exact words, but I know they were about how we must sacredly concern ourselves with the people and the holy earth. I know his words were about how we must regard ourselves and others with compassion and love; I know that his knowledge was vast, as a medicine man and an elder of his kiva, and I listened as a boy should. My grandfather represented for me a link to the past that is important for me to hold in my memory because it is not only memory but knowledge that substantiates my present existence. He and the grandmothers and grandfathers before him thought about us as they lived, confirmed in their belief of a continuing life, and they brought our present beings into existence by the beliefs they held. The consciousness of that belief is what informs my present concerns with language, poetry, and fiction.

My first poem was for Mother's Day when I was in the fifth grade, and it was the first poem that was ever published, too, in the Skull Valley School newsletter. Of course I don't remember how the juvenile poem went, but it must have been certain in its expression of love and reverence for the woman who was the most important person in my young life. The poem didn't signal any prophecy of my future as a poet, but it must have come from the forming idea that there were things one could do with language and writing. My mother, years later, remembers how I was a child who always told stories—that is, tall tales—who always had explanations for things probably better left unspoken, and she says that I also liked to perform in school plays. In remembering, I do know that I was coming to that age when the emotions and thoughts in me began to moil to the surface. There was much to experience and express in that age when youth has a precociousness that is broken easily or made to flourish. We were a poor family, always on the verge of financial disaster, though our parents always managed to feed us and keep us in clothing. We had the problems, unfortunately ordinary, of many Indian families who face poverty on a daily basis, never enough of anything, the feeling of a denigrating self-consciousness, alcoholism in the family and community, the feeling that something was falling apart though we tried desperately to hold it all together.

My father worked for the railroad for many years as a laborer and later as a welder. We moved to Skull Valley, Arizona, for one year in the early 1950s, and it was then that I first came in touch with a non-Indian, non-Acoma world. Skull Valley was a farming and ranching community, and my younger brothers and sisters and I went to a one-room school. I had never really had much contact with white people except from a careful and suspicious distance, but now here I was, totally surrounded by them, and there was nothing to do but bear the experience and learn from it. Although I perceived there was not much difference between *them* and *us* in certain respects, there was a distinct feeling that we were not the same either. This thought had been inculcated in me, especially by an Acoma expression—*Gaimuu Mericano*—that spoke of the "fortune" of being an American. In later years as a social activist and committed writer, I would try to offer a strong positive view of our collective Indianness through my writing. Nevertheless, my father was an inadequately paid laborer, and we were far from our home land for economic-social reasons, and my feelings and thoughts about that experience during that time would become a part of how I became a writer.

Soon after, I went away from my home and family to go to   10
boarding school, first in Santa Fe and then in Albuquerque. This was in the 1950s, and this had been the case for the past half-century for Indians: we had to leave home in order to become truly American by joining the mainstream, which was deemed to be the proper course of our lives. On top of this was termination, a U.S. government policy which dictated that Indians sever their relationship to the federal government and remove themselves from their lands and go to American cities for jobs and education. It was an era which bespoke the intent of U.S. public policy that Indians were no longer to be Indians. Naturally, I did not perceive this in any analytical or purposeful sense; rather, I felt an unspoken anxiety and resentment against unseen forces that determined our destiny to be un-Indian, embarrassed and uncomfortable with our grandparents' customs and strictly held values. We were to set our goals as American working men and women, singlemindedly industrious, patriotic, and unquestioning, building for a future which ensured that the U.S. was the greatest nation in the world. I felt fearfully uneasy with this, for by then I felt the loneliness, alienation, and isolation imposed upon me by the separation from my family, home, and community.

Something was happening; I could see that in my years at Catholic school and the U.S. Indian school. I remembered my grandparents' and parents' words: educate yourself in order to help your people. In that era and the generation who had the same experience I had, there was an unspoken vow: we were caught in a system inexorably, and we had to learn that system well in order to fight back. Without the motive of a fight-back we would not be able to survive as the people our heritage had lovingly bequeathed us. My diaries and notebooks began then, and though none have survived to the present, I know they contained the varied moods of a youth filled with loneliness, anger, and discomfort that seemed to have unknown causes. Yet at the same time, I realize now, I was coming to know myself clearly in a way that I would later articulate in writing. My love of language, which allowed me to deal with the world, to delve into it, to experiment and discover, held for me a vision of awe and wonder, and by then grammar teachers had noticed I was a good speller, used verbs and tenses correctly, and wrote complete sentences. Although I imagine that they might have surmised this as unusual for an Indian student whose original language was not English, I am grateful for their perception and attention.

During the latter part of that era in the 1950s of Indian termination and the Cold War, a portion of which still exists today, there were the beginnings of a bolder and more vocalized resistance against the current U.S. public policies of repression, racism, and cultural ethnocide. It seemed to be inspired by the civil rights movement led by black people in the U.S. and by decolonization and liberation struggles worldwide. Indian people were being relocated from their rural homelands at an astonishingly devastating rate, yet at the same time they resisted the U.S. effort by maintaining determined ties with their heritage, returning often to their native communities and establishing Indian centers in the cities they were removed to. Indian rural communities, such as Acoma Pueblo, insisted on their land claims and began to initiate legal battles in the areas of natural and social, political and economic human rights. By the retention and the inspiration of our native heritage, values, philosophies, and language, we would know ourselves as a strong and enduring people. Having a modest and latent consciousness of this as a teenager, I began to write about the experience of being Indian in America. Although I had only a romanticized image of what a writer was, which came from the pulp rendered by American popular literature, and I really didn't know anything about writing, I sincerely felt a need to say things, to speak, to release the energy of the impulse to help my people.

My writing in my late teens and early adulthood was fashioned after the American short stories and poetry taught in the high schools of the 1940s and 1950s, but by the 1960s, after I had gone to college and dropped out and served in the military, I began to develop topics and themes from my Indian background. The experience in my village of Deetziyamah and Acoma Pueblo was readily accessible. I had grown up within the oral tradition of speech, social and religious ritual, elders' counsel and advice, countless and endless stories, everyday event, and the visual art that was symbolically representative of life all around. My mother was a potter of the well-known Acoma clayware, a traditional art form that had been passed to her from her mother and the generations of mothers before. My father carved figures from wood and did beadwork. This was not unusual, as Indian people know; there was always some kind of artistic endeavor that people set themselves to, although they did not necessarily articulate it as "Art" in the sense of Western civilization. One lived and expressed an artful life, whether it was in ceremonial singing and dancing, architecture, painting, speaking, or in the way one's social-cultural life was structured. When I turned my attention to my own heritage, I did so because this was my identity, the substance of who I was, and I wanted to write about what that meant. My desire was to write about the integrity and dignity of an Indian identity, and at the same time I wanted to look at what this was within the context of an America that had too often denied its Indian heritage.

To a great extent my writing has a natural political-cultural bent simply because I was nurtured intellectually and emotionally within an atmosphere of Indian resistance. Aacquu did not die in 1598 when it was burned and razed by European conquerors, nor did the people become hopeless when their children were taken away to U.S. schools far from home and new ways were imposed upon them. The *Aaquumeh hano*, despite losing much of their land and surrounded by a foreign civilization, have not lost sight of their native heritage. This is the factual case with most other Indian peoples, and the clear explanation for this has been the fight-back we have found it necessary to wage. At times, in the past, it was outright armed struggle, like that of present-day Indians in Central and South America with whom we must identify; currently, it is often in the legal arena, and it is in the field of literature. In 1981, when I was invited to the White House for an event celebrating American poets and poetry, I did not immediately accept the invitation. I questioned myself about the possibility that I was merely being exploited as an Indian, and I hedged against accepting. But then I recalled the elders going among our people in the poor days of the 1950s, asking for donations—a dollar here and there, a sheep, perhaps a piece of pottery—in order to finance a trip to the nation's capital. They were to make another countless appeal on behalf of our people, to demand justice, to reclaim lost land even though there was only spare hope they would be successful. I went to the White House realizing that I was to do no less than they and those who had fought in the Pueblo Revolt of 1680, and I read my poems and sang songs that were later described as "guttural" by a Washington, D.C., newspaper. I suppose it is more or less understandable why such a view of Indian literature is held by many, and it is also clear why there should be a polit-

ical stand taken in my writing and those of my sister and brother
Indian writers.

15   The 1960s and afterward have been an invigorating and liberating
period for Indian people. It has been only a little more than twenty
years since Indian writers began to write and publish extensively,
but we are writing and publishing more and more; we can only go
forward. We come from an ageless, continuing oral tradition that
informs us of our values, concepts, and notions as native people, and
it is amazing how much of this tradition is ingrained so deeply in
our contemporary writing, considering the brutal efforts of cultural
repression that was not long ago outright U.S. policy. We were not
to speak our languages, practice our spiritual beliefs, or accept the
values of our past generations; and we were discouraged from pressing for our natural rights as Indian human beings. In spite of the fact
that there is to some extent the same repression today, we persist
and insist in living, believing, hoping, loving, speaking, and writing
as Indians. This is embodied in the language we know and share in
our writing. We have always had this language, and it is the language, spoken and unspoken, that determines our existence, that
brought our grandmothers and grandfathers and ourselves into being
in order that there be a continuing life.

Response

1.   According to Ortiz, the Acoma language gives the past present
     reality and "determines our existence." Explain the impor-
     tance of his original language in Ortiz's view. Considering that
     Ortiz writes in English, how is his writing influenced by his
     knowledge of Acoma? How does he make writing a continua-
     tion of the oral tradition?
2.   Ortiz speaks without resentment about being forced to learn
     English as a child. What benefits did he find in knowing it,
     both as a child and later as an adult?
3.   By helping his father build traditional homes of stone and mud,
     Ortiz learned that the work "takes time, persistence, patience,
     and the belief that the walls that come to stand will do so for a
     long, long time, perhaps even forever" (paragraph 4). How did
     that knowledge influence him as a writer?
4.   Consider how the 1950s policy of "Indian termination" de-
     scribed by Ortiz contrasted with the racial segregation in the
     South during the same period: Native Americans, with a strong
     sense of their cultural heritage, were pressured to assimilate

into the mainstream of U.S. society; African Americans, cut off from their history and cultural origins, were systematically excluded. How could the two policies serve similar functions?

5. Sent away from home to boarding school "in order to become truly American by joining the mainstream" (paragraph 10), Ortiz felt anxious and alienated. How did he and others of his generation respond to this experience? What did Ortiz see as a positive purpose for his mainstream education?

6. If you know more than one language, do you like Ortiz find that your knowledge of one influences your use of the other? What is the significance of each in your life?

Boxing on Paper
Ishmael Reed

In this essay from his book Writin' Is Fightin' *(1988),*
Reed extends the metaphor in the title to explain his
view of being a politically independent African
American male writer.

In 1953, I was working in a drugstore on William Street in Buffalo,
New York. As I left one evening to go home, a man pulled up to the
curb and told me that he needed somebody to help him deliver
newspapers. There were stacks of them in the backseat of his old
brown beat-up Packard, which was just a shade darker than he was.
His name was A. J. Smitherman, editor of *The Empire Star Weekly*,
a Buffalo newspaper. How would you like to have this job every
week? he asked after we'd taken copies of his newspaper to all of the
newsstands on his route. I had been writing before then, and date
my first commissioned work to 1952, when my mother asked me to
write a birthday poem for one of her fellow employees at Satler's
Department Store on Fillmore.

As a youngster, living in the projects, I also composed mini-
sermons that I'd deliver during Sunday School from the pulpit at
Saint Luke's Church, an old Afro-American Episcopal Zion church
located on Eagle Street. But working at *The Empire Star* brought me

into contact with articulate black people like Mary Crosby, Mr. Smitherman, and his son, Toussaint. Within a year, they even let me try my hand at writing columns, and I wrote jazz articles in what was to become a pungent writing style.

I drifted away from the *Star* in high school, having other things on my mind and needing more spending money than Mr. Smitherman was able to pay me. He was a relentless man who was barely able to bring out his newspaper every week. When he died, *The Buffalo Evening News* noted that he had to struggle against adversity. That's one of the things I remember about this gentle, intellectual editor and poet. His calm in the face of calamity.

As fate would have it, in 1960, after I'd dropped out of college and found myself, a father, living in the Talbert Mall Projects, attempting to support a family on forty dollars per week, I volunteered to do some work for the *Star*, which was then edited by Joe Walker, a dynamic young militant who was causing a stir in the city because of his fight against segregated schools and on behalf of Black Power. It was then that the lively style of my writing was put to the test. Fighting for a traffic light for my Talbert Mall neighbors (it's still there); debating the current mayor, James Griffith, on the subject of school segregation; defending black prostitutes who'd been brutalized by the police; and, at the same time, writing poetry and plays. The *Star* folded.

An Irish-American poet named David Sharpe liked a play of mine, and I traveled to New York with him one weekend. We spent most of the time at Chumley's, a restaurant located on Bedford Street in the Village. I was impressed. The book jackets of authors who'd drunk there, including Edna Saint Vincent Millay, lined the wall, and years later I felt that I'd arrived because mine went up. A screenwriter read my play standing at the bar (a play that was later lost in an abandoned car); he liked it.

After that, there was no keeping me from New York, and a few weeks later, Dave and I went down on the Greyhound bus. I carried all of my belongings in a blue plastic bag I'd purchased for ten cents at the laundromat, and noticing my embarrassment, Dave carried it for me. It was 1962.

In New York, I joined the Umbra Workshop, to which Amiri Baraka credits the origin of the type of black aesthetic that so influenced the Black Arts Repertory School. It was in that workshop that I began to become acquainted with the techniques of the Afro-American literary style.

In 1965, I ran a newspaper in Newark, New Jersey, where I featured some of the same issues I'd covered in the *Star*, including a controversial piece on a welfare mother, which offended some blacks because she didn't sport the proper coiffure. It was during my tenure as editor of the *Advance* newspaper that I wrote an article about the police. Under heavy criticism, they'd invited members of the community to travel with them as a way of monitoring their activities. Representatives from the local civil rights organizations refused, but, in the interest of fair play, I accompanied them on their rounds one Saturday night, and because I commented that they had a tough job, I was called a right-winger by some black intellectuals.

I don't have a predictable, computerized approach to political and social issues in a society in which you're either for it or agin' it. Life is much more complex. And so for my early articles about black-on-black crime, I've been criticized by the left, and for my sympathy with some "left-wing" causes I've been criticized by the right, though from time to time I've noticed that there doesn't seem to be a dime's worth of difference between the zealotry of the left and that of the right.

10   I think that a certain amount of philosophical skepticism is necessary, and so regardless of the criticisms I receive from the left, the right, and the middle, I think it's important to maintain a prolific writing jab, as long as my literary legs hold up, because even during these bland and yuppie times, there are issues worth fighting about. Issues that require fresh points of view.

It was quite generous, I thought, for critic Mel Watkins to compare my writing style with that of Muhammad Ali's boxing style. My friend the late Richard Brautigan even saluted me after the publication of *Mumbo Jumbo*, my third novel, with the original front-page description of Jack Johnson's defeat of Jim Jeffries, printed by the *San Francisco Daily*, 4 July 1910. This, too, amounted to overpraise. If I had to compare my style with anyone's it would probably be with that of Larry Holmes. I don't mince my words. Nor do I pull any punches, and though I've delivered some low blows over the years, I'm becoming more accurate, and my punches are regularly landing above the waistline. I'm not a body snatcher like Mike McCallum, and I usually aim for the head.

A black boxer's career is the perfect metaphor for the career of a black male. Every day is like being in the gym, sparring with impersonal opponents as one faces the rudeness and hostility that a black male must confront in the United States, where he is the object of both fear and fascination. My difficulty in communicating this point of view used to really bewilder me, but over the years I've learned that it takes an extraordinary amount of effort to understand someone from a background different from your own, especially when your life doesn't really depend upon it. And so, during this period, when black males seem to be on somebody's endangered-species list, I can understand why some readers and debating opponents might have problems appreciating where I'm coming from.

On a day in the 1940s, the story of the deportation of Jews to European concentration camps was carried in the back pages of a New York newspaper, while news of the weather made the front page. Apparently it was a hot day, and most people were concerned about getting to the beach. And so, during this period when American society begins to resemble those of feudal lore, where the income chasm between the rich and the poor is widening, when downtown developers build concrete and steel vanity monuments to themselves—driving out the writers, the artists, the poor, and leaving the neighborhoods to roaming drug-death squads (since all of the cops are guarding these downtown Brasilias)—it seems that most people are interested in getting to the beach and getting tanned so that they'll resemble the very people the media, the "educational" system, and the cultural leadership have taught them to despise (that's what I meant by blacks being objects of fear and fascination). The widespread adoption of such Afro-American forms as rock and roll can be viewed as a kind of cultural tanning.

And so as long as I can be a professional like Larry Holmes, that is, have the ability to know my way around my craft, I'll probably still be controversial. Arguing on behalf of the homeless, but at the same time defending Atlanta's middle-class leadership against what I considered to be unfair charges made by the great writer James Baldwin (no relation). And as I continue to practice this sometimes uncanny and taxing profession, I hope to become humbler.

I've had a good shot. It's almost a miracle for a black male writer to last as long as I have, and though some may regard me as a "token," I'm fully aware that, regardless of how some critics protect their fragile egos by pretending that black talent is rare, black talent is bountiful. I've read and heard a lot of manuscripts authored by the fellas over the years. The late Hoyt Fuller was right when he said that for one published Ishmael Reed, there are dozens of talented writers in the ghettos and elsewhere, who remain unpublished. And having lasted this long, I've been able to witness the sad demise of a lot of "tokens" who believed what their literary managers told them. Who believed that they were indeed unique and unusual.

Just think of all of the cocky boxers who got punched out by "nobodies" as they took on an unknown to warm up for their fight with the champion. In this business, spoilers are all over the place.

I was shocked to hear Secretary of State George Shultz acknowledge during the Iran-Contragate hearings what our cultural leadership, and "educational" defenders of Western civilization, fail to realize. That people are smart all over the world. I know that. I'm aware of the fellas, writing throughout the country in the back of beat-up trailers, in jails, on kitchen tables, at their busboy jobs, during the rest period on somebody's night shift, or in between term papers. All the guys burnt-out, busted, disillusioned, collecting their hundredth rejection slip, being discouraged by people who say they'll never be a champion, or even a contender. This book is for them. Writin' is Fightin'.

Response

1. How would you describe Reed's attitude toward his early writing? What influences does he recognize as having shaped his development as a writer? What sort of personality emerges in this essay?

2. In Reed's view, why is it "important to maintain a prolific writing jab" (paragraph 10)? How does Reed characterize his own writing style? What does he value, in either a writer or a fighter?

3. "It takes an extraordinary amount of effort to understand someone from a background different from your own, especially when your life doesn't really depend upon it," says Reed in paragraph 12. Evaluate this statement, either from the perspective of understanding others or from that of being understood yourself.

4. This society has failed to acknowledge the abundance of talent among African Americans, according to Reed. He refers to "the fellas" and "the guys" writing under adverse circumstances without recognition or encouragement. Why do you think Reed omits any mention of women in his remarks?

Seven Long Times
Piri Thomas

In this passage from his autobiographical book Seven
Long Times *(1974), Thomas gives a glimpse of prison
life and recalls his first attempts to write, while he
was serving a fifteen-year sentence for armed robbery.*

Most of us inmates were between twenty and thirty-five years
old and full of vim and vigor. We strove mightily to work off our
excess energies by playing handball, baseball, football, and by taking
up the still more strenuous pastime of weight lifting. Weights
weren't easy to come by in prison and ordering them from the outside cost a bundle of money.

So we made our own simply by getting two empty five-gallon
paint cans, filling them with borrowed cement, and joining them
with a four-foot iron bar from the plumbing shop, also borrowed. We
would have a weight of over a hundred pounds. If we couldn't get a
metal bar for the grip, we'd make one out of wood. But that was
dangerous, for if it broke while you were doing a press, you could
suffer a painful injury.

When the weather was bad, we had the choice of staying in our
cells or going to the recreation hall. But the "recreation" was in
name only. The hall had nothing except a shuffleboard painted on
the smooth cement floor, green metal tables, and benches. It was a

large hall, freezing in wintertime and muggy and damp when it rained.

The recreation consisted of checkers, chess, dirty hearts, whist, bridge, seven-card rummy, five-hundred rummy, and every kind of poker and blackjack you could name.

5   If you had tailor-mades, you could gamble. Otherwise, the cheapest form of recreation was just plain old bullshitting, and gossiping about anything or anybody. Topics ranged from sex, art, sex, philosophy, sex, and life in general to conditions in prison, sex, politics, sex, and drugs, and on to used, reused, overused, and abused master plans for breaking out of the goddamn place. And without much hope of it ever happening, we could sit around and wish the seven plagues that fell on Biblical Egypt would strike the official prison ruling class, from the warden on down. But if one was tired of all the bullshit, one could always sit alone in some corner, turn into one's mind, and think positive or brood negative. It was the last stronghold of privacy.

Sport substitution helped me work off prison pressure, but when lockup time rolled around and the next fourteen to sixteen hours were to be spent in a cell, even dynamic tension got tiring. Dynamic tension is the science of building muscles without weights, simply by using the pressure and strain of one part of your body against another, and doing breathing exercises. But how long can one stay interested in doing pushups, even on one hand?

The radio we got in our cells by plugging earphones into a wall socket always had the same station on the air. It seemed whoever worked the dial in the communication room knew only one station.

I started to sketch and draw pictures, first with an ordinary pencil. As I got into it, I began to deal with pastels, but I could only do so much of that before it was a bore. Moreover, there wasn't a limitless supply of chalks and paper, and if you couldn't afford to purchase your supplies, there were no freebies given by the state prison system.

There was a light-skinned West Indian named Isaac who was about twenty-eight years old. He kept pretty much to himself and no one knew what he was in for. We got somewhat friendly and I found out he was an avid reader with a pretty decent private library. My head had been changing toward the better, and after two years of not really using my mind, I had begun dealing in getting an education as well as a better understanding of myself and my life via reading. From Isaac I got Richard Wright's *Native Son*, Lillian Smith's *Strange Fruit*, and many other books that were relevant to my life.

10   All this reading and the discussions I had with Isaac and others

got my mind to thinking. While reading John Oliver Killen's *Young-blood*, a strong desire surged through my blood, a thirst to write, and write I did despite the fact that I didn't know where to put commas and quotation marks and I wasn't too sure about adverbs and pronouns. But that didn't stop me. I just let it all pour out. I almost literally vomited words on paper.

One day in my cell, I remembered an incident that happened to me as a young boy in Babylon, Long Island, and wrote about it because it was related to my surging feeling toward writing.

At the beginning of World War II, my father hit the numbers and with his new airplane factory job, we moved to a house in the country way out on Long Island. I was enrolled in Babylon High School where the lack of blacks and Puerto Ricans was so apparent that the two or three of us there looked like little brown specks floating in a sea of milk.

I had a young English teacher who was so beautiful to me at age of fifteen that I promptly fell in love with her, from afar. One day she asked the class to write a composition on anything we wished. I proceeded to write a two-and-a-half-page declaration of love. I wrote of my passion for her beauty, her wondrous hazel eyes, the softness of her curly chestnut-brown hair, the warmth of her well-stacked body. I included that I didn't particularly care for her adjectives, pronouns, verbs, and so forth, but could manage to live with them for her sake. All in all it was a composition of love and beauty.

I turned the composition in and carefully avoided meeting my English teacher's eyes, lest the burning love-light in mine betray me.

A few days later, we were called up to her desk one by one to   15
retrieve our compositions. When my turn came, I went quickly to avoid her eyes. Looking from the corner of my eyes, I reached for my composition.

"Turn your paper over and read what's there." She smiled as she spoke.

I turned it over and there written in red pencil at the end was this note:

> *SON,*
>   *Your punctuation is lousy, your grammar*
> *is nonexistent. Yet if you want to be a writer,*
> *you will be.*
>   *P.S. We both love my wife.*
>   *[Signed],*
>   HER HUSBAND

All I could do was stare heartbroken at my English teacher, and

her understanding smile almost made me blush through my brown
skin.

I had by this time a little library of hand-picked books gotten
from inmates who wanted to sell them or give them away because
they were going home. I felt kind of like an intellectual and would
sometimes have fantasies about having some of my own books
alongside those of Killens, Wright, Smith, and others. Regardless, I
had found something to do that was me. It was my safety valve. I
had found how to express myself on paper and escape from the ugliness of that prison cell inside me.

20   My writings at first were recollections of free side—in the form
of short stories and poems—and these progressed into writing my
observations and feelings of the goings-on around me in a strange,
brutal, ice-cold world called "prison." The system had tried to soften
the harshness by labeling it "correctional institution" and by changing us from "prisoners" to "inmates." I often wondered if the offi-
cials' next step of fantasy would be to have this hell called "hotel"
and us "guests." I wrote these thoughts down. I wrote about us humans in every aspect of our continual debasement, hiding my papers
in fear of getting caught by the guards with such anti-prison-system
writings.

We were subject at any time to a shakedown—a search of one's
cell and person, usually without warning. Sometimes the guards
would spring the shakedown in the wee hours of the morning, looking for contraband, weapons, and un-American writings, the last
being anything that told the truth about what was happening inside
the joint. Guards did not expect us to love the prison, but we had
better not in any shape or form smear the integrity of the place, let
alone the honor and fair-mindedness of its keepers. We, the kept,
didn't have the right to be so ungrateful.

When I first started to set my mind to a routine of reading and
learning, I had gotten some light kidding about it. I often wondered
if it is just human nature to put down, even if in jest, the efforts of
someone trying to do better. Many times the inmates would sit
around and talk about past crimes, each trying to outdo the other
with heroic details. There would be looks of admiration and words
of praise, but when the conversation turned to bettering one's mind
with books or discussions, there'd be some polite, "Yeah, yeah, that's
great," and the attempt was buried under another round of negative
bullshit.

I remember one day I had come from the prison library where
an old white con librarian by the name of Joe had laid two heavy
books on me, one was a dictionary and the other dealt with philos-

ophy. I approached Pancho and Bayamon, who were leaning up against the prison wall. Pancho, noticing the books under my arm, asked, "Hey, what's happening with them heavies under your arm?"

"I got them in the library. Joe the librarian recommended them to me. He said that this book on philosophy was a conglomeration of many schools of thought as to what the manifestation of life is all about."

"*Coño*," whistled Bayamon. "What he say?"   25

"Yeah," said Pancho, looking a little hurt that a couple of words like *conglomeration* and *manifestation* could send him up a dead end. "What the hell does that mean?"

Oh boy. That's when I went into my grandstanding. I cleared my throat and feeling like some doctor of letters or something, hung it out for my two illiterate *hermanos*.

"*Conglomeration* means many things put together and *manifestation* is what comes out of it. Diggit!"

Pancho nodded and looked very wise. Bayamon only said, "Man, that's some heavy shit."

"Anyway, I got these books from the old man to broaden my   30
intellect. Man, I'm tired of reading westerns, murder mysteries, and bullshit short heists."

"*Tu qué*? I didn't know your intellect needed broadening." Bayamon moved around me and I just watched him inspect my backside.

"Whatta you think. Pancho? His intellect is pretty broad now. Don't you think?"

I just stood there patiently, waiting for him to get his cracks in so I could continue what to me was serious conversation.

"Maybe it can stand to be a little broader." Pancho helped Bayamon out. "You know the saying, 'The broader, the badder.'"

"It's pronounced *better*, not *badder*."   35

"You see, Pancho. Piri's intellect is getting broader all the time."

I waited for them to stop laughing. I laughed only to be a good sport, and finally got going again.

"Be serious, you guys. Like I said, one book is on philosophy and the other's a dictionary to broad—to enlarge my vocabulary."

"Wow, *amigo*." Pancho was on a teasing streak. I almost knew what was coming. "Ain't your vocabulary enlarged enough? *Caramba*, you beat it often enough."

"Wow, ain't *nada* sacred. *Coño*, if I jack off, that's my busi-   40
ness."

"Well, keep your shades down. The reflection shows in the window across from your cell."

"You know something, *pendejo*," I smiled friendly-like. "You're a manifestation of a conglomeration of a real genuine twenty-two-carat *maricón*."

Pancho went into some mincing girlish step, said in a high voice, "Oh, please, tell me more," and swished his behind from side to side, ending with, "I do so want to broaden my intellect."

Bayamon and Pancho roared with laughter. I had to burst out laughing, too.

45   "O.K., O.K., see you around, lowbrows." I started to walk away.

"Hey, *panita*. Don't go away mad. I was only kidding."

"I ain't mad. It's just that there is a lot to be learned in books, man, and like I'm into some heavy stuff."

"Heavy is right," roared Pancho. "Them two fucking words must have weighed at least a couple hundred pounds apiece."

I waved a disgusted but friendly see-ya-around, checked out across the cellblock, and found myself trying to quote something I had read. What I remembered was: "Many times in history great minds have been ridiculed by others because of their faithful quest for knowledge." After that barrage of ribbing, it made me feel a little better to join the ranks of history's greats who suffered the slings and arrows but never copped a plea.

Response

1. What motivated Thomas to start writing? What different functions did writing serve for him? How did his purpose gradually shift?

2. This passage contains explicit sexual language, as do many of Thomas's stories. Look for sexual imagery in Thomas's descriptions of his feelings and experience. Analyze different ways sexual talk was used in the incidents he describes. What was the intent and effect of these ways of talking?

3. Thomas says, "I often wondered if it is just human nature to put down, even if in jest, the efforts of someone trying to do better" (paragraph 22). What do you think?

4. What is the image of "history's greats" that Thomas holds as a model for himself? In what sense does he see himself becoming like those "who suffered the slings and arrows but never copped a plea," as he mentions in his last paragraph?

How to Write with Style
Kurt Vonnegut, Jr.

In this essay from his book Palm Sunday *(1981),
Vonnegut expresses some opinions about what makes
good writing, as he reflects on his own development
as a writer. He says he wrote this essay for the
International Paper Company, which "for obvious
reasons, hopes that Americans will continue to read
and write."*

Newspaper reporters and technical writers are trained to reveal almost nothing about themselves in their writings. This makes them freaks in the world of writers, since almost all of the other ink-stained wretches in that world reveal a lot about themselves to readers. We call these revelations, accidental and intentional, elements of literary style.

These revelations are fascinating to us as readers. They tell us what sort of person it is with whom we are spending time. Does the writer sound ignorant or informed, crazy or sane, stupid or bright, crooked or honest, humorless or playful—? And on and on.

When you yourself put words on paper, remember that the most damning revelation you can make about yourself is that you do not know what is interesting and what is not. Don't you yourself like or dislike writers mainly for what they choose to show you or make you think about? Did you ever admire an empty-headed writer for his or her mastery of the language? No.

So your own winning literary style must begin with interesting ideas in your head. Find a subject you care about and which you in your heart feel others should care about. It is this genuine caring, and not your games with language, which will be the most compelling and seductive element in your style.

5   I am not urging you to write a novel, by the way—although I would not be sorry if you wrote one, provided you genuinely cared about something. A petition to the mayor about a pothole in front of your house or a love letter to the girl next door will do.

Do not ramble, though.

As for your use of language: Remember that two great masters of our language, William Shakespeare and James Joyce, wrote sentences which were almost childlike when their subjects were most profound. "To be or not to be?" asks Shakespeare's Hamlet. The longest word is three letters long. Joyce, when he was frisky, could put together a sentence as intricate and glittering as a necklace for Cleopatra, but my favorite sentence in his short story "Eveline" is this one: "She was tired." At that point in the story, no other words could break the heart of a reader as those words do.

Simplicity of language is not only reputable, but perhaps even sacred. The Bible opens with a sentence well within the writing skills of a lively fourteen-year-old: "In the beginning God created the heavens and the earth."

It may be that you, too, are capable of making necklaces for Cleopatra, so to speak. But your eloquence should be the servant of the ideas in your head. Your rule might be this: If a sentence, no matter how excellent, does not illuminate my subject in some new and useful way, scratch it out. Here is the same rule paraphrased to apply to storytelling, to fiction: Never include a sentence which does not either remark on character or advance the action.

10   The writing style which is most natural for you is bound to echo speech you heard when a child. English was the novelist Joseph Conrad's third language, and much that seems piquant in his use of English was no doubt colored by his first language, which was Polish. And lucky indeed is the writer who has grown up in Ireland, for the English spoken there is so amusing and musical. I myself grew up in Indianapolis, Indiana, where common speech sounds like a band saw cutting galvanized tin, and employs a vocabulary as unornamental as a monkey wrench.

In some of the more remote hollows of Appalachia, children still grow up hearing songs and locutions of Elizabethan times. Yes, and many Americans grow up hearing a language other than English, or an English dialect a majority of Americans cannot understand.

All these varieties of speech are beautiful, just as the varieties of butterflies are beautiful. No matter what your first language, you should treasure it all your life. If it happens not to be standard English, and if it shows itself when you write standard English, the result is usually delightful, like a very pretty girl with one eye that is green and one that is blue.

I myself find that I trust my own writing most, and others seem to trust it most, too, when I sound most like a person from Indianapolis, which is what I am. What alternatives do I have? The one most vehemently recommended by teachers has no doubt been pressed on you, as well: that I write like cultivated Englishmen of a century or more ago.

I used to be exasperated by such teachers, but am no more. I understand now that all those antique essays and stories with which I was to compare my own work were not magnificent for their datedness or foreignness, but for saying precisely what their authors meant them to say. My teachers wished me to write accurately, always selecting the most effective words, and relating the words to one another unambiguously, rigidly, like parts of a machine. The teachers did not want to turn me into an Englishman after all. They hoped that I would become understandable—and therefore understood.

And there went my dream of doing with words what Pablo Picasso did with paint or what any number of jazz idols did with music. If I broke all the rules of punctuation, had words mean whatever I wanted them to mean, and strung them together higgledy-piggledy, I would simply not be understood. So you, too, had better avoid Picasso-style or jazz-style writing, if you have something worth saying and wish to be understood.

If it were only teachers who insisted that modern writers stay close to literary styles of the past, we might reasonably ignore them. But readers insist on the very same thing. They want our pages to look very much like pages they have seen before.

Why? It is because they themselves have a tough job to do, and they need all the help they can get from us. They have to identify thousands of little marks on paper, and make sense of them immediately. They have to *read*, an art so difficult that most people do not really master it even after having studied it all through grade school and high school—for twelve long years.

So this discussion, like all discussions of literary styles, must finally acknowledge that our stylistic options as writers are neither numerous nor glamorous, since our readers are bound to be such imperfect artists. Our audience requires us to be sympathetic and patient teachers, ever willing to simplify and clarify—whereas we would rather soar high above the crowd, singing like nightingales.

That is the bad news. The good news is that we Americans are governed under a unique Constitution, which allows us to write whatever we please without fear of punishment. So the most meaningful aspect of our styles, which is what we choose to write about, is unlimited.

20   Also: we are members of an egalitarian society, so there is no reason for us to write, in case we are not classically educated aristocrats, as though we were classically educated aristocrats.

Response

1. Vonnegut says in paragraph 1 that writers, other than newspaper reporters and technical writers, "reveal a lot about themselves to readers." What does Vonnegut reveal about himself to you in this essay? How does this affect your response to his essay?
2. Vonnegut gives his views about how to write well. Express several "rules" for good writing that you can derive from his essay. What does he seem to consider most important?
3. How does Vonnegut underscore his point in paragraph 6? Does he follow his own advice in other respects, in this essay?
4. According to Vonnegut, what do readers demand of writers?
5. Vonnegut says, "No matter what your first language, you should treasure it all your life. If it happens not to be standard English, and if it shows itself when you write standard English, the result is usually delightful, like a very pretty girl with one eye that is green and one that is blue" (paragraph 12). What do you think of Vonnegut's point of view? Do you think it might be controversial?

II
IDENTITY
AND COMMUNITY

The New World Man

Rudolfo Anaya

Anaya wrote this essay after returning from his second trip to Spain, in 1988. It was published the following year in the Before Columbus Review. *Looking toward the 500th anniversary of Columbus' voyage to the "New World," Anaya reflected on his own cultural identity and how it had been shaped by historical events.*

. . .

The great majority of the *Mexicanos* of the Southwest are *Indo-hispanos*, part of *La Raza* of the New World, the fruit of the Spanish father and the Indian mother. We have taken pride in our Hispanic heritage, that is, we know the history of the Spanish father, his language, and his character. We know that in this country it has been more seductive to identify with one's white, European ancestry. But the focus of that identification with that which is Spanish has, until recently, caused us to neglect our indigenous native American roots, and thus we have not known and honored the heritage of our mother, the Indian mothers of Mexico and the Southwest.

. . .

Located at the heart of what is now the Southwest United States, the people of *Nuevo México* have retained the essence of what

Rudolfo Anaya, "The New World Man," in *Before Columbus Review* (1:2 and 3), Fall-Winter 1989. Reprinted by permission of Before Columbus Foundation.

it means to be Hispanic, having preserved the Spanish language, the Catholic religion, and the folktales and folkways which came to us from Spain. But our nature was also formed by intermarriage with the Pueblo Indians of the Rio Grande. Our Spanish heritage and character are evident; it is a legacy left by those who came from Spain to settle in *Nuevo México*.

Those ancestors imbued the history of *Nuevo México* with their particular world view. For more than four centuries those ancestors lived in the isolated frontier of northernmost New Spain. But they did not survive and multiply in a vacuum; they survived and evolved because they adopted many of the ways of the Pueblos. The Spanish character underwent change as it encountered the native Americans of the Southwest, and from that interaction and intermarriage a unique American person and perspective were born.

We need to describe the totality of that world view which was formed in what we now call the Southwest, understanding that we are heirs not only of our Spanish character but of our Native American nature as well. The Spanish character is the aggressive, conquest-oriented part of our identity; the Native American nature is the more harmonious, earth-oriented side. I believe we must give attention to the characteristics of both sides of our identity in order to be more spiritually and psychologically centered when relating to the world. To pay attention only to one side of our sensibility is to be less self-actualizing, therefore less knowledgeable of self. If we are to understand our potential, it is important that we know the indigenous side of our history, not just the European.

. . .

5   The Americas represent a wonderful experiment in the synthesis of divergent world views, and each one of us is a representative of that process. The illuminations of self that are revealed as we explore and understand our true natures can be one of the most rewarding experiences of our lives, for so much of the sensitive part of life is a search and understanding of the inner self. To define ourselves as we really are and not as others wish us to be allows us to become authentic, and that definition carries with it the potential of our humanism.

Our Hispanic ancestors in the mid-sixteenth century settled along the Rio Grande of *Nuevo México*, bringing to the land their language. They gave names to the land and its features. It is in the naming that one engages in the sacred, that is, by naming one creates a *sacred sense of time*, a historic sense of time. By engaging in naming, our ancestors imposed themselves on history and gave definition to history. The language used in that naming ceremony is our birthright.

I live in Albuquerque, a name that invokes some of the history of the Iberian peninsula. In Spain I spoke my *Nuevo Mexicano* Spanish, a dialect that was preserved by my ancestors and which evolved in the mountains and valleys of New Mexico. But language changes with the passage of time and the vicissitudes of survival, and so I returned to Spain more proficient in English than in Spanish. All my novels and stories are written in English. While my parents' generation still communicated only in Spanish, my generation converses almost completely in English, a function of our professional lives. Still we struggle to retain our Spanish language, not only because it relates us to that part of our heritage, but also because it connects us to our brethren in Mexico and Latin America.

I returned to Spain to share with Spaniards the nature of my New World consciousness. At times I felt uncomfortable in believing I had to conform to the Spanish character, but the truth is that I now realize we who return to Spain no longer need to feel constrained to conform to the Spanish character. My generation of *Hispanos* liberated ourselves from that constraint by naming ourselves Chicanos. For us, using the word Chicano was our declaration of independence, the first step toward our true identity and the institution of a process by which we rediscovered our history.

By naming ourselves Chicanos we stamped an era with our communal identity, we reaffirmed our humanity by exploring and understanding the nature of our mothers, the indigenous American women. Those of us of Mexican heritage took the word Chicano from *Mexicano*, dropping the first syllable and keeping the *Xicano*. We are proud of that heritage even though we are not Mexican citizens, and although we are citizens of the United States we are not Anglo-Americans. The word Chicano defined the *space in time* as we struggled to define our contemporary history, and therefore Chicano came closer to embracing our Native American heritage.

Our first declaration of independence was from Anglo-America, that is, we insisted on the right to our *Indohispano* heritage. Now I believe the declaration has to go further. We have to insist on being the *señores of our own time*, to borrow a phrase from Miguel León Portilla. To be the *señores and señoras of our own time* is to continue to create our definition and sense of destiny in time; for me it means a bonding of the character of our Spanish heritage with our Indian American heritage. 10

. . .

One of the most interesting questions we ask ourselves as human beings is that of identity. Who am I? We seek to know our roots, to know ourselves. When we encounter the tap root of our history we feel authentic and able to identify self, family and community. Finding self should also mean finding humanity, declaring personal independence also means declaring that independence for all individuals.

How did you begin this journey of self-knowledge, people ask me. I listened to the *cuentos* of the old people, the stories of their history, and in retelling those stories and starting my own odyssey, I had to turn within. I had to know myself. Everyone does. The spiritual beliefs and mysticism of the Catholic Church and the love of the earth were elements of my childhood, so I turned to those sources in my stories. The folkways of my community became the web of the fictions I create, for the elements of drama exist within the stories of the folk. Even today, when I feel I have outgrown some of the themes I explored as a young writer, I know my best writing still comes when I return to the essence of my culture.

. . .

When I first traveled in Spain in 1980 I went into Andalucia. There in those wide expanses and mountains which reminded me of New Mexico, I felt at home. But a person needs more than the landscape to feel connected; we need the deeper connection to the communal body, we need to feel connected to our community.

The broad, political history of the independence of the Spanish colonies in the Americas is well known; now we must turn to an exploration of our personal and communal identity. That is what Chicano writers and artists have been doing since the cultural movement of the 1960s. The definition of Chicano culture must come from a multicultural perspective. Many streams of history define us and will continue to define us, for we are the synthesis which is the Americas.

15   Christ and Quetzalcóatl are not opposing spiritual figures; they fulfill the humanistic yearning toward harmonious resolution. Harmony within, harmony with neighbors, harmony with the cosmos. The Virgin of Spanish Catholicism and the Aztec Tonantzin culminate in the powerful and all-loving *Virgen de Guadalupe*. And *los santos* of the Catholic Church and those more personal saints of my mother's altar merge with and share the sacred space of the *Kachinas* of the Indian pueblos.

This metaphor, *Los santos are the kachinas*, has become a guiding metaphor of synthesis for me. The Old World and the New World have become one in me. Perhaps it is this syncretic sensibility of harmony which is the ideal of New World character. The New World cultures accepted the spiritual manifestations of Catholicism; Christ and the saints entered the religious cosmology of Indian America. A new age of cultural and spiritual blending came to unite humanity's course in the Americas. It was an age born in suffering, but the very act of birth created the children who were heirs to a new world view.

The New World view is syncretic and encompassing. It is one of the most humanistic views in the world, and yet it is a view not well-known in the world. The pressure of political realities and negative views of the mestizo populations of the Americas have constrained the flowering of our nature. Still, that view of self-knowledge and harmony is carried in the heart of the New World person.

What is important to me as a writer is to find the words by which to describe myself and my relationship to others. I now have the insight that allows me to speak of my history, and to posit myself at the center of that history. There I stand poised at the center of power, the knowing of myself, the heart and soul of the New World man alive in me.

This is a time of reflection for those of us who are the mestizos of the New World, and I believe the reflections in my writings and my attention to the myths and legends of Mesoamerica and the Rio Grande help expand the definition of our *Indohispano* heritage.

My trip to Spain was beneficial for me. I brought back memories of the Alhambra where I felt my soul stir to Moorish rhythm, and in the paintings of Goya's dark period I saw his apocryphal vision of an era ending. At La Sagrada Familia of Gaudi I bowed to genius, in the Valle de los Caidos I reflected on the Civil War . . . and on the wide expanses of Andalucia I thought of home. In all these places my memory stirred, and still I yearned for my home in *Nuevo México*, the mountains I know, the sacred places of my way of life. In that yearning the message whispered its secret, it was time for me to state my declaration of independence, time to center myself in the consciousness of the New World.

I was the New World man I had sought, with one foot in the glorious *mestisaje* of *México* and the other in the earth of the *Indohispanos of Nuevo México*; my dreams are woven of New World earth and history. I could walk anywhere in the world and feel attached, but it was *Nuevo México* that centered me, it was the indigenous soul of the Americas that held my secret.

It is important to know that the search for identity is not an esoteric search and not a divisive process. It is a way to reaffirm our humanity. We are all on this search, we all advocate justice, basic human rights, and the right of all to declare their independence of consciousness. . . .

History and the collective memory are vast. One delves into these powerful forces and finds that one is part of every other human being. I am extremely proud of my New World heritage, but I know the tree of mankind is one, and I share my roots with every other person. It seems appropriate to end on this archetype of the tree. The tree, or the tree of life, is also a dominant symbol of the Americas, and its syncretic image combines the tree of Quetzalcóatl and the cross of Christ. My ancestors nourished the tree of life; now it is up to me to care for all it symbolizes.

Response

1. "The Americas represent a wonderful experiment in the synthesis of divergent world views," says Anaya in paragraph 5, "and each one of us is a representative of that process." Do you think his remark applies to yourself and to people you know? Do different world views merge in your experience?

2. According to Anaya, names for places and people are significant because they give "definition to history." He suggests in paragraph 9 that Chicano people, by taking that name, began the process of rediscovering their history. To what extent can the same be said about names used by other racial or ethnic groups in this country to identify themselves?

3. Anaya says that "to define ourselves as we really are and not as others wish us to be allows us to become authentic" (paragraph 5). We accomplish this, he suggests, "when we encounter the tap root of our history" (paragraph 11). Explain his metaphor. In what sense can a knowledge of history "authenticate" people?

4. Anaya illustrates the synthesis of different cultures in his New World view. From where does he draw his examples? How does his view complement that of Ishmael Reed in "America: The Multinational Society"?

5. Anaya's New World view represents a harmonious blending of influences from different cultures. The attempt to define one's identity, he concludes, "is not a divisive process. It is a way to reaffirm our humanity." How does the tree symbolize his view? Do you agree with him that "finding self should also mean finding humanity"?

Lifeline

Gloria Anzaldua

This story, to appear in Anzaldua's forthcoming book
Entreguerras entremundos/Civil Wars Among the
Worlds, *deals with the issues of sexual preference and
identity, and with the common experience of
rejection.*

La Prieta met Suel at the university during the Summer session. Prieta was studying comp lit and Suel education. They were
both in graduate programs full of whites in a school full of whites.
Both were floundering in the sea of white faces and they gravitated
to each other as to life preservers. For hours they would sit in the
air-conditioned commons buoying each other with iced drinks, *pla-
ticando* about their courses, their families, movies, books, everything and anything. They would walk across the spacious lawns of
the UT campus and then wind their way down a ravine to Waller
Creek, where they would sit close together on the rocks and listen
to the gurgle of the trickling water, fanning each other's hot faces
with large green leaves while their feet, submerged in the water,
cooled.

Suel was 12 years older than la Prieta. She bordered on skinny

Gloria E. Anzaldúa, "Lifeline," in *Entreguerras entremundos/Civil Wars
Among the Worlds* from *Prieta*. San Francisco: Aunt Lute, to appear. Printed by permission of Aunt Lute Books, San Francisco, CA.

and was tall and leggy. Prieta was short and chunky. Suel never wore make-up, wore her *pelo* pulled back in a bun. When Prieta asked her to wear her hair down, Suel replied, "Don't be silly, it's too hot to wear down." As Suel looked at la Prieta, a brightness washed over her eyes, and something in it, both naked and curtained, refused to hold la Prieta's gaze. La Prieta had seen a similar look in *niños que tenían hambre* who were hungry and were ashamed of their hunger, children who knew that food was something they would never have enough of.

One hot summer day turned into another and Prieta smiled a lot. She attributed her smiles to Suel's presence. Suel was always poised at the edge of calmness. Prieta eased into that tranquility like easing into cool deep water. Once Prieta asked Suel what she saw in her and Suel had replied, "I never know what you're going to say or do. You have such strong feelings. Sometimes they frighten me." As the summer heat intensified Prieta became more and more aware that the fragile thread connecting the two was becoming stronger every day.

One day six days away from the end of the Summer session, they were lying on Suel's bed, having been up all night working on papers. Their heads felt hollow from too much coffee and lack of sleep. In a few days they would return to *el valle* to their respective hometowns. Their pueblos were 69 miles apart. The more Prieta thought about the 69 miles, the farther apart their towns seemed. She wondered if their *familias* would think it strange if one drove to visit the other. She had never considered visiting Suel before— they had not been that close. It would look suspicious. It was peculiar, the closeness that had developed between them was different from the closeness she had with her sister or with her other girl friends. Prieta had felt this closeness before with other women.

5   As they lay side by side, with arms and thighs touching, la Prieta debated silently, whether to risk saying something about the spark she'd first glimpsed in Suel's eyes at their meeting two Summer sessions back, and that she had since then seen every time Suel looked at her. She wanted to talk about the dense air that breathed between them when they sat close together. She wanted to get closer to Suel. She wanted to touch her and hold her. And she was afraid to bring this up with Suel.

"Do you want to talk about it?" la Prieta finally asked, touching the soft skin at the inside of Suel's elbow. Suel pulled her arm away.

"Talk about what?" Suel responded in a low voice.

"I think we should decide what to do about it."

"Do about what?" Suel's voice seemed sharper.

"*Tú sabes*. That special feeling between us and this intense   10
bonding. We both recognize it."

"What feeling? What bonding?"

"You know," Prieta said impatiently, "the erotic feelings *marimachos* have for certain *mujeres*." Suel turned her head and stared at her. Slowly, she moved away, then, averting her face, she sat up, got up and walked out.

La Prieta waited for two hours. Not wanting to fall asleep on Suel's bed in case Suel returned still angry at her, she returned to her dorm. The next day and the next and the next, la Prieta went to all their usual hangouts. She asked everyone who knew them, but no one had seen Suel. As a last resort, she went to the Dean's office. She was told that Suel had had a family emergency and had left without finishing her course work. After that Prieta went to classes, studied and kept to herself. She did not go out with anyone.

A month later, when la Prieta had gotten *las ganas* and her nerve up, she called Suel's house. Suel's sister answered and yelled out to Suel to come to the phone. At the other end la Prieta heard Suel's voice say, "*Dile que no estoy en casa.* Tell her I moved away and you don't know where I am."

A month went by, then another and another. Prieta psyched   15
herself up and called her again. The mother answered this time. She told la Prieta that Suel didn't live there anymore and hung up before Prieta could say a word.

A year later at a conference, Prieta saw Suel sitting in the middle of the almost empty auditorium. Standing at the mouth of the auditorium her heart leaped. She felt like she was falling and Suel was the only net that could catch her and bring her home. Smiling and with the lightest step she'd had in over a year, she made straight for the row where Suel sat. She saw Suel's thin neck under the familiar bun and felt a tenderness surge through her body, softening her heart. Suddenly she was afraid and her body tensed. What if Suel turned her back on her again? Then once more hope pushed fear back into its hiding place deep in Prieta's belly. Prieta slowly walked toward Suel. She saw Suel's head turn, saw her eyes register shock, saw her get up and, head bent, hurry down the row to the other side and circle back to the entrance. As she watched Suel leave, la Prieta felt the lifeline slipping through her hands.

Response

1. The metaphor contained in the title "Lifeline" is extended through the story. How does it shed light on la Prieta's experience?

2. What do you think was Suel's perception of herself and of her relationship with la Prieta? What support does the story give for your interpretation?

3. Anzaldua uses Spanish to develop her characters and the cultural context for the story. What bearing, if any, do you think the fact that the women are Latina has on the story?

4. Consider how elements of this story—denial, ambiguity, misinterpretation, rejection—echo experiences familiar to most of us at one time or another. Can you translate any of these elements of experience into circumstances other than those depicted by Anzaldua?

5. What do you think is Anzaldua's intent in writing this story? In what ways does the story carry out the author's views as expressed in "Speaking in Tongues: A Letter to Third World Women Writers" (Section V)?

The Discovery of What It Means to Be an American

James Baldwin

In 1948 Baldwin left the United States, saying he couldn't write in this country. He spent most of the next nine years living in Paris, where he wrote much of his best-known work. He wrote the following essay upon his return to New York. It first appeared in the New York Times Book Review *of January 1959 and is included in Baldwin's second collection of nonfiction,* Nobody Knows My Name *(1961). In it Baldwin explores how living in Europe helped him gain a sense of his American identity.*

"It is a complex fate to be an American," Henry James observed, and the principal discovery an American writer makes in Europe is just how complex this fate is. America's history, her aspirations, her peculiar triumphs, her even more peculiar defeats, and her position in the world—yesterday and today—are all so profoundly and stubbornly unique that the very word "America" remains a new, almost completely undefined and extremely controversial proper noun. No one in the world seems to know exactly

what it describes, not even we motley millions who call ourselves
Americans.

I left America because I doubted my ability to survive the fury
of the color problem here. (Sometimes I still do.) I wanted to prevent
myself from becoming *merely* a Negro; or, even, merely a Negro
writer. I wanted to find out in what way the *specialness* of my experience could be made to connect me with other people instead of
dividing me from them. (I was as isolated from Negroes as I was
from whites, which is what happens when a Negro begins, at bottom, to believe what white people say about him.)

In my necessity to find the terms on which my experience
could be related to that of others, Negroes and whites, writers and
non-writers, I proved, to my astonishment, to be as American as any
Texas G.I. And I found my experience was shared by every American writer I knew in Paris. Like me, they had been divorced from
their origins, and it turned out to make very little difference that
the origins of white Americans were European and mine were African—they were no more at home in Europe than I was.

The fact that I was the son of a slave and they were the sons of
free men meant less, by the time we confronted each other on European soil, than the fact that we were both searching for our separate
identities. When we had found these, we seemed to be saying, why,
then, we would no longer need to cling to the shame and bitterness
which had divided us so long.

5   It became terribly clear in Europe, as it never had been here,
that we knew more about each other than any European ever could.
And it also became clear that, no matter where our fathers had been
born, or what they had endured, the fact of Europe had formed us
both, was part of our identity and part of our inheritance.

I had been in Paris a couple of years before any of this became
clear to me. When it did, I, like many a writer before me upon the
discovery that his props have all been knocked out from under him,
suffered a species of breakdown and was carried off to the mountains of Switzerland. There, in that absolutely alabaster landscape,
armed with two Bessie Smith records and a typewriter, I began to
try to re-create the life that I had first known as a child and from
which I had spent so many years in flight.

It was Bessie Smith, through her tone and her cadence, who
helped me to dig back to the way I myself must have spoken when
I was a pickaninny, and to remember the things I had heard and seen
and felt. I had buried them very deep. I had never listened to Bessie
Smith in America (in the same way that, for years, I would not touch
watermelon), but in Europe she helped to reconcile me to being a
"nigger."

I do not think that I could have made this reconciliation here. Once I was able to accept my role—as distinguished, I must say, from my "place"—in the extraordinary drama which is America, I was released from the illusion that I hated America.

The story of what can happen to an American Negro writer in Europe simply illustrates, in some relief, what can happen to any American writer there. It is not meant, of course, to imply that it happens to them all, for Europe can be very crippling, too; and, anyway, a writer, when he has made his first breakthrough, has simply won a crucial skirmish in a dangerous, unending and unpredictable battle. Still, the breakthrough is important, and the point is that an American writer, in order to achieve it, very often has to leave this country.

The American writer, in Europe, is released, first of all, from   10
the necessity of apologizing for himself. It is not until he *is* released from the habit of flexing his muscles and proving that he is just a "regular guy" that he realizes how crippling this habit has been. It is not necessary for him, there, to pretend to be something he is not, for the artist does not encounter in Europe the same suspicion he encounters here. Whatever the Europeans may actually think of artists, they have killed enough of them off by now to know that they are as real—and as persistent—as rain, snow, taxes or businessmen.

Of course, the reason for Europe's comparative clarity concerning the different functions of men in society is that European society has always been divided into classes in a way that American society never has been. A European writer considers himself to be part of an old and honorable tradition—of intellectual activity, of letters—and his choice of a vocation does not cause him any uneasy wonder as to whether or not it will cost him all his friends. But this tradition does not exist in America.

On the contrary, we have a very deep-seated distrust of real intellectual effort (probably because we suspect that it will destroy, as I hope it does, that myth of America to which we cling so desperately). An American writer fights his way to one of the lowest rungs on the American social ladder by means of pure bull-headedness and an indescribable series of odd jobs. He probably *has* been a "regular fellow" for much of his adult life, and it is not easy for him to step out of that lukewarm bath.

We must, however, consider a rather serious paradox: though American society is more mobile than Europe's, it is easier to cut across social and occupational lines there than it is here. This has something to do, I think, with the problem of status in American life. Where everyone has status, it is also perfectly possible, after all, that no one has. It seems inevitable, in any case, that a man may become uneasy as to just what his status is.

But Europeans have lived with the idea of status for a long time. A man can be as proud of being a good waiter as of being a good actor, and, in neither case, feel threatened. And this means that the actor and the waiter can have a freer and more genuinely friendly relationship in Europe than they are likely to have here. The waiter does not feel, with obscure resentment, that the actor has "made it," and the actor is not tormented by the fear that he may find himself, tomorrow, once again a waiter.

15   This lack of what may roughly be called social paranoia causes the American writer in Europe to feel—almost certainly for the first time in his life—that he can reach out to everyone, that he is accessible to everyone and open to everything. This is an extraordinary feeling. He feels, so to speak, his own weight, his own value.

It is as though he suddenly came out of a dark tunnel and found himself beneath the open sky. And, in fact, in Paris, I began to see the sky for what seemed to be the first time. It was borne in on me—and it did not make me feel melancholy—that this sky had been there before I was born and would be there when I was dead. And it was up to me, therefore, to make of my brief opportunity the most that could be made.

I was born in New York, but have lived only in pockets of it. In Paris, I lived in all parts of the city—on the Right Bank and the Left, among the bourgeoisie and among les misérables, and knew all kinds of people, from pimps and prostitutes in Pigalle to Egyptian bankers in Neuilly. This may sound extremely unprincipled or even obscurely immoral: I found it healthy. I love to talk to people, all kinds of people, and almost everyone, as I hope we still know, loves a man who loves to listen.

This perpetual dealing with people very different from myself caused a shattering in me of preconceptions I scarcely knew I held. The writer is meeting in Europe people who are not American, whose sense of reality is entirely different from his own. They may love or hate or admire or fear or envy this country—they see it, in any case, from another point of view, and this forces the writer to reconsider many things he had always taken for granted. This reassessment, which can be very painful, is also very valuable.

This freedom, like all freedom, has its dangers and its responsibilities. One day it begins to be borne in on the writer, and with great force, that he is living in Europe as an American. If he were living there as a European, he would be living on a different and far less attractive continent.

20   This crucial day may be the day on which an Algerian taxi-driver tells him how it feels to be an Algerian in Paris. It may be the day on which he passes a café terrace and catches a glimpse of the

tense, intelligent and troubled face of Albert Camus. Or it may be the day on which someone asks him to explain Little Rock and he begins to feel that it would be simpler—and, corny as the words may sound, more honorable—to *go* to Little Rock than sit in Europe, on an American passport, trying to explain it.

This is a personal day, a terrible day, the day to which his entire sojourn has been tending. It is the day he realizes that there are no untroubled countries in this fearfully troubled world; that if he has been preparing himself for anything in Europe, he has been preparing himself—for America. In short, the freedom that the American writer finds in Europe brings him, full circle, back to himself, with the responsibility for his development where it always was: in his own hands.

Even the most incorrigible maverick has to be born somewhere. He may leave the group that produced him—he may be forced to—but nothing will efface his origins, the marks of which he carries with him everywhere. I think it is important to know this and even find it a matter for rejoicing, as the strongest people do, regardless of their station. On this acceptance, literally, the life of a writer depends.

. . .

American writers do not have a fixed society to describe. The only society they know is one in which nothing is fixed and in which the individual must fight for his identity. This is a rich confusion, indeed, and it creates for the American writer unprecedented opportunities.

That the tensions of American life, as well as the possibilities, are tremendous is certainly not even a question. But these are dealt with in contemporary literature mainly compulsively; that is, the book is more likely to be a symptom of our tension than an examination of it. The time has come, God knows, for us to examine ourselves, but we can only do this if we are willing to free ourselves of the myth of America and try to find out what is really happening here.

Every society is really governed by hidden laws, by unspoken   25
but profound assumptions on the part of the people, and ours is no exception. It is up to the American writer to find out what these laws and assumptions are. In a society much given to smashing taboos without thereby managing to be liberated from them, it will be no easy matter.

It is no wonder, in the meantime, that the American writer keeps running off to Europe. He needs sustenance for his journey and the best models he can find. Europe has what we do not have yet, a sense of the mysterious and inexorable limits of life, a sense, in a word, of tragedy. And we have what they sorely need: a new sense of life's possibilities.

In this endeavor to wed the vision of the Old World with that of the New, it is the writer, not the statesman, who is our strongest arm. Though we do not wholly believe it yet, the interior life is a real life, and the intangible dreams of people have a tangible effect on the world.

Response

1. Explain the isolation Baldwin felt when he first went to Paris. Why had he not listened to Bessie Smith before?

2. In his "Autobiographical Notes" (Section I), Baldwin said that "before [the writer] can look forward in any meaningful sense, he must first be allowed to take a long look back." How did he do this after he left the United States, and what was it about living in Europe that allowed him to do it?

3. What elements of their experience connected Baldwin and other Americans in Europe, and allowed him to discover "what it means to be an American"?

4. Explain the distinction Baldwin makes between his "role" and his "place" in American society (paragraph 8). How did this distinction enable him to stop hating America? Explain how acceptance of his origins ultimately brought Baldwin "full circle, back to himself, with the responsibility for his development where it always was: in his own hands" (paragraph 21).

5. In this essay Baldwin discusses the role of writers in American society. Recall what he says on this topic in "Autobiographical Notes," and explain why, in Baldwin's view, serious writers did not get the attention and respect in America that they had in Europe. When he wrote this essay in 1961, Baldwin believed that in this country "we have a very deep-seated distrust of real intellectual effort (probably because we suspect that it will destroy. . .that myth of America to which we cling so desperately)" (paragraph 12). Consider how Baldwin reiterated that view in "A Talk to Teachers" (Section V). To what extent do you think his observation applies today?

6. In *American Hunger* (Section V) Richard Wright discusses how racism can be internalized and resurface as hatred against members of one's own race, with debilitating effects on self-esteem. Based on your reading of this essay and of Baldwin's "Autobiographical Notes," as well as of Wright, consider how Baldwin's experience illustrates Wright's analysis. How did both Baldwin and Wright get beyond that state of mind?

Keeping Close to Home
bell hooks

The subtitle of this essay, from the book **Talking Back** *(1989), is "Class and Education." In it hooks looks back to the time when she first left her home in Kentucky, to enroll at Stanford University. Drawing on that experience, she considers the cultural distance that education can create between working-class students and their parents.*

We are both awake in the almost dark of 5 a.m. Everyone else is sound asleep. Mama asks the usual questions. Telling me to look around, make sure I have everything, scolding me because I am uncertain about the actual time the bus arrives. By 5:30 we are waiting outside the closed station. Alone together, we have a chance to really talk. Mama begins. Angry with her children, especially the ones who whisper behind her back, she says bitterly, "Your childhood could not have been that bad. You were fed and clothed. You did not have to do without—that's more than a lot of folks have and I just can't stand the way y'all go on." The hurt in her voice saddens me. I have always wanted to protect mama from hurt, to ease her burdens. Now I am part of what troubles. Confronting me, she says accusingly, "It's not just the other children. You talk too much about the past. You don't just listen." And I do talk. Worse, I write about it.

bell hooks, "Keeping Close to Home," in *Talking Back: Thinking Feminist, Thinking Black.* Boston: South End Press, 1989. Reprinted with permission from the publisher.

Mama has always come to each of her children seeking different responses. With me she expresses the disappointment, hurt, and anger of betrayal: anger that her children are so critical, that we can't even have the sense to like the presents she sends. She says, "From now on there will be no presents. I'll just stick some money in a little envelope the way the rest of you do. Nobody wants criticism. Everybody can criticize me but I am supposed to say nothing." When I try to talk, my voice sounds like a twelve year old. When I try to talk, she speaks louder, interrupting me, even though she has said repeatedly, "Explain it to me, this talk about the past." I struggle to return to my thirty-five year old self so that she will know by the sound of my voice that we are two women talking together. It is only when I state firmly in my very adult voice, "Mama, you are not listening," that she becomes quiet. She waits. Now that I have her attention, I fear that my explanations will be lame, inadequate. "Mama," I begin, "people usually go to therapy because they feel hurt inside, because they have pain that will not stop, like a wound that continually breaks open, that does not heal. And often these hurts, that pain has to do with things that have happened in the past, sometimes in childhood, often in childhood, or things that we believe happened." She wants to know, "What hurts, what hurts are you talking about?" "Mom, I can't answer that. I can't speak for all of us, the hurts are different for everybody. But the point is you try to make the hurt better, to heal it, by understanding how it came to be. And I know you feel mad when we say something happened or hurt that you don't remember being that way, but the past isn't like that, we don't have the same memory of it. We remember things differently. You know that. And sometimes folk feel hurt about stuff and you just don't know or didn't realize it, and they need to talk about it. Surely you understand the need to talk about it."

Our conversation is interrupted by the sight of my uncle walking across the park toward us. We stop to watch him. He is on his way to work dressed in a familiar blue suit. They look alike, these two who rarely discuss the past. This interruption makes me think about life in a small town. You always see someone you know. Interruptions, intrusions are part of daily life. Privacy is difficult to maintain. We leave our private space in the car to greet him. After the hug and kiss he has given me every year since I was born, they talk about the day's funerals. In the distance the bus approaches. He walks away knowing that they will see each other later. Just before I board the bus I turn, staring into my mother's face. I am momentarily back in time, seeing myself eighteen years ago, at this same bus stop, staring into my mother's face, continually turning back, waving farewell as I returned to college—that experience which first took me away from our town, from family. Departing was as painful then as it is now. Each movement away makes return harder. Each separation intensifies distance, both physical and emotional.

To a southern black girl from a working-class background who had never been on a city bus, who had never stepped on an escalator, who had never travelled by plane, leaving the comfortable confines of a small town Kentucky life to attend Stanford University was not just frightening; it was utterly painful. My parents had not been delighted that I had been accepted and adamantly opposed my going so far from home. At the time, I did not see their opposition as an expression of their fear that they would lose me forever. Like many working-class folks, they feared what college education might do to their children's minds even as they unenthusiastically acknowledged its importance. They did not understand why I could not attend a college nearby, an all-black college. To them, any college would do. I would graduate, become a school teacher, make a decent living and a good marriage. And even though they reluctantly and skeptically supported my educational endeavors, they also subjected them to constant harsh and bitter critique. It is difficult for me to talk about my parents and their impact on me because they have always felt wary, ambivalent, mistrusting of my intellectual aspirations even as they have been caring and supportive. I want to speak about these contradictions because sorting through them, seeking resolution and reconciliation has been important to me both as it affects my development as a writer, my effort to be fully self-realized, and my longing to remain close to the family and community that provided the groundwork for much of my thinking, writing, and being.

Studying at Stanford, I began to think seriously about class dif-   5 ferences. To be materially underprivileged at a university where most folks (with the exception of workers) are materially privileged provokes such thought. Class differences were boundaries no one wanted to face or talk about. It was easier to downplay them, to act as though we were all from privileged backgrounds, to work around them, to confront them privately in the solitude of one's room, or to pretend that just being chosen to study at such an institution meant that those of us who did not come from privilege were already in transition toward privilege. To not long for such transition marked one as rebellious, as unlikely to succeed. It was a kind of treason not to believe that it was better to be identified with the world of material privilege than with the world of the working class, the poor. No wonder our working-class parents from poor backgrounds feared our entry into such a world, intuiting perhaps that we might learn to be ashamed of where we had come from, that we might never return home, or come back only to lord it over them.

Though I hung with students who were supposedly radical and

chic, we did not discuss class. I talked to no one about the sources of my shame, how it hurt me to witness the contempt shown the brown-skinned Filipina maids who cleaned our rooms, or later my concern about the $100 a month I paid for a room off-campus which was more than half of what my parents paid for rent. I talked to no one about my efforts to save money, to send a little something home. Yet these class realities separated me from fellow students. We were moving in different directions. I did not intend to forget my class background or alter my class allegiance. And even though I received an education designed to provide me with a bourgeois sensibility, passive acquiescence was not my only option. I knew that I could resist. I could rebel. I could shape the direction and focus of the various forms of knowledge available to me. Even though I sometimes envied and longed for greater material advantages (particularly at vacation times when I would be one of few if any students remaining in the dormitory because there was no money for travel), I did not share the sensibility and values of my peers. That was important—class was not just about money; it was about values which showed and determined behavior. While I often needed more money, I never needed a new set of beliefs and values. For example, I was profoundly shocked and disturbed when peers would talk about their parents without respect, or would even say that they hated their parents. This was especially troubling to me when it seemed that these parents were caring and concerned. It was often explained to me that such hatred was "healthy and normal." To my white, middle-class California roommate, I explained the way we were taught to value our parents and their care, to understand that they were not obligated to give us care. She would always shake her head, laughing all the while, and say, "Missy, you will learn that it's different here, that we think differently." She was right. Soon, I lived alone, like the one Mormon student who kept to himself as he made a concentrated effort to remain true to his religious beliefs and values. Later in graduate school I found that classmates believed "lower class" people had no beliefs and values. I was silent in such discussions, disgusted by their ignorance.

. . .

Maintaining connections with family and community across class boundaries demands more than just summary recall of where one's roots are, where one comes from. It requires knowing, naming, and being evermindful of those aspects of one's past that have enabled and do enable one's self-development in the present, that sustain and support, that enrich. One must also honestly confront barriers that do exist, aspects of that past that do diminish. My parents' ambivalence about my love for reading led to intense conflict. They (especially my mother) would work to ensure that I had access to books, but would threaten to burn the books or throw them away if I did not conform to other expectations. Or they would insist that reading too much would drive me insane. Their ambivalence nurtured in me a like uncertainty about the value and significance of intellectual endeavor which took years for me to unlearn. While this aspect of our class reality was one that wounded and diminished, their vigilant insistence that being smart did not make me a "better" or "superior" person (which often got on my nerves because I think I wanted to have that sense that it did indeed set me apart, make me better) made a profound impression. From them I learned to value and respect various skills and talents folk might have, not just to value people who read books and talk about ideas. They and my grandparents might say about somebody, "Now he don't read nor write a lick, but he can tell a story," or as my grandmother would say, "call out the hell in words."

. . .

I do not know that my mother's mother ever acknowledged my college education except to ask me once, "How can you live so far away from your people?" Yet she gave me sources of affirmation and nourishment, sharing the legacy of her quilt-making, of family history, of her incredible way with words. Recently, when our father retired after more than thirty years of work as a janitor, I wanted to pay tribute to this experience, to identify links between his work and my own as writer and teacher. Reflecting on our family past, I recalled ways he had been an impressive example of diligence and hard work, approaching tasks with a seriousness of concentration I work to mirror and develop, with a discipline I struggle to maintain. Sharing these thoughts with him keeps us connected, nurtures our respect for each other, maintaining a space, however large or small, where we can talk.

Open, honest communication is the most important way we maintain relationships with kin and community as our class experience and backgrounds change. It is as vital as the sharing of resources. Often financial assistance is given in circumstances where there is no meaningful contact. However helpful, this can also be an expression of estrangement and alienation. Communication between black folks from various experiences of material privilege was much easier when we were all in segregated communities sharing common experiences in relation to social institutions. Without this grounding, we must work to maintain ties, connection. We must assume greater responsibility for making and maintaining contact, connections that can shape our intellectual visions and inform our radical commitments.

10   The most powerful resource any of us can have as we study and teach in university settings is full understanding and appreciation of the richness, beauty, and primacy of our familial and community backgrounds. Maintaining awareness of class differences, nurturing ties with the poor and working-class people who are our most intimate kin, our comrades in struggle, transforms and enriches our intellectual experience. Education as the practice of freedom becomes not a force which fragments or separates, but one that brings us closer, expanding our definitions of home and community.

Response

1. Notice how, in the first four paragraphs of the essay, hooks uses a recent anecdote to set the context for her story about going away to college. How does the anecdote work to accomplish this? In what sense does it illustrate hooks's point that "each separation intensifies distance"?

2. Explain the contradictions and ambivalence in hooks's parents' attitudes toward her education. Why is it so important for her to resolve and reconcile the contradictions?

3. At Stanford, hooks says, "class differences were boundaries no one wanted to face or talk about" (paragraph 5). Why didn't hooks and her student-friends discuss social class? Why was it considered traitorous not to long for "transition toward privilege"? And why didn't hooks want to move in that direction?

4. Hooks says that her university education was "designed to provide [her] with a bourgeois sensibility" (paragraph 6). To what extent do you think this is true of any university education, including your own? Hooks says she resisted this influence; "I could shape the direction and focus of the various forms of knowledge available to me," she asserts. Can you? How and why might you do this?

5. At the end of this essay hooks suggests that it is important to maintain ties, not only for educated children of working-class families, but more generally for "black folks from various experiences of material privilege." What is her broader social message?

6. What were or are your parents' attitudes about reading, learning, being smart? How have they affected your own values pertaining to your education? To what extent do you think your parents' and your own attitudes toward education have been shaped by social class?

The Names
N. Scott Momaday

*This passage is an excerpt from Momaday's
autobiographical book* The Names, *published in
1976. It reflects Momaday's concern with the
continuity of tradition through storytelling. In this
excerpt he reflects on the connection between himself
and his ancestry, particularly his grandfather
Mammedaty.*

Children trust in language. They are open to the power and
beauty of language, and here they differ from their elders, most of
whom have come to imagine that they have found words out, and
so much of magic is lost upon them. Creation says to the child:
Believe in this tree, for it has a name.

If you say to a child, "The day is almost gone," he will take
you at your word and will find much wonder in it. But if you say
this to a man whom the world has disappointed, he will be bound
to doubt it. *Almost* will have no precision for him, and he will mistake your meaning. I can remember that someone held out his hand
to me, and in it was a bird, its body broken. *It is almost dead.* I was
overcome with the mystery of it, that the dying bird should exist
entirely in its dying. J. V. Cunningham has a poem, "On the Calcu-
lus":

N. Scott Momaday, from *The Names*. New York: Harper and Row, 1976. Reprinted with permission.

From almost nought to almost all I flee,
And *almost* has almost confounded me;
Zero my limit, and infinity.

I can almost see into the summer of a year in my childhood. I
am again in my grandmother's house, where I have come to stay for
a month or six weeks—or for a time that bears no common shape in
my mind, neither linear nor round, but it is a deep dimension, and I
am lonely in it. Earlier in the day—or in the day before, or in another
day—my mother and father have driven off. Somewhere on a road,
in Texas, perhaps, they are moving away from me, or they are settled in a room away, away, thinking of me or not, my father scratching his head, my mother smoking a cigarette and holding a little dog
in her lap. There is a silence between them and between them and
me. I am thoughtful. I see into the green, transparent base of a kerosene lamp; there is a still circle within it, the surface of a deeper
transparency. Do I bring my hands to my face? Do I turn or nod my
head? Something of me has just now moved upon the metal throat
of the lamp, some distortion of myself, nonetheless recognizable,
and I am distracted. I look for my image then in the globe, rising a
little in my chair, but I see nothing but my ghost, another transparency, glass upon glass, the wall beyond, another distortion. I take up
a pencil and set the point against a sheet of paper and define the
head of a boy, bowed slightly, facing right. I fill in quickly only a
few details, the line of the eye, the curve of the mouth, the ear, the
hair—all in a few simple strokes. Yet there is life and expression in
the face, a conjugation that I could not have imagined in these mark-
ings. The boy looks down at something that I cannot see, something
that lies apart from the picture plane. It might be an animal, or a
leaf, or the drawing of a boy. He is thoughtful and well-disposed. It
seems to me that he will smile in a moment, but there is no laughter
in him. He is contained in his expression—and fixed, as if the foundation upon which his flesh and bones are set cannot be shaken. I
like him certainly, but I don't know who or where or what he is,
except that he is the inscrutable reflection of my own vague certainty. And then I write, in my child's hand, beneath the drawing,
"This is someone. Maybe this is Mammedaty. This is Mammedaty
when he was a boy." And I wonder at the words. *What are they?*
They stand, they lean and run upon the page of a manuscript—I have
made a manuscript, rude and illustrious. The page bears the likeness
of a boy—so simply crude the likeness to some pallid shadow on my
blood—and his name consists in the letters there, the words, the
other likeness, the little, jumbled drawings of a ritual, the nominal
ceremony in which all homage is returned, the legend of the boy's

having been, of his going on. I have said it; I have set it down. I trace
the words; I touch myself to the words, and they stand for me. My
mind lives among them, moving ever, ever going on. I lay the page
aside, I imagine. I pass through the rooms of the house, slowly, paus-
ing at familiar objects: a quiver of arrows on the wall, old photographs in oval frames, beaded emblems, a Bible, an iron bedstead, a
calendar for the year 1942. Mammedaty lies ten years in the ground
at Rainy Mountain Cemetery. What is there, *just there*, in the earth,
in the bronze casket, under Keahdinekeah's shawl? I go out into the
yard; the shadows are long to the east, and the sunlight has deepened
and the red earth is darkened now to umber and the grasses are burnished. Across the road, where the plain is long and undulant and
bears the soft sheen of rose gentian and rose mallow, there are figures like fossils in the prisms of the air. I see a boy standing still in
the distance, only his head and shoulders visible above the long,
luminous grass, and from the place where he stands there comes the
clear call of a meadowlark. It is so clear, so definite in the great
plain! I believe that it circles out and out, that it touches like ancient light upon the thistles at Saddle Mountain, upon the broken
floor of Boke's store, upon the thin shadows that follow on the current of the Washita. And round on the eastern shelves I see the
crooked ravines which succeed to the sky, a whirlwind tracing a red,
slanting line across the middle distance, and there in the roiling dust
a knoll, a gourd dance and give-away, and Mammedaty moves among
the people, answers to his name; low thunder rolls upon the drum.
A boy leads a horse into the circle, the horse whipping its haunches
around, rattling its blue hooves on the hard earth, rolling its eyes
and blowing. There are eagle feathers fixed with ribbons in the
braided mane, a bright red blanket on the back of the black, beautiful hunting horse. The boy's arms are taut with the living weight,
the wild will and resistance of the horse, swinging the horse round
in a tight circle, to the center of the circle where Mammedaty stands
waiting to take the reins and walk, with dignity, with the whole life
of the hunting horse, away. It is good and honorable to be made such
a gift—the gift of this horse, this hunting horse—and honorable to
be the boy, the intermediary in whose hands the gift is passed. My
fingers are crisped, my fingertips bear hard upon the life of this black
horse. *Oh my grandfather, take hold of this horse. It is good that
you should be given this horse to hold in your hands, that you
should lead it away from this holy circle, that such a thing should
happen in your name.* And the southern moon descends; light like
phosphorus appears in the earth, blue and bone, clusters of blue-
black bunch grass, pocks in pewter. Flames gutter momently in the
arbor and settle to the saffron lamps; fireflies flicker on the lawn;

frogs begin to tell of the night; and crickets tell of the night, but there is neither beginning nor end in their telling. The old people arrive, the thin-limbed, deep-eyed men in their hats and braids, the round-faced women in their wide half sleeves and fringed shawls, apron-bound, carrying pots and pans and baskets of food—fried bread, boiled cracked corn, melons, pies and cakes—and for hours my grandmother has been cooking meat, boiled beef, fried chicken, chicken-fried beefsteaks, white and brown gravies. *Cohn' Tsotohah, Tsoai-talee, come here; I want to tell you something.* I sit at an old man's knee. I don't know who he is, and I am shy and uncomfortable at first; but there is delight in his eyes, and I see that he loves me. There are many people in the arbor; everyone listens. *Cohn', do you see the moon?* The full, white moon has receded into the southeast; it is a speckled moon; through the arbor screen it shimmers in the far reaches of the night. *Well, do you see?—there is a man in the moon. This is how it happened: Saynday was hungry. Oh, everyone was hungry then; the buffalo were keeping away, you know. Then Saynday's wife said to him, "Saynday, tomorrow the men are going on a hunt. You must go with them and bring back buffalo meat." "Well, yes," said Saynday. And the next day he went out on the hunt. Everyone found buffalo, except Saynday. Saynday could find no buffalo, and so he brought some tomatoes home to his wife. She was angry, but she said to him, "Saynday, tomorrow the men are going hunting again. Now I tell you that you must go with them, and you must bring back buffalo meat." "Well, yes," said Saynday. And again he went on the hunt. Everyone found buffalo, except Saynday. He could find no buffalo, and so he brought tomatoes home to his wife again. She was very angry, but she said to him, "Saynday, tomorrow the men are going hunting again. You must go with them, and you must bring back buffalo meat." "Well, yes," said Saynday. And Saynday went out on the hunt for the third time. And it was just the same: everyone found buffalo, except Saynday. Saynday could find no buffalo, and so he brought tomatoes home to his wife again. She was so angry that she began to beat him with a broom. Saynday ran, but she ran after him, beating him with the broom. He ran faster and faster, until he got away, and then he wanted to hide. He hid in the moon. There he is now in the moon, and he will not come down because he is afraid of his wife.* My people laugh with me; I am created in the old man's story, in his delight. There is a black bank and lightning in the north, the moon higher and holding off, the Big Dipper on a nail at the center of the sky. I lie down on the wide bench at my grandmother's back. The prayer meeting goes on, the singing of Christian hymns in Kiowa, now and then a gourd dance song.

There would be old men and old women in my life.

I invented history. In April's thin white light, in the white landscape of the Staked Plains, I looked for tracks among the tufts of coarse, brittle grass, amid the stones, beside the tangle of dusty hedges. When I look back upon those days—days of infinite promise and steady adventure and the certain sanctity of childhood—I see how much was there in the balance. The past and the future were simply the large contingencies of a given moment; they bore upon the present and gave it shape. One does not pass through time, but time enters upon him, in his place. As a child, I knew this surely, as a matter of fact; I am not wise to doubt it now. Notions of the past and future are essentially notions of the present. In the same way an idea of one's ancestry and posterity is really an idea of the self. About this time I was formulating an idea of myself.

. . .

I asked Billy Don if his mom and dad told him stories when he went to bed and he laughed once upon a time there were three pigs Rootie and Tootie and Pootie and Mickey Mouse and Minnie Mouse Scotty had a brand-new red car and it was snowing outside Billy Don began to laugh he got so tickled and we were all surprised because gosh it was right there in school what is it Billy Don the teacher said and he said oh nothing you wouldn't understand I was just thinking and we all laughed like heck it was so funny Ida was sent out of the room and I felt funny about that that she was sent outside and knew that we were all talking about her gee and Miss Marshall said you must not be cruel some people do not have as much as you do and Ida can't help it her clothes are old and dirty I found her crying in the bathroom and you must not be cruel you must make her feel that you are all her friends and then we all went out of our way to be friendly even Charles you're an Indian Charles said and I said yes Indians are no good he said and I said you're a liar he can't stand to be called that gosh anything but that and he's so tough so I took it back

Grandma I miss you I feel sorry for you when I come to see you and see you and go away I know you're lonely I like to see you I love to see you in the arbor cooking and talking to us you goot boy you say Scotty you goot boy and you used to carry me on your back in your shawl and hold me in your lap and I came to sleep with you and you're so soft and warm and I like the smell of you your hair is so thick and heavy it is so black except for the gray here and there you buy me candy corn and candy orange slices jellybeans animal crackers I like to watch you sew and make beadwork let's go to town grandma to the store you have so much money always Uncle Jimmy has money sometimes he buys me something down by Lonewolf his land everyone says he's going to give me some land someday oh yes

Miss Marshall my dad's people the Kiowas they have a lot of land in
Oklahoma my uncle is going to give me some land quite a lot of it
someday no ma'am he's not a farmer but he owns farmland yes
ma'am it's very strange well yes ma'am I'm a Kiowa yes ma'am I'm
sure it's not Keeowa no ma'am I can't say the Lord's Prayer in Kiowa
I can't say much of anything really my dad can yes ma'am I *am*
proud to be so American I know it ma'am Lay that pistol down babe

    Oh I feel so dumb I can't answer all those questions I don't
know how to be a Kiowa Indian my grandmother lives in a house
it's like your house Miss Marshall or Billy Don's house only it
doesn't have lights and light switches and the toilet is outside and
you have to carry wood in from the woodpile and water from the
well but that isn't what makes it Indian it's my grandma the way
she is the way she looks her hair in braids the clothes somehow yes
the way she talks she doesn't speak English so well Scotty you goot
boy she says wait I know why it's an Indian house because there are
pictures of Indians on the walls photographs of people with long
braids and buckskin clothes dresses and shirts and moccasins and
necklaces and beadwork yes that's it and there is Indian stuff all
around blankets and shawls bows and arrows everyone there acts
like an Indian everyone even me and my dad when we're there we
eat meat and everyone talks Kiowa and the old people wear Indian
clothes well those dresses dark blue and braids and hats and there is
laughing Indians laugh a lot and they sing oh yes they love to sing
sometimes when an old man comes to visit he sits in the living
room and pretty soon he just begins to sing loud with his eyes closed
but really loud and his head nodding and in the arbor there are sometimes pretty often a lot of people and lots to eat and everyone sings
and sometimes there are drums too and it goes on through the night
that's Indian my dad sets out poles on the river and we eat catfish
that's Indian and grandma goes to Rainy Mountain Baptist Church
that's Indian and my granddad Mammedaty is buried at Rainy
Mountain and some of the stones there have peyote pictures on them
and you can hear bobwhites there and see terrapins and scissortails
and that's Indian too

    . . .

    My name that's Indian my names Tsotohah Tsoai-talee Kiowa
George gave me that name Kiowa George Poolaw on his gravestone
at Rainy Mountain Pohd-lohk those funny names Pohd-lohk Kau-
au-ointy that's Indian Mammedaty Huan-toa and mom Natachee too
that's Indian the round dance holding hands moving round sideways
singing the dresses swaying those beautiful shawls and moccasins
beadwork the war dancers feather bustles bells quills we went some-

where Carnegie or Anadarko or Hobart that time there was a dance
and give-away oh it was fine all the colors everyone was wearing
such fine clothes the dancers had fans and rattles there was one big
drum those men four or five were beating that drum like making
thunder the ground seemed to shake and the dancers their feet
seemed to make the thunder how do they do it keep time that way
so perfectly that's Indian and when they stopped the give-away those
women put lots of things down on the ground heck anybody could
just go out there and take them blankets and stuff money too but
sometimes they call out the names Indian names and those people
come out and get gifts dad got a blanket Pendleton blanket plaid red
and blue and green mom got a shawl black with red flowers that old
man gave me some money two dollars two dollar bills they were
new they were folded once the long way like paper airplanes and
Jimmy and Lester gave me money too they always give me money
that's Indian that give-away it's funny it takes such a long time you
get bored well I get bored if you don't get anything and have to watch
just sit there talking maybe resting and the boy the water boy comes
around with a bucket of water and a dipper and the dancers drink
it's so hot and all the names are called out Goombi Poolaw Tsoodle
Tonamah Poorbuffalo Whitehorse those funny names Marland told
me someone's name was Chester Meat and he got so tickled it was
somehow it was really funny like Billy Don that time and we all
laughed Chester Meat and we all really laughed that's Indian Chester Meat you'd be so nice to come home to dad said one time Mammedaty got a horse at the give-away a black horse really a good one
well I guess it was the best horse in the world it was black dad said
and it had a red blanket on its back and it pranced and danced around
and there were feathers in its hair its mane and tail and that time
too a girl dad said a beautiful girl in a buckskin dress beautiful beadwork white buckskin she had hair so black and black eyes dad said
she was given a name at the give-away and it was good dad said a
good thing to be given a name there and the girl was very beautiful
and everyone was honored everyone honored her because of that
maybe I would have married her if I had been there did she look like
Faye Emerson no Minnehaha that's Indian

. . .

But I was yet a child, and I lay low at Hobbs, feeling for the   10
years in which I should find my whole self. And I had the strong,
deceptive patience of a child, had not to learn it as patience but only
to persist in it. Patience is what children have; it is especially theirs
to have. I grew tall, and I entered into the seventh grade. I sat looking into books; there were birds on the lawn, chirping. Girls ambled

in the dark corridors in white socks and saddle oxfords, and there were round, sweet syllables on their tongues. Time receded into Genesis on an autumn day in 1946.

West of Jemez Pueblo there is a great red mesa, and in the folds of the earth at its base there is a canyon, the dark red walls of which are sheer and shadow-stained; they rise vertically to a remarkable height. You do not suspect that the canyon is there, but you turn a corner and the walls contain you; you look into a corridor of geologic time. When I went into that place I left my horse outside, for there was a strange light and quiet upon the walls, and the shadows closed upon me. I looked up, straight up, to the serpentine strip of the sky. It was clear and deep, like a river running across the top of the world. The sand in which I stood was deep, and I could feel the cold of it through the soles of my shoes. And when I walked out, the light and heat of the day struck me so hard that I nearly fell. On the side of a hill in the plain of the Hissar I saw my horse grazing among sheep. The land inclined into the distance, to the Pamirs, to the Fedchenko Glacier. The river which I had seen near the sun had run out into the endless ether above the Karakoram range and the Plateau of Tibet.

Response _____

1. In the beginning of this passage Momaday moves from looking at himself to reflecting upon his grandfather Mammedaty. In the dust of a whirlwind Momaday imagines a vision of his grandfather and becomes a participant in the imaginary scene himself. Connect this vision in paragraph 3 with the story his father has told him about Mammedaty at a give-away, related later (in paragraph 9). "I invented history," Momaday says; how and why did he do this?

2. At the prayer meeting, an old man addresses Momaday as "Cohn", a Kiowa term of endearment meaning "grandson," and relates a humorous legend (paragraph 3). How is Momaday "created in the old man's story"?

3. Questioned by his teacher, in paragraph 8 Momaday says "I don't know how to be a Kiowa Indian." Why not? In the rambling interior monologue that follows, what does he show he knows?

4. Many Native American stories are not structured in terms of linear chronology; events don't necessarily have a starting point

and an ending point. Instead, the story can freely incorporate events from other times that affect our understanding of the present situation. Look for imagery in this passage that connects ancient time with the present. How does Momaday treat time in his narrative? What is the effect?

5. A portion of this passage is written without sentences and punctuation. Also, Momaday seems to ignore conventional paragraphing in places. How is this style of writing connected to the content? What effect do these stylistic decisions achieve, and what view of language does the story convey?

The Long Journey and
the Short Ride
Toshio Mori

This autobiographical story, written in 1959, was published twenty years later in the collection The Chauvinist and Other Stories. *Mori's younger brother Kazuo served in a combat team made up exclusively of Japanese-American men, and he was wounded in Italy. After the war the Mori family was able to return from Topaz Relocation Center in Utah to San Leandro and revive their nursery business.*

The other day my brother and I got to talking of the World War II days. It seemed so long ago, we agreed. The mild California climate of San Leandro was much to our liking, inasmuch being our hometown. We were back home again.

My brother looked pensively out into the yard and beyond the nearby hills as if he were re-living the past, momentarily forgetting his helpless legs and wheelchair living.

"Do you remember the last leave you got before you went overseas?" I said.

His eyes kept staring eastward over the hills but I knew he had

Toshio Mori, "The Long Journey and the Short Ride," in *The Chauvinist and Other Stories*. Asian American Studies Center, Los Angeles: U.C.L.A., 1979. Reprinted with permission.

heard me. Once again I saw him in his khaki uniform—young and healthy sergeant of the 442nd Infantry Regiment. Again I saw Mom alive and excited as ever as she saw in flesh her youngest son. She had not seen him in two years—she as an enemy alien in the Utah detention camp and her son in the army cap. Ironic? But it was so. A few Nisei in the camp would ask why in the sam hill had he chosen to spend his leave in a dump like Topaz War Relocation Center—why not the bright lights and the free "outside" world?

"I came to spend a few days with my family," he would say.   5
Then others would ask why he remained in the army. "Because I trust the government of my country," he would say.

Our mother and father were living then. We had been a tight little family group. As my brother's eyes dreamily stared into the past, I could imagine how much he had missed the family life during the war years and since then, not counting what he had gone through at the front.

"Do you remember the time Mom and I saw you off on your last leave?" I said.

My brother nodded his head and smiled. "Sure do," he said.

How many times he had heard the story I have forgotten, but I am continually retelling it because of its lasting impression on me— of my country and the little people representing it in time of war and turmoil.

At the gatehouse in front of the administration building we   10
stood in line waiting for our names to be checked off the passenger list. Mother and I were accompanying my brother to Delta station to see him off for the last time.

It was a rare occasion for us to leave the camp and go "outside" to the town. We had to have a special permit with a reasonable and specific purpose.

As we passed the gate and boarded the bus to Delta an internal security clerk counted the heads for a final check-up. Finally we were on our way. At our first glance back, we saw nothing but the fence enclosure. Gradually our perspective restored, we saw our hospital building and water tank. Now the Military Police barracks were becoming blurred and a speck in the distance. Mother and I were "outside" for the first time.

We faced the future with misgivings and apprehension—especially the immediate present. What will it be like to be on the "outside?" For being cooped up as we were, perhaps, our imagination played tricks. We had been away for so long from the normal atmosphere.

About midway to the town of Delta the bus slowed down. Up ahead stood the MP gatehouse. A soldier climbed aboard to check the passenger list. He tallied the number of names on his paper and the number of heads on the bus. Having satisfied himself, the MP jumped off and waved the bus away.

15   To my brother it must have been all a puzzle. In the first place, he must have asked himself, what we were doing out in the middle of the Utah desert. Fortunately for me, he never did ask me why— why his family had been evacuated from their home on the West Coast.

From my standpoint as a camp resident, I had a different puzzle. How will a camp resident be received on the "outside?"

The train was on time. Once at the station there was little time for brooding. I shook hands with my brother. Mother took him aside for the last few precious minutes. She said, "Be careful, my boy. Take good care of yourself."

"Don't worry, Mom. I'll be back," my brother said.

The station platform was quite filled with groups of white folks. In my concern for my brother and mother, I had not noticed anything unusual—incidents unpleasant or otherwise.

20   It was long after the train whistle had died down that I observed the bleak loneliness of the station. A moment ago a trainload of people with a purpose of duty was here and now I must go back to my camp, I thought. As I guided my mother down the dirt road toward the town, the vast emptiness of the desert sunset depressed me. A fitting description for my "inside" life, I thought.

Walking with my head down and watching our feet raise puffs of dust in the air, I had not at first noticed the car stopping alongside of us nor the voice calling us. A friendly middle-aged couple and their teenage daughter were smiling at us. "Going back to town? Hop in," the white man said. At the same time the girl in the rear seat opened the door for us.

The swift change of climate dumbfounded me. All the way to town, which was only a few blocks away from the station, we exchanged family news with the white folks. They had just seen their boy off after a short shore leave. They had noticed Mother and I with my brother at the station. For all the good their friendly gesture had done for me, all I could say in words was a simple thanks. It was a short ride, sure enough, but the most memorable, coming at the right moment for us—especially for me.

Home again together after going our separate ways, we made the most of it. Many days along with many events had gone by since then. My brother who had fought almost a year in France and Italy was wounded in the last Italian campaign of the war. Then a series of hospital transfers finally ended at the Letterman in San Francisco. Our mother and father and I returned from camp to California when the war with Japan was reaching near the climax. Mother and I made numerous visits to see my brother at the DeWitt Hospital in Auburn, California and the Letterman before she died. She never saw him discharged for home. Then Father passed on.

Today the spring sun is shining bright in San Leandro. From the kitchen in his new home my brother and I gazed at the familiar surroundings now interspersed with the town's growth. He had built his new home under the disabled veteran's benefit. It was his pride and joy. "You're doing all right," I said.

My brother nodded and said, "Thought I'd never make it. It   25 sure was a long journey home—for both of us."

Mother always used to worry about getting my brother married early and settled down, even during the war years. After he had returned home totally paralyzed and had to live on a wheelchair I too was worried. I was afraid that he would never find a wife. After he had completed furnishing his new house I used to egg him on, if only to encourage him. "Now all you need is a bride."

Today he is married. He had found his life partner just about a year ago.

"Mom got the roughest part of the deal," I said. "She never saw you recover."

There was a tinge of sorrow in my brother's voice. Not with bitterness and despair but with calm and contentment, he said, "If only she could see me now."

Response

1. Mori recalls his mother: "she as an enemy alien in the Utah detention camp and her son in the army cap. Ironic? But it was so" (paragraph 4). In this story, as in "Tomorrow Is Coming, Children" (Section V), Mori juxtaposes opposite aspects of situations as a subtle comment on them. Find other ironic situations in this story, and consider the effect of the irony.

2. Mori looks back on the "puzzle" of his family's wartime experience. "Fortunately for me," he says of his brother, "he never did ask me why—why his family had been evacuated from their home on the West Coast" (paragraph 15). How might this comment be interpreted? How do you think Mori felt about his brother's military service?

3. What attitude toward the war experience does Mori express
    through this story?

4. Many of Mori's stories quietly celebrate the ability of ordinary
    people through small acts to transcend the indifference and
    cruelties of the larger society. In "Confessions of an Unknown
    Writer" (Section I) Mori says, "It is the capability of man which
    is so natural to occur that I am taking myself as the story and
    firmly believe its worth." How does this story illustrate that
    theme?

No-No Boy
John Okada

*The following excerpt comes from the opening
chapter of Okada's 1976 novel. The story examines
an individual's struggle for identity and a
community's struggle to cope with the pain, guilt,
and anger left by World War II. While the novel
realistically portrays the Japanese-American
community of Seattle where Okada grew up, it is not
strictly autobiographical; Okada himself was not a
No-No Boy. But his characters, and his understanding
of the deep conflict and ambivalence they share, are
drawn from his own experience.*

Two weeks after his twenty-fifth birthday, Ichiro got off a bus
at Second and Main in Seattle. He had been gone four years, two in
camp and two in prison.

Walking down the street that autumn morning with a small,
black suitcase, he felt like an intruder in a world to which he had
no claim. It was just enough that he should feel this way, for, of his
own free will, he had stood before the judge and said that he would
not go in the army. At the time there was no other choice for him.
That was when he was twenty-three, a man of twenty-three. Now,
two years older, he was even more of a man.

John Okada, from *No-No Boy*. Seattle: University of Washington Press, 1976.
Reprinted with permission.

Christ, he thought to himself, just a goddamn kid is all I was. Didn't know enough to wipe my own nose. What the hell have I done? What am I doing back here? Best thing I can do would be to kill some son of a bitch and head back to prison.

He walked toward the railroad depot where the tower with the clocks on all four sides was. It was a dirty looking tower of ancient brick. It was a dirty city. Dirtier, certainly, than it had a right to be after only four years.

5   Waiting for the light to change to green, he looked around at the people standing at the bus stop. A couple of men in suits, half a dozen women who failed to arouse him even after prolonged good behavior, and a young Japanese with a lunch bucket. Ichiro studied him, searching in his mind for the name that went with the round, pimply face and the short-cropped hair. The pimples were gone and the face had hardened, but the hair was still cropped. The fellow wore green, army-fatigue trousers and an Eisenhower jacket—Eto Minato. The name came to him at the same time as did the horrible significance of the army clothes. In panic, he started to step off the curb. It was too late. He had been seen.

"Itchy!" That was his nickname.

Trying to escape, Ichiro urged his legs frenziedly across the street.

"Hey, Itchy!" The caller's footsteps ran toward him.

An arm was placed across his back. Ichiro stopped and faced the other Japanese. He tried to smile, but could not. There was no way out now.

10   "I'm Eto. Remember?" Eto smiled and extended his palm. Reluctantly, Ichiro lifted his own hand and let the other shake it.

The round face with the round eyes peered at him through silver-rimmed spectacles. "What the hell! It's been a long time, but not that long. How've you been? What's doing?"

"Well . . . that is, I'm . . ."

"Last time must have been before Pearl Harbor. God, it's been quite a while, hasn't it? Three, no, closer to four years, I guess. Lotsa Japs coming back to the Coast. Lotsa Japs in Seattle. You'll see 'em around. Japs are funny that way. Gotta have their rice and saké and other Japs. Stupid, I say. The smart ones went to Chicago and New York and lotsa places back east, but there's still plenty coming back out this way." Eto drew cigarettes from his breast pocket and held out the package. "No? Well, I'll have one. Got the habit in the army. Just got out a short while back. Rough time, but I made it. Didn't get out in time to make the quarter, but I'm planning to go to school. How long you been around?"

Ichiro touched his toe to the suitcase. "Just got in. Haven't been home yet."

"When'd you get discharged?"   15

A car grinding its gears started down the street. He wished he were in it. "I . . . that is . . . I never was in."

Eto slapped him good-naturedly on the arm. "No need to look so sour. So you weren't in. So what? Been in camp all this time?"

"No." He made an effort to be free of Eto with his questions. He felt as if he were in a small room whose walls were slowly closing in on him. "It's been a long time, I know, but I'm really anxious to see the folks."

"What the hell. Let's have a drink. On me. I don't give a damn if I'm late to work. As for your folks, you'll see them soon enough. You drink, don't you?"

"Yeah, but not now."   20

"Ahh." Eto was disappointed. He shifted his lunch box from under one arm to the other.

"I've really got to be going."

The round face wasn't smiling any more. It was thoughtful. The eyes confronted Ichiro with indecision which changed slowly to enlightenment and then to suspicion. He remembered. He knew.

The friendliness was gone as he said: "No-no boy, huh?"

Ichiro wanted to say yes. He wanted to return the look of de-   25
spising hatred and say simply yes, but it was too much to say. The walls had closed in and were crushing all the unspoken words back down into his stomach. He shook his head once, not wanting to evade the eyes but finding it impossible to meet them. Out of his big weakness the little ones were branching, and the eyes he didn't have the courage to face were ever present. If it would have helped to gouge out his own eyes, he would have done so long ago. The hate-churned eyes with the stamp of unrelenting condemnation were his cross and he had driven the nails with his own hands.

"Rotten bastard. Shit on you." Eto coughed up a mouthful of sputum and rolled his words around it: "Rotten, no-good bastard."

Surprisingly, Ichiro felt relieved. Eto's anger seemed to serve as a release to his own naked tensions. As he stooped to lift the suitcase a wet wad splattered over his hand and dripped onto the black leather. The legs of his accuser were in front of him. God in a pair of green fatigues, U.S. Army style. They were the legs of the jury that had passed sentence upon him. Beseech me, they seemed to say, throw your arms about me and bury your head between my knees and seek pardon for your great sin.

"I'll piss on you next time," said Eto vehemently.

He turned as he lifted the suitcase off the ground and hurried away from the legs and the eyes from which no escape was possible.

Jackson Street started at the waterfront and stretched past the   30
two train depots and up the hill all the way to the lake, where the

houses were bigger and cleaner and had garages with late-model cars in them. For Ichiro, Jackson Street signified that section of the city immediately beyond the railroad tracks between Fifth and Twelfth Avenues. That was the section which used to be pretty much Japanese town. It was adjacent to Chinatown and most of the gambling and prostitution and drinking seemed to favor the area.

Like the dirty clock tower of the depot, the filth of Jackson Street had increased. Ichiro paused momentarily at an alley and peered down the passage formed by the walls of two sagging buildings. There had been a door there at one time, a back door to a movie house which only charged a nickel. A nickel was a lot of money when he had been seven or nine or eleven. He wanted to go into the alley to see if the door was still there.

Being on Jackson Street with its familiar store fronts and taverns and restaurants, which were somehow different because the war had left its mark on them, was like trying to find one's way out of a dream that seemed real most of the time but wasn't really real because it was still only a dream. The war had wrought violent changes upon the people, and the people, in turn, working hard and living hard and earning a lot of money and spending it on whatever was available, had distorted the profile of Jackson Street. The street had about it the air of a carnival without quite succeeding at becoming one. A shooting gallery stood where once had been a clothing store; fish and chips had replaced a jewelry shop; and a bunch of Negroes were horsing around raucously in front of a pool parlor. Everything looked older and dirtier and shabbier.

He walked past the pool parlor, picking his way gingerly among the Negroes, of whom there had been only a few at one time and of whom there seemed to be nothing but now. They were smoking and shouting and cussing and carousing and the sidewalk was slimy with their spittle.

"Jap!"

His pace quickened automatically, but curiosity or fear or indignation or whatever it was made him glance back at the white teeth framed in a leering dark brown which was almost black.

"Go back to Tokyo, boy." Persecution in the drawl of the persecuted.

The white teeth and brown-black leers picked up the cue and jigged to the rhythmical chanting of "Jap-boy, To-ki-yo; Jap-boy, To-ki-yo . . ."

Friggin' niggers, he uttered savagely to himself and, from the same place deep down inside where tolerance for the Negroes and the Jews and the Mexicans and the Chinese and the too short and too fat and too ugly abided because he was Japanese and knew what it was like better than did those who were white and average and middle class and good Democrats or liberal Republicans, the hate which was unrelenting and terrifying seethed up.

Then he was home. It was a hole in the wall with groceries crammed in orderly confusion on not enough shelving, into not enough space. He knew what it would be like even before he stepped in. His father had described the place to him in a letter, composed in simple Japanese characters because otherwise Ichiro could not have read it. The letter had been purposely repetitive and painstakingly detailed so that Ichiro should not have any difficulty finding the place. The grocery store was the same one the Ozakis had operated for many years. That's all his father had had to say. Come to the grocery store which was once the store of the Ozakis. The Japanese characters, written simply so that he could read them, covered pages of directions as if he were a foreigner coming to the city for the first time.

Thinking about the letter made him so mad that he forgot   40
about the Negroes. He opened the door just as he had a thousand times when they had lived farther down the block and he used to go to the Ozakis' for a loaf of bread or a jar of pickled scallions, and the bell tinkled just as he knew it would. All the grocery stores he ever knew had bells which tinkled when one opened the door and the familiar sound softened his inner turmoil.

"Ichiro?" The short, round man who came through the curtains at the back of the store uttered the name preciously as might an old woman. "Ya, Ichiro, you have come home. How good that you have come home!" The gently spoken Japanese which he had not heard for so long sounded strange. He would hear a great deal of it now that he was home, for his parents, like most of the old Japanese, spoke virtually no English. On the other hand, the children, like Ichiro, spoke almost no Japanese. Thus they communicated, the old speaking Japanese with an occasional badly mispronounced word or two of English; and the young, with the exception of a simple word or phrase of Japanese which came fairly effortlessly to the lips, resorting almost constantly to the tongue the parents avoided.

The father bounced silently over the wood flooring in slippered feet toward his son. Fondly, delicately, he placed a pudgy hand on Ichiro's elbow and looked up at his son who was Japanese but who had been big enough for football and tall enough for basketball in high school. He pushed the elbow and Ichiro led the way into the back, where there was a kitchen, a bathroom, and one bedroom. He looked around the bedroom and felt like puking. It was neat and clean and scrubbed. His mother would have seen to that. It was just the idea of everybody sleeping in the one room. He wondered if his folks still pounded flesh.

He backed out of the bedroom and slumped down on a stool. "Where's Ma?"

"Mama is gone to the bakery." The father kept his beaming eyes on his son who was big and tall. He shut off the flow of water and shifted the metal teapot to the stove.

45 "What for?"

"Bread," his father said in reply, "bread for the store."

"Don't they deliver?"

"Ya, they deliver." He ran a damp rag over the table, which was spotlessly clean.

"What the hell is she doing at the bakery then?"

50 "It is good business, Ichiro." He was at the cupboard, fussing with the tea cups and saucers and cookies. "The truck comes in the morning. We take enough for the morning business. For the afternoon, we get soft, fresh bread. Mama goes to the bakery."

Ichiro tried to think of a bakery nearby and couldn't. There was a big Wonder Bread bakery way up on Nineteenth, where a nickel used to buy a bagful of day-old stuff. That was thirteen and a half blocks, all uphill. He knew the distance by heart because he'd walked it twice every day to go to grade school, which was a half-block beyond the bakery or fourteen blocks from home.

"What bakery?"

The water on the stove began to boil and the old man flipped the lid on the pot and tossed in a pinch of leaves. "Wonder Bread."

"Is that the one up on Nineteenth?"

55 "Ya."

"How much do you make on bread?"

"Let's see," he said pouring the tea, "Oh, three, four cents. Depends."

"How many loaves does Ma get?"

"Ten or twelve. Depends."

60 Ten loaves at three or four cents' profit added up to thirty or forty cents. He compromised at thirty-five cents and asked the next question: "The bus, how much is it?"

"Oh, let's see." He sipped the tea noisily, sucking it through his teeth in well regulated gulps. "Let's see. Fifteen cents for one time. Tokens are two for twenty-five cents. That is twelve and one-half cents."

Twenty-five cents for bus fare to get ten loaves of bread which turned a profit of thirty-five cents. It would take easily an hour to make the trip up and back. He didn't mean to shout, but he shouted: "Christ, Pa, what else do you give away?"

His father peered over the teacup with a look of innocent surprise.

It made him madder. "Figure it out. Just figure it out. Say you make thirty-five cents on ten loaves. You take a bus up and back and there's twenty-five cents shot. That leaves ten cents. On top of that, there's an hour wasted. What are you running a business for? Your health?"

Slup went the tea through his teeth, slup, slup, slup. "Mama walks." He sat there looking at his son like a benevolent Buddha.   65

Ichiro lifted the cup to his lips and let the liquid burn down his throat. His father had said "Mama walks" and that made things right with the world. The overwhelming simplicity of the explanation threatened to evoke silly giggles which, if permitted to escape, might lead to hysterics. He clenched his fists and subdued them.

At the opposite end of the table the father had slupped the last of his tea and was already taking the few steps to the sink to rinse out the cup.

"Goddammit, Pa, sit down!" He'd never realized how nervous a man his father was. The old man had constantly been doing something every minute since he had come. It didn't figure. Here he was, round and fat and cheerful-looking and, yet, he was going incessantly as though his trousers were crawling with ants.

"Ya, Ichiro, I forget you have just come home. We should talk." He resumed his seat at the table and busied his fingers with a box of matches.

Ichiro stepped out of the kitchen, spotted the cigarettes behind   70 the cash register, and returned with a pack of Camels. Lighting a match, the old man held it between his fingers and waited until the son opened the package and put a cigarette in his mouth. By then the match was threatening to sear his fingers. He dropped it hastily and stole a sheepish glance at Ichiro, who reached for the box and struck his own match.

"Ichiro." There was a timorousness in the father's voice. Or was it apology?

"Yeah."

"Was it very hard?"

"No. It was fun." The sarcasm didn't take.

"You are sorry?" He was waddling over rocky ground on a   75 pitch-black night and he didn't like it one bit.

"I'm okay, Pa. It's finished. Done and finished. No use talking about it."

"True," said the old man too heartily. "it is done and there is no use to talk." The bell tinkled and he leaped from the chair and fled out of the kitchen.

Using the butt of the first cigarette, Ichiro lit another. He heard his father's voice in the store.

"Mama. Ichiro. Ichiro is here."

80   The sharp, lifeless tone of his mother's words flipped through the silence and he knew that she hadn't changed.

"The bread must be put out."

In other homes mothers and fathers and sons and daughters rushed into hungry arms after week-end separations to find assurance in crushing embraces and loving kisses. The last time he saw his mother was over two years ago. He waited, seeing in the sounds of the rustling waxed paper the stiff, angular figure of the woman stacking the bread on the rack in neat, precise piles.

His father came back into the kitchen with a little less bounce and began to wash the cups. She came through the curtains a few minutes after, a small, flat-chested, shapeless woman who wore her hair pulled back into a tight bun. Hers was the awkward, skinny body of a thirteen-year-old which had dried and toughened through the many years following but which had developed no further. He wondered how the two of them had ever gotten together long enough to have two sons.

"I am proud that you are back," she said. "I am proud to call you my son."

85   It was her way of saying that she had made him what he was and that the thing in him which made him say no to the judge and go to prison for two years was the growth of a seed planted by the mother tree and that she was the mother who had put this thing in her son and that everything that had been done and said was exactly as it should have been and that that was what made him her son because no other would have made her feel the pride that was in her breast.

He looked at his mother and swallowed with difficulty the bitterness that threatened to destroy the last fragment of understanding for the woman who was his mother and still a stranger because, in truth, he could not know what it was to be a Japanese who breathed the air of America and yet had never lifted a foot from the land that was Japan.

"I've been talking with Pa," he said, not knowing or caring why except that he had to say something.

"After a while, you and I, we will talk also." She walked through the kitchen into the bedroom and hung her coat and hat in a wardrobe of cardboard which had come from Sears Roebuck. Then she came back through the kitchen and out into the store.

The father gave him what was meant to be a knowing look and uttered softly: "Doesn't like my not being in the store when she is out. I tell her the bell tinkles, but she does not understand."

"Hell's bells," he said in disgust. Pushing himself out of the chair violently, he strode into the bedroom and flung himself out on one of the double beds.

Lying there, he wished the roof would fall in and bury forever the anguish which permeated his every pore. He lay there fighting with his burden, lighting one cigarette after another and dropping ashes and butts purposely on the floor. It was the way he felt, stripped of dignity, respect, purpose, honor, all the things which added up to schooling and marriage and family and work and happiness.

It was to please her, he said to himself with teeth clamped together to imprison the wild, meaningless, despairing cry which was forever straining inside of him. Pa's okay, but he's a nobody. He's a goddamned, fat, grinning, spineless nobody. Ma is the rock that's always hammering, pounding, pounding, pounding in her unobtrusive, determined, fanatical way until there's nothing left to call one's self. She's cursed me with her meanness and the hatred that you cannot see but which is always hating. It was she who opened my mouth and made my lips move to sound the words which got me two years in prison and an emptiness that is more empty and frightening than the caverns of hell. She's killed me with her meanness and hatred and I hope she's happy because I'll never know the meaning of it again.

"Ichiro."

He propped himself up on an elbow and looked at her. She had hardly changed. Surely, there must have been a time when she could smile and, yet, he could not remember.

"Yeah?"

"Lunch is on the table."

As he pushed himself off the bed and walked past her to the kitchen, she took broom and dustpan and swept up the mess he had made.

There were eggs, fried with soy sauce, sliced cold meat, boiled cabbage, and tea and rice. They all ate in silence, not even disturbed once by the tinkling of the bell. The father cleared the table after they had finished and dutifully retired to watch the store. Ichiro had smoked three cigarettes before his mother ended the silence.

"You must go back to school."

100   He had almost forgotten that there had been a time before the war when he had actually gone to college for two years and studiously applied himself to courses in the engineering school. The statement staggered him. Was that all there was to it? Did she mean to sit there and imply that the four intervening years were to be casually forgotten and life resumed as if there had been no four years and no war and no Eto who had spit on him because of the thing he had done?

"I don't feel much like going to school."

"What will you do?"

"I don't know."

"With an education, your opportunities in Japan will be unlimited. You must go and complete your studies."

105   "Ma," he said slowly, "Ma, I'm not going to Japan. Nobody's going to Japan. The war is over. Japan lost. Do you hear? Japan lost."

"You believe that?" It was said in the tone of an adult asking a child who is no longer a child if he really believed that Santa Claus was real.

"Yes, I believe it. I know it. America is still here. Do you see the great Japanese army walking down the streets? No. There is no Japanese army any more."

"The boat is coming and we must be ready."

"The boat?"

110   "Yes." She reached into her pocket and drew out a worn envelope.

The letter had been mailed from Sao Paulo, Brazil, and was addressed to a name that he did not recognize. Inside the envelope was a single sheet of flimsy, rice paper covered with intricate flourishes of Japanese characters.

"What does it say?"

She did not bother to pick up the letter. "To you who are a loyal and honorable Japanese, it is with humble and heartfelt joy that I relay this momentous message. Word has been brought to us that the victorious Japanese government is presently making preparations to send ships which will return to Japan those residents in foreign countries who have steadfastly maintained their faith and loyalty to our Emperor. The Japanese government regrets that the responsibilities arising from the victory compels them to delay in the sending of the vessels. To be among the few who remain to receive this honor is a gratifying tribute. Heed not the propaganda of the radio and newspapers which endeavor to convince the people with lies about the allied victory. Especially, heed not the lies of your traitorous countrymen who have turned their backs on the country of their birth and who will suffer for their treasonous acts. The day of glory is close at hand. The rewards will be beyond our greatest expectations. What we have done, we have done only as Japanese, but the government is grateful. Hold your heads high and make ready for the journey, for the ships are coming."

"Who wrote that?" he asked incredulously. It was like a weird nightmare. It was like finding out that an incurable strain of insanity pervaded the family, an intangible horror that swayed and taunted beyond the grasp of reaching fingers.

"A friend in South America. We are not alone."   115

"We *are* alone," he said vehemently. "This whole thing is crazy. You're crazy. I'm crazy. All right, so we made a mistake. Let's admit it."

"There has been no mistake. The letter confirms."

"Sure it does. It proves there's crazy people in the world besides us. If Japan won the war, what the hell are we doing here? What are you doing running a grocery store? It doesn't figure. It doesn't figure because we're all wrong. The minute we admit that, everything is fine. I've had a lot of time to think about all this. I've thought about it, and every time the answer comes out the same. You can't tell me different any more."

She sighed ever so slightly. "We will talk later when you are feeling better." Carefully folding the letter and placing it back in the envelope, she returned it to her pocket. "It is not I who tell you that the ship is coming. It is in the letter. If you have come to doubt your mother—and I'm sure you do not mean it even if you speak in weakness—it is to be regretted. Rest a few days. Think more deeply and your doubts will disappear. You are my son, Ichiro."

No, he said to himself as he watched her part the curtains and   120 start into the store. There was a time when I was your son. There was a time that I no longer remember when you used to smile a mother's smile and tell me stories about gallant and fierce warriors who protected their lords with blades of shining steel and about the old woman who found a peach in the stream and took it home and, when her husband split it in half, a husky little boy tumbled out to fill their hearts with boundless joy. I was that boy in the peach and you were the old woman and we were Japanese with Japanese feelings and Japanese pride and Japanese thoughts because it was all right then to be Japanese and feel and think all the things that Japanese do even if we lived in America. Then there came a time when I was only half Japanese because one is not born in America and raised in America and taught in America and one does not speak and swear and drink and smoke and play and fight and see and hear in America among Americans in American streets and houses without becoming American and loving it. But I did not love enough, for you were still half my mother and I was thereby still half Japanese and when the war came and they told me to fight for America, I was not strong enough to fight you and I was not strong enough to fight the bitterness which made the half of me which was you bigger than the half of me which was America and really the whole of me that I could not see or feel. Now that I know the truth when it is too late and the half of me which was you is no longer there, I am only half of me and the half that remains is American by law because the government was wise and strong enough to know why it was that I could not fight for America and did not strip me of my birthright. But it is not enough to be American only in the eyes of the law and it is not enough to be only half an American and know that it is an empty half. I am not your son and I am not Japanese and I am not American. I can go someplace and tell people that I've got an inverted stomach and that I am an American, true and blue and Hail Columbia, but the army wouldn't have me because of the stomach. That's easy and I would do it, only I've got to convince myself first and that I cannot do. I wish with all my heart that I were Japanese or that I were American. I am neither and I blame you and I blame myself and I blame the world which is made up of many countries which fight with each other and kill and hate and destroy but not enough, so that they must kill and hate and destroy again and again and again. It is so easy and simple that I cannot understand it at all. And the reason I do not understand it is because I do not understand you who were the half of me that is no more and because I do not understand what it was about that half that made me destroy the half of me which was American and the half which might have become the whole of me if I had said yes I will go and fight in your army because that is what I believe and want and cherish and love. . .

Defeatedly, he crushed the stub of a cigarette into an ash tray filled with many other stubs and reached for the package to get another. It was empty and he did not want to go into the store for more because he did not feel much like seeing either his father or mother. He went into the bedroom and tossed and groaned and half slept.

Response

1. "The war had wrought violent changes upon the people," writes Okada (paragraph 32). In what different ways is this observation developed in the text?

2. With the characters introduced in this chapter—Ichiro, Eto, and the parents—Okada presents a spectrum of attitudes about the

war and about national identity within the Japanese-American community. Analyze these different viewpoints and consider what might motivate them.

3. Near the end of this passage Ichiro responds in his thoughts to his mother, in a long paragraph that author Frank Chin (in his Afterword to Okada's book) has called "one of the most powerfully moving passages in Asian American writing." Given what is revealed of Ichiro's character, explain why he refused military service, and the emotional consequences of his action for him.

4. Keeping in mind that Okada himself was not a No-No Boy, we know that Ichiro does not directly represent the author in an autobiographical sense. Based on this passage, what do you think is the author's point of view about the war and about the issue of identity? Find support in the text for your analysis.

5. "I am not Japanese and I am not American," says Ichiro in despair. Compare his dilemma with that expressed by James Baldwin in his "Autobiographical Notes" (Section I) and "The Discovery of What It Means to Be an American." What are the causes of each man's condition, and what solutions are available to them?

America:
The Multinational Society
Ishmael Reed

This essay from the collection Writin' Is Fightin'
*(1988) presents an optimistic but cautionary view of
the possibilities facing U.S. society. It reflects Reed's
continuing concern with political and religious
repression.*

On the day before Memorial Day, 1983, a poet called me to
describe a city he had just visited. He said that one section included
mosques, built by the Islamic people who dwelled there. Attending
his reading, he said, were large numbers of Hispanic people, forty
thousand of whom lived in the same city. He was not talking about
a fabled city located in some mysterious region of the world. The
city he'd visited was Detroit.

A few months before, as I was leaving Houston, Texas, I heard
it announced on the radio that Texas's largest minority was Mexican American, and though a foundation recently issued a report critical of bilingual education, the taped voice used to guide the passengers on the air trams connecting terminals in Dallas Airport is in
both Spanish and English. If the trend continues, a day will come
when it will be difficult to travel through some sections of the coun-

try without hearing commands in both English and Spanish; after all, for some western states, Spanish was the first written language and the Spanish style lives on in the western way of life.

Shortly after my Texas trip, I sat in an auditorium located on the campus of the University of Wisconsin at Milwaukee as a Yale professor—whose original work on the influence of African cultures upon those of the Americas has led to his ostracism from some monocultural intellectual circles—walked up and down the aisle, like an old-time southern evangelist, dancing and drumming the top of the lectern, illustrating his points before some serious Afro-American intellectuals and artists who cheered and applauded his performance and his mastery of information. The professor was "white." After his lecture, he joined a group of Milwaukeeans in a conversation. All of the participants spoke Yoruban, though only the professor had ever traveled to Africa.

One of the artists told me that his paintings, which included African and Afro-American mythological symbols and imagery, were hanging in the local McDonald's restaurant. The next day I went to McDonald's and snapped pictures of smiling youngsters eating hamburgers below paintings that could grace the walls of any of the country's leading museums. The manager of the local McDonald's said, "I don't know what you boys are doing, but I like it," as he commissioned the local painters to exhibit in his restaurant.

Such blurring of cultural styles occurs in everyday life in the   5
United States to a greater extent than anyone can imagine and is probably more prevalent than the sensational conflict between people of different backgrounds that is played up and often encouraged by the media. The result is what the Yale professor, Robert Thompson, referred to as a cultural bouillabaisse, yet members of the nation's present educational and cultural Elect still cling to the notion that the United States belongs to some vaguely defined entity they refer to as "Western civilization," by which they mean, presumably, a civilization created by the people of Europe, as if Europe can be viewed in monolithic terms. Is Beethoven's Ninth Symphony, which includes Turkish marches, a part of Western civilization, or the late nineteenth- and twentieth-century French paintings, whose creators were influenced by Japanese art? And what of the cubists, through whom the influence of African art changed modern painting, or the surrealists, who were so impressed with the art of the Pacific Northwest Indians that, in their map of North America, Alaska dwarfs the lower forty-eight in size?

Are the Russians, who are often criticized for their adoption of "Western" ways by Tsarist dissidents in exile, members of Western civilization? And what of the millions of Europeans who have black African and Asian ancestry, black Africans having occupied several countries for hundreds of years? Are these "Europeans" members of Western civilization, or the Hungarians, who originated across the Urals in a place called Greater Hungary, or the Irish, who came from the Iberian Peninsula?

Even the notion that North America is part of Western civilization because our "system of government" is derived from Europe is being challenged by Native American historians who say that the founding fathers, Benjamin Franklin especially, were actually influenced by the system of government that had been adopted by the Iroquois hundreds of years prior to the arrival of large numbers of Europeans.

Western civilization, then, becomes another confusing category like Third World, or Judeo-Christian culture, as man attempts to impose his small-screen view of political and cultural reality upon a complex world. Our most publicized novelist recently said that Western civilization was the greatest achievement of mankind, an attitude that flourishes on the street level as scribbles in public restrooms: "White Power," "Niggers and Spics Suck," or "Hitler was a prophet," the latter being the most telling, for wasn't Adolph Hitler the archetypal monoculturalist who, in his pigheaded arrogance, believed that one way and one blood was so pure that it had to be protected from alien strains at all costs? Where did such an attitude, which has caused so much misery and depression in our national life, which has tainted even our noblest achievements, begin? An attitude that caused the incarceration of Japanese-American citizens during World War II, the persecution of Chicanos and Chinese Americans, the near-extermination of the Indians, and the murder and lynchings of thousands of Afro-Americans.

Virtuous, hardworking, pious, even though they occasionally would wander off after some fancy clothes, or rendezvous in the woods with the town prostitute, the Puritans are idealized in our schoolbooks as "a hardy band" of no-nonsense patriarchs whose discipline razed the forest and brought order to the New World (a term that annoys Native American historians). Industrious, responsible, it was their "Yankee ingenuity" and practicality that created the work ethic. They were simple folk who produced a number of good poets, and they set the tone for the American writing style, of lean and spare lines, long before Hemingway. They worshiped in churches whose colors blended in with the New England snow, churches with simple structures and ornate lecterns.

10   The Puritans were a daring lot, but they had a mean streak. They hated the theater and banned Christmas. They punished people in a cruel and inhuman manner. They killed children who dis-

obeyed their parents. When they came in contact with those whom they considered heathens or aliens, they behaved in such a bizarre and irrational manner that this chapter in the American history comes down to us as a late-movie horror film. They exterminated the Indians, who taught them how to survive in a world unknown to them, and their encounter with the calypso culture of Barbados resulted in what the tourist guide in Salem's Witches' House refers to as the Witchcraft Hysteria.

The Puritan legacy of hard work and meticulous accounting led to the establishment of a great industrial society; it is no wonder that the American industrial revolution began in Lowell, Massachusetts, but there was the other side, the strange and paranoid attitudes toward those different from the Elect.

The cultural attitudes of that early Elect continue to be voiced in everyday life in the United States: the president of a distinguished university, writing a letter to the *Times*, belittling the study of African civilizations; the television network that promoted its show on the Vatican art with the boast that this art represented "the finest achievements of the human spirit." A modern up-tempo state of complex rhythms that depends upon contacts with an international community can no longer behave as if it dwelled in a "Zion Wilderness" surrounded by beasts and pagans.

When I heard a schoolteacher warn the other night about the invasion of the American educational system by foreign curriculums, I wanted to yell at the television set, "Lady, they're already here." It has already begun because the world is here. The world has been arriving at these shores for at least ten thousand years from Europe, Africa, and Asia. In the late nineteenth and early twentieth centuries, large numbers of Europeans arrived, adding their cultures to those of the European, African, and Asian settlers who were already here, and recently millions have been entering the country from South America and the Caribbean, making Yale Professor Bob Thompson's bouillabaisse richer and thicker.

One of our most visionary politicians said that he envisioned a time when the United States could become the brain of the world, by which he meant the repository of all of the latest advanced information systems. I thought of that remark when an enterprising poet friend of mine called to say that he had just sold a poem to a computer magazine and that the editors were delighted to get it because they didn't carry fiction or poetry. Is that the kind of world we desire? A humdrum homogenous world of all brains but no heart, no fiction, no poetry; a world of robots with human attendants bereft of imagination, of culture? Or does North America deserve a more exciting destiny? To become a place where the cultures of the world crisscross. This is possible because the United States is unique in the world: The world is here.

Response

1. Reed opens his essay with a series of examples, leading to a generalization in paragraph 5. How do these introductory examples define his notion of "cultural blurring"? How does Reed's concept differ from the popular idea of America as a "melting pot"? To what extent does your own experience support or contradict Reed's view?

2. How does Reed evaluate the concept of "Western civilization" in paragraphs 5 through 8? On what basis does he call it a "confusing category"?

3. A "small-screen view of political and cultural reality" is inherently dangerous, Reed suggests in paragraph 8, and he asks, "Where did such an attitude . . . begin?" His answer lies in a somewhat unconventional analysis of the early Puritans, with their notion of the Elect. Explain the connection Reed makes between Puritan beliefs and present-day monocultural attitudes.

4. Reed cautions against a limited vision of the United States as scientific and technological leader in the world. Instead, in his conclusion he raises the possibility of "a more exciting destiny." How do you interpret his proposal?

My Baseball Years

Philip Roth

Roth wrote this essay at the invitation of The New York Times; *it appeared on the opening day of the baseball season in 1973. Later it was published in* Reading Myself and Others, *a collection of Roth's nonfiction.*

In one of his essays George Orwell writes that, though he was not very good at the game, he had a long, hopeless love affair with cricket until he was sixteen. My relations with baseball were similar. Between the ages of nine and thirteen, I must have put in a forty-hour week during the snowless months over at the neighborhood playfield—softball, hardball, and stickball pick-up games—while simultaneously holding down a full-time job as a pupil at the local grammar school. As I remember it, news of two of the most cataclysmic public events of my childhood—the death of President Roosevelt and the bombing of Hiroshima—reached me while I was out playing ball. My performance was uniformly erratic; generally okay for those easygoing pick-up games, but invariably lacking the calm and the expertise that the naturals displayed in stiff competition. My taste, and my talent, such as it was, was for the flashy, whiz-bang catch rather than the towering fly; running and leaping I loved, all the do-or-die stuff—somehow I lost confidence waiting and wait-

ing for the ball lofted right at me to descend. I could never make the
high school team, yet I remember that, in one of the two years I
vainly (in both senses of the word) tried out, I did a good enough
imitation of a baseball player's *style* to be able to fool (or amuse) the
coach right down to the day he cut the last of the dreamers from the
squad and gave out the uniforms.

Though my disappointment was keen, my misfortune did not
necessitate a change in plans for the future. Playing baseball was not
what the Jewish boys of our lower-middle-class neighborhood were
expected to do in later life for a living. Had I been cut from the high
school itself, *then* there would have been hell to pay in my house,
and much confusion and shame in me. As it was, my family took
my chagrin in stride and lost no more faith in me than I actually did
in myself. They probably would have been shocked if I had made the
team.

Maybe I would have been too. Surely it would have put me on
a somewhat different footing with this game that I loved with all
my heart, not simply for the fun of playing it (fun was secondary,
really), but for the mythic and aesthetic dimension that it gave to
an American boy's life—particularly to one whose grandparents
could hardly speak English. For someone whose roots in America
were strong but only inches deep, and who had no experience, such
as a Catholic child might, of an awesome hierarchy that was real
and felt, baseball was a kind of secular church that reached into
every class and region of the nation and bound millions upon millions of us together in common concerns, loyalties, rituals, enthu-
siasms, and antagonisms. Baseball made me understand what patriotism was about, at its best.

Not that Hitler, the Bataan Death March, the battle for the
Solomons, and the Normandy invasion didn't make of me and my
contemporaries what may well have been the most patriotic generation of schoolchildren in American history (and the most willingly
and successfully propagandized). But the war we entered when I was
eight had thrust the country into what seemed to a child—and not
only to a child—a struggle to the death between Good and Evil.
Fraught with perilous, unthinkable possibilities, it inevitably nourished a patriotism grounded in moral virtue and bloody-minded hate,
the patriotism that fixes a bayonet to a Bible. It seems to me that
through baseball I was put in touch with a more humane and tender
brand of patriotism, lyrical rather than martial or righteous in spirit,
and without the reek of saintly zeal, a patriotism that could not so
easily be sloganized, or contained in a high-sounding formula to
which you had to pledge something vague but all-encompassing
called your "allegiance."

5   To sing the National Anthem in the school auditorium every

week, even during the worst of the war years, generally left me cold. The enthusiastic lady teacher waved her arms in the air and we obliged with the words: "See! Light! Proof! Night! There!" But nothing stirred within, strident as we might be—in the end, just another school exercise. It was different, however, on Sundays out at Ruppert Stadium, a green wedge of pasture miraculously walled in among the factories, warehouses, and truck depots of industrial Newark. It would, in fact, have seemed to me an emotional thrill forsaken if, before the Newark Bears took on the hated enemy from across the marshes, the Jersey City Giants, we hadn't first to rise to our feet (my father, my brother, and I—along with our inimical countrymen, the city's Germans, Italians, Irish, Poles, and, out in the Africa of the bleachers, Newark's Negroes) to celebrate the America that had given to this unharmonious mob a game so grand and beautiful.

Just as I first learned the names of the great institutions of higher learning by trafficking in football pools for a neighborhood bookmaker rather than from our high school's college adviser, so my feel for the American landscape came less from what I learned in the classroom about Lewis and Clark than from following the major-league clubs on their road trips and reading about the minor leagues in the back pages of *The Sporting News*. The size of the continent got through to you finally when you had to stay up to 10:30 p.m. in New Jersey to hear via radio "ticker-tape" Cardinal pitcher Mort Cooper throw the first strike of the night to Brooklyn shortstop Pee Wee Reese out in "steamy" Sportsmen's Park in St. Louis, Missouri. And however much we might be told by teacher about the stock-yards and the Haymarket riot, Chicago only began to exist for me as a real place, and to matter in American history, when I became fearful (as a Dodger fan) of the bat of Phil Cavarretta, first baseman for the Chicago Cubs.

Not until I got to college and was introduced to literature did I find anything with a comparable emotional atmosphere and aesthetic appeal. I don't mean to suggest that it was a simple exchange, one passion for another. Between first discovering the Newark Bears and the Brooklyn Dodgers at seven or eight and first looking into Conrad's *Lord Jim* at age eighteen, I had done some growing up. I am only saying that my discovery of literature, and fiction particularly, and the "love affair"—to some degree hopeless, but still earnest—that has ensued, derives in part from this childhood infatuation with baseball. Or, more accurately perhaps, baseball—with its lore and legends, its cultural power, its seasonal associations, its native authenticity, its simple rules and transparent strategies, its longueurs and thrills, its spaciousness, its suspensefulness, its heroics, its nuances, its lingo, its "characters," its peculiarly hypnotic tedium, its mythic transformation of the immediate—was the literature of my boyhood.

Baseball, as played in the big leagues, was something completely outside my own life that could nonetheless move me to ecstasy and to tears; like fiction it could excite the imagination and hold the attention as much with minutiae as with high drama. Mel Ott's cocked leg striding into the ball, Jackie Robinson's pigeon-toed shuffle as he moved out to second base, each was to be as deeply affecting over the years as that night—"inconceivable," "inscrutable," as any night Conrad's Marlow might struggle to comprehend— the night that Dodger wild man, Rex Barney (who never lived up to "our" expectations, who should have been "our" Koufax), not only went the distance without walking in half a dozen runs, but, of all things, threw a no-hitter. A thrilling mystery, marvelously enriched by the fact that a light rain had fallen during the early evening, and Barney, figuring the game was going to be postponed, had eaten a hot dog just before being told to take the mound.

This detail was passed on to us by Red Barber, the Dodger radio sportscaster of the forties, a respectful, mild Southerner with a subtle rural tanginess to his vocabulary and a soft country-parson tone to his voice. For the adventures of "dem bums" of Brooklyn—a region then the very symbol of urban wackiness and tumult—to be narrated from Red Barber's highly alien but loving perspective constituted a genuine triumph of what my English professors would later teach me to call "point of view." James himself might have admired the implicit cultural ironies and the splendid possibilities for oblique moral and social commentary. And as for the detail about Rex Barney eating his hot dog, it was irresistible, joining as it did the spectacular to the mundane, and furnishing an adolescent boy with a glimpse of an unexpectedly ordinary, even humdrum, side to male heroism.

10   Of course, in time, neither the flavor and suggestiveness of Red Barber's narration nor "epiphanies" as resonant with meaning as Rex Barney's pre-game hot dog could continue to satisfy a developing literary appetite; nonetheless, it was just this that helped to sustain me until I was ready to begin to respond to the great inventors of narrative detail and masters of narrative voice and perspective like James, Conrad, Dostoevsky, and Bellow.

Response

1. Roth attributes his early learning of civic and moral values to baseball rather than to religion or school. In what sense did baseball serve him as "a kind of secular church" (paragraph 3)?

2. "Baseball made me understand what patriotism was about, at its best," Roth says at the end of paragraph 3. What is that best sense of patriotism, in his view? How does it compare with the patriotism of school or with public attitudes engendered by wartime events?

3. Roth compares the "mythic and aesthetic dimension" of baseball (paragraph 3) with the "emotional atmosphere and aesthetic appeal" of literature (paragraph 7). Examine the connections he makes. How did love of baseball prepare him for love of literature? From this essay, what do you know about Roth that made him susceptible to the appeal of first baseball, and later literature?

4. Notice how Roth illustrates his statement that "baseball . . . was the literature of my boyhood" (paragraph 7). Identify, in his discussion of baseball that follows, the phrases usually used to comment on literature.

5. Recalling the "unharmonious mob" in the bleachers, his "inimical countrymen" (paragraph 5), Roth acknowledges the racial and ethnic diversity of which he was a part, as "someone whose roots in America were strong but only inches deep" (paragraph 3). Compare the notion of Americanness that emerges in this essay with that of James Baldwin in "The Discovery of What It Means to Be an American."

Like Mexicans

Gary Soto

This essay is the first one in Soto's book Small Faces *(1986), which he dedicated to his wife Carolyn. Like many of Soto's prose pieces, it recalls the anxious uncertainty of a particular time in the author's life and ends on a positive note of regained confidence and sense of harmony.*

My grandmother gave me bad advice and good advice when I was in my early teens. For the bad advice, she said that I should become a barber because they made good money and listened to the radio all day. "Honey, they don't work como burros," she would say every time I visited her. She made the sound of donkeys braying. "Like that, honey!" For the good advice, she said that I should marry a Mexican girl. "No Okies, hijo"—she would say—"Look my son. He marry one and they fight every day about I don't know what and I don't know what." For her, everyone who wasn't Mexican, black, or Asian were Okies. The French were Okies, the Italians in suits were Okies. When I asked about Jews, whom I had read about, she asked for a picture. I rode home on my bicycle and returned with a calendar depicting the important races of the world. "Pues si, son Okies tambien!" she said, nodding her head. She waved the calendar

Gary Soto, "Like Mexicans," in *Small Faces*. Houston, Texas: Arte Publico Press, 1986. Reprinted by permission of the publisher.

away and we went to the living room where she lectured me on the virtues of the Mexican girl: first, she could cook and, second, she acted like a woman, not a man, in her husband's home. She said she would tell me about a third when I got a little older.

I asked my mother about it—becoming a barber and marrying Mexican. She was in the kitchen. Steam curled from a pot of boiling beans, the radio was on, looking as squat as a loaf of bread. "Well, if you want to be a barber—they say they make good money." She slapped a round steak with a knife, her glasses slipping down with each strike. She stopped and looked up. "If you find a good Mexican girl, marry her of course." She returned to slapping the meat and I went to the backyard where my brother and David King were sitting on the lawn feeling the inside of their cheeks.

"This is what girls feel like," my brother said, rubbing the inside of his cheek. David put three fingers inside his mouth and scratched. I ignored them and climbed the back fence to see my best friend, Scott, a second-generation Okie. I called him and his mother pointed to the side of the house where his bedroom was a small aluminum trailer, the kind you gawk at when they're flipped over on the freeway, wheels spinning in the air. I went around to find Scott pitching horseshoes.

I picked up a set of rusty ones and joined him. While we played, we talked about school and friends and record albums. The horseshoes scuffed up dirt, sometimes ringing the iron that threw out a meager shadow like a sundial. After three argued-over games, we pulled two oranges apiece from his tree and started down the alley still talking school and friends and record albums. We pulled more oranges from the alley and talked about who we would marry. "No offense, Scott," I said with an orange slice in my mouth, "but I would never marry an Okie." We walked in step, almost touching, with a sled of shadows dragging behind us. "No offense, Gary," Scott said, "but I would *never* marry a Mexican." I looked at him: a fang of orange slice showed from his munching mouth. I didn't think anything of it. He had his girl and I had mine. But our seventh-grade vision was the same: to marry, get jobs, buy cars and maybe a house if we had money left over.

We talked about our future lives until, to our surprise, we were   5
on the downtown mall, two miles from home. We bought a bag of popcorn at Penneys and sat on a bench near the fountain watching Mexican and Okie girls pass. "That one's mine," I pointed with my chin when a girl with eyebrows arched into black rainbows ambled by. "She's cute," Scott said about a girl with yellow hair and a mouthful of gum. We dreamed aloud, our chins busy pointing out

girls. We agreed that we couldn't wait to become men and lift them onto our laps.

But the woman I married was not Mexican but Japanese. It was a surprise to me. For years, I went about wide-eyed in my search for the brown girl in a white dress at a dance. I searched the playground at the baseball diamond. When the girls raced for grounders, their hair bounced like something that couldn't be caught. When they sat together in the lunchroom, heads pressed together, I knew they were talking about us Mexican guys. I saw them and dreamed them. I threw my face into my pillow, making up sentences that were good as in the movies.

But when I was twenty, I fell in love with this other girl who worried my mother, who had my grandmother asking once again to see the calendar of the Important Races of the World. I told her I had thrown it away years before. I took a much-glanced-at snapshot from my wallet. We looked at it together, in silence. Then grandma reclined in her chair, lit a cigarette, and said, "Es pretty." She blew and asked with all her worry pushed up to her forehead: "Chinese?"

I was in love and there was no looking back. She was the one. I told my mother who was slapping hamburger into patties. "Well, sure if you want to marry her," she said. But the more I talked, the more concerned she became. Later I began to worry. Was it all a mistake? "Marry a Mexican girl," I heard my mother say in my mind. I heard it at breakfast. I heard it over math problems, between Western Civilization and cultural geography. But then one afternoon while I was hitchhiking home from school, it struck me like a baseball in the back: my mother wanted me to marry someone of my own social class—a poor girl. I considered my fiancee, Carolyn, and she didn't look poor, though I knew she came from a family of farm workers and pull-yourself-up-by-your-bootstraps ranchers. I asked my brother, who was marrying Mexican poor that fall, if I should marry a poor girl. He screamed "Yeah" above his terrible guitar playing in his bedroom. I considered my sister who had married Mexican. Cousins were dating Mexican. Uncles were remarrying poor women. I asked Scott, who was still my best friend, and he said, "She's too good for you, so you better not."

I worried about it until Carolyn took me home to meet her parents. We drove in her Plymouth until the houses gave way to farms and ranches and finally her house fifty feet from the highway. When we pulled into the drive, I panicked and begged Carolyn to make a U-turn and go back so we could talk about it over a soda. She pinched my cheek, calling me a "silly boy." I felt better, though, when I got out of the car and saw the house: the chipped paint, a cracked window, boards for a walk to the back door. There were rusting cars near the barn. A tractor with a net of spiderwebs under a mulberry. A field. A bale of barbed wire like children's scribbling leaning against an empty chicken coop. Carolyn took my hand and pulled me to my future mother-in-law who was coming out to greet us.

We had lunch: sandwiches, potato chips, and iced tea. Carolyn   10
and her mother talked mostly about neighbors and the congregation at the Japanese Methodist Church in West Fresno. Her father, who was in khaki work clothes, excused himself with a wave that was almost a salute and went outside. I heard a truck start, a dog bark, and then the truck rattle away.

Carolyn's mother offered another sandwich, but I declined with a shake of my head and a smile. I looked around when I could, when I was not saying over and over that I was a college student, hinting that I could take care of her daughter. I shifted my chair. I saw newspapers piled in corners, dusty cereal boxes and vinegar bottles in corners. The wallpaper was bubbled from rain that had come in from a bad roof. Dust. Dust lay on lamp shades and window sills. These people are just like Mexicans, I thought. Poor people.

Carolyn's mother asked me through Carolyn if I would like a *sushi*. A plate of black and white things were held in front of me. I took one, wide-eyed, and turned it over like a foreign coin. I was biting into one when I saw a kitten crawl up the window screen over the sink. I chewed and the kitten opened its mouth of terror as she crawled higher, wanting in to paw the leftovers from our plates. I looked at Carolyn who said that the cat was just showing off. I looked up in time to see it fall. It crawled up, then fell again.

We talked for an hour and had apple pie and coffee, slowly. Finally, we got up with Carolyn taking my hand. Slightly embarrassed, I tried to pull away but her grip held me. I let her have her way as she led me down the hallway with her mother right behind me. When I opened the door, I was startled by a kitten clinging to the screen door, its mouth screaming "cat food, dog biscuits, *sushi* . . ." I opened the door and the kitten, still holding on, whined in the language of hungry animals. When I got into Carolyn's car, I looked back: the cat was still clinging. I asked Carolyn if it were possibly hungry, but she said the cat was being silly. She started the car, waved to her mother, and bounced us over the rain-poked drive, patting my thigh for being her lover baby. Carolyn waved again. I looked back, waving, then gawking at a window screen where there were now three kittens clawing and screaming to get in. Like Mexicans, I thought. I remembered the Molinas and how the cats clung to their screens—cats they shot down with squirt guns. On the highway, I felt happy, pleased by it all. I patted Carolyn's thigh. Her people were like Mexicans, only different.

Response

1. Marry a Mexican girl, advised Soto's grandmother and mother. Why did they say this? What values lay behind their advice?
2. How does Soto the adult author, looking back, regard his mother's and grandmother's efforts and advice? What attitude does he take toward the home life of his youth?
3. In what ways were Carolyn's family "like Mexicans, only different"? Look for the details Soto uses to show this. Why did he feel "happy, pleased by it all" as they drove away?
4. Soto realized what his mother was really advising: she "wanted me to marry someone of my own social class" (paragraph 8). What was his response? Other parents advise their children to marry someone of their own religion or race. What do you think of this sort of advice?

III
OTHER GENERATIONS
AND TRADITIONS

Bless Me, Ultima
Rudolfo Anaya

*This is the first chapter from Anaya's 1972 novel
about life in rural New Mexico and a boy's
relationship with Ultima, an old curandera (faith
healer) who comes to live with his family. Anaya
writes in a style of magic realism, blending mythical
and real-life elements in such a way that the
boundary between the two is blurred.*

Ultima came to stay with us the summer I was almost seven.
When she came the beauty of the llano unfolded before my eyes, and
the gurgling waters of the river sang to the hum of the turning earth.
The magical time of childhood stood still, and the pulse of the living
earth pressed its mystery into my living blood. She took my hand,
and the silent, magic powers she possessed made beauty from the
raw, sun-baked llano, the green river valley, and the blue bowl which
was the white sun's home. My bare feet felt the throbbing earth and
my body trembled with excitement. Time stood still, and it shared
with me all that had been, and all that was to come. . . .

Let me begin at the beginning. I do not mean the beginning
that was in my dreams and the stories they whispered to me about
my birth, and the people of my father and mother, and my three
brothers—but the beginning that came with Ultima.

Rudolfo Anaya, from *Bless Me, Ultima.* Berkeley, California: Tonatiuh-Quinto
Sol International Publishers, 1972. Reprinted by permission.

The attic of our home was partitioned into two small rooms. My sisters, Deborah and Theresa, slept in one and I slept in the small cubicle by the door. The wooden steps creaked down into a small hallway that led into the kitchen. From the top of the stairs I had a vantage point into the heart of our home, my mother's kitchen. From there I was to see the terrified face of Chávez when he brought the terrible news of the murder of the sheriff; I was to see the rebellion of my brothers against my father; and many times late at night I was to see Ultima returning from the llano where she gathered the herbs that can be harvested only in the light of the full moon by the careful hands of a curandera.

That night I lay very quietly in my bed, and I heard my father and mother speak of Ultima.

5 "Está sola," my father said, "ya no queda gente en el pueblito de Las Pasturas—"

He spoke in Spanish, and the village he mentioned was his home. My father had been a vaquero all his life, a calling as ancient as the coming of the Spaniard to Nuevo Méjico. Even after the big rancheros and the tejanos came and fenced the beautiful llano, he and those like him continued to work there, I guess because only in that wide expanse of land and sky could they feel the freedom their spirits needed.

"¡Qué lástima," my mother answered, and I knew her nimble fingers worked the pattern on the doily she crocheted for the big chair in the sala.

I heard her sigh, and she must have shuddered too when she thought of Ultima living alone in the loneliness of the wide llano. My mother was not a woman of the llano, she was the daughter of a farmer. She could not see beauty in the llano and she could not understand the coarse men who lived half their lifetimes on horseback. After I was born in Las Pasturas she persuaded my father to leave the llano and bring her family to the town of Guadalupe where she said there would be opportunity and school for us. The move lowered my father in the esteem of his compadres, the other vaqueros of the llano who clung tenaciously to their way of life and freedom. There was no room to keep animals in town so my father had to sell his small herd, but he would not sell his horse so he gave it to a good friend, Benito Campos. But Campos could not keep the animal penned up because somehow the horse was very close to the spirit of the man, and so the horse was allowed to roam free and no vaquero on that llano would throw a lazo on that horse. It was as if someone had died, and they turned their gaze from the spirit that walked the earth.

It hurt my father's pride. He saw less and less of his old compadres. He went to work on the highway and on Saturdays after they collected their pay he drank with his crew at the Longhorn, but he was never close to the men of the town. Some weekends the llaneros would come into town for supplies and old amigos like Bonney or Campos or the Gonzales brothers would come by to visit. Then my father's eyes lit up as they drank and talked of the old days and told the old stories. But when the western sun touched the clouds with orange and gold the vaqueros got in their trucks and headed home, and my father was left to drink alone in the long night. Sunday morning he would get up very crudo and complain about having to go to early mass.

"—She served the people all her life, and now the people are scattered, driven like tumbleweeds by the winds of war. The war sucks everything dry," my father said solemnly, "it takes the young boys overseas, and their families move to California where there is work—"

"Ave María Purísima," my mother made the sign of the cross for my three brothers who were away at war. "Gabriel," she said to my father, "it is not right that la Grande be alone in her old age—"

"No," my father agreed.

"When I married you and went to the llano to live with you and raise your family, I could not have survived without la Grande's help. Oh, those were hard years—"

"Those were good years," my father countered. But my mother would not argue.

"There isn't a family she did not help," she continued, "no road was too long for her to walk to its end to snatch somebody from the jaws of death, and not even the blizzards of the llano could keep her from the appointed place where a baby was to be delivered—"

"Es verdad," my father nodded.

"She tended me at the birth of my sons—" And then I knew her eyes glanced briefly at my father. "Gabriel, we cannot let her live her last days in loneliness—"

"No," my father agreed, "it is not the way of our people."

"It would be a great honor to provide a home for la Grande," my mother murmured. My mother called Ultima la Grande out of respect. It meant the woman was old and wise.

"I have already sent word with Campos that Ultima is to come and live with us," my father said with some satisfaction. He knew it would please my mother.

"I am grateful," my mother said tenderly, "perhaps we can re-pay a little of the kindness la Grande has given to so many."

"And the children?" my father asked. I knew why he expressed concern for me and my sisters. It was because Ultima was a curan-

10

15

20

dera, a woman who knew the herbs and remedies of the ancients, a miracle-worker who could heal the sick. And I had heard that Ultima could lift the curses laid by brujas, that she could exorcise the evil the witches planted in people to make them sick. And because a curandera had this power she was misunderstood and often suspected of practicing witchcraft herself.

I shuddered and my heart turned cold at the thought. The cuentos of the people were full of the tales of evil done by brujas.

"She helped bring them into the world, she cannot be but good for the children," my mother answered.

25 "Está bien," my father yawned, "I will go for her in the morning."

So it was decided that Ultima should come and live with us. I knew that my father and mother did good by providing a home for Ultima. It was the custom to provide for the old and the sick. There was always room in the safety and warmth of la familia for one more person, be that person stranger or friend.

It was warm in the attic, and as I lay quietly listening to the sounds of the house falling asleep and repeating a Hail Mary over and over in my thoughts, I drifted into the time of dreams. Once I had told my mother about my dreams and she said they were visions from God and she was happy, because her own dream was that I should grow up and become a priest. After that I did not tell her about my dreams, and they remained in me forever and ever . . .

In my dream I flew over the rolling hills of the llano. My soul wandered over the dark plain until it came to a cluster of adobe huts. I recognized the village of Las Pasturas and my heart grew happy. One mud hut had a lighted window, and the vision of my dream swept me towards it to be witness at the birth of a baby.

I could not make out the face of the mother who rested from the pains of birth, but I could see the old woman in black who tended the just-arrived, steaming baby. She nimbly tied a knot on the cord that had connected the baby to its mother's blood, then quickly she bent and with her teeth she bit off the loose end. She wrapped the squirming baby and laid it at the mother's side, then she returned to cleaning the bed. All linen was swept aside to be washed, but she carefully wrapped the useless cord and the afterbirth and laid the package at the feet of the Virgin on the small altar. I sensed that these things were yet to be delivered to someone.

30 *Now the people who had waited patiently in the dark were allowed to come in and speak to the mother and deliver their gifts to the baby. I recognized my mother's brothers, my uncles from El Puerto de las Lunas. They entered ceremoniously. A patient hope stirred in their dark, brooding eyes.*

This one will be a Luna, the old man said, he will be a farmer and keep our customs and traditions. Perhaps God will bless our family and make the baby a priest.

And to show their hope they rubbed the dark earth of the river valley on the baby's forehead, and they surrounded the bed with the fruits of their harvest so the small room smelled of fresh green chile and corn, ripe apples and peaches, pumpkins and green beans.

Then the silence was shattered with the thunder of hoofbeats; vaqueros surrounded the small house with shouts and gunshots, and when they entered the room they were laughing and singing and drinking.

Gabriel, they shouted, you have a fine son! He will make a fine vaquero! And they smashed the fruits and vegetables that surrounded the bed and replaced them with a saddle, horse blankets, bottles of whiskey, a new rope, bridles, chapas, and an old guitar. And they rubbed the stain of earth from the baby's forehead because man was not to be tied to the earth but free upon it.

These were the people of my father, the vaqueros of the llano. 35 *They were an exuberant, restless people, wandering across the ocean of the plain.*

We must return to our valley, the old man who led the farmers spoke. We must take with us the blood that comes after the birth. We will bury it in our fields to renew their fertility and to assure that the baby will follow our ways. He nodded for the old woman to deliver the package at the altar.

No! the llaneros protested, it will stay here! We will burn it and let the winds of the llano scatter the ashes.

It is blasphemy to scatter a man's blood on unholy ground, the farmers chanted. The new son must fulfill his mother's dream. He must come to El Puerto and rule over the Lunas of the valley. The blood of the Lunas is strong in him.

He is a Márez, the vaqueros shouted. His forefathers were conquistadores, men as restless as the seas they sailed and as free as the land they conquered. He is his father's blood!

Curses and threats filled the air, pistols were drawn, and the 40 *opposing sides made ready for battle. But the clash was stopped by the old woman who delivered the baby.*

Cease! she cried, and the men were quiet. I pulled this baby into the light of life, so I will bury the afterbirth and the cord that once linked him to eternity. Only I will know his destiny.

The dream began to dissolve. When I opened my eyes I heard my father cranking the truck outside. I wanted to go with him, I wanted to see Las Pasturas, I wanted to see Ultima. I dressed hurriedly, but I was too late. The truck was bouncing down the goat path that led to the bridge and the highway.

I turned, as I always did, and looked down the slope of our hill to the green of the river, and I raised my eyes and saw the town of Guadalupe. Towering above the housetops and the trees of the town was the church tower. I made the sign of the cross on my lips. The only other building that rose above the housetops to compete with the church tower was the yellow top of the schoolhouse. This fall I would be going to school.

My heart sank. When I thought of leaving my mother and going to school a warm, sick feeling came to my stomach. To get rid of it I ran to the pens we kept by the molino to feed the animals. I had fed the rabbits that night and they still had alfalfa and so I only changed their water. I scattered some grain for the hungry chickens and watched their mad scramble as the rooster called them to peck. I milked the cow and turned her loose. During the day she would forage along the highway where the grass was thick and green, then she would return at nightfall. She was a good cow and there were very few times when I had to run and bring her back in the evening. Then I dreaded it, because she might wander into the hills where the bats flew at dusk and there was only the sound of my heart beating as I ran and it made me sad and frightened to be alone.

45   I collected three eggs in the chicken house and returned for breakfast.

"Antonio," my mother smiled and took the eggs and milk, "come and eat your breakfast."

I sat across the table from Deborah and Theresa and ate my atole and the hot tortilla with butter. I said very little. I usually spoke very little to my two sisters. They were older than I and they were very close. They usually spent the entire day in the attic, playing dolls and giggling. I did not concern myself with those things.

"Your father has gone to Las Pasturas," my mother chattered, "he has gone to bring la Grande." Her hands were white with the flour of the dough. I watched carefully. "—And when he returns, I want you children to show your manners. You must not shame your father or your mother—"

"Isn't her real name Ultima?" Deborah asked. She was like that, always asking grown-up questions.

50   "You will address her as la Grande," my mother said flatly. I looked at her and wondered if this woman with the black hair and laughing eyes was the woman who gave birth in my dream.

"Grande," Theresa repeated.

"Is it true she is a witch?" Deborah asked. Oh, she was in for it. I saw my mother whirl then pause and control herself.

"No!" she scolded. "You must not speak of such things! Oh, I don't know where you learn such ways—" Her eyes flooded with tears. She always cried when she thought we were learning the ways of my father, the ways of the Márez. "She is a woman of learning," she went on and I knew she didn't have time to stop and cry, "she has worked hard for all the people of the village. Oh, I would never have survived those hard years if it had not been for her—so show her respect. We are honored that she comes to live with us, understand?"

"Sí, mamá," Deborah said half willingly.

"Sí, mamá," Theresa repeated.   55

"Now run and sweep the room at the end of the hall. Eugene's room—" I heard her voice choke. She breathed a prayer and crossed her forehead. The flour left white stains on her, the four points of the cross. I knew it was because my three brothers were at war that she was sad, and Eugene was the youngest.

"Mamá." I wanted to speak to her. I wanted to know who the old woman was who cut the baby's cord.

"Sí." She turned and looked at me.

"Was Ultima at my birth?" I asked.

"¡Ay Dios mío!" my mother cried. She came to where I sat and   60 ran her hand through my hair. She smelled warm, like bread. "Where do you get such questions, my son. Yes," she smiled, "la Grande was there to help me. She was there to help at the birth of all of my children—"

"And my uncles from El Puerto were there?"

"Of course," she answered, "my brothers have always been at my side when I needed them. They have always prayed that I would bless them with a—"

I did not hear what she said because I was hearing the sounds of the dream, and I was seeing the dream again. The warm cereal in my stomach made me feel sick.

"And my father's brother was there, the Márez' and their friends, the vaqueros—"

"Ay!" she cried out, "Don't speak to me of those worthless   65 Márez and their friends!"

"There was a fight?" I asked.

"No," she said, "a silly argument. They wanted to start a fight with my brothers—that is all they are good for. Vaqueros, they call themselves, they are worthless drunks! Thieves! Always on the move, like gypsies, always dragging their families around the country like vagabonds—"

As long as I could remember she always raged about the Márez family and their friends. She called the village of Las Pasturas beautiful; she had gotten used to the loneliness, but she had never accepted its people. She was the daughter of farmers.

But the dream was true. It was as I had seen it. Ultima knew.
70 "But you will not be like them." She caught her breath and
stopped. She kissed my forehead. "You will be like my brothers. You
will be a Luna, Antonio. You will be a man of the people, and perhaps a priest." She smiled.

A priest, I thought, that was her dream. I was to hold mass on
Sundays like father Byrnes did in the church in town. I was to hear
the confessions of the silent people of the valley, and I was to ad-
minister the holy Sacrament to them.

"Perhaps," I said.

"Yes," my mother smiled. She held me tenderly. The fragrance
of her body was sweet.

"But then," I whispered, "who will hear my confession?"
75 "What?"

"Nothing," I answered. I felt a cool sweat on my forehead and
I knew I had to run, I had to clear my mind of the dream. "I am going
to Jasón's house," I said hurriedly and slid past my mother. I ran out
the kitchen door, past the animal pens, towards Jasón's house. The
white sun and the fresh air cleansed me.

On this side of the river there were only three houses. The
slope of the hill rose gradually into the hills of juniper and mesquite
and cedar clumps. Jasón's house was farther away from the river
than our house. On the path that led to the bridge lived huge, fat Fío
and his beautiful wife. Fío and my father worked together on the
highway. They were good drinking friends.

"¡Jasón!" I called at the kitchen door. I had run hard and was
panting. His mother appeared at the door.

"Jasón no está aquí," she said. All of the older people spoke
only in Spanish, and I myself understood only Spanish. It was only
after one went to school that one learned English.
80 "¿Dónde está?" I asked.

She pointed towards the river, northwest, past the railroad
tracks to the dark hills. The river came through those hills and there
were old Indian grounds there, holy burial grounds Jasón told me.
There in an old cave lived his Indian. At least everybody called him
Jasón's Indian. He was the only Indian of the town, and he talked
only to Jasón. Jasón's father had forbidden Jasón to talk to the Indian, he had beaten him, he had tried in every way to keep Jasón
from the Indian.

But Jasón persisted. Jasón was not a bad boy, he was just Jasón.
He was quiet and moody, and sometimes for no reason at all wild,
loud sounds came exploding from his throat and lungs. Sometimes
I felt like Jasón, like I wanted to shout and cry, but I never did.

I looked at his mother's eyes and I saw they were sad. "Thank you," I said, and returned home. While I waited for my father to return with Ultima I worked in the garden. Every day I had to work in the garden. Every day I reclaimed from the rocky soil of the hill a few more feet of earth to cultivate. The land of the llano was not good for farming, the good land was along the river. But my mother wanted a garden and I worked to make her happy. Already we had a few chile and tomato plants growing. It was hard work. My fingers bled from scraping out the rocks and it seemed that a square yard of ground produced a wheelbarrow full of rocks which I had to push down to the retaining wall.

The sun was white in the bright blue sky. The shade of the clouds would not come until the afternoon. The sweat was sticky on my brown body. I heard the truck and turned to see it chugging up the dusty goat path. My father was returning with Ultima.

"¡Mamá!" I called. My mother came running out, Deborah and   85
Theresa trailed after her.

"I'm afraid," I heard Theresa whimper.

"There's nothing to be afraid of," Deborah said confidently. My mother said there was too much Márez blood in Deborah. Her eyes and hair were very dark, and she was always running. She had been to school two years and she spoke only English. She was teaching Theresa and half the time I didn't understand what they were saying.

"Madre de Dios, but mind your manners!" my mother scolded. The truck stopped and she ran to greet Ultima. "Buenos días le de Dios, Grande," my mother cried. She smiled and hugged and kissed the old woman.

"Ay, María Luna," Ultima smiled, "Buenos días te de Dios, a ti y a tu familia." She wrapped the black shawl around her hair and shoulders. Her face was brown and very wrinkled. When she smiled her teeth were brown. I remembered the dream.

"Come, come!" my mother urged us forward. It was the cus-   90
tom to greet the old. "Deborah!" my mother urged. Deborah stepped forward and took Ultima's withered hand.

"Buenos días, Grande," she smiled. She even bowed slightly. Then she pulled Theresa forward and told her to greet la Grande. My mother beamed. Deborah's good manners surprised her, but they made her happy, because a family was judged by its manners.

"What beautiful daughters you have raised," Ultima nodded to my mother. Nothing could have pleased my mother more. She looked proudly at my father who stood leaning against the truck, watching and judging the introductions.

"Antonio," he said simply. I stepped forward and took Ultima's hand. I looked up into her clear brown eyes and shivered. Her face was old and wrinkled, but her eyes were clear and sparkling, like the eyes of a young child.

"Antonio," she smiled. She took my hand and I felt the power of a whirlwind sweep around me. Her eyes swept the surrounding hills and through them I saw for the first time the wild beauty of our hills and the magic of the green river. My nostrils quivered as I felt the song of the mockingbirds and the drone of the grasshoppers mingle with the pulse of the earth. The four directions of the llano met in me, and the white sun shone on my soul. The granules of sand at my feet and the sun and sky above me seemed to dissolve into one strange, complete being.

95   A cry came to my throat, and I wanted to shout it and run in the beauty I had found.

"Antonio." I felt my mother prod me. Deborah giggled because she had made the right greeting, and I who was to be my mother's hope and joy stood voiceless.

"Buenos días le de Dios, Ultima," I muttered. I saw in her eyes my dream. I saw the old woman who had delivered me from my mother's womb. I knew she held the secret of my destiny.

"¡Antonio!" My mother was shocked I had used her name instead of calling her Grande. But Ultima held up her hand.

"Let it be," she smiled. "This was the last child I pulled from your womb, María. I knew there would be something between us."

100 My mother who had started to mumble apologies was quiet. "As you wish, Grande," she nodded.

"I have come to spend the last days of my life here, Antonio," Ultima said to me.

"You will never die, Ultima," I answered. "I will take care of you—" She let go of my hand and laughed. Then my father said, "pase, Grande, pase. Nuestra casa es su casa. It is too hot to stand and visit in the sun—"

"Sí, sí," my mother urged. I watched them go in. My father carried on his shoulders the large blue-tin trunk which later I learned contained all of Ultima's earthly possessions, the black dresses and shawls she wore, and the magic of her sweet smelling herbs.

As Ultima walked past me I smelled for the first time a trace of the sweet fragrance of herbs that always lingered in her wake. Many years later, long after Ultima was gone and I had grown to be a man, I would awaken sometimes at night and think I caught a scent of her fragrance in the cool-night breeze.

105 And with Ultima came the owl. I heard it that night for the first time in the juniper tree outside of Ultima's window. I knew it was her owl because the other owls of the llano did not come that near the house. At first it disturbed me, and Deborah and Theresa too. I heard them whispering through the partition. I heard Deborah

reassuring Theresa that she would take care of her, and then she took Theresa in her arms and rocked her until they were both asleep.

I waited. I was sure my father would get up and shoot the owl with the old rifle he kept on the kitchen wall. But he didn't, and I accepted his understanding. In many cuentos I had heard the owl was one of the disguises a bruja took, and so it struck a chord of fear in the heart to hear them hooting at night. But not Ultima's owl. Its soft hooting was like a song, and as it grew rhythmic it calmed the moonlit hills and lulled us to sleep. Its song seemed to say that it had come to watch over us.

I dreamed about the owl that night, and my dream was good. La Virgen de Guadalupe was the patron saint of our town. The town was named after her. In my dream I saw Ultima's owl lift la Virgen on her wide wings and fly her to heaven. Then the owl returned and gathered up all the babes of Limbo and flew them up to the clouds of heaven.

The Virgin smiled at the goodness of the owl.

Response

1. The boy's mother and father reflect different elements of their Spanish heritage. Note how the contrast between them is portrayed, both in real life and in the boy's dream. What values does each represent?

2. When Ultima is described it is in terms that draw on Native American ceremony and tradition—in particular, a sense of timelessness and connection with the natural world. Find indications of her indigenous character. How do the parents regard her? How does the boy respond to her?

3. La Virgen de Guadalupe is a synthesis of Indian goddess and Spanish Catholic Virgin. She is historically a deity of indigenous people in the American Southwest, an Earth Mother who ensured health, fertility, and the growth of crops; with the Spanish conquest in the sixteenth century, this goddess merged with the Virgin Mary and became patroness of the Mexican people. How does Ultima also reflect that blending of cultures?

4. In traditional stories an owl can be the embodiment of a witch, but Ultima's owl is benevolent. What role does it seem to play?

5. In his essay "The New World Man" (Section II) Anaya explains how the particular viewpoint of the New Mexican mestizos is harmonious and encompassing, "one of the most humanistic views in the world." How does this story reflect that New World view?

Railroad Standard Time

Frank Chin

*"This is how I come home," Chin says in the final
paragraph of this story, which is a collage of
reminiscences, images, and thoughts going through
his mind as he drives back home for his mother's
funeral. This is the first story in his book* The
Chinaman Pacific and Frisco R.R. Co. *(1988).*

"This was your Grandfather's," Ma said. I was twelve, maybe fourteen years old when Grandma died. Ma put it on the table. The big
railroad watch, Elgin. Nineteen-jewel movement. American made.
Lever set. Stem wound. Glass facecover. Railroad standard all the
way. It ticked on the table between stacks of dirty dishes and cold
food. She brought me in here to the kitchen, always to the kitchen
to loose her thrills and secrets, as if the sound of running water and
breathing the warm soggy ghosts of stale food, floating grease, old
spices, ever comforted her, as if the kitchen was a paradise for conspiracy, sanctuary for us *juk sing* Chinamen from the royalty of pure-
talking China-born Chinese, old, mourning, and belching in the
other rooms of my dead grandmother's last house. Here, private, to
say in Chinese, "This was your grandfather's," as if now that her
mother had died and she'd been up all night long, not weeping, tough

Frank Chin, "Railroad Standard Time," in *The Chinaman Pacific and Frisco
R.R. Co.* Minneapolis: Coffee House Press, 1988. Copyright © 1988 by Frank Chin.
Reprinted by permission of the publisher.

and lank, making coffee and tea and little foods for the broken-hearted family in her mother's kitchen, Chinese would be easier for me to understand. As if my mother would say all the important things of the soul and blood to her son, me, only in Chinese from now on. Very few people spoke the language at me the way she did. She chanted a spell up over me that conjured the meaning of what she was saying in the shape of old memories come to call. Words I'd never heard before set me at play in familiar scenes new to me, and ancient.

She lay the watch on the table, eased it slowly off her fingertips down to the tabletop without a sound. She didn't touch me, but put it down and held her hands in front of her like a bridesmaid holding an invisible bouquet and stared at the watch. As if it were talking to her, she looked hard at it, made faces at it, and did not move or answer the voices of the old, calling her from other rooms, until I picked it up.

A two-driver, high stepping locomotive ahead of a coal tender and baggage car, on double track between two semaphores showing a stop signal was engraved on the back.

"Your grandfather collected railroad watches," Ma said. "This one is the best." I held it in one hand and then the other, hefted it, felt out the meaning of "the best," words that rang of meat and vegetables, oils, things we touched, smelled, squeezed, washed, and ate, and I turned the big cased thing over several times. "Grandma gives it to you now," she said. It was big in my hand. Gold. A little greasy. Warm.

I asked her what her father's name had been, and the manic heat of her all-night burnout seemed to go cold and congeal. "Oh," she finally said, "it's one of those Chinese names I . . ." in English, faintly from another world, woozy and her throat and nostrils full of bubbly sniffles, the solemnity of the moment gone, the watch in my hand turned to cheap with the mumbling of a few awful English words. She giggled herself down to nothing but breath and moving lips. She shuffled backward, one step at a time, fox trotting dreamily backwards, one hand dragging on the edge of the table, wobbling the table, rattling the dishes, spilling cold soup. Back down one side of the table, she dropped her butt a little with each step then muscled it back up. There were no chairs in the kitchen tonight. She knew, but still she looked. So this dance and groggy mumbling about the watch being no good, in strange English, like an Indian medicine man in a movie.

I wouldn't give it back or trade it for another out of the collection. This one was mine. No other. It had belonged to my grandfather. I wore it braking on the Southern Pacific, though it was two

5

jewels short of new railroad standard and an outlaw watch that could get me fired. I kept it on me, arrived at my day-off courthouse wedding to its time, wore it as a railroad relic/family heirloom/grin-bringing affectation when I was writing background news in Seattle, reporting from the shadows of race riots, grabbing snaps for the 11:00 P.M., timing today's happenings with a nineteenth-century escapement. (Ride with me, Grandmother.) I was wearing it on my twenty-seventh birthday, the Saturday I came home to see my son asleep in the back of a strange station wagon, and Sarah inside, waving, shouting through an open window, "Goodbye Daddy," over and over.

I stood it. Still and expressionless as some good Chink, I watched Barbara drive off, leave me, like some blonde white goddess going home from the jungle with her leather patches and briar pipe sweetheart writer and my kids. I'll learn to be a sore loser. I'll learn to hit people in the face. I'll learn to cry when I'm hurt and go for the throat instead of being polite and worrying about being obnoxious to people walking out of my house with my things, taking my kids away. I'll be more than quiet, embarrassed. I won't be likable anymore.

I hate my novel about a Chinatown mother like mine dying, now that Ma's dead. But I'll keep it. I hated after reading *Father and Glorious Descendant*, *Fifth Chinese Daughter*, *The House That Tai Ming Built*. Books scribbled up by a sad legion of snobby autobiographical Chinatown saps all on their own. Christians who never heard of each other, hardworking people who sweat out the exact same Chinatown book, the same cunning "Confucius says" joke, just like me. I kept it then and I'll still keep it. Part cookbook, memories of Mother in the kitchen slicing meat paper-thin with a cleaver. Mumbo jumbo about spices and steaming. The secret of Chinatown rice. The hands come down toward the food. The food crawls with culture. The thousand-year-old living Chinese meat makes dinner a safari into the unknown, a blood ritual. Food pornography. Black magic. Between the lines, I read a madman's detailed description of the preparation of shrunken heads. I never wrote to mean anything more than word fun with the food Grandma cooked at home. Chinese food. I read a list of what I remembered eating at my grandmother's table and knew I'd always be known by what I ate, that we come from a hungry tradition. Slop eaters following the wars on all fours. Weed cuisine and mud gravy in the shadow of corpses. We plundered the dust for fungus. Buried things. Seeds plucked out of the wind to feed a race of lace-boned skinnys, in high-school English, become transcendental Oriental art to make the dyke-ish spinster teacher cry. We always come to fake art and write the Chinatown book like bugs come to fly in the light. I hate my book now that ma's dead, but I'll keep it. I know she's not the woman I wrote up like my mother, and dead, in a book that was like everybody else's Chinatown book. Part word map of Chinatown San Francisco, shop to shop down Grant Avenue. Food again. The wind sucks the shops out and you breathe warm roast ducks dripping fat, hooks into the neck, through the head, out an eye. Stacks of iced fish, blue and fluorescent pink in the neon. The air is thin soup, sharp up the nostrils.

All mention escape from Chinatown into the movies. But we all forgot to mention how stepping off the streets into a faceful of Charlie Chaplin or a Western on a ripped and stained screen that became caught in the grip of winos breathing in unison in their sleep and billowed in and out, that shuddered when cars went by . . . we all of us Chinamans watched our own MOVIE ABOUT ME! I learned how to box watching movies shot by James Wong Howe. Cartoons were our nursery rhymes. Summers inside those neon-and-stucco downtown hole-in-the-wall Market Street Frisco movie houses blowing three solid hours of full-color seven-minute cartoons was school, was rows and rows of Chinamans learning English in a hurry from Daffy Duck.

When we ate in the dark and recited the dialogue of cartoon   10 mice and cats out loud in various tones of voice with our mouths full, we looked like people singing hymns in church. We learned to talk like everybody in America. Learned to need to be afraid to stay alive, keep moving. We learned to run, to be cheerful losers, to take a sudden pie in the face, talk American with a lot of giggles. To us a cartoon is a desperate situation. Of the movies, cartoons were the high art of our claustrophobia. They understood us living too close to each other. How, when you're living too close to too many people, you can't wait for one thing more without losing your mind. Cartoons were a fine way out of waiting in Chinatown around the rooms. Those of our Chinamans who every now and then break a reverie with, "Thank you, Mighty Mouse," mean it. Other folks thank Porky Pig, Snuffy Smith, Woody Woodpecker.

The day my mother told me I was to stay home from Chinese school one day a week starting today, to read to my father and teach him English while he was captured in total paralysis from a vertebra in the neck on down, I stayed away from cartoons. I went to a matinee in a white neighborhood looking for the MOVIE ABOUT ME and was the only Chinaman in the house. I liked the way Peter Lorre ran along non-stop routine hysterical. I came back home with Peter Lorre. I turned out the lights in Pa's room. I put a candle on the dresser and wheeled Pa around in his chair to see me in front of the dresser mirror, reading Edgar Allen Poe out loud to him in the voice of Peter Lorre by candlelight.

The old men in the Chinatown books are all fixtures for

Chinese ceremonies. All the same. Loyal filial children kowtow to the old and whiff food laid out for the dead. The dead eat the same as the living but without the sauces. White food. Steamed chicken. Rice we all remember as children scrambling down to the ground, to all fours and bonking our heads on the floor, kowtowing to a dead chicken.

My mother and aunts said nothing about the men of the family except they were weak. I like to think my grandfather was a good man. Even the kiss-ass steward service, I like to think he was tough, had a few laughs and ran off with his pockets full of engraved watches. Because I never knew him, not his name, nor anything about him, except a photograph of him as a young man with something of my mother's face in his face, and a watch chain across his vest. I kept his watch in good repair and told everyone it would pass to my son someday, until the day the boy was gone. Then I kept it like something of his he'd loved and had left behind, saving it for him maybe, to give to him when he was a man. But I haven't felt that in a long time.

The watch ticked against my heart and pounded my chest as I went too fast over bumps in the night and the radio on, on an all-night run downcoast, down country, down old Highway 99, Interstate 5, I ran my grandfather's time down past road signs that caught a gleam in my headlights and came at me out of the night with the names of forgotten high school girlfriends, BELLEVUE KIRKLAND, ROBERTA GERBER, AURORA CANBY, and sang with the radio to Jonah and Sarah in Berkeley, my Chinatown in Oakland and Frisco, to raise the dead. Ride with me, Grandfather, this is your grandson the ragmouth, called Tampax, the burned scarred boy, called Barbecue, going to San Francisco to bury my mother, your daughter, and spend Chinese New Year's at home. When we were sitting down and into our dinner after Grandma's funeral, and ate in front of the table set with white food for the dead, Ma said she wanted no white food and money burning after her funeral. Her sisters were there. Her sisters took charge of her funeral and the dinner afterwards. The dinner would most likely be in a Chinese restaurant in Frisco. Nobody had these dinners at home anymore. I wouldn't mind people having dinner at my place after my funeral, but no white food.

15   The whiz goes out of the tires as their roll bites into the steel grating of the Carquinez Bridge. The noise of the engine groans and echoes like a bomber in flight through the steel roadway. Light from the water far below shines through the grate, and I'm driving high, above a glow. The voice of the tires hums a shrill rubber screechy mosquito hum that vibrates through the chassis and frame of the car into my meatless butt, into my tender asshole, my pelvic bones,

the roots of my teeth. Over the Carquinez Bridge to CROCKETT MAR-
TINEZ closer to home, roll the tires of Ma's Chevy, my car now,
carrying me up over the water southwest toward rolls of fog. The fat
man's coming home on a sneaky breeze. Dusk comes a drooly mess
of sunlight, a slobber of cheap pawnshop gold, a slow building heat
across the water, all through the milky air through the glass of the
window into the closed atmosphere of a driven car, into one side of
my bomber's face. A bomber, flying my mother's car into the unknown charted by the stars and the radio, feels the coming of some
old night song climbing hand over hand, bass notes plunking as
steady and shady as reminiscence to get on my nerves one stupid
beat after the other crossing the high rhythm six-step of the engine.
I drive through the shadows of the bridge's steel structure all over
the road. Fine day. I've been on the road for sixteen hours straight
down the music of Seattle, Spokane, Salt Lake, Sacramento, Los Angeles, and Wolfman Jack lurking in odd hours of darkness, at peculiar altitudes of darkness, favoring the depths of certain Oregon valleys and heat and moonlight of my miles. And I'm still alive.
Country'n'western music for the night road. It's pure white music.
Like "The Star-Spangled Banner," it was the first official American
music out of school into my jingling earbones sung by sighing white
big tits in front of the climbing promise of FACE and Every Good Boy
Does Fine chalked on the blackboard.

She stood up singing, one hand cupped in the other as if to
catch drool slipping off her lower lip. Our eyes scouted through her
blouse to elastic straps, lacy stuff, circular stitching, buckles, and in
the distance, finally some skin. The color of her skin spread through
the stuff of her blouse like melted butter through bread nicely to our
tongues and was warm there. She sat flopping them on the keyboard
as she breathed, singing "Home on the Range" over her shoulder,
and pounded the tune out with her palms. The lonesome prairie was
nothing but her voice, some hearsay country she stood up to sing *a
capella* out of her. Simple music you can count. You can hear the
words clear. The music's run through Clorox and Simonized, beating so insistently right and regular that you feel to sing it will deo-
dorize you, make you clean. The hardhat hit parade. I listen to it a
lot on the road. It's that get-outta-town beat and tune that makes
me go.

Mrs. Morales was her name. Aurora Morales. The music
teacher us boys liked to con into singing for us. Come-on opera, we
wanted from her, not them Shirley Temple tunes the girls wanted
to learn, but big notes, high long ones up from the navel that drilled
through plaster and steel and skin and meat for bone marrow and
electric wires on one long titpopping breath.

This is how I come home, riding a mass of spasms and death throes, warm and screechy inside, itchy, full of ghostpiss, as I drive right past what's left of Oakland's dark wooden Chinatown and dark streets full of dead lettuce and trampled carrot tops, parallel all the time in line with the tracks of the Western Pacific and Southern Pacific railroads.

Response

1. Chin uses derogatory terms and embarrassing characterizations to express his contempt for stereotypes and to suggest their painful consequences as well. Find different ways in which he does this in this story. Do you think he intends to make readers uncomfortable? How effective do you find this approach?

2. This story expresses Chin's concern with distinguishing what is real and what is "fake" in Chinese tradition and identity. He condemns assimilation when it means misrepresenting true Asian-American history and culture—as in everybody's "Chinatown book," catering to a mainstream audience. How does he develop that theme in this story? What do you think of his view?

3. Note the rich visual detail in Chin's description of the watch. What was its value to Chin's mother? What is its significance to Chin? Find language in the story that indicates what it meant to him.

4. Chin plays with words a lot. What do you think he means to communicate about how he comes home, in the last paragraph? Why does he say he drives "parallel all the time in line with the tracks of the Western Pacific and Southern Pacific railroads"?

The Power of Horses

Elizabeth Cook-Lynn

This story, from Cook-Lynn's 1990 book of the same title, is about a contemporary reliving of a mythic story. In this way it reflects the author's emphasis on historical themes and her commitment to make her writing promote the survival and continued development of Native American people.

The mother and daughter steadied themselves, feet planted squarely, foreheads glistening with perspiration, and each grasped a handle of the large, steaming kettle.

"Ready?"

"Uh-huh."

"Take it, then," the mother said. "Careful." Together they lifted the tub of boiled beets from the flame of the burners on the gas stove and set it heavily on the table across the room. The girl let the towel which had served as a makeshift pot holder drop to the floor as the heat penetrated to the skin, and she slapped her hand against the coolness of the smooth, painted wall and then against her thigh, feeling the roughness of the heavy jeans with tingling fingers. To stop the tingling, she cupped her fingers to her mouth and blew on them, then raised her apologetic eyes and looked at her mother. Without speaking, as if that was the end of it, she sank into the chrome chair and picked up the towel and began wiping the sweat from her face. The sun came relentlessly through the thin gauze curtains, and the hot wind blew gently across the stove, almost extinguishing the gas flames of the burners, making the blue edges turn yellow and then orange and then white. The towel was damp now and stained purple from the beets, and the girl leaned back in the chair and laid the towel across her face, feeling her own hot breath around her nose and mouth.

5   "Your hands get used to it, Marleen," the mother said, not even glancing at the girl, nor at her own rough, brown hands, "just have to keep at it," saying this not so much from believing it as from the need to stop this feeling of futility in the girl and the silence between them. The mother gingerly grasped the bleached stems of several beets and dropped them into a pan of cold water, rolling one and then another of the beets like balls in her hands, pushing the purple-black skins this way and that, quickly, deftly removing the peel and stem and tossing the shiny vegetable into another container. Finishing one, she hurriedly picked up another, as if by hurrying she could forestall the girl's rebellion.

The woman's arms, like her hands, were large, powerful. But, despite the years of heavy work, her sloping shoulders and smooth, long neck were part of a tender femininity only recently showing small signs of decline and age. The dark stains on her dark face might have seemed like age spots or a disfigurement on someone else, but on the woman they spread delicately across her cheeks, forehead, and neck like a sweep of darkened cloud, making her somehow vulnerable and defenseless.

"Your hands'll get used to it, Marleen," she repeated, again attempting to keep the girl's unwillingness in check, and an avenue to reasonable tolerance and cooperation open.

The brief rest with the towel on her face seemed to diminish the girl's weariness, and for an instant more she sat silently, breathing peacefully into the damp towel. As the girl drew the towel across her face and away from her eyes, something like fear began to rise in her, and she peered out the window, where she saw her father standing with a white man she had never seen before. Her father was looking straight ahead down the draw where the horses stood near the corral. They always want something from him, she thought, and as she watched the white man put a cigarette in his mouth and turn sideways out of the wind, the flame of his lighter licking toward his bony profile, she wondered what it was this time. She watched the man's quick mannerisms, and she saw that he began to talk earnestly and gesture toward his green pickup truck, which was parked close to the barbed-wire fence encircling the house and yard.

The girl was startled out of her musings at the sound of her mother's "*yu-u-u-u*," the softly uttered indication of disapproval, insistent, always compelling a change in the girl's behavior. And she turned quickly to get started with her share of the hot beets, handling them inexpertly, but peeling their hot skins away as best she could. After a few minutes, during which the women worked in silence, only the monotonous hiss of the burning gas flame between them, the girl, surprised, thought: her sounds of disapproval aren't because I'm wasting time; instead, they are made because she is afraid my father and the white man will see me watching them. Spontaneously, defensively, she said, "They didn't see me." She looked into the brown-stained face but saw only her mother's careful pretense of being preoccupied with the beets, as she picked up a small knife to begin slicing them. All last winter, every time I came home, I spied on him for you, thought the girl, even riding my horse over to Chekpa's through the snow to see if he was there. And when I came back and told you that he was, you acted as if you hadn't heard anything, like now. So this is not the beginning of the story, nor is it the part of the story that matters, probably, thought the girl, and she started to recognize a long, long history of acrimony between her parents, thinking, in hindsight, that it would have been better if she had stayed at Stephen Mission. But then, she remembered her last talk with Brother Otto at the Mission as he sat before her, one leg languidly draped over the other, his collar open, showing his sparse red chest hairs, his watery, pale eyes looking at her searchingly, and she knew that it wasn't better to have stayed there.

He had sat quivering with sympathy as she had tried to tell   10
him that to go home was to be used by her mother against her father. I rode over to Chekpa's, she told him, hating herself that she was letting out the symptoms of her childish grief, despising him for his delicate white skin, his rapt gaze, the vicariousness of his measly existence, and *Até* was there, cutting wood for the eldest of the Tatiopa women, Rosalie, the one he was supposed to marry, you know, but, instead, he married my mother. My mother sent me there, and when I rode into the yard and saw him, he stood in uncertainty, humiliated in the eyes of Chekpa, his old friend, as well as all of those in the Tatiopa family. Worse yet, she knew, humiliated in the eyes of his nine-year-old daughter.

In her memory of that awful moment, she didn't speak, nor did her father, and so she had ridden out of the yard as abruptly as she had come and home at a dead gallop, standing easily in the stirrups, her face turned toward her right shoulder out of the wind, watching

the slush fly behind the horse's hooves. She didn't cut across Ar-
chie's field as she usually did, but took the long way, riding as hard
as she could alongside the road. When she got to the gate she reined
in, dismounted, and led her horse through the gate and then, slowly,
down the sloping hill to the tack shed. She stood for a long time
with her head against the wide, smooth leather of the stirrup shaft,
her eyes closed tightly and the smell of wet horse hair in her nostrils. Much later she had recited the event as fully as she could bear
to the mission school priest, much as she had been taught to recite
the events of her sinful life: I have taken the Lord's name in vain, I
have taken the Lord's name in vain, I have tak. . . .

Damn beets, damn all these damn beets, the girl thought, and
she turned away from the table back to the stove, where she stirred
the second, smaller, pot of sliced beets, and she looked out through
the gauze curtains to see if her father and the white man were still
there. They had just run the horses into the corral from the small
fenced pasture where they usually grazed when they were brought
down to the place.

"He must be getting ready to sell them, is he?" she asked her
mother.

Her mother said nothing.

"How come? I didn't know he was going to sell," the girl said
slowly, noticing that her horse, two quarterhorse brood mares, and
a half-Shetland black-and-white gelding she had always called
"Shōta" had been cut out of the herd and were standing at the far
corner of the pasture, grazing. The heat shimmered above the long
buffalo grass, and the girl's thoughts drifted, and, vaguely, she heard
her mother say, "You'd better spoon those sliced ones into these hot
jars, Marleen," and then, almost to herself, her mother started talking as if in recognition of what the girl did not know about the factual and philosophical sources from which present life emerges. "I
used to have land, myself, daughter," she began, "and on it my
grandfather had many horses. What happened to it was that some
white men from Washington came and took it away from me when
my grandfather died because, they said, they were going to breed
game birds there; geese, I think.

"There was no one to do anything about it," she continued,
"there was only this old woman who was a mother to me, and she
really didn't know what to do, who to see, or how to prevent this
from happening.

"Among the horses there on my land was a pair of brood mares
just like those two out there." She pointed with her chin to the two
bays at the end of the pasture. And, looking at the black-and-white
horse called Shōta, she said, "And there was also another strange,

mysterious horse, *su'ka wak a'*," *i-e-e-e*, she had used the word for "mysterious dog" in the Dakotah language. And the mother and daughter stood looking out the window at the *shōta* horse beside the bays, watching them pick their way through the shimmering heat and through the tall grass, slowly, unhurried. The beets were forgotten, momentarily, and the aging woman remembered the magic of those horses and especially the one that resembled the *shōta* horse, thinking about that time, that primordial time when an old couple of the tribe received a gift horse from a little bird, and the horse produced many offspring for the old man and woman, and the people were never poor after that. Her grandfather, old Bowed Head, the man with many horses, had told her that story often during her childhood when he wished to speak of those days when all creatures knew one another . . . and it was a reassuring thing. "I wish this tribe to be strong and good," the mysterious horse had told the old man, "and so I keep giving my offspring every year and the tribe will have many horses and this good thing will be among you always."

"They were really fast horses," said the mother, musing still, filling in the texture of her imagination and memory, "they were known throughout our country for their speed, and the old man allowed worthy men in the tribe to use them in war or to go on a hunt with them. It is an old story," the woman concluded, as though the story were finished, as though commenting upon its history made everything comprehensible.

As the girl watched her mother's extraordinary vitality, which rose during the telling of these events, she also noted the abruptness with which the story seemed to end and the kind of formidable reserve and closure which fell upon the dark, stained features as the older woman turned again to the stove.

"What happened to the horses?" the girl wanted to know. "Did someone steal them? Did they die?"   20

After a long silence her mother said, "Yes, I suppose so," and the silence again deepened between them as they fell to filling hot jars with sliced beets and sealing hot lids upon them, wiping and stroking them meticulously and setting them one by one on a dim pantry shelf.

The girl's frustration was gone now, and she seemed mindless of the heat, her own physical discomfort, and the miserableness of the small, squalid kitchen where she and her mother moved quietly about, informed now with the wonder of the past, the awesomeness of the imagination.

The sun moved west and the kitchen fell into shadow, the wind died down, and the mother and daughter finished their tedious task

and carried the large tub of hot water out through the entryway a
few feet from the door and emptied its contents upon the ground.
The girl watched the red beet juice stain the dry, parched earth in
which there was no resistance, and she stepped away from the red-
ness of the water, which gushed like strokes of a painter's brush,
suddenly black and ominous, as it sank into the ground. She looked
up to see the white man's green pickup truck disappear over the rise,
the dust billowing behind the heavy wheels, settling gently in the
heat.

The nameless fear struck at her again and she felt a knot being
drawn tightly inside her and she looked anxiously toward the corral.
Nothing around her seemed to be moving, the air suddenly still, the
sweat standing out in beads on her face and her hands, oddly, moist
and cold. As she ran toward the corral, she saw her mother out of
the corner of her eye, still grasping one handle of the boiler tub,
strangely composed, her head and shoulders radiant in the sun.

25   At the corral, moments later, she saw her father's nearly lifeless form lying facedown in the dirt, his long gray hair spread out
like a fan above him, pitifully untidy for a man who ordinarily took
meticulous care with his appearance. He had his blue cotton scarf
which he used as a handkerchief clutched tightly in his right hand,
and he was moaning softly.

The odor of whiskey on his breath was strong as she helped
him turn over and sit up, and in that instant the silent presence of
the past lay monumentally between them, so that he did not look
at her nor did he speak. In that instant she dimly perceived her own
innocence and was filled with regret that she would never know
those times to which *Até* would return, if he could, again and again.
She watched as he walked unsteadily toward the house, rumpled
and drunk, a man of grave dignity made comic and sad and helpless
by circumstances which his daughter could only regard with won-
derment.

*Keyapi: Late one night, when the old man had tied the horses near
his lodge, someone crept through the draw and made ready to steal
them; it was even said that they wanted to kill the wonderful
horses. The mysterious gift horse called to the sleeping old man and
told him that an evil lurked nearby. And he told the old man that
since such a threat as this had come upon them and all the people
of the tribe, the power of the horses would be diminished, and no
more colts would be born and the people would have to go back to
their miserable ways.*

As her father made his way to the house, walking stiffly past
her mother, who pretended to be scrubbing the black residue from

the boiler, the girl turned and walked quickly away from the corral in the opposite direction.

I must look: she thought, into the distance, and as she lifted her eyes and squinted into the evening light, she saw the Fort George road across the river, beyond the bend in the river, so far away that it would take most of the day for anyone to get there from where she walked. I must look: at the ground in front of me where my grandmothers made paths to the ti(n)psina beds and carried home with them long braided strands over their shoulders. I must look: she thought, into the past for the horse that speaks to humans.

She took long strides and walked into the deepening dusk. She   30
walked for a long time before returning to the darkened house, where she crept into her bed and lay listening to the summer's night insect sounds, thinking apocalyptic thoughts in regard to what her mother's horse story might have to do with the day's events.

She awoke with a start, her father shaking her shoulder. "You must ride with me today, daughter, before the horse buyer comes back," he said. "I wish to take the horses way out to the far side of the north pasture. I am ready to go, so please hurry."

The girl dressed quickly, and just as dawn was breaking, she and her father, each leading two horses, with the others following, set out over the prairie hills. These were the hills, she knew, to which the people had come when the Uprising was finished and the U.S. Cavalry fell to arguing with missionaries and settlers about the "Indian problem." These were the hills, dark blue in this morning light, which she knew as repositories of sacred worlds unknown to all but its most ancient tenants.

When they reached the ridge above Dry Creek, the girl and her father stopped and let the horses go their way, wildly. The *shōta* horse led them down the steep prairie hills and into the dry creek bed and, one by one, the horses of the herd disappeared into the stand of heavy cottonwood trees which lined the ravine.

She stood beside her father and watched them go. "Why were you going to sell them?" she asked abruptly.

"There are too many," he replied, "and the grass is short this   35
summer. It's been too hot," he said, wiping his face with the blue handkerchief, and he repeated, "The grass is short this summer."

With that, they mounted their horses and rode home together.

Response

1. Members of the family—Marleen's mother, her father, and herself—exhibit different ways of relating to the larger society: stoic endurance, demoralization, or a restless sense of rebel-

lion. Look for ways each character is described, to expand on this idea.

2. This story is three stories in one. Locate the three; what is the message of this repetition? How do the earlier stories explain the ending of the one Cook-Lynn tells? What is "the power of horses"?

3. While the two women engage in the ritual of processing the beets, Marleen's mother makes her aware of "the factual and philosophical sources from which present life emerges" (paragraph 15). By telling the story she enables Marleen to recognize "the wonder of the past, the awesomeness of the imagination" (paragraph 22). What does Marleen's father do for Marleen by taking her with him to free the horses?

4. In her essay "You May Consider Speaking About Your Art" (Section I) Cook-Lynn says she feels it is her responsibility as a writer "to 'consecrate' history." There is a "ceremonial aspect" to being a Dakotah writer, she says; she must add to "that body of creative expression which accounts for the continued survival and development of a people, a nation." How do you see her fulfilling that responsibility in this story?

No Name Woman

Maxine Hong Kingston

This story comes from Woman Warrior: Memoirs of a
Girlhood Among Ghosts *(1975). The book is, as the
title suggests, a collection of autobiographical stories
about growing up as the daughter of Chinese
immigrant parents in California and trying to make
sense out of living in two cultures. Near the end of
that book, Kingston says, "I continue to sort out
what's just my childhood, just my imagination, just
my family, just the village, just movies, just living."*

"You must not tell anyone," my mother said, "what I am about
to tell you. In China your father had a sister who killed herself. She
jumped into the family well. We say that your father has all brothers
because it is as if she had never been born.

"In 1924 just a few days after our village celebrated seventeen
hurry-up weddings—to make sure that every young man who went
'out on the road' would responsibly come home—your father and
his brothers and your grandfather and his brothers and your aunt's
new husband sailed for America, the Gold Mountain. It was your
grandfather's last trip. Those lucky enough to get contracts waved
goodbye from the decks. They fed and guarded the stowaways and

helped them off in Cuba, New York, Bali, Hawaii. 'We'll meet in California next year,' they said. All of them sent money home.

"I remember looking at your aunt one day when she and I were dressing; I had not noticed before that she had such a protruding melon of a stomach. But I did not think, 'She's pregnant,' until she began to look like other pregnant women, her shirt pulling and the white tops of her black pants showing. She could not have been pregnant, you see, because her husband had been gone for years. No one said anything. We did not discuss it. In early summer she was ready to have the child, long after the time when it could have been possible.

"The village had also been counting. On the night the baby was to be born the villagers raided our house. Some were crying. Like a great saw, teeth strung with lights, files of people walked zigzag across our land, tearing the rice. Their lanterns doubled in the disturbed black water, which drained away through the broken bunds. As the villagers closed in, we could see that some of them, probably men and women we knew well, wore white masks. The people with long hair hung it over their faces. Women with short hair made it stand up on end. Some had tied white bands around their foreheads, arms, and legs.

5   "At first they threw mud and rocks at the house. Then they threw eggs and began slaughtering our stock. We could hear the animals scream their deaths—the roosters, the pigs, a last great roar from the ox. Familiar wild heads flared in our night windows; the villagers encircled us. Some of the faces stopped to peer at us, their eyes rushing like searchlights. The hands flattened against the panes, framed heads, and left red prints.

"The villagers broke in the front and the back doors at the same time, even though we had not locked the doors against them. Their knives dripped with the blood of our animals. They smeared blood on the doors and walls. One woman swung a chicken, whose throat she had slit, splattering blood in red arcs about her. We stood together in the middle of our house, in the family hall with the pictures and tables of the ancestors around us, and looked straight ahead.

"At that time the house had only two wings. When the men came back, we would build two more to enclose our courtyard and a third one to begin a second courtyard. The villagers pushed through both wings, even your grandparents' rooms, to find your aunt's, which was also mine until the men returned. From this room a new wing for one of the younger families would grow. They ripped up her clothes and shoes and broke her combs, grinding them underfoot. They tore her work from the loom. They scattered the cooking

fire and rolled the new weaving in it. We could hear them in the kitchen breaking our bowls and banging the pots. They overturned the great waist-high earthenware jugs; duck eggs, pickled fruits, vegetables burst out and mixed in acrid torrents. The old woman from the next field swept a broom through the air and loosed the spirits-of-the-broom over our heads. 'Pig.' 'Ghost.' 'Pig,' they sobbed and scolded while they ruined our house.

"When they left, they took sugar and oranges to bless themselves. They cut pieces from the dead animals. Some of them took bowls that were not broken and clothes that were not torn. Afterward we swept up the rice and sewed it back up into sacks. But the smells from the spilled preserves lasted. Your aunt gave birth in the pigsty that night. The next morning when I went for the water, I found her and the baby plugging up the family well.

"Don't let your father know that I told you. He denies her. Now that you have started to menstruate, what happened to her could happen to you. Don't humiliate us. You wouldn't like to be forgotten as if you had never been born. The villagers are watchful."

Whenever she had to warn us about life, my mother told stories that ran like this one, a story to grow up on. She tested our strength to establish realities. Those in the emigrant generations who could not reassert brute survival died young and far from home. Those of us in the first American generations have had to figure out how the invisible world the emigrants built around our childhoods fits in solid America.

The emigrants confused the gods by diverting their curses, misleading them with crooked streets and false names. They must try to confuse their offspring as well, who, I suppose, threaten them in similar ways—always trying to get things straight, always trying to name the unspeakable. The Chinese I know hide their names; sojourners take new names when their lives change and guard their real names with silence.

Chinese-Americans, when you try to understand what things in you are Chinese, how do you separate what is peculiar to childhood, to poverty, insanities, one family, your mother who marked your growing with stories, from what is Chinese? What is Chinese tradition and what is the movies?

If I want to learn what clothes my aunt wore, whether flashy or ordinary, I would have to begin, "Remember Father's drowned-in-the-well sister?" I cannot ask that. My mother has told me once and for all the useful parts. She will add nothing unless powered by Necessity, a riverbank that guides her life. She plants vegetable gardens rather than lawns; she carries the odd-shaped tomatoes home from the fields and eats food left for the gods.

10

Whenever we did frivolous things, we used up energy; we flew high kites. We children came up off the ground over the melting cones our parents brought home from work and the American movie on New Year's Day—*Oh, You Beautiful Doll* with Betty Grable one year, and *She Wore a Yellow Ribbon* with John Wayne another year. After the one carnival ride each, we paid in guilt; our tired father counted his change on the dark walk home.

15   Adultery is extravagance. Could people who hatch their own chicks and eat the embryos and the heads for delicacies and boil the feet in vinegar for party food, leaving only the gravel, eating even the gizzard lining—could such people engender a prodigal aunt? To be a woman, to have a daughter in starvation time was a waste enough. My aunt could not have been the lone romantic who gave up everything for sex. Women in the old China did not choose. Some man had commanded her to lie with him and be his secret evil. I wonder whether he masked himself when he joined the raid on her family.

Perhaps she had encountered him in the fields or on the mountain where the daughters-in-law collected fuel. Or perhaps he first noticed her in the marketplace. He was not a stranger because the village housed no strangers. She had to have dealings with him other than sex. Perhaps he worked an adjoining field, or he sold her the cloth for the dress she sewed and wore. His demand must have surprised, then terrified her. She obeyed him; she always did as she was told.

When the family found a young man in the next village to be her husband, she had stood tractably beside the best rooster, his proxy, and promised before they met that she would be his forever. She was lucky that he was her age and she would be the first wife, an advantage secure now. The night she first saw him, he had sex with her. Then he left for America. She had almost forgotten what he looked like. When she tried to envision him, she only saw the black and white face in the group photograph the men had had taken before leaving.

The other man was not, after all, much different from her husband. They both gave orders: she followed. "If you tell your family, I'll beat you. I'll kill you. Be here again next week." No one talked sex, ever. And she might have separated the rapes from the rest of living if only she did not have to buy her oil from him or gather wood in the same forest. I want her fear to have lasted just as long as rape lasted so that the fear could have been contained. No drawn-out fear. But women at sex hazarded birth and hence lifetimes. The fear did not stop but permeated everywhere. She told the man, "I think I'm pregnant." He organized the raid against her.

On nights when my mother and father talked about their life back home, sometimes they mentioned an "outcast table" whose business they still seemed to be settling, their voices tight. In a commensal tradition, where food is precious, the powerful older people made wrongdoers eat alone. Instead of letting them start separate new lives like the Japanese, who could become samurais and geishas, the Chinese family, faces averted but eyes glowering sideways, hung on to the offenders and fed them leftovers. My aunt must have lived in the same house as my parents and eaten at an outcast table. My mother spoke about the raid as if she had seen it, when she and my aunt, a daughter-in-law to a different household, should not have been living together at all. Daughters-in-law lived with their husbands' parents, not their own; a synonym for marriage in Chinese is "taking a daughter-in-law." Her husband's parents could have sold her, mortgaged her, stoned her. But they had sent her back to her own mother and father, a mysterious act hinting at disgraces not told me. Perhaps they had thrown her out to deflect the avengers.

She was the only daughter; her four brothers went with her father, husband, and uncles "out on the road" and for some years became western men. When the goods were divided among the family, three of the brothers took land, and the youngest, my father, chose an education. After my grandparents gave their daughter away to her husband's family, they had dispensed all the adventure and all the property. They expected her alone to keep the traditional ways, which her brothers, now among the barbarians, could fumble without detection. The heavy, deep-rooted women were to maintain the past against the flood, safe for returning. But the rare urge west had fixed upon our family, and so my aunt crossed boundaries not delineated in space.

The work of preservation demands that the feelings playing about in one's guts not be turned into action. Just watch their passing like cherry blossoms. But perhaps my aunt, my forerunner, caught in a slow life, let dreams grow and fade and after some months or years went toward what persisted. Fear at the enormities of the forbidden kept her desires delicate, wire and bone. She looked at a man because she liked the way the hair was tucked behind his ears, or she liked the question-mark line of a long torso curving at the shoulder and straight at the hip. For warm eyes or a soft voice or a slow walk—that's all—a few hairs, a line, a brightness, a sound, a pace, she gave up family. She offered us up for a charm that vanished with tiredness, a pigtail that didn't toss when the wind died. Why, the wrong lighting could erase the dearest thing about him.

It could very well have been, however, that my aunt did not take subtle enjoyment of her friend, but, a wild woman, kept rollicking company. Imagining her free with sex doesn't fit, though. I don't know any women like that, or men either. Unless I see her life branching into mine, she gives me no ancestral help.

To sustain her being in love, she often worked at herself in the mirror, guessing at the colors and shapes that would interest him, changing them frequently in order to hit on the right combination. She wanted him to look back.

On a farm near the sea, a woman who tended her appearance reaped a reputation for eccentricity. All the married women blunt-cut their hair in flaps about their ears or pulled it back in tight buns. No nonsense. Neither style blew easily into heart-catching tangles. And at their weddings they displayed themselves in their long hair for the last time. "It brushed the backs of my knees," my mother tells me. "It was braided, and even so, it brushed the backs of my knees."

25   At the mirror my aunt combed individuality into her bob. A bun could have been contrived to escape into black streamers blowing in the wind or in quiet wisps about her face, but only the older women in our picture album wear buns. She brushed her hair back from her forehead, tucking the flaps behind her ears. She looped a piece of thread, knotted into a circle between her index fingers and thumbs, and ran the double strand across her forehead. When she closed her fingers as if she were making a pair of shadow geese bite, the string twisted together catching the little hairs. Then she pulled the thread away from her skin, ripping the hairs out neatly, her eyes watering from the needles of pain. Opening her fingers, she cleaned the thread, then rolled it along her hairline and the tops of her eyebrows. My mother did the same to me and my sisters and herself. I used to believe that the expression "caught by the short hairs" meant a captive held with a depilatory string. It especially hurt at the temples, but my mother said we were lucky we didn't have to have our feet bound when we were seven. Sisters used to sit on their beds and cry together, she said, as their mothers or their slaves removed the bandages for a few minutes each night and let the blood gush back into their veins. I hope that the man my aunt loved appreciated a smooth brow, that he wasn't just a tits-and-ass man.

Once my aunt found a freckle on her chin, at a spot that the almanac said predestined her for unhappiness. She dug it out with a hot needle and washed the wound with peroxide.

More attention to her looks than these pullings of hairs and pickings at spots would have caused gossip among the villagers. They owned work clothes and good clothes, and they wore good clothes for feasting the new seasons. But since a woman combing her hair hexes beginnings, my aunt rarely found an occasion to look her best. Women looked like great sea snails—the corded wood, babies, and laundry they carried were the whorls on their backs. The Chinese did not admire a bent back; goddesses and warriors stood straight. Still there must have been a marvelous freeing of beauty when a worker laid down her burden and stretched and arched.

Such commonplace loveliness, however, was not enough for my aunt. She dreamed of a lover for the fifteen days of New Year's, the time for families to exchange visits, money, and food. She plied her secret comb. And sure enough she cursed the year, the family, the village, and herself.

Even as her hair lured her imminent lover, many other men looked at her. Uncles, cousins, nephews, brothers would have looked, too, had they been home between journeys. Perhaps they had already been restraining their curiosity, and they left, fearful that their glances, like a field of nesting birds, might be startled and caught. Poverty hurt, and that was their first reason for leaving. But another, final reason for leaving the crowded house was the never-said.

She may have been unusually beloved, the precious only 30 daughter, spoiled and mirror gazing because of the affection the family lavished on her. When her husband left, they welcomed the chance to take her back from the in-laws; she could live like the little daughter for just a while longer. There are stories that my grandfather was different from other people, "crazy ever since the little Jap bayoneted him in the head." He used to put his naked penis on the dinner table, laughing. And one day he brought home a baby girl, wrapped up inside his brown western-style greatcoat. He had traded one of his sons, probably my father, the youngest, for her. My grandmother made him trade back. When he finally got a daughter of his own, he doted on her. They must have all loved her, except perhaps my father, the only brother who never went back to China, having once been traded for a girl.

Brothers and sisters, newly men and women, had to efface their sexual color and present plain miens. Disturbing hair and eyes, a smile like no other, threatened the ideal of five generations living under one roof. To focus blurs, people shouted face to face and yelled from room to room. The immigrants I know have loud voices, unmodulated to American tones even after years away from the village where they called their friendships out across the fields. I have not been able to stop my mother's screams in public libraries or over telephones. Walking erect (knees straight, toes pointed forward, not pigeon-toed, which is Chinese-feminine) and speaking in an inaudible voice, I have tried to turn myself American-feminine. Chinese communication was loud, public. Only sick people had to whisper.

But at the dinner table, where the family members came nearest one another, no one could talk, not the outcasts nor any eaters. Every word that falls from the mouth is a coin lost. Silently they gave and accepted food with both hands. A preoccupied child who took his bowl with one hand got a sideways glare. A complete moment of total attention is due everyone alike. Children and lovers have no singularity here, but my aunt used a secret voice, a separate attentiveness.

She kept the man's name to herself throughout her labor and dying; she did not accuse him that he be punished with her. To save her inseminator's name she gave silent birth.

He may have been somebody in her own household, but intercourse with a man outside the family would have been no less abhorrent. All the village were kinsmen, and the titles shouted in loud country voices never let kinship be forgotten. Any man within visiting distance would have been neutralized as a lover—"brother," "younger brother," "older brother"—one hundred and fifteen relationship titles. Parents researched birth charts probably not so much to assure good fortune as to circumvent incest in a population that has but one hundred surnames. Everybody has eight million relatives. How useless then sexual mannerisms, how dangerous.

As if it came from an atavism deeper than fear, I used to add "brother" silently to boys' names. It hexed the boys, who would or would not ask me to dance, and made them less scary and as familiar and deserving of benevolence as girls.

35 But, of course, I hexed myself also—no dates. I should have stood up, both arms waving, and shouted out across libraries, "Hey, you! Love me back." I had no idea, though, how to make attraction selective, how to control its direction and magnitude. If I made myself American-pretty so that the five or six Chinese boys in the class fell in love with me, everyone else—the Caucasian, Negro, and Japanese boys—would too. Sisterliness, dignified and honorable, made much more sense.

Attraction eludes control so stubbornly that whole societies designed to organize relationships among people cannot keep order, not even when they bind people to one another from childhood and raise them together. Among the very poor and the wealthy, brothers married their adopted sisters, like doves. Our family allowed some romance, paying adult brides' prices and providing dowries so that their sons and daughters could marry strangers. Marriage promises to turn strangers into friendly relatives—a nation of siblings.

In the village structure, spirits shimmered among the live creatures, balanced and held in equilibrium by time and land. But one human being flaring up into violence could open up a black hole, a maelstrom that pulled in the sky. The frightened villagers, who depended on one another to maintain the real, went to my aunt to show her a personal, physical representation of the break she had made in the "roundness." Misallying couples snapped off the future, which was to be embodied in true offspring. The villagers punished her for acting as if she could have a private life, secret and apart from them.

If my aunt had betrayed the family at a time of large grain yields and peace, when many boys were born, and wings were being built on many houses, perhaps she might have escaped such severe punishment. But the men—hungry, greedy, tired of planting in dry soil—had been forced to leave the village in order to send food-money home. There were ghost plagues, bandit plagues, wars with the Japanese, floods. My Chinese brother and sister had died of an unknown sickness. Adultery, perhaps only a mistake during good times, became a crime when the village needed food.

The round moon cakes and round doorways, the round tables of graduated sizes that fit one roundness inside another, round windows and rice bowls—these talismans had lost their power to warn this family of the law: a family must be whole, faithfully keeping the descent line by having sons to feed the old and the dead, who in turn look after the family. The villagers came to show my aunt and her lover-in-hiding a broken house. The villagers were speeding up the circling of events because she was too shortsighted to see that her infidelity had already harmed the village, that waves of consequences would return unpredictably, sometimes in disguise, as now, to hurt her. This roundness had to be made coin-sized so that she would see its circumference: punish her at the birth of her baby. Awaken her to the inexorable. People who refused fatalism because they could invent small resources insisted on culpability. Deny accidents and wrest fault from the stars.

After the villagers left, their lanterns now scattering in various directions toward home, the family broke their silence and cursed her. "Aiaa, we're going to die. Death is coming. Death is coming. Look what you've done. You've killed us. Ghost! Dead ghost! Ghost! You've never been born." She ran out into the fields, far enough from the house so that she could no longer hear their voices, and pressed herself against the earth, her own land no more. When she felt the birth coming, she thought that she had been hurt. Her body seized together. "They've hurt me too much," she thought. "This is gall, and it will kill me." With forehead and knees against the earth, her body convulsed and then relaxed. She turned on her back, lay on the ground. The black well of sky and stars went out and out and out forever; her body and her complexity seemed to disappear. She was one of the stars, a bright dot in blackness, without home, without a companion, in eternal cold and silence. An agoraphobia rose in her, speeding higher and higher, bigger and bigger; she would not be able to contain it; there would no end to fear.

Flayed, unprotected against space, she felt pain return, focusing her body. This pain chilled her—a cold, steady kind of surface pain. Inside, spasmodically, the other pain, the pain of the child, heated her. For hours she lay on the ground, alternately body and space. Sometimes a vision of normal comfort obliterated reality: she saw the family in the evening gambling at the dinner table, the young people massaging their elders' backs. She saw them congratulating one another, high joy on the mornings the rice shoots came up. When these pictures burst, the stars drew yet further apart. Black space opened.

She got to her feet to fight better and remembered that old-fashioned women gave birth in their pigsties to fool the jealous, pain-dealing gods, who do not snatch piglets. Before the next spasms could stop her, she ran to the pigsty, each step a rushing out into emptiness. She climbed over the fence and knelt in the dirt. It was good to have a fence enclosing her, a tribal person alone.

Laboring, this woman who had carried her child as a foreign growth that sickened her every day, expelled it at last. She reached down to touch the hot, wet, moving mass, surely smaller than anything human, and could feel that it was human after all—fingers, toes, nails, nose. She pulled it up on to her belly, and it lay curled there, butt in the air, feet precisely tucked one under the other. She opened her loose shirt and buttoned the child inside. After resting, it squirmed and thrashed and she pushed it up to her breast. It turned its head this way and that until it found her nipple. There, it made little snuffling noises. She clenched her teeth at its preciousness, lovely as a young calf, a piglet, a little dog.

She may have gone to the pigsty as a last act of responsibility: she would protect this child as she had protected its father. It would look after her soul, leaving supplies on her grave. But how would this tiny child without family find her grave when there would be no marker for her anywhere, neither in the earth nor the family hall? No one would give her a family hall name. She had taken the child with her into the wastes. At its birth the two of them had felt the same raw pain of separation, a wound that only the family pressing tight could close. A child with no descent line would not soften her life but only trail after her, ghostlike, begging her to give it purpose. At dawn the villagers on their way to the fields would stand around the fence and look.

Full of milk, the little ghost slept. When it awoke, she hard-   45
ened her breasts against the milk that crying loosens. Toward morning she picked up the baby and walked to the well.

Carrying the baby to the well shows loving. Otherwise aban-
don it. Turn its face into the mud. Mothers who love their children
take them along. It was probably a girl; there is some hope of forgiveness for boys.

"Don't tell anyone you had an aunt. Your father does not want
to hear her name. She has never been born." I have believed that sex
was unspeakable and words so strong and fathers so frail that "aunt"
would do my father mysterious harm. I have thought that my family, having settled among immigrants who had also been their neighbors in the ancestral land, needed to clean their name, and a wrong
word would incite the kinspeople even here. But there is more to
this silence: they want me to participate in her punishment. And I
have.

In the twenty years since I heard this story I have not asked for
details nor said my aunt's name; I do not know it. People who can
comfort the dead can also chase after them to hurt them further—a
reverse ancestor worship. The real punishment was not the raid
swiftly inflicted by the villagers, but the family's deliberately forgetting her. Her betrayal so maddened them, they saw to it that she
would suffer forever, even after death. Always hungry, always needing, she would have to beg food from other ghosts, snatch and steal
it from those whose living descendants give them gifts. She would
have to fight the ghosts massed at crossroads for the buns a few
thoughtful citizens leave to decoy her away from village and home
so that the ancestral spirits could feast unharassed. At peace, they
could act like gods, not ghosts, their descent lines providing them
with paper suits and dresses, spirit money, paper houses, paper automobiles, chicken, meat, and rice into eternity—essences delivered
up in smoke and flames, steam and incense rising from each rice
bowl. In an attempt to make the Chinese care for people outside the
family, Chairman Mao encourages us now to give our paper replicas
to the spirits of outstanding soldiers and workers, no matter whose
ancestors they may be. My aunt remains forever hungry. Goods are
not distributed evenly among the dead.

My aunt haunts me—her ghost drawn to me because now, after
fifty years of neglect, I alone devote pages of paper to her, though
not origamied into houses and clothes. I do not think she always
means me well. I am telling on her, and she was a spite suicide,
drowning herself in the drinking water. The Chinese are always very

frightened of the drowned one, whose weeping ghost, wet hair hanging and skin bloated, waits silently by the water to pull down a substitute.

Response

1. What was the mother's purpose in telling her daughter the story about her aunt? Where do you find evidence of her intent? What parts of this essay are the mother's story, and what parts the daughter's speculation? How can you tell?

2. Kingston imagines different explanations for her aunt's experience. "Unless I see her life branching into mine," she comments, "she gives me no ancestral help" (paragraph 22). What kind of person does she imagine her aunt to have been? What does her speculation about her aunt's character reveal about her own?

3. As she imagines her aunt's story, Kingston recreates the social context in which her aunt lived. What aspects of that society contributed, in her mind, to her aunt's downfall? What was the social significance of her aunt's transgression—both to her village and to the family? How does Kingston herself relate to the social values that surrounded her aunt, and those of her own family?

4. Early in the essay Kingston comments, "Those of us in the first American generations have had to figure out how the invisible world the emigrants built around our childhoods fit in solid America" (paragraph 10). And she asks in paragraph 12, "Chinese Americans, when you try to understand what things in you are Chinese, how do you separate what is peculiar to childhood, to poverty, insanities, one family, your mother who marked your growing with stories, from what is Chinese?" How do these questions shed light on her essay? To what extent could questions like these apply to the experience of others besides Chinese Americans?

From the Poets
in the Kitchen

Paule Marshall

*This autobiographical essay first appeared in 1983 in
a series in* The New York Times Book Review *called
"The Making of a Writer." It was published the same
year in a collection of Marshall's stories and novellas,*
Reena and Other Stories. *In it Marshall examines
early influences on her development as a writer.
Recalling her childhood in the Barbadian community
of Brooklyn, she credits the women around her
mother's kitchen table for passing on "the rich legacy
of language and culture" that shaped her writing.*

Some years ago, when I was teaching a graduate seminar in
fiction at Columbia University, a well known male novelist visited
my class to speak on his development as a writer. In discussing his
formative years, he didn't realize it but he seriously endangered
his life by remarking that women writers are luckier than those of
his sex because they usually spend so much time as children around
their mothers and their mothers' friends in the kitchen.

What did he say that for? The women students immediately
forgot about being in awe of him and began readying their attack for
the question and answer period later on. Even I bristled. There again
was that awful image of women locked away from the world in the

kitchen with only each other to talk to, and their daughters locked in with them.

But my guest wasn't really being sexist or trying to be provocative or even spoiling for a fight. What he meant—when he got around to explaining himself more fully—was that, given the way children are (or were) raised in our society, with little girls kept closer to home and their mothers, the woman writer stands a better chance of being exposed, while growing up, to the kind of talk that goes on among women, more often than not in the kitchen; and that this experience gives her an edge over her male counterpart by instilling in her an appreciation for ordinary speech.

It was clear that my guest lecturer attached great importance to this, which is understandable. Common speech and the plain, workaday words that make it up are, after all, the stock in trade of some of the best fiction writers. They are the principal means by which characters in a novel or story reveal themselves and give voice sometimes to profound feelings and complex ideas about themselves and the world. Perhaps the proper measure of a writer's talent is skill in rendering everyday speech—when it is appropriate to the story—as well as the ability to tap, to exploit, the beauty, poetry and wisdom it often contains.

5　　"If you say what's on your mind in the language that comes to you from your parents and your street and friends you'll probably say something beautiful." Grace Paley tells this, she says, to her students at the beginning of every writing course.

It's all a matter of exposure and a training of the ear for the would-be writer in those early years of apprenticeship. And, according to my guest lecturer, this training, the best of it, often takes place in as unglamorous a setting as the kitchen.

He didn't know it, but he was essentially describing my experience as a little girl. I grew up among poets. Now they didn't look like poets—whatever that breed is supposed to look like. Nothing about them suggested that poetry was their calling. They were just a group of ordinary housewives and mothers, my mother included, who dressed in a way (shapeless house-dresses, dowdy felt hats and long, dark, solemn coats) that made it impossible for me to imagine they had ever been young.

Nor did they do what poets were supposed to do—spend their days in an attic room writing verses. They never put pen to paper except to write occasionally to their relatives in Barbados. "I take my pen in hand hoping these few lines will find you in health as they leave me fair for the time being," was the way their letters invariably began. Rather, their day was spent "scrubbing floor," as they described the work they did.

Several mornings a week these unknown bards would put an apron and a pair of old house shoes in a shopping bag and take the train or streetcar from our section of Brooklyn out to Flatbush. There, those who didn't have steady jobs would wait on certain designated corners for the white housewives in the neighborhood to come along and bargain with them over pay for a day's work cleaning their houses. This was the ritual even in the winter.

Later, armed with the few dollars they had earned, which in 10 their vocabulary became "a few raw-mouth pennies," they made their way back to our neighborhood, where they would sometimes stop off to have a cup of tea or cocoa together before going home to cook dinner for their husbands and children.

The basement kitchen of the brownstone house where my family lived was the usual gathering place. Once inside the warm safety of its walls the women threw off the drab coats and hats, seated themselves at the large center table, drank their cups of tea or cocoa, and talked. While my sister and I sat at a smaller table over in a corner doing our homework, they talked—endlessly, passionately, poetically, and with impressive range. No subject was beyond them. True, they would indulge in the usual gossip: whose husband was running with whom, whose daughter looked slightly "in the way" (pregnant) under her bridal gown as she walked down the aisle. That sort of thing. But they also tackled the great issues of the time. They were always, for example, discussing the state of the economy. It was the mid and late 30's then, and the aftershock of the Depression, with its soup lines and suicides on Wall Street, was still being felt.

Some people, they declared, didn't know how to deal with adversity. They didn't know that you had to "tie up your belly" (hold in the pain, that is) when things got rough and go on with life. They took their image from the bellyband that is tied around the stomach of a newborn baby to keep the navel pressed in.

They talked politics. Roosevelt was their hero. He had come along and rescued the country with relief and jobs, and in gratitude they christened their sons Franklin and Delano and hoped they would live up to the names.

If F.D.R. was their hero, Marcus Garvey was their God. The name of the fiery, Jamaican-born black nationalist of the 20's was constantly invoked around the table. For he had been their leader when they first came to the United States from the West Indies shortly after World War I. They had contributed to his organization, the United Negro Improvement Association (UNIA), out of their meager salaries, bought shares in his ill-fated Black Star Shipping Line, and at the height of the movement they had marched as mem-

bers of his "nurses' brigade" in their white uniforms up Seventh
Avenue in Harlem during the great Garvey Day parades. Garvey: He
lived on through the power of their memories.

15   And their talk was of war and rumors of wars. They raged
against World War II when it broke out in Europe, blaming it on the
politicians. "It's these politicians. They're the ones always starting
up all this lot of war. But what they care? It's the poor people got to
suffer and mothers with their sons." If it was *their* sons, they swore
they would keep them out of the Army by giving them soap to eat
each day to make their hearts sound defective. Hitler? He was for
them "the devil incarnate."

Then there was home. They reminisced often and at length
about home. The old country. Barbados—or Bimshire, as they affec-
tionately called it. The little Caribbean island in the sun they loved
but had to leave. "Poor—poor but sweet" was the way they remembered it.

And naturally they discussed their adopted home. America
came in for both good and bad marks. They lashed out at it for the
racism they encountered. They took to task some of the people they
worked for, especially those who gave them only a hard-boiled egg
and a few spoonfuls of cottage cheese for lunch. "As if anybody can
scrub floor on an egg and some cheese that don't have no taste to
it!"

Yet although they caught H in "this man country," as they
called America, it was nonetheless a place where "you could at least
see your way to make a dollar." That much they acknowledged.
They might even one day accumulate enough dollars, with both
them and their husbands working, to buy the brownstone houses
which, like my family, they were only leasing at that period. This
was their consuming ambition: to "buy house" and to see the children through.

There was no way for me to understand it at the time, but the
talk that filled the kitchen those afternoons was highly functional.
It served as therapy, the cheapest kind available to my mother and
her friends. Not only did it help them recover from the long wait on
the corner that morning and the bargaining over their labor, it restored them to a sense of themselves and reaffirmed their self-worth.
Through language they were able to overcome the humiliations of
the work-day.

20   But more than therapy, that freewheeling, wide-ranging, exuberant talk functioned as an outlet for the tremendous creative
energy they possessed. They were women in whom the need for self-
expression was strong, and since language was the only vehicle
readily available to them they made of it an art form that—in keep-

ing with the African tradition in which art and life are one—was an
integral part of their lives.

And their talk was a refuge. They never really ceased being
baffled and overwhelmed by America—its vastness, complexity and
power. Its strange customs and laws. At a level beyond words they
remained fearful and in awe. Their uneasiness and fear were even
reflected in their attitude toward the children they had given birth
to in this country. They referred to those like myself, the little
Brooklyn-born Bajans (Barbadians), as "these New York children"
and complained that they couldn't discipline us properly because of
the laws here. "You can't beat these children as you would like, you
know, because the authorities in this place will dash you in jail for
them. After all, these is New York children." Not only were we
different, American, we had, as they saw it, escaped their ultimate
authority.

Confronted therefore by a world they could not encompass,
which even limited their rights as parents, and at the same time
finding themselves permanently separated from the world they had
known, they took refuge in language. "Language is the only home-
land," Czeslaw Milosz, the emigré Polish writer and Nobel Laure-
ate, has said. This is what it became for the women at the kitchen
table.

It served another purpose also, I suspect. My mother and her
friends were after all the female counterpart of Ralph Ellison's invisible man. Indeed, you might say they suffered a triple invisibility,
being black, female and foreigners. They really didn't count in
American society except as a source of cheap labor. But given the
kind of women they were, they couldn't tolerate the fact of their
invisibility, their powerlessness. And they fought back, using the
only weapon at their command: the spoken word.

Those late afternoon conversations on a wide range of topics
were a way for them to feel they exercised some measure of control
over their lives and the events that shaped them. "Soully-gal, talk
yuh talk!" they were always exhorting each other. "In this man
world you got to take yuh mouth and make a gun!" They were in
control, if only verbally and if only for the two hours or so that they
remained in our house.

For me, sitting over in the corner, being seen but not heard,   25
which was the rule for children in those days, it wasn't only what
the women talked about—the content—but the way they put
things—their style. The insight, irony, wit and humor they brought
to their stories and discussions and their poet's inventiveness and
daring with language—which of course I could only sense but not
define back then.

They had taken the standard English taught them in the pri-

mary schools of Barbados and transformed it into an idiom, an in-
strument that more adequately described them—changing around
the syntax and imposing their own rhythm and accent so that the
sentences were more pleasing to their ears. They added the few African sounds and words that had survived, such as the derisive suck-
teeth sound and the word "yam," meaning to eat. And to make it
more vivid, more in keeping with their expressive quality, they
brought to bear a raft of metaphors, parables, Biblical quotations,
sayings and the like:

"The sea ain' got no back door," they would say, meaning that
it wasn't like a house where if there was a fire you could run out the
back. Meaning that it was not to be trifled with. And meaning perhaps in a larger sense that man should treat all of nature with caution and respect.

"I has read hell by heart and called every generation blessed!"
They sometimes went in for hyperbole.

A woman expecting a baby was never said to be pregnant. They
never used that word. Rather, she was "in the way" or, better yet,
"tumbling big." "Guess who I butt up on in the market the other
day tumbling big again!"

30   And a woman with a reputation of being too free with her sexual favors was known in their book as a "thoroughfare"—the sense
of men like a steady stream of cars moving up and down the road of
her life. Or she might be dubbed "a free-bee," which was my favorite
of the two. I liked the image it conjured up of a woman scandalous
perhaps but independent, who flitted from one flower to another in
a garden of male beauties, sampling their nectar, taking her pleasure
at will, the roles reversed.

And nothing, no matter how beautiful, was ever described as
simply beautiful. It was always "beautiful-ugly": the beautiful-ugly
dress, the beautiful-ugly house, the beautiful-ugly car. Why the word
"ugly," I used to wonder, when the thing they were referring to was
beautiful, and they knew it. Why the antonym, the contradiction,
the linking of opposites? It used to puzzle me greatly as a child.

There is the theory in linguistics which states that the idiom
of a people, the way they use language, reflects not only the most
fundamental views they hold of themselves and the world but their
very conception of reality. Perhaps in using the term "beautiful-
ugly" to describe nearly everything, my mother and her friends were
expressing what they believed to be a fundamental dualism in life:
the idea that a thing is at the same time its opposite, and that these
opposites, these contradictions make up the whole. But theirs was
not a Manichaean brand of dualism that sees matter, flesh, the body,
as inherently evil, because they constantly addressed each other as

"soully-gal"—soul: spirit; gal: the body, flesh, the visible self. And it was clear from their tone that they gave one as much weight and importance as the other. They had never heard of the mind/body split.

As for God, they summed up His essential attitude in a phrase. "God," they would say, "don' love ugly and He ain' stuck on pretty."

Using everyday speech, the simple commonplace words—but always with imagination and skill—they gave voice to the most complex ideas. Flannery O'Connor would have approved of how they made ordinary language work, as she put it, "double-time," stretching, shading, deepening its meaning. Like Joseph Conrad they were always trying to infuse new life in the "old old words worn thin . . . by . . . careless usage." And the goals of their oral art were the same as his: "to make you hear, to make you feel . . . to make you *see*." This was their guiding esthetic.

By the time I was 8 or 9, I graduated from the corner of the   35
kitchen to the neighborhood library, and thus from the spoken to the written word. The Macon Street Branch of the Brooklyn Public Library was an imposing half block long edifice of heavy gray masonry, with glass-paneled doors at the front and two tall metal torches symbolizing the light that comes of learning flanking the wide steps outside.

The inside was just as impressive. More steps—of pale marble with gleaming brass railings at the center and sides—led up to the circulation desk, and a great pendulum clock gazed down from the balcony stacks that faced the entrance. Usually stationed at the top of the steps like the guards outside Buckingham Palace was the custodian, a stern-faced West Indian type who for years, until I was old enough to obtain an adult card, would immediately shoo me with one hand into the Children's Room and with the other threaten me into silence, a finger to his lips. You would have thought he was the chief librarian and not just someone whose job it was to keep the brass polished and the clock wound. I put him in a story called "Barbados" years later and had terrible things happen to him at the end.

I sheltered from the storm of adolescence in the Macon Street library, reading voraciously, indiscriminately, everything from Jane Austen to Zane Grey, but with a special passion for the long, full-blown, richly detailed 18th- and 19th-century picaresque tales: "Tom Jones," "Great Expectations," "Vanity Fair."

But although I loved nearly everything I read and would enter fully into the lives of the characters—indeed, would cease being myself and become them—I sensed a lack after a time. Something I couldn't quite define was missing. And then one day, browsing in the poetry section, I came across a book by someone called Paul Laurence Dunbar, and opening it I found the photograph of a wistful, sad-eyed poet who to my surprise was black. I turned to a poem at random. "Little brown-baby wif spa'klin' / eyes / Come to yo' pappy an' set on his knee." Although I had a little difficulty at first with the words in dialect, the poem spoke to me as nothing I had read before of the closeness, the special relationship I had had with my father, who by then had become an ardent believer in Father Divine and gone to live in Father's "kingdom" in Harlem. Reading it helped to ease somewhat the tight knot of sorrow and longing I carried around in my chest that refused to go away. I read another poem. "'Lias! 'Lias! Bless de Lawd! / Don' you know de day's / erbroad? / Ef you don' get up, you scamp / Dey'll be trouble in dis camp." I laughed. It reminded me of the way my mother sometimes yelled at my sister and me to get out of bed in the mornings.

And another: "Seen my lady home las' night / Jump back, honey, jump back. / Hel' huh han' an' sque'z it tight . . ." About love between a black man and a black woman. I had never seen that written about before and it roused in me all kinds of delicious feelings and hopes.

40   And I began to search then for books and stories and poems about "The Race" (as it was put back then), about my people. While not abandoning Thackeray, Fielding, Dickens and the others, I started asking the reference librarian, who was white, for books by Negro writers, although I must admit I did so at first with a feeling of shame—the shame I and many others used to experience in those days whenever the word "Negro" or "colored" came up.

No grade school literature teacher of mine had ever mentioned Dunbar or James Weldon Johnson or Langston Hughes. I didn't know that Zora Neale Hurston existed and was busy writing and being published during those years. Nor was I made aware of people like Frederick Douglass and Harriet Tubman—their spirit and example—or the great 19th-century abolitionist and feminist Sojourner Truth. There wasn't even Negro History Week when I attended *P.S. 35* on Decatur Street!

What I needed, what all the kids—West Indian and native black American alike—with whom I grew up needed, was an equivalent of the Jewish shul, someplace where we could go after school—the schools that were shortchanging us—and read works by those like ourselves and learn about our history.

It was around that time also that I began harboring the dangerous thought of someday trying to write myself. Perhaps a poem about an apple tree, although I had never seen one. Or the story of a girl who could magically transplant herself to wherever she wanted to be in the world—such as Father Divine's kingdom in Harlem. Dunbar—his dark, eloquent face, his large volume of poems—permitted me to dream that I might someday write, and with something of the power with words my mother and her friends possessed.

When people at readings and writers' conferences ask me who my major influences were, they are sometimes a little disappointed when I don't immediately name the usual literary giants. True, I am indebted to those writers, white and black, whom I read during my formative years and still read for instruction and pleasure. But they were preceded in my life by another set of giants whom I always acknowledge before all others: the group of women around the table long ago. They taught me my first lessons in the narrative art. They trained my ear. They set a standard of excellence. This is why the best of my work must be attributed to them; it stands as testimony to the rich legacy of language and culture they so freely passed on to me in the wordshop of the kitchen.

Response

1. Marshall begins her essay by recalling a lecturer's observation that girls growing up in our culture have more immediate access than boys to the ordinary speech of adults. Marshall's experience confirms the observation. Why, in her view, is this a special advantage? Do you share her point of view?

2. "I grew up among poets," Marshall says in paragraph 7. She then gives substance to her statement in a detailed and neatly organized discussion of their topics, the functions of their talk, and the ways in which they used language like poets—their style. Identify the paragraphs that correspond to each of these points: What did the women talk about? What functions did their talk serve? How did they make poetic use of language? Consider how Marshall's comments about speech can also apply to writing.

3. Marshall observes that her mother and her friends "suffered a triple invisibility, being black, female and foreigners" (paragraph 23). How did the women adapt to life in America? How did they carry out the axiom that "in this man world you got to take yuh mouth and make a gun"?

4. How were the schools "shortchanging" Marshall and the kids she grew up with (paragraph 42)? What did Marshall and her peers need, and why?

5. The poet Paul Laurence Dunbar "permitted" Marshall to dream

about becoming a writer (paragraph 42). How did Dunbar's influence combine with that of Marshall's mother and her friends to shape her development? From her essay what can we infer about her goals and motivations as a writer?

6. Early in her essay Marshall quotes the writer Grace Paley saying, "If you say what's on your mind in the language that comes to you from your parents and your street and friends you'll probably say something beautiful." In what ways does Marshall's essay extend Paley's point? To what extent is this viewpoint supported by writers such as Kurt Vonnegut, Jr. ("How to Write with Style," Section I) and others? What is your point of view on this issue?

The Seam of the Snail
Cynthia Ozick

In this essay from her book Metaphor and Memory *(1989) Ozick writes about her mother in contrast to herself. In doing so she writes about different approaches to life and different standards of excellence. In the essay she also reveals something of her approach to writing.*

In my Depression childhood, whenever I had a new dress, my cousin Sarah would get suspicious. The nicer the dress was, and especially the more expensive it looked, the more suspicious she would get. Finally she would lift the hem and check the seams. This was to see if the dress had been bought or if my mother had sewed it. Sarah could always tell. My mother's sewing had elegant outsides, but there was something catch-as-catch-can about the insides. Sarah's sewing, by contrast, was as impeccably finished inside as out; not one stray thread dangled.

My uncle Jake built meticulous grandfather clocks out of rosewood; he was a perfectionist, and sent to England for the clockworks. My mother built serviceable radiator covers and a serviceable cabinet, with hinged doors, for the pantry. She built a pair of bookcases for the living room. Once, after I was grown and in a house of my own, she fixed the sewer pipe. She painted ceilings, and also landscapes; she reupholstered chairs. One summer she planted a whole yard of tall corn. She thought herself capable of doing anything, and did everything she imagined. But nothing was perfect. There was always some clear flaw, never visible head-on. You had to look underneath, where the seams were. The corn thrived, though not in rows. The stalks elbowed one another like gossips in a dense little village.

"Miss Brrrroooobaker," my mother used to mock, rolling her Russian r's, whenever I crossed a *t* she had left uncrossed, or corrected a word she had misspelled, or became impatient with a *v* that had tangled itself up with a *w* in her speech. ("*Vvv*entriloquist," I would say. "*Vvv*entriloquist," she would obediently repeat. And the next time it would come out "wiolinist.") Miss Brubaker was my high school English teacher, and my mother invoked her name as an emblem of raging finical obsession. "Miss Brrrroooobaker," my mother's voice hoots at me down the years, as I go on casting and recasting sentences in a tiny handwriting on monomaniacally uniform paper. The loops of my mother's handwriting—it was the Palmer Method—were as big as soup bowls, spilling generous splashy ebullience. She could pull off, at five minutes' notice, a satisfying dinner for ten concocted out of nothing more than originality and panache. But the napkin would be folded a little off center, and the spoon might be on the wrong side of the knife. She was an optimist who ignored trifles; for her, God was not in the details but in the intent. And all these culinary and agricultural efflorescences were extracurricular, accomplished in the crevices and niches of a fourteen-hour business day. When she scribbled out her family memoirs, in heaps of dog-eared notebooks, or on the backs of old bills, or on the margins of last year's calendar, I would resist typing them; in the speed of the chase she often omitted words like "the," "and," "will." The same flashing and bountiful hand fashioned and fired ceramic pots, and painted brilliant autumn views and vases of imaginary flowers and ferns, and decorated ordinary Woolworth platters with lavish enameled gardens. But bits of the painted petals would chip away.

Lavish: my mother was as lavish as nature. She woke early and saturated the hours with work and inventiveness, and read late into the night. She was all profusion, abundance, fabrication. Angry at her children, she would run after us whirling the cord of the electric iron, like a lasso or a whip; but she never caught us. When, in seventh grade, I was afraid of failing the Music Appreciation final exam because I could not tell the difference between "To a Wild Rose" and "Barcarole," she got the idea of sending me to school with a

gauze sling rigged up on my writing arm, and an explanatory note
that was purest fiction. But the sling kept slipping off. My mother
gave advice like mad—she boiled over with so much passion for the
predicaments of strangers that they turned into permanent cronies.
She told intimate stories about people I had never heard of.

Despite the gargantuan Palmer loops (or possibly because of   5
them), I have always known that my mother's was a life of—intri-
cately abashing word!—excellence: insofar as excellence means ripe
generosity. She burgeoned, she proliferated; she was endlessly leafy
and flowering. She wore red hats, and called herself a gypsy. In her
girlhood she marched with the suffragettes and for Margaret Sanger
and called herself a Red. She made me laugh, she was so varied: like
a tree on which lemons, pomegranates, and prickly pears absurdly
all hang together. She had the comedy of prodigality.

My own way is a thousand times more confined. I am a pinched
perfectionist, the ultimate fruition of Miss Brubaker; I attend to
crabbed minutiae and am self-trammeled through taking pains. I am
a kind of human snail, locked in and condemned by my own nature.
The ancients believed that the moist track left by the snail as it
crept was the snail's own essence, depleting its body little by little;
the farther the snail toiled, the smaller it became, until it finally
rubbed itself out. That is how perfectionists are. Say to us Excellence, and we will show you how we use up our substance and wear
ourselves away, while making scarcely any progress at all. The fact
that I am an exacting perfectionist in a narrow strait only, and nowhere else, is hardly to the point, since nothing matters to me so
much as a comely and muscular sentence. It is my narrow strait,
this snail's road; the track of the sentence I am writing now; and
when I have eked out the wet substance, ink or blood, that is its
mark, I will begin the next sentence. Only in treading out sentences
am I perfectionist; but then there is nothing else I know how to do,
or take much interest in. I miter every pair of abutting sentences as
scrupulously as Uncle Jake fitted one strip of rosewood against another. My mother's worldly and bountiful hand has escaped me. The
sentence I am writing is my cabin and my shell, compact, self-suffi-
cient. It is the burnished horizon—a merciless planet where flaw-
lessness is the single standard, where even the inmost seams, however hidden from a laxer eye, must meet perfection. Here
"excellence" is not strewn casually from a tipped cornucopia, here
disorder does not account for charm, here trifles rule like tyrants.

I measure my life in sentences pressed out, line by line, like
the lustrous ooze on the underside of the snail, the snail's secret
open seam, its wound, leaking attar. My mother was too mettle-
some to feel the force of a comma. She scorned minutiae. She mea-

sured her life according to what poured from the horn of plenty, which was her own seamless, ample, cascading, elastic, susceptible, inexact heart. My narrower heart rides between the tiny twin horns of the snail, dwindling as it goes.

And out of this thinnest thread, this ink-wet line of words, must rise a visionary fog, a mist, a smoke, forging cities, histories, sorrows, quagmires, entanglements, lives of sinners, even the life of my furnace-hearted mother: so much wilderness, waywardness, plenitude on the head of the precise and impeccable snail, between the horns. (Ah, if this could be!)

Response

1. When Ozick first published this essay, in *Ms.* magazine, she entitled it "Excellence." Explain the different notions of excellence she presents. Do you think she values one over the other?
2. Analyze the snail image to understand Ozick's vision of herself as a writer. How do the attributes of the snail elucidate that vision?
3. In this essay we see Ozick doing what she describes herself as doing: turning out meticulously crafted sentences. Collect different descriptive words and phrases from her portrayals of both her mother and herself to see how she builds the contrast.
4. How does Ozick connect herself and her mother in the last paragraph? What does Ozick want to accomplish through her writing?

The Loom

R. A. Sasaki

This is the title story from Sasaki's book The Loom
*and Other Stories (1991). In it the author reflects upon
her mother's life; the story offers insight into the
history of San Francisco's Japanese-American
community as well.*

It was when Cathy died that the other Terasaki sisters began
to think that something was wrong with their mother. Sharon and
Jo were home for the weekend, and when the phone call came they
had gone up to her room with the shocking news, barely able to
speak through their tears. Sharon had to raise her voice so her mother
could hear the awful words, choked out like bits of shattered glass,
while Jo watched what seemed like anger pull her mother's face into
a solemn frown.

"You see?" their mother said. Her voice, harsh and trembling
with a shocking vehemence, startled the two sisters even in their
grief. "Daddy told her not to go mountain climbing. He said it was
too dangerous. She didn't listen."

Recalling her words later, Jo felt chilled.

They had always known about their mother's "ways"—the way
she would snip off their straight black hair when they were children
as soon as it grew past their ears, saying that hair too long would

give people the wrong idea. Then later, when they were grown and defiant and wore their hair down to their waists, she would continue to campaign by lifting the long strands and snipping at them with her fingers. There was also the way she would tear through the house in a frenzy of cleaning just before they left on a family vacation, "in case there's a fire or someone breaks in and *yoso no hito* have to come in." They never understood if it was the firemen, the police, or the burglar before whose eyes she would be mortally shamed if her house were not spotless. There was even the way she cooked. She was governed not by inspiration or taste, but by what "they" did. The clothes she chose for them were what "they" were wearing these days. Who is this "they"? her daughters always wanted to ask her. Her idiosyncrasies were a source of mild frustration to which the girls were more or less resigned. "Oh, Mom," they would groan, or, to each other: "That's just Mom."

5   But this.

"It was as though she didn't feel anything at all," Jo recounted to her eldest sister, Linda, who had come home from Germany for the funeral. "It was as though all she could think about was that Cathy had broken the rules."

It wasn't until their father had come home that their mother cried, swept along in the wake of his massive grief. He had been away on a weekend fishing trip, and they had tried to get in touch with him, but failed. Jo had telephoned the highway patrol and park rangers at all his favorite fishing spots, saying, "No, don't tell him that his daughter has died. Would you just tell him to come home as soon as possible?" And it was Jo who was standing at the window watching when his truck turned the corner for home. The three women went down to the basement together. He and his fishing buddy had just emerged from the dusty, fish-odorous truck, and he was rolling up the garage door when they reached him. He was caught between the bright spring sunlight and the dark coolness of the basement. His hand still on the garage door, he heard the news of his daughter's death. Their mother told him, with a hint of fear in her voice. He cried, as children cry who have awakened in the night to a nameless terror, a nameless grief; for a suspended moment, as he stood alone sobbing his dead daughter's name, the three women deferred to the sanctity of his suffering. Then Sharon moved to encircle him in her arms, clinging flimsily to him against the tremendous isolation of grief.

It was only then that their mother had cried, but it seemed almost vicarious, as if she had needed their father to process the raw stuff of life into personal emotion. Not once since the death had she talked about her own feelings. Not ever, her daughters now realized.

"It would probably do Mom good to get away for a while," Linda said. "I was thinking of taking her to Germany with me when I go back, just for a few weeks. She's never been anywhere. A change of scene might be just what she needs. Don't you think?"

"I suppose it's worth a try," Jo said. 10

So it was decided that when Linda flew back to join her husband, who was stationed in Heidelberg, their mother would go with her and stay a month. Except for a visit to Japan with her own mother when she was sixteen, it was their mother's first trip abroad. At first she was hesitant, but their father encouraged her; he would go too if he didn't have to stay and run the business.

It was hard to imagine their mother outside the context of their house. She had always been there when the children came back from school; in fact, the sisters had never had babysitters. Now, as they watched her at the airport, so small and sweet with her large purse clutched tightly in both hands and her new suitcase neatly packed and properly tagged beside her, they wondered just who was this little person, this person who was their mother?

She had grown up in San Francisco, wearing the two faces of a second-generation child born of immigrant parents. The two faces never met; there was no common thread running through both worlds. The duality was unplanned, untaught. Perhaps it had begun the first day of school when she couldn't understand the teacher and Eleanor Leland had called her a "Jap" and she cried. Before then there had never been a need to sort out her identity; she had met life headlong and with the confidence of a child.

Her world had been the old Victorian flat in which her mother took in boarders—the long, narrow corridor, the spiral stairway, the quilts covered with bright Japanese cloth, and the smell of fish cooking in the kitchen. She had accepted without question the people who padded in and out of her world on stockinged feet; they all seemed to be friends of the family. She never wondered why most of them were men, and it never occurred to her child's mind to ask why they didn't have their own families. The men often couldn't pay, but they were always grateful. They lounged in doorways and had teasing affectionate words for her and her sister. Then they would disappear, for a month, for six months, a year. Time, to a child, was boundless and unmeasurable. Later, crates of fruit would arrive and be stacked in the corridor. "From Sato-san," her mother would say, or, "*Kudoh-san kara.*"

The young men sometimes came back to visit with new hats 15 set jauntily on their heads, if luck was good. But often luck was not good, and they came back to stay, again and again, each stay longer than the last; and each time they would tease less and drink more with her father in the back room. The slap of cards rose over the low mumble of their longing and despair. All this she accepted as her world.

The Victorian house which contained her world was on Pine Street, and so it was known as "Pine" to the young adventurers from her parents' native Wakayama prefecture in Japan who made their way from the docks of Osaka to the lettuce fields and fruit orchards of California. "Stay at Pine," the word passed along the grapevine, "Moriwaki-san will take care of you."

It was a short walk down the Buchanan Street hill from Pine to the flats where the Japanese community had taken root and was thriving like a tree whose seed had blown in from the Pacific and had held fast in this nook, this fold in the city's many gradations. When she was a little older her world expanded beyond the Victorian called Pine. It expanded toward the heart of this community, toward the little shops from which her mother returned each day, string bag bulging with newspaper-wrapped parcels and a long white radish or two. She played hide-and-seek among the barrels of pickles and sacks of rice piled high in the garage that claimed to be the American Fish Market while her mother exchanged news of the comings and goings of the community over the fish counter. "Ship coming in Friday? Do you think Yamashita-san's picture bride will come? She's in for a surprise!"

At the age of five she roller-skated to the corner of her block, then on sudden impulse turned the corner and started down the Buchanan Street hill. Her elder sister, Keiko, who had expected her to turn around and come right back, threw down her jump rope and ran after her, screaming for her to stop. But she didn't stop. She made it all the way to the bottom, cheeks flushed red and black hair flying, before shooting off the curb and crumpling in the street. Her hands and knees were scraped raw, but she was laughing.

Before that first day of school there had been no need to look above Pine Street, where the city reached upwards to the Pacific Heights area and the splendid mansions of the rich white people. The only Japanese who went to Pacific Heights were the ones employed to do housecleaning as day laborers. She had always known what was on the other side of Pine Street, and accepted easily that it was not part of her world.

20   When it came time for her to go to school, she was not sent to the same school as the other Japanese-American children because Pine was on the edge of Japantown and in a different school district. She was the only Japanese in her class. And from the instant Eleanor Leland pulled up the corners of her eyes at her, sneering "Jap!", a

kind of radar system went to work in her. Afterward she always acted with caution in new surroundings, blending in like a chameleon for survival. There were two things she would never do again: one was to forget the girl's name who had called her a Jap, and the other was to cry.

She did her best to blend in. Though separated from the others by her features and her native tongue, she tried to be as inconspicuous as possible. If she didn't understand what the teacher said, she watched the other children and copied them. She listened carefully to the teacher and didn't do anything that might provoke criticism. If she couldn't be outstanding she at least wanted to be invisible.

She succeeded. She muted her colors and blended in. She was a quiet student and the other children got used to her; some were even nice to her. But she was still not really a part of their world because she was not really herself.

At the end of each school day she went home to the dark, narrow corridors of the old Victorian and the soothing, unconscious jumble of two tongues that was the two generations' compromise for the sake of communication. Theirs was a comfortable language, like a comfortable old sweater that had been well washed and rendered shapeless by wear. She would never wear it outside of the house. It was a personal thing, like a hole in one's sock, which was perfectly all right at home but would be a horrible embarrassment if seen by *yoso no hito*.

In the outside world—the *hakujin* world—there was a watchdog at work who rigorously edited out Japanese words and mannerisms when she spoke. Her words became formal, carefully chosen and somewhat artificial. She never thought they conveyed what she really felt, what she really was, because what she really was was unacceptable. In the realm of behavior, the watchdog was a tyrant. Respectability, as defined by popular novels and Hollywood heroines, must be upheld at all costs. How could she explain about the young men lounging in the doorways of her home and drinking in the back room with her father? How could she admit to the stories of the immigrant women who came to her mother desperate for protection from the beatings by their frenzied husbands? It was all so far from the drawing rooms of Jane Austen and the virtue and gallantry of Hollywood. The Japanese who passed through her house could drink, gamble, and philander, but she would never acknowledge it. She could admit to no weakness, no peculiarity. She would be irreproachable. She would be American.

Poverty was irreproachably American in the Depression years.   25
Her father's oriental art goods business on Union Square had sur-

vived the 1906 earthquake only to be done in by the dishonesty of a
hakujin partner who absconded with the gross receipts and the company car. The family survived on piecework and potatoes. Her
mother organized a group of immigrant ladies to crochet window-
shade rings. They got a penny apiece from the stores on Grant Avenue. Her father strung plastic birds onto multicolored rings. As they
sat working in the back room day after day, they must have dreamed
of better times. They had all gambled the known for the unknown
when they left Japan to come to America. Apparently it took more
than hard work. They could work themselves to death for pennies.
Entrepreneurial ventures were risky. They wanted to spare their sons
and daughters this insecurity and hardship. Education was the key
that would open the magical doors to a better future. Not that they
hadn't been educated in Japan, indeed some of them were better educated than the people whose houses they cleaned on California
Street. But they felt the key was an American education, a college
education. Immigrant sons and immigrant daughters would fulfill
their dreams.

She and her peers acquiesced in this dream. After all, wasn't it
the same as their own? To succeed, to be irreproachable, to be American? She would be a smart career girl in a tailored suit, beautiful
and bold—an American girl.

After the Depression her father opened a novelty store on Grant
Avenue, and she was able to go to college. She set forth into the
unknown with a generation of immigrant sons and daughters, all
fortified by their mutual vision of the American dream.

They did everything right. They lived at home to save ex-
penses. Each morning they woke up at dawn to catch the bus to the
ferry building. They studied on the ferry as it made the bay crossing,
and studied on the train from the Berkeley marina to Shattuck Avenue, a few blocks from the majestic buildings of the University of
California. They studied for hours in the isolation of the library on
campus. They brought bag lunches from the dark kitchens of old
Japantown flats and ate on the manicured grass or at the Japanese
Students' Club off campus. They went to football games and rooted
for the home team. They wore bobby socks and Cal sweaters. The
women had pompadours and the men parted their hair in the middle. They did everything correctly. But there was one thing they did
not do: they did not break out of the solace of their own society to
establish contact with the outside world.

In a picture dated 1939 of the graduating members of the Nisei
Students' Club, there are about sixty of them in caps and gowns
standing before California Hall. She is there, among the others,
glowing triumphantly. No whisper of Pearl Harbor to cast a shadow

on those bright faces. Yet all these young graduates would soon be clerking in Chinatown shops or pruning American gardens. Their degrees would get them nowhere, not because they hadn't done right, but because it was 1939 and they had Japanese faces. There was nowhere for them to go.

When the war came, her application for a teaching job had already been on file for two years. Since graduation she had been helping at her father's Grant Avenue store. Now she had to hand-letter signs for the store saying "Bargain Sale: Everything Must Go." Her father's back slumped in defeat as he watched the business he had struggled to build melt away overnight. America was creating a masterpiece and did not want their color.

They packed away everything they could not carry. Tom the Greek, from whom they rented Pine, promised to keep their possessions in the basement, just in case they would be able to come back someday. The quilts of bright Japanese cloth, Imari dishes hand-carried by her mother from Japan, letters, photos, window-shade rings made in hard times, a copy of her junior college newspaper in which she had written a column, her Cal yearbook, faded pictures of bright Hollywood starlets—she put all her dreams in boxes for indefinite keeping. As they were told, they took along only what was practical, only what would serve in the uncertain times to come—blankets, sweaters, pots, and pans. Then, tagged like baggage, they were escorted by the U.S. Army to their various pick-up points in the city. And when the buses took them away, it was as though they had never been.

They were taken to Tanforan Racetrack, south of the city, which was to be their new home. The stables were used as barracks, and horse stalls became "apartments" for families. As she viewed the dirt and manure left by the former occupants, she realized, "So this is what they think of me." Realization was followed by shame. She recalled how truly she had believed she was accepted, her foolish confidence, and her unfounded dreams. She and her *nisei* friends had been spinning a fantasy world that was unacknowledged by the larger fabric of society. She had been so carried away by the aura of Berkeley that she had forgotten the legacy left her by Eleanor Leland. Now, the damp, dusty floor and stark cots reminded her sharply of her place. She was twenty-four. They lived in Tanforan for one year.

After a year they were moved to the Topaz Relocation Center in the wastelands of Utah. Topaz, Jewel of the Desert, they called it sardonically. Outside the barbed wire fence, the sagebrush traced aimless patterns on the shifting gray sands. Her sister Keiko could not endure it; she applied for an office job in Chicago and left the camp. Her brother enrolled at a midwestern university. She stayed and looked after her parents.

After a time she began to have trouble with her hearing. At first, it was only certain frequencies she could not hear, like some desert insects. Then it was even human voices, particularly when there was background noise. She couldn't be sure, but sometimes she wondered if it was a matter of choice, that if she only concentrated, she would be able to hear what someone was saying. But the blowing dust seemed to muffle everything anyway.

35   She left camp only once, and briefly, to marry the young man who had courted her wordlessly in the prewar days. He was a *kibei*, born in America and taken back to Japan at the age of eight. He had then returned to San Francisco to seek his fortune at the age of eighteen. He got off the boat with seven dollars in his pocket. He was one of those restless, lonely young men who would hang out at the Japantown pool hall, work at odd jobs by day, and go to school at night. He lived with a single-minded simplicity that seemed almost brash to someone like her who had grown up with so many unspoken rules. He wanted this sophisticated, college-educated American girl to be his wife, and she was completely won over. So she got leave from camp, and he from his unit, which was stationed at Fort Bragg, and they met in Chicago to cast a humble line into the uncertain future, a line they hoped would pull them out of this war into another, better life. Then they each returned to their respective barracks.

As defeat loomed inevitable for Japan, more and more people were allowed to leave the camps. Some of them made straight for the Midwest or East Coast, where feelings did not run so high against their presence, but her family could think only of going back home. The longing for San Francisco had become so strong that there was no question as to where they would go when they were released. They went straight back to Pine, and their hearts fell when they saw the filth and damage caused by three years of shifting tenancy. But they set about restoring it nevertheless because it was the only thing left of their lives.

The three years that had passed seemed like wasted years. The experience had no connection to the rest of her life; it was like a pocket in time, or a loose string. It was as though she had fallen asleep and dreamed the experience. But there was certainly no time to think about that now; they were busy rebuilding their lives.

She was pregnant with her first child. Her husband pleated skirts at a factory that hired Japanese. Later he ventured into the wholesale flower business where the future might be brighter. His hours were irregular; he rose in the middle of the night to deliver fresh flowers to market. Her sister, who had come back from Chicago to rejoin the family, took an office job with the government. Her parents were too old to start over. Her father hired out to do day work, but it shamed him so much that he did not want anyone else to know.

Then she was busy with the babies, who came quickly, one after another, all girls. She was absorbed in their nursing and bodily functions, in the sucking, smacking world of babies. How could she take time to pick up the pieces of her past selves, weave them together into a pattern, when there were diapers to be changed and washed, bowel movements to be recorded, and bottles sterilized? Her world was made up of Linda's solicitude for her younger sister Cathy, Cathy's curiosity, and the placidity of the third baby Sharon. Then there was Jo, who demanded so much attention because of her frail health. The house was filled with babies. Her husband was restless, fiercely independent—he wanted to raise his family in a place of his own.

So they moved out to the Avenues, leaving the dark corridors   40
and background music of mixed tongues for a sturdy little house in a predominantly *hakujin* neighborhood, where everyone had a yard enclosed by a fence.

When first their father, then their mother, died, Keiko also moved out of Pine and closed it up for good. The old Victorian was too big for one person to live in alone. But before all the old things stored away and forgotten in the basement were thrown out or given away, was there anything she wanted to keep? Just her college yearbook from Cal. That was all she could think of. She couldn't even remember what had been so important, to have been packed away in those boxes so carefully when the war had disrupted their lives. She couldn't take the time with four babies to sift through it all now. It would take days. No, just her yearbook. That was all.

Sealed off in her little house in the fog-shrouded Avenues, the past seemed like a dream. Her parents, the old Victorian, the shuffling of slippered guests, and the low mumble of Japanese, all gone from her life. Her college friends were scattered all over the country, or married and sealed off in their own private worlds. But she felt no sense of loss. Their lives, after all, were getting better. There was no time to look back on those days before the war. The girls were growing. They needed new clothes for school. She must learn to sew. Somer & Kaufman was having a sale on school shoes. Could she make this hamburger stretch for two nights?

Linda was a bright and obedient child. She was very much the big sister. Jo, the youngest, was volatile, alternating between loving and affectionate, and strong and stubborn. Sharon was a quiet child, buffered from the world on both sides by sisters. She followed her sister, Cathy, demanding no special attention. Cathy was friendly and fearless, an unredeemable tomboy. When she slid down banisters and bicycled down the big hill next to their house in the Avenues, her mother's eyes would narrow as if in recognition, watching her.

As a mother, she was without fault. Her girls were always neatly dressed and on time. They had decent table manners, remembered to excuse themselves and say thank you. They learned to read quickly and loved books because she always read to them. She chose the books carefully and refused to read them any slang or bad grammar. Her children would be irreproachable.

45   She conscientiously attended PTA meetings, although this was a trial for her. She wasn't able to tell people about her hearing problem; somehow she was unable to admit to such a deficiency. So she did her best, sometimes pretending to hear when she didn't, nodding her head and smiling. She wanted things to go smoothly; she wanted to appear normal.

Linda, Cathy, and Jo excelled in school and were very popular. Linda held class offices and was invariably the teacher's pet. "A nice girl," her teachers said. Cathy was outgoing and athletic, and showed great talent in art and design—"a beautiful girl," in her teachers' estimation. Jo was rebellious, read voraciously, and wrote caustic essays and satires. Teachers sometimes disliked her, but they all thought she was "intelligent." Sharon was termed "shy." Although she liked the arts, Cathy was the artist of the family. And though Sharon read quite a bit, Jo was thought of as the reader. Sharon was not popular like Linda, and of all the Terasaki girls, she had to struggle the hardest, often unsuccessfully, to make the honor roll. But all in all, the girls vindicated their mother, and it was a happy time, the happiest time of her life.

Then they were grown up and gone. They left one by one. The house emptied room by room until it seemed there was nothing but silence. She had to answer the phone herself now, if she heard it ring. She dreaded doing so because she could never be sure if she was hearing correctly. Sometimes she let the telephone ring, pretending not to be home. The one exception was when her sister called every night. Then she would exchange news on the phone for an hour.

When her daughters came home to visit she came alive. Linda was doing the right things. She had a nice Japanese-American boyfriend; she was graduating from college; and she was going to get married.

Cathy was a bit of a free spirit, and harder to understand. She

wore her hair long and straight, and seldom came home from Berkeley. When she did she seemed to find fault. Why didn't her mother
get a hearing aid? Did she enjoy being left out of the hearing world?
But Cathy had friends, interesting friends, *hakujin* friends, whom
she sometimes brought home with her. She moved easily in all
worlds, and her mother's heart swelled with pride to see it.

Sharon sometimes came home, sometimes stayed away. When   50
she did come home she did not have much to say. She was not happy
in school. She liked throwing pots and weaving.

Then there was Jo, who would always bring a book or notebook
home, and whose "evil pen" would pause absently in midstroke
when her mother hovered near, telling her little bits of information
that were new since the last visit. Jo, whose thoughts roamed far
away, would gradually focus on the little figure of her mother. She
had led such a sheltered life.

And then Cathy had died, and her mother didn't even cry.

Linda sent pictures from Germany of their mother in front of Heidelberg Castle, cruising down the Rhine. "She's just like a young
girl," her letters proclaimed triumphantly. "She's excited about
everything." But when their mother came home she talked about
her trip for about a week. Then the old patterns prevailed, as if the
house were a mold. In a month, Germany seemed like another loose
thread in the fabric of her life. When Jo visited two months later,
her mother was once again effaced, a part of the house almost, in
her faded blouse and shapeless skirt, joylessly adding too much sea-
soned salt to the dinner salad.

"If only," Jo wrote Linda facetiously, "we could ship her out to
some exotic place every other month."

In the fall Jo went to New York to study. "I have to get away,"   55
she wrote Linda. "The last time I went home I found myself discussing the machine washability of acrylics with Mom. There has
got to be more to life than that." In the spring she had her mother
come for a visit. No trip to the top of the Empire State Building, no
Staten Island ferry, with Jo. She whisked her mother straight from
Kennedy Airport to her cramped flat in the Village, and no sooner
had they finished dinner than Jo's boyfriend, Michael, arrived.

Her mother was gracious. "Where do you live, Michael?" she
asked politely.

He and Jo exchanged looks. "Here," he said.

Despite her mother's anxiety about the safety of New York
streets, the two of them walked furiously in the dusk and circled
Washington Square several times, mother shocked and disap-

pointed, daughter reassuring. At the end of an hour they returned to
the flat for tea, and by the end of the evening the three of them had
achieved an uneasy truce.

"I knew you wouldn't be happy about it," Jo said to her, "but I
wanted you to know the truth. I hate pretending."

60   "Things were different when we were your age," her mother
said. "What's Daddy going to say?"

She stayed for two weeks. Every morning Michael cooked
breakfast, and the three of them ate together. Her attitude toward
the situation softened from one of guarded assessment to tentative
acceptance. Michael was very articulate, Jo as level-headed as ever.
Their apartment was clean and homey. She began to relax over
morning coffee at the little round table by the window.

She remembered the trip she made to Chicago during the war
to get married. She had traveled from Topaz to Chicago by train. It
was her first trip alone. Her parents and camp friends had seen her
off at Topaz, and her sister and future husband had met her at the
station in Chicago. But as the train followed its track northeastward
across the country, she had been alone in the world. She remembered vividly the quality of light coming through the train window,
and how it had bathed the passing countryside in a golden wash.
Other passengers had slept, but she sat riveted at the window. Perhaps the scenery seemed so beautiful because of the bleakness and
sensory deprivation of Topaz. She didn't know why she remembered
it now.

Jo took her to the Metropolitan and to the Statue of Liberty. In
a theater on Broadway they sat in the front row to see Deborah Kerr,
her all-time favorite, and afterwards she declared she had heard every
word.

When she left she shook Michael's hand and hugged Jo, saying,
"I'll talk to Daddy."

65   But by the time Jo came home to visit a year later, the house,
or whatever it was, had done its work. Her mother was again lost to
her, a sweet little creature unable to hear very well, relaying little
bits of information.

"I give up," said Jo. "We seem to lose ground every time. We
dig her out, then she crawls back in, only deeper."

Linda loyally and staunchly defended the fortress in which her
mother seemed to have taken refuge.

Jo wanted to break through. "Like shock treatment," she said.
"It's the only way to bring her out."

Sharon, the middle daughter, gave her mother a loom.

70   And so, late in life, she took up weaving. She attended a class and
took detailed notes, then followed them step by step, bending to the

loom with painstaking attention, threading the warp tirelessly, endlessly winding, threading, tying. She made sampler after sampler,
using the subdued, muted colors she liked: five inches of one weave,
two inches of another, just as the teacher instructed.

For a year she wove samplers, geometric and repetitious, all in
browns and neutral shades, the colors she preferred. She was fascinated by some of the more advanced techniques she began to learn.
One could pick up threads from the warp selectively, so there could
be a color on the warp that never appeared in the fabric if it were
not picked up and woven into the fabric. With this technique she
could show a flash of color, repeat flashes of the color, or never show
it at all. The color would still be there, startling the eye when the
piece was turned over. The back side would reveal long lengths of a
color that simply hadn't been picked up from the warp and didn't
appear at all in the right side of the fabric.

She took to her loom with new excitement, threading the warp
with all the shades of her life: gray, for the cold, foggy mornings
when she had warmed Jo's clothes by the heater vent as Jo, four,
stood shivering in her pajamas; brown, the color of the five lunch
bags she had packed each morning with a sandwich, cut in half and
wrapped in waxed paper, napkin, fruit, and potato chips; dark brown,
like the brownies they had baked "to make Daddy come home" from
business trips. Sharon and Jo had believed he really could smell
them, because he always came home.

Now when the daughters came home they always found something new she had woven. Linda, back from Germany, dropped by
often to leave her daughter, Terry, at "*Bachan's* house" before dash-
ing off to work. When Linda's husband picked her up, Terry never
wanted to leave "Bachi" and would cling to her, crying at the door.

She continued to weave: white, the color of five sets of sheets,
which she had washed, hung out, and ironed each week—also the
color of the bathroom sink and the lather of shampoo against four
small black heads; blue, Cathy's favorite color.

Sharon came by from time to time, usually to do a favor or   75
bring a treat. She would cook Mexican food or borrow a tool or help
trim trees in the garden. She was frustrated with the public school
system where she had been substitute teaching and was now working part time in a gallery.

Sometimes Sharon brought yarn for her mother to weave:
golden brown, the color of the Central Valley in summer. The family had driven through the valley on their way to the mountains
almost every summer. They would arrive hot and sweating and hurry
into the cool, emerald green waters of the Merced River. The children's floats flashed yellow on the dark green water. Yellow, too,
were the beaten eggs fried flat, rolled, and eaten cold, with dark

brown pickled vegetables and white rice balls. She always sat in the shade.

Jo was working abroad and usually came home to visit once a year. She and Michael had broken up. During the visits the house would fill with Jo and her friends. They would sit in the back room to talk. Jo visited her mother's weaving class and met her weaving friends.

"So this is the daughter," one of them said. "Your mother's been looking forward to your visit. The only time she misses class is when her daughters are home."

Soon it was time for Jo to leave again. "Mom's colors," she remarked to Sharon as she fingered the brown muffler her mother had woven for her.

80   "Put it on," said Sharon.

Jo did, and as she moved toward the light, hidden colors leaped from the brown fabric. It came alive in the sunlight.

"You know, there's actually red in here," she marveled, "and even bits of green. You'd never know it unless you looked real close."

"Most people don't," Sharon said.

The two sisters fell silent, sharing a rare moment together before their lives diverged again. Their mother's muffler was warm about Jo's neck.

85   At the airport, Jo's mother stood next to Jo's father, leaning slightly toward him as an object of lighter mass naturally tends toward a more substantial one. She was crying.

When Jo was gone she returned to the house, and her loom. And amidst the comings and goings of the lives around her, she sat, a woman bent over a loom, weaving the diverse threads of life into one miraculous, mystical fabric with timeless care.

Response

1. What insight into her mother's life has the author (in the persona of Jo) gained by the time she tells this story? How does she use the central metaphor—of fabric woven on a loom—to communicate her perception?

2. What lesson did the mother take from the childhood incident with Eleanor Leland, related in paragraphs 13 and 20? How was that lesson reinforced by later events in her life? How did it shape her character and behavior?

3. Look through the story to find recurring language that extends

the imagery of weaving fabric. How does Sasaki use this imagery to portray the social and political circumstances of life for her mother's generation?

4. In the end, what do we learn about the mother's life through the descriptions of the fabric she weaves? How is the daughters' relationship with their mother portrayed?

Yellow Woman
Leslie Marmon Silko

In this story, which appeared in her book Storyteller
*(1981), Silko draws on the oral tradition of Yellow
Woman stories among the Laguna and Acoma people
in New Mexico. The central character in these stories
experiences special adventures, such as abduction by
a ka'tsina, a messenger from the spirit world. In this
tradition yellow is the color for woman. While she
takes various forms, Yellow Woman is a spiritual
representation of woman, central to the harmony and
balance of the tribe.*

One

My thigh clung to his with dampness, and I watched
the sun rising up through the tamaracks and willows. The small
brown water birds came to the river and hopped across the mud,
leaving brown scratches in the alkali-white crust. They bathed in
the river silently. I could hear the water, almost at our feet where
the narrow fast channel bubbled and washed green ragged moss and
fern leaves. I looked at him beside me, rolled in the red blanket on
the white river sand. I cleaned the sand out of the cracks between

Leslie Marmon Silko, "Yellow Woman," in *The Man to Send Rain Clouds*,
edited by Kenneth Rosen. New York: Viking Penguin, 1974. Reprinted by permission
of the author.

my toes, squinting because the sun was above the willow trees. I looked at him for the last time, sleeping on the white river sand.

I felt hungry and followed the river south the way we had come the afternoon before, following our footprints that were already blurred by lizard tracks and bug trails. The horses were still lying down, and the black one whinnied when he saw me but he did not get up—maybe it was because the corral was made out of thick cedar branches and the horses had not yet felt the sun like I had. I tried to look beyond the pale red mesas to the pueblo. I knew it was there, even if I could not see it, on the sandrock hill above the river, the same river that moved past me now and had reflected the moon last night.

The horse felt warm underneath me. He shook his head and pawed the sand. The bay whinnied and leaned against the gate trying to follow, and I remembered him asleep in the red blanket beside the river. I slid off the horse and tied him close to the other horse. I walked north with the river again, and the white sand broke loose in footprints over footprints.

"Wake up."

He moved in the blanket and turned his face to me with his eyes still closed. I knelt down to touch him.

"I'm leaving."

He smiled now, eyes still closed. "You are coming with me, remember?" He sat up now with his bare dark chest and belly in the sun.

"Where?"

"To my place."

"And will I come back?"

He pulled his pants on. I walked away from him, feeling him behind me and smelling the willows.

"Yellow Woman," he said.

I turned to face him. "Who are you?" I asked.

He laughed and knelt on the low, sandy bank, washing his face in the river. "Last night you guessed my name, and you knew why I had come."

I stared past him at the shallow moving water and tried to remember the night, but I could only see the moon in the water and remember his warmth around me.

"But I only said that you were him and that I was Yellow Woman—I'm not really her—I have my own name and I come from the pueblo on the other side of the mesa. Your name is Silva and you are a stranger I met by the river yesterday afternoon."

He laughed softly. "What happened yesterday has nothing to do with what you will do today, Yellow Woman."

"I know—that's what I'm saying—the old stories about the ka'tsina spirit and Yellow Woman can't mean us."

My old grandpa like to tell those stories best. There is one about Badger and Coyote who went hunting and were gone all day and when the sun was going down they found a house. There was a girl living there alone, and she had light hair and eyes and she told them that they could sleep with her. Coyote wanted to be with her all night so he sent Badger into a prairie-dog hole, telling him he thought he saw something in it. As soon as Badger crawled in, Coyote blocked up the entrance with rocks and hurried back to Yellow Woman.

20   "Come here," he said gently.

He touched my neck and I moved close to him to feel his breathing and to hear his heart. I was wondering if Yellow Woman had known who she was—if she knew that she would become part of the stories. Maybe she'd had another name that her husband and relatives called her so that only the ka'tsina from the north and the storytellers would know her as Yellow Woman. But I didn't go on; I felt him all around me, pushing me down into the white river sand.

Yellow Woman went away with the spirit from the north and lived with him and his relatives. She was gone for a long time, but then one day she came back and she brought twin boys.

"Do you know the story?"

"What story?" He smiled and pulled me close to him as he said this. I was afraid lying there on the red blanket. All I could know was the way he felt, warm, damp, his body beside me. This is the way it happens in the stories, I was thinking, with no thought beyond the moment she meets the ka'tsina spirit and they go.

25   "I don't have to go. What they tell in stories was real only then, back in time immemorial, like they say."

He stood up and pointed at my clothes tangled in the blanket. "Let's go," he said.

I walked beside him, breathing hard because he walked fast, his hand around my wrist. I had stopped to pull away from him, because his hand felt cool and the sun was high, drying the river bed into alkali. I will see someone, eventually I will see someone, and then I will be certain that he is only a man—some man from nearby—and I will be sure that I am not Yellow Woman. Because she is from out of time past and I live now and I've been to school and there are highways and pickup trucks that Yellow Woman never saw.

It was an easy ride north on horseback. I watched the change from the cottonwood trees along the river to the junipers that brushed past us in the foothills, and finally there were only piñons,

and when I looked up at the rim of the mountain plateau I could see
pine trees growing on the edge. Once I stopped to look down, but
the pale sandstone had disappeared and the river was gone and the
dark lava hills were all around. He touched my hand, not speaking,
but always singing softly a mountain song and looking into my eyes.

I felt hungry and wondered what they were doing at home
now—my mother, my grandmother, my husband, and the baby.
Cooking breakfast, saying, "Where did she go?—maybe kidnaped,"
and Al going to the tribal police with the details: "She went walking
along the river."

The house was made with black lava rock and red mud. It was　　30
high above the spreading miles of arroyos and long mesas. I smelled
a mountain smell of pitch and buck brush. I stood there beside the
black horse, looking down on the small, dim country we had passed,
and I shivered.

"Yellow Woman, come inside where it's warm."

Two

He lit a fire in the stove. It was an old stove with a
round belly and an enamel coffeepot on top. There was only the
stove, some faded Navajo blankets, and a bedroll and cardboard box.
The floor was made of smooth adobe plaster, and there was one small
window facing east. He pointed at the box.

"There's some potatoes and the frying pan." He sat on the floor
with his arms around his knees pulling them close to his chest and
he watched me fry the potatoes. I didn't mind him watching me
because he was always watching me—he had been watching me
since I came upon him sitting on the river bank trimming leaves
from a willow twig with his knife. We ate from the pan and he wiped
the grease from his fingers on his Levis.

"Have you brought women here before?" He smiled and kept
chewing, so I said, "Do you always use the same tricks?"

"What tricks?" He looked at me like he didn't understand.　　35

"The story about being a ka'tsina from the mountains. The
story about Yellow Woman."

Silva was silent, his face was calm.

"I don't believe it. Those stories couldn't happen now," I said.

He shook his head and said softly, "But someday they will talk
about us, and they will say, 'Those two lived long ago when things
like this happened.'"

He stood up and went out. I ate the rest of the potatoes and　　40
thought about things—about the noise the stove was making and

the sound of the mountain wind outside. I remembered yesterday and the day before, and then I went outside.

I walked past the corral to the edge where the narrow trail cut through the black rim rock. I was standing in the sky with nothing around me but the wind that came down from the blue mountain peak behind me. I could see faint mountain images in the distance, miles across the vast spread of mesas and valleys and plains. I wondered who was over there to feel the mountain wind on those sheer blue edges—who walks on the pine needles in those blue mountains.

"Can you see the pueblo?" Silva was standing behind me.

I shook my head. "We're too far away."

"From here I can see the world." He stepped out on the edge. "The Navajo reservation begins over there." He pointed to the east. "The Pueblo boundaries are over here." He looked below us to the south, where the narrow trail seemed to come from. "The Texans have their ranches over there, starting with that valley, the Concho Valley. The Mexicans run some cattle over there too."

45   "Do you ever work for them?"

"I steal from them," Silva answered. The sun was dropping behind us and shadows were filling the land below. I turned away from the edge that dropped forever into the valleys below.

"I'm cold," I said; "I'm going inside." I started wondering about this man who could speak the Pueblo language so well but who lived on a mountain and rustled cattle. I decided that this man Silva must be Navajo, because Pueblo men didn't do things like that.

"You must be a Navajo."

Silva shook his head gently. "Little Yellow Woman," he said, "you never give up, do you? I have told you who I am. The Navajo people know me, too." He knelt down and unrolled the bedroll and spread the extra blankets out on a piece of canvas. The sun was down, and the only light in the house came from outside—the dim orange light from sundown.

50   I stood there and waited for him to crawl under the blankets.

"What are you waiting for?" he said, and I lay down beside him. He undressed me slowly like the night before beside the river— kissing my face gently and running his hands up and down my belly and legs. He took off my pants and then he laughed.

"Why are you laughing?"

"You are breathing so hard."

I pulled away from him and turned my back to him.

55   He pulled me around and pinned me down with his arms and chest. "You don't understand, do you, little Yellow Woman? You will do what I want."

And again he was all around me with his skin slippery against mine, and I was afraid because I understood that his strength could hurt me. I lay underneath him and I knew that he could destroy me. But later, while he slept beside me, I touched his face and I had a feeling—the kind of feeling for him that overcame me that morning along the river. I kissed him on the forehead and he reached out for me.

When I woke up in the morning he was gone. It gave me a strange feeling because for a long time I sat there on the blankets and looked around the little house for some object of his—some proof that he had been there or maybe that he was coming back. Only the blankets and the cardboard box remained. The .30-30 that had been leaning in the corner was gone, and so was the knife I had used the night before. He was gone, and I had my chance to go now. But first I had to eat, because I knew it would be a long walk home.

I found some dried apricots in the cardboard box, and I sat down on a rock at the edge of the plateau rim. There was no wind and the sun warmed me. I was surrounded by silence. I drowsed with apricots in my mouth, and I didn't believe that there were highways or railroads or cattle to steal.

When I woke up, I stared down at my feet in the black mountain dirt. Little black ants were swarming over the pine needles around my foot. They must have smelled the apricots. I thought about my family far below me. They would be wondering about me, because this had never happened to me before. The tribal police would file a report. But if old Grandpa weren't dead he would tell them what happened—he would laugh and say, "Stolen by a ka'tsina, a mountain spirit. She'll come home—they usually do." There are enough of them to handle things. My mother and grandmother will raise the baby like they raised me. Al will find someone else, and they will go on like before, except that there will be a story about the day I disappeared while I was walking along the river. Silva had come for me; he said he had. I did not decide to go. I just went. Moonflowers blossom in the sand hills before dawn, just as I followed him. That's what I was thinking as I wandered along the trail through the pine trees.

It was noon when I got back. When I saw the stone house I remembered that I had meant to go home. But that didn't seem important any more, maybe because there were little blue flowers growing in the meadow behind the stone house and the gray squirrels were playing in the pines next to the house. The horses were standing in the corral, and there was a beef carcass hanging on the shady side of a big pine in front of the house. Flies buzzed around the clotted blood that hung from the carcass. Silva was washing his

60

hands in a bucket full of water. He must have heard me coming because he spoke to me without turning to face me.

"I've been waiting for you."

"I went walking in the big pine trees."

I looked into the bucket full of bloody water with brown-and-white animal hairs floating in it. Silva stood there letting his hand drip, examining me intently.

"Are you coming with me?"

65   "Where?" I asked him.

"To sell the meat in Marquez."

"If you're sure it's O.K."

"I wouldn't ask you if it wasn't," he answered.

He sloshed the water around in the bucket before he dumped it out and set the bucket upside down near the door. I followed him to the corral and watched him saddle the horses. Even beside the horses he looked tall, and I asked him again if he wasn't Navajo. He didn't say anything; he just shook his head and kept cinching up the saddle.

70   "But Navajos are tall."

"Get on the horse," he said, "and let's go."

The last thing he did before we started down the steep trail was to grab the .30-30 from the corner. He slid the rifle into the scabbard that hung from his saddle.

"Do they ever try to catch you?" I asked.

"They don't know who I am."

75   "Then why did you bring the rifle?"

"Because we are going to Marquez where the Mexicans live."

Three

The trail leveled out on a narrow ridge that was steep on both sides like an animal spine. On one side I could see where the trail went around the rocky gray hills and disappeared into the southeast where the pale sandrock mesas stood in the distance near my home. On the other side was a trail that went west, and as I looked far into the distance I thought I saw the little town. But Silva said no, that I was looking in the wrong place, that I just thought I saw houses. After that I quit looking off into the distance; it was hot and the wildflowers were closing up their deep-yellow petals. Only the waxy cactus flowers bloomed in the bright sun, and I saw every color that a cactus blossom can be; the white ones and the red ones were still buds, but the purple and the yellow were blossoms, open full and the most beautiful of all.

Silva saw him before I did. The white man was riding a big gray horse, coming up the trail toward us. He was traveling fast and the gray horse's feet sent rocks rolling off the trail into the dry tumbleweeds. Silva motioned for me to stop and we watched the white man. He didn't see us right away, but finally his horse whinnied at our horses and he stopped. He looked at us briefly before he loped the gray horse across the three hundred yards that separated us. He stopped his horse in front of Silva, and his young fat face was shadowed by the brim of his hat. He didn't look mad, but his small, pale eyes moved from the blood-soaked gunny sacks hanging from my saddle to Silva's face and then back to my face.

"Where did you get the fresh meat?" the white man asked.

"I've been hunting," Silva said, and when he shifted his weight   80
in the saddle the leather creaked.

"The hell you have, Indian. You've been rustling cattle. We've been looking for the thief for a long time."

The rancher was fat, and sweat began to soak through his white cowboy shirt and the wet cloth stuck to the thick rolls of belly fat. He almost seemed to be panting from the exertion of talking, and he smelled rancid, maybe because Silva scared him.

Silva turned to me and smiled. "Go back up the mountain, Yellow Woman."

The white man got angry when he heard Silva speak in a language he couldn't understand. "Don't try anything, Indian. Just keep riding to Marquez. We'll call the state police from there."

The rancher must have been unarmed because he was very   85
frightened and if he had a gun he would have pulled it out then. I turned my horse around and the rancher yelled, "Stop!" I looked at Silva for an instant and there was something ancient and dark—something I could feel in my stomach—in his eyes, and when I glanced at his hand I saw his finger on the trigger of the .30-30 that was still in the saddle scabbard. I slapped my horse across the flank and the sacks of raw meat swung against my knees as the horse leaped up the trail. It was hard to keep my balance, and once I thought I felt the saddle slipping backward; it was because of this that I could not look back.

I didn't stop until I reached the ridge where the trail forked. The horse was breathing deep gasps and there was a dark film of sweat on its neck. I looked down in the direction I had come from, but I couldn't see the place. I waited. The wind came up and pushed warm air past me. I looked up at the sky, pale blue and full of thin clouds and fading vapor trails left by jets.

I think four shots were fired—I remember hearing four hollow explosions that reminded me of deer hunting. There could have been more shots after that, but I couldn't have heard them because my horse was running again and the loose rocks were making too much noise as they scattered around his feet.

Horses have a hard time running downhill, but I went that way instead of uphill to the mountain because I thought it was safer. I felt better with the horse running southeast past the round gray hills that were covered with cedar trees and black lava rock. When I got to the plain in the distance I could see the dark green patches of tamaracks that grew along the river; and beyond the river I could see the beginning of the pale sandrock mesas. I stopped the horse and looked back to see if anyone was coming; then I got off the horse and turned the horse around, wondering if it would go back to its corral under the pines on the mountain. It looked back at me for a moment and then plucked a mouthful of green tumbleweeds before it trotted back up the trail with its ears pointed forward, carrying its head daintily to one side to avoid stepping on the dragging reins. When the horse disappeared over the last hill, the gunny sacks full of meat were still swinging and bouncing.

Four

I walked toward the river on a wood-hauler's road that I knew would eventually lead to the paved road. I was thinking about waiting beside the road for someone to drive by, but by the time I got to the pavement I had decided it wasn't very far to walk if I followed the river back the way Silva and I had come.

90   The river water tasted good, and I sat in the shade under a cluster of silvery willows. I thought about Silva, and I felt sad at leaving him; still, there was something strange about him, and I tried to figure it out all the way back home.

I came back to the place on the river bank where he had been sitting the first time I saw him. The green willow leaves that he had trimmed from the branch were still lying there, wilted in the sand. I saw the leaves and I wanted to go back to him—to kiss him and to touch him—but the mountains were too far away now. And I told myself, because I believe it, he will come back sometime and be waiting again by the river.

I followed the path up from the river into the village. The sun was getting low, and I could smell supper cooking when I got to the screen door of my house. I could hear their voices inside—my mother was telling my grandmother how to fix the Jell-o and my husband, Al, was playing with the baby. I decided to tell them that some Navajo had kidnaped me, but I was sorry that old Grandpa wasn't alive to hear my story because it was the Yellow Woman stories he liked to tell best.

Response

1. The woman has heard the stories about Yellow Woman from her grandfather. "What they tell in stories was real only then, back in time immemorial," she insists in paragraph 25. But Silva says, "Someday they will talk about us, and they will say, 'Those two lived long ago when things like this happened'" (paragraph 38). What is the woman's attitude toward the stories? What does Silko accomplish by having her narrator mention Yellow Woman stories in the beginning?

2. Who is Silva? What indications does the story give of his identity? What are the woman's feelings toward him?

3. After the woman leaves Silva, details of civilized modern life begin to appear within the imagery of the natural landscape. Find examples, and consider their effect in the story.

4. Despite the sacred nature of stories in the tribal tradition, they are seen as inextricably connected with daily life; in other words, the distinction between sacred and ordinary is somehow irrelevant. Keeping this in mind, consider how Silko presents the events of this story. Like all Yellow Woman stories, it is told from the woman's point of view. Mirroring her perceptions, it goes back and forth between mundane details of real life and suggestions of a mystical experience. This could be read as a story about a woman's casual affair with a cattle rustler, or a modern woman meeting a messenger from the ancient spirit world, or even an experience imagined by a restless woman recalling her grandfather's stories. Do you think it is important to decide? What can readers infer from this ambiguity?

Seventeen Syllables

Hisaye Yamamoto

> *This is the title story from Yamamoto's book*
> Seventeen Syllables and Other Stories *(1988); it was*
> *first published in* Partisan Review *in 1949. This story,*
> *based on Yamamoto's own mother's experience,*
> *treats two themes that recur in her writing: the*
> *restricted lives of first-generation Japanese immigrant*
> *women and the conflicts of language and culture in*
> *their relationships with their American-born Nisei*
> *(second-generation) children.*

The first Rosie knew that her mother had taken to writing poems was one evening when she finished one and read it aloud for her daughter's approval. It was about cats, and Rosie pretended to understand it thoroughly and appreciate it no end, partly because she hesitated to disillusion her mother about the quantity and quality of Japanese she had learned in all the years now that she had been going to Japanese school every Saturday (and Wednesday, too, in the summer). Even so, her mother must have been skeptical about the depth of Rosie's understanding, because she explained afterwards about the kind of poem she was trying to write.

See, Rosie, she said, it was a *haiku*, a poem in which she must pack all her meaning into seventeen syllables only, which were divided into three lines of five, seven, and five syllables. In the one she had just read, she had tried to capture the charm of a kitten, as well as comment on the superstition that owning a cat of three colors meant good luck.

"Yes, yes, I understand. How utterly lovely," Rosie said, and her mother, either satisfied or seeing through the deception and resigned, went back to composing.

The truth was that Rosie was lazy; English lay ready on the tongue but Japanese had to be searched for and examined, and even then put forth tentatively (probably to meet with laughter). It was so much easier to say yes, yes, even when one meant no, no. Besides, this was what was in her mind to say: I was looking through one of your magazines from Japan last night, Mother, and towards the back I found some *haiku* in English that delighted me. There was one that made me giggle off and on until I fell asleep—

It is morning, and lo!
I lie awake, comme il faut,
sighing for some dough.

Now, how to reach her mother, how to communicate the melancholy song? Rosie knew formal Japanese by fits and starts, her mother had even less English, no French. It was much more possible to say yes, yes.

It developed that her mother was writing the *haiku* for a daily newspaper, the *Mainichi Shimbun*, that was published in San Francisco. Los Angeles, to be sure, was closer to the farming community in which the Hayashi family lived and several Japanese vernaculars were printed there, but Rosie's parents said they preferred the tone of the northern paper. Once a week, the *Mainichi* would have a section devoted to *haiku*, and her mother became an extravagant contributor, taking for herself the blossoming pen name, Ume Hanazono.

So Rosie and her father lived for awhile with two women, her mother and Ume Hanazono. Her mother (Tome Hayashi by name) kept house, cooked, washed, and, along with her husband and the Carrascos, the Mexican family hired for the harvest, did her ample share of picking tomatoes out in the sweltering fields and boxing them in tidy strata in the cool packing shed. Ume Hanazono, who came to life after the dinner dishes were done, was an earnest, muttering stranger who often neglected speaking when spoken to and stayed busy at the parlor table as late as midnight scribbling with pencil on scratch paper or carefully copying characters on good paper with her fat, pale green Parker.

The new interest had some repercussions on the household routine. Before, Rosie had been accustomed to her parents and herself taking their hot baths early and going to bed almost immediately afterwards, unless her parents challenged each other to a game of flower cards or unless company dropped in. Now if her father wanted to play cards, he had to resort to solitaire (at which he always cheated fearlessly), and if a group of friends came over, it was bound to contain someone who was also writing *haiku*, and the small assemblage would be split in two, her father entertaining the non-literary members and her mother comparing ecstatic notes with the visiting poet.

If they went out, it was more of the same thing. But Ume Hanazono's life span, even for a poet's, was very brief—perhaps three months at most.

10   One night they went over to see the Hayano family in the neighboring town to the west, an adventure both painful and attractive to Rosie. It was attractive because there were four Hayano girls, all lovely and each one named after a season of the year (Haru, Natsu, Aki, Fuyu), painful because something had been wrong with Mrs. Hayano ever since the birth of her first child. Rosie would sometimes watch Mrs. Hayano, reputed to have been the belle of her native village, making her way about a room, stooped, slowly shuffling, violently trembling (*always* trembling), and she would be reminded that this woman, in this same condition, had carried and given issue to three babies. She would look wonderingly at Mr. Hayano, handsome, tall, and strong, and she would look at her four pretty friends. But it was not a matter she could come to any decision about.

On this visit, however, Mrs. Hayano sat all evening in the rocker, as motionless and unobtrusive as it was possible for her to be, and Rosie found the greater part of the evening practically anaesthetic. Too, Rosie spent most of it in the girls' room, because Haru, the garrulous one, said almost as soon as the bows and other greetings were over, "Oh, you must see my new coat!"

It was a pale plaid of grey, sand, and blue, with an enormous collar, and Rosie, seeing nothing special in it, said, "Gee, how nice."

"Nice?" said Haru, indignantly. "Is that all you can say about it? It's gorgeous! And so cheap, too. Only seventeen-ninety-eight, because it was a sale. The saleslady said it was twenty-five dollars regular."

"Gee," said Rosie. Natsu, who never said much and when she

said anything said it shyly, fingered the coat covetously and Haru
pulled it away.

"Mine," she said, putting it on. She minced in the aisle be-   15
tween the two large beds and smiled happily. "Let's see how your
mother likes it."

She broke into the front room and the adult conversation and
went to stand in front of Rosie's mother, while the rest watched
from the door. Rosie's mother was properly envious. "May I inherit
it when you're through with it?"

Haru, pleased, giggled and said yes, she could, but Natsu reminded gravely from the door, "You promised me, Haru."

Everyone laughed but Natsu, who shamefacedly retreated into
the bedroom. Haru came in laughing, taking off the coat. "We were
only kidding, Natsu," she said. "Here, you try it on now."

After Natsu buttoned herself into the coat, inspected herself
solemnly in the bureau mirror, and reluctantly shed it, Rosie, Aki,
and Fuyu got their turns, and Fuyu, who was eight, drowned in it
while her sisters and Rosie doubled up in amusement. They all went
into the front room later, because Haru's mother quaveringly called
to her to fix the tea and rice cakes and open a can of sliced peaches
for everybody. Rosie noticed that her mother and Mr. Hayano were
talking together at the little table—they were discussing a *haiku*
that Mr. Hayano was planning to send to the *Mainichi*, while her
father was sitting at one end of the sofa looking through a copy of
Life, the new picture magazine. Occasionally, her father would comment on a photograph, holding it toward Mrs. Hayano and speaking
to her as he always did—loudly, as though he thought someone such
as she must surely be at least a trifle deaf also.

The five girls had their refreshments at the kitchen table, and   20
it was while Rosie was showing the sisters her trick of swallowing
peach slices without chewing (she chased each slippery crescent
down with a swig of tea) that her father brought his empty teacup
and untouched saucer to the sink and said, "Come on, Rosie, we're
going home now."

"Already?" asked Rosie.

"Work tomorrow," he said.

He sounded irritated, and Rosie, puzzled, gulped one last yellow slice and stood up to go, while the sisters began protesting, as
was their wont.

"We have to get up at five-thirty," he told them, going into the
front room quickly, so that they did not have their usual chance to
hang onto his hands and plead for an extension of time.

Rosie, following, saw that her mother and Mr. Hayano were   25
sipping tea and still talking together, while Mrs. Hayano concen-

trated, quivering, on raising the handleless Japanese cup to her lips with both her hands and lowering it back to her lap. Her father, saying nothing, went out the door, onto the bright porch, and down the steps. Her mother looked up and asked, "Where is he going?"

"Where is he going?" Rosie said. "He said we were going home now."

"Going home?" Her mother looked with embarrassment at Mr. Hayano and his absorbed wife and then forced a smile. "He must be tired," she said.

Haru was not giving up yet. "May Rosie stay overnight?" she asked, and Natsu, Aki, and Fuyu came to reinforce their sister's plea by helping her make a circle around Rosie's mother. Rosie, for once having no desire to stay, was relieved when her mother, apologizing to the perturbed Mr. and Mrs. Hayano for her father's abruptness at the same time, managed to shake her head no at the quartet, kindly but adamant, so that they broke their circle and let her go.

Rosie's father looked ahead into the windshield as the two joined him. "I'm sorry," her mother said. "You must be tired." Her father, stepping on the starter, said nothing. "You know how I get when it's *haiku*," she continued, "I forget what time it is." He only grunted.

30   As they rode homeward silently, Rosie, sitting between, felt a rush of hate for both—for her mother for begging, for her father for denying her mother. I wish this old Ford would crash, right now, she thought, then immediately, no, no, I wish my father would laugh, but it was too late: already the vision had passed through her mind of the green pick-up crumpled in the dark against one of the mighty eucalyptus trees they were just riding past, of the three contorted, bleeding bodies, one of them hers.

Rosie ran between two patches of tomatoes, her heart working more rambunctiously than she had ever known it to. How lucky it was that Aunt Taka and Uncle Gimpachi had come tonight, though, how very lucky. Otherwise she might not have really kept her half-promise to meet Jesus Carrasco. Jesus was going to be a senior in September at the same school she went to, and his parents were the ones helping with the tomatoes this year. She and Jesus, who hardly remembered seeing each other at Cleveland High where there were so many other people and two whole grades between them, had become great friends this summer—he always had a joke for her when he periodically drove the loaded pick-up up from the fields to the shed where she was usually sorting while her mother and father did the packing, and they laughed a great deal together over infinitesimal repartee during the afternoon break for chilled watermelon or ice cream in the shade of the shed.

What she enjoyed most was racing him to see which could finish picking a double row first. He, who could work faster, would
tease her by slowing down until she thought she would surely pass
him this time, then speeding up furiously to leave her several
sprawling vines behind. Once he had made her screech hideously by
crossing over, while her back was turned, to place atop the tomatoes
in her green-stained bucket a truly monstrous, pale green worm (it
had looked more like an infant snake). And it was when they had
finished a contest this morning, after she had pantingly pointed a
green finger at the immature tomatoes evident in the lugs at the end
of his row and he had returned the accusation (with justice), that he
had startlingly brought up the matter of their possibly meeting outside the range of both their parents' dubious eyes.

"What for?" she had asked.

"I've got a secret I want to tell you," he said.

"Tell me now," she demanded.   35

"It won't be ready till tonight," he said.

She laughed. "Tell me tomorrow then."

"It'll be gone tomorrow," he threatened.

"Well, for seven hakes, what is it?" she had asked, more than
twice, and when he had suggested that the packing shed would be
an appropriate place to find out, she had cautiously answered maybe.
She had not been certain she was going to keep the appointment
until the arrival of mother's sister and her husband. Their coming
seemed a sort of signal of permission, of grace, and she had definitely
made up her mind to lie and leave as she was bowing them welcome.

So as soon as everyone appeared settled back for the evening,   40
she announced loudly that she was going to the privy outside, "I'm
going to the *benjo!*" and slipped out the door. And now that she was
actually on her way, her heart pumped in such an undisciplined way
that she could hear it with her ears. It's because I'm running, she
told herself, slowing to a walk. The shed was up ahead, one more
patch away, in the middle of the fields. Its bulk, looming in the
dimness, took on a sinisterness that was funny when Rosie reminded herself that it was only a wooden frame with a canvas roof
and three canvas walls that made a slapping noise on breezy days.

Jesus was sitting on the narrow plank that was the sorting platform and she went around to the other side and jumped backwards
to seat herself on the rim of a packing stand. "Well, tell me," she
said without greeting, thinking her voice sounded reassuringly familiar.

"I saw you coming out the door," Jesus said. "I heard you running part of the way, too."

"Uh-huh," Rosie said. "Now tell me the secret."

"I was afraid you wouldn't come." he said.

45   Rosie delved around on the chicken-wire bottom of the stall for number two tomatoes, ripe, which she was sitting beside, and came up with a left-over that felt edible. She bit into it and began sucking out the pulp and seeds. "I'm here," she pointed out.

"Rosie, are you sorry you came?"

"Sorry? What for?" she said. "You said you were going to tell me something."

"I will, I will," Jesus said, but his voice contained disappointment, and Rosie fleetingly felt the older of the two, realizing a brand-new power which vanished without category under her recognition.

"I have to go back in a minute," she said. "My aunt and uncle are here from Wintersburg. I told them I was going to the privy."

50   Jesus laughed. "You funny thing," he said. "You slay me!"

"Just because you have a bathroom *inside*," Rosie said. "Come on, tell me."

Chuckling, Jesus came around to lean on the stand facing her. They still could not see each other very clearly, but Rosie noticed that Jesus became very sober again as he took the hollow tomato from her hand and dropped it back into the stall. When he took hold of her empty hand, she could find no words to protest; her vocabulary had become distressingly constricted and she thought desperately that all that remained intact now was yes and no and oh, and even these few sounds would not easily come out. Thus, kissed by Jesus, Rosie fell for the first time entirely victim to a helplessness delectable beyond speech. But the terrible, beautiful sensation lasted no more than a second, and the reality of Jesus' lips and tongue and teeth and hands made her pull away with such strength that she nearly tumbled.

Rosie stopped running as she approached the lights from the windows of home. How long since she had left? She could not guess, but gasping yet, she went to the privy in back and locked herself in. Her own breathing deafened her in the dark, close space, and she sat and waited until she could hear at last the nightly calling of the frogs and crickets. Even then, all she could think to say was oh, my, and the pressure of Jesus' face against her face would not leave.

No one had missed her in the parlor, however, and Rosie walked in and through quickly, announcing that she was next going to take a bath. "Your father's in the bathhouse," her mother said, and Rosie, in her room, recalled that she had not seen him when she entered. There had been only Aunt Taka and Uncle Gimpachi with her mother at the table, drinking tea. She got her robe and straw sandals and crossed the parlor again to go outside. Her mother was telling them about the *haiku* competition in the *Mainichi* and the poem she had entered.

Rosie met her father coming out of the bathhouse. "Are you   55
through, Father?" she asked. "I was going to ask you to scrub my back."

"Scrub your own back," he said shortly, going toward the main house.

"What have I done now?" she yelled after him. She suddenly felt like doing a lot of yelling. But he did not answer, and she went into the bathhouse. Turning on the dangling light, she removed her denims and T-shirt and threw them in the big carton for dirty clothes standing next to the washing machine. Her other things she took with her into the bath compartment to wash after her bath. After she had scooped a basin of hot water from the square wooden tub, she sat on the grey cement of the floor and soaped herself at exaggerated leisure, singing "Red Sails in the Sunset" at the top of her voice and using da-da-da where she suspected her words. Then, standing up, still singing, for she was possessed by the notion that any attempt now to analyze would result in spoilage and she believed that the larger her volume the less she would be able to hear herself think,she obtained more hot water and poured it on until she was free of lather. Only then did she allow herself to step into the steaming vat, one leg first, then the remainder of her body inch by inch until the water no longer stung and she could move around at will.

She took a long time soaking, afterwards remembering to go around outside to stoke the embers of the tin-lined fireplace beneath the tub and to throw on a few more sticks so that the water might keep its heat for her mother, and when she finally returned to the parlor, she found her mother still talking *haiku* with her aunt and uncle, the three of them on another round of tea. Her father was nowhere in sight.

At Japanese school the next day (Wednesday, it was), Rosie was grave and giddy by turns. Preoccupied at her desk in the row for students on Book Eight, she made up for it at recess by performing wild mimicry for the benefit of her friend Chizuko. She held her nose and whined a witticism or two in what she considered was the manner of Fred Allen; she assumed intoxication and a British accent to go over the climax of the Rudy Vallee recording of the pub conversation about William Ewart Gladstone; she was the child Shirley Temple piping, "On the Good Ship Lollipop"; she was the gentleman soprano of the Four Inkspots trilling, "If I Didn't Care." And she felt reasonably satisfied when Chizuko wept and gasped, "Oh, Rosie, you ought to be in the movies!"

60   Her father came after her at noon, bringing her sandwiches of minced ham and two nectarines to eat while she rode, so that she could pitch right into the sorting when they got home. The lugs were piling up, he said, and the ripe tomatoes in them would probably have to be taken to the cannery tomorrow if they were not ready for the produce haulers tonight. "This heat's not doing them any good. And we've got no time for a break today."

It *was* hot, probably the hottest day of the year, and Rosie's blouse stuck damply to her back even under the protection of the canvas. But she worked as efficiently as a flawless machine and kept the stalls heaped, with one part of her mind listening in to the parental murmuring about the heat and the tomatoes and with another part planning the exact words she would say to Jesus when he drove up with the first load of the afternoon. But when at last she saw that the pick-up was coming, her hands went berserk and the tomatoes started falling in the wrong stalls, and her father said, "Hey, hey! Rosie, watch what you're doing!"

"Well, I have to go to the *benjo*," she said, hiding panic.

"Go in the weeds over there," he said, only half-joking.

"Oh, Father!" she protested.

65   "Oh, go on home," her mother said. "We'll make out for awhile."

In the privy Rosie peered through a knothole toward the fields, watching as much as she could of Jesus. Happily she thought she saw him look in the direction of the house from time to time before he finished unloading and went back toward the patch where his mother and father worked. As she was heading for the shed, a very presentable black car purred up the dirt driveway to the house and its driver motioned to her. Was this the Hayashi home, he wanted to know. She nodded. Was she a Hayashi? Yes, she said, thinking that he was a good-looking man. He got out of the car with a huge, flat package and she saw that he warmly wore a business suit. "I have something here for your mother then," he said, in a more elegant Japanese than she was used to.

She told him where her mother was and he came along with her, patting his face with an immaculate white handkerchief and saying something about the coolness of San Francisco. To her surprised mother and father, he bowed and introduced himself as, among other things, the *haiku* editor of the *Mainichi Shimbun*, saying that since he had been coming as far as Los Angeles anyway, he had decided to bring her the first prize she had won in the recent contest.

"First prize?" her mother echoed, believing and not believing, pleased and overwhelmed. Handed the package with a bow, she bobbed her head up and down numerous times to express her utter gratitude.

"It is nothing much," he added, "but I hope it will serve as a token of our great appreciation for your contributions and our great admiration of your considerable talent."

"I am not worthy," she said, falling easily into his style. "It is   70
I who should make some sign of my humble thanks for being permitted to contribute."

"No, no, to the contrary," he said, bowing again.

But Rosie's mother insisted, and then saying that she knew she was being unorthodox, she asked if she might open the package because her curiosity was so great. Certainly she might. In fact, he would like her reaction to it, for personally, it was one of his favorite *Hiroshiges*.

Rosie thought it was a pleasant picture, which looked to have been sketched with delicate quickness. There were pink clouds, containing some graceful calligraphy, and a sea that was a pale blue except at the edges, containing four sampans with indications of people in them. Pines edged the water and on the far-off beach there was a cluster of thatched huts towered over by pine-dotted mountains of grey and blue. The frame was scalloped and gilt.

After Rosie's mother pronounced it without peer and somewhat prodded her father into nodding agreement, she said Mr. Kuroda must at least have a cup of tea after coming all this way, and although Mr. Kuroda did not want to impose, he soon agreed that a cup of tea would be refreshing and went along with her to the house, carrying the picture for her.

"Ha, your mother's crazy!" Rosie's father said, and Rosie   75
laughed uneasily as she resumed judgment on the tomatoes. She had emptied six lugs when he broke into an imaginary conversation with Jesus to tell her to go and remind her mother of the tomatoes, and she went slowly.

Mr. Kuroda was in his shirtsleeves expounding some *haiku* theory as he munched a rice cake, and her mother was rapt. Abashed in the great man's presence, Rosie stood next to her mother's chair until her mother looked up inquiringly, and then she started to whisper the message, but her mother pushed her gently away and reproached, "You are not being very polite to our guest."

"Father says the tomatoes . . ." Rosie said aloud, smiling foolishly.

"Tell him I shall only be a minute," her mother said, speaking the language of Mr. Kuroda.

When Rosie carried the reply to her father, he did not seem to hear and she said again, "Mother says she'll be back in a minute."

80   "All right, all right," he nodded, and they worked again in silence. But suddenly, her father uttered an incredible noise, exactly like the cork of a bottle popping, and the next Rosie knew, he was stalking angrily toward the house, almost running in fact, and she chased after him crying, "Father! Father! What are you going to do?"

He stopped long enough to order her back to the shed. "Never mind!" he shouted. "Get on with the sorting!"

And from the place in the fields where she stood, frightened and vacillating, Rosie saw her father enter the house. Soon Mr. Kuroda came out alone, putting on his coat. Mr. Kuroda got into his car and backed out down the driveway onto the highway. Next her father emerged, also alone, something in his arms (it was the picture, she realized), and, going over to the bathhouse woodpile, he threw the picture on the ground and picked up the axe. Smashing the picture, glass and all (she heard the explosion faintly), he reached over for the kerosene that was used to encourage the bath fire and poured it over the wreckage. I am dreaming, Rosie said to herself, I am dreaming, but her father, having made sure that his act of cremation was irrevocable, was even then returning to the fields.

Rosie ran past him and toward the house. What had become of her mother? She burst into the parlor and found her mother at the back window watching the dying fire. They watched together until there remained only a feeble smoke under the blazing sun. Her mother was very calm.

"Do you know why I married your father?" she said without turning.

85   "No," said Rosie. It was the most frightening question she had ever been called upon to answer. Don't tell me now, she wanted to say, tell me tomorrow, tell me next week, don't tell me today. But she knew she would be told now, that the telling would combine with the other violence of the hot afternoon to level her life, her world to the very ground.

It was like a story out of the magazines illustrated in sepia, which she had consumed so greedily for a period until the information had somehow reached her that those wretchedly unhappy autobiographies, offered to her as the testimonials of living men and women, were largely inventions: Her mother, at nineteen, had come to America and married her father as an alternative to suicide.

At eighteen she had been in love with the first son of one of the well-to-do families in her village. The two had met whenever and wherever they could, secretly, because it would not have done for his family to see him favor her—her father had no money; he was a drunkard and a gambler besides. She had learned she was with child; an excellent match had already been arranged for her lover.

Despised by her family, she had given premature birth to a stillborn son, who would be seventeen now. Her family did not turn her out, but she could no longer project herself in any direction without refreshing in them the memory of her indiscretion. She wrote to Aunt Taka, her favorite sister in America, threatening to kill herself if Aunt Taka would not send for her. Aunt Taka hastily arranged a marriage with a young man of whom she knew, but lately arrived from Japan, a young man of simple mind, it was said, but of kindly heart. The young man was never told why his unseen betrothed was so eager to hasten the day of meeting.

The story was told perfectly, with neither groping for words nor untoward passion. It was as though her mother had memorized it by heart, reciting it to herself so many times over that its nagging vileness had long since gone.

"I had a brother then?" Rosie asked, for this was what seemed to matter now; she would think about the other later, she assured herself, pushing back the illumination which threatened all that darkness that had hitherto been merely mysterious or even glamorous. "A half-brother?"

"Yes."

90

"I would have liked a brother," she said.

Suddenly, her mother knelt on the floor and took her by the wrists. "Rosie," she said urgently. "Promise me you will never marry!" Shocked more by the request than the revelation, Rosie stared at her mother's face. Jesus, Jesus, she called silently, not certain whether she was invoking the help of the son of the Carrascos or of God, until there returned sweetly the memory of Jesus' hand, how it had touched her and where. Still her mother waited for an answer, holding her wrists so tightly that her hands were going numb. She tried to pull free. Promise, her mother whispered fiercely, promise. Yes, yes, I promise, Rosie said. But for an instant she turned away, and her mother, hearing the familiar glib agreement, released her. Oh you, you, you, her eyes and twisted mouth said, you fool. Rosie, covering her face, began at last to cry, and the embrace and consoling hand came much later than she expected.

Response

1. Two plots unfold in this story: Rosie's and her mother's. Rosie's story, about her first sexual encounter and awakening to the possibility of romantic love, stands in counterpoint to her mother's, about the destruction of her creative identity and death of romantic love. What is the effect of her mother's story

on Rosie? How does her mother's experience become inter-
twined with her own in the end?

2. How does the ending of the story mirror the beginning? How
    have mother's and daughter's outlooks changed? What barriers
    stand between them? What does each understand and fail to
    understand about the other?

3. What traits of character do Rosie and her mother have in com-
    mon? In the conclusion of the story, why does Rosie's mother
    make her shocking proposal to Rosie? Why does her mother's
    "embrace and consoling hand" come to Rosie "much later than
    she expected"?

4. In her introduction to the book *Seventeen Syllables and Other
    Stories*, King-Kok Cheung observes that "Yamamoto seldom
    casts her characters as heroes or villains, and rarely presents
    personal interaction in simple black and white terms." She also
    says that in Yamamoto's stories, "characters are often caught
    in circumstances that render unqualified approval or condem-
    nation difficult." Do you think that these comments apply in
    the case of Rosie's father? What do you think motivates Mr.
    Hayashi to behave as he does? How does his wife's story, in the
    end, shed light on his behavior?

5. Compare this story to Maxine Hong Kingston's "No Name
    Woman." What similar themes are treated in the two stories?
    How do the authors' perspectives on these themes compare?

IV
A SENSE OF TIME
AND PLACE

Fifth Avenue, Uptown: A Letter from Harlem

James Baldwin

James Baldwin wrote this essay upon returning to the neighborhood in Harlem where he had lived as a child. It was published in 1960 in Baldwin's second collection of essays, Nobody Knows My Name.

There is a housing project standing now where the house in which we grew up once stood, and one of those stunted city trees is snarling where our doorway used to be. This is on the rehabilitated side of the avenue. The other side of the avenue—for progress takes time—has not been rehabilitated yet and it looks exactly as it looked in the days when we sat with our noses pressed against the window-pane, longing to be allowed to go "across the street." The grocery store which gave us credit is still there, and there can be no doubt that it is still giving credit. The people in the project certainly need it—far more, indeed, than they ever needed the project. The last time I passed by, the Jewish proprietor was still standing among his shelves, looking sadder and heavier but scarcely any older. Farther down the block stands the shoe-repair store in which our shoes were repaired until reparation became impossible and in which, then, we bought all our "new" ones. The Negro proprietor is still in the window, head down, working at the leather.

These two, I imagine, could tell a long tale if they would (perhaps they would be glad to if they could), having watched so many, for so long, struggling in the fishhooks, the barbed wire, of this avenue.

The avenue is elsewhere the renowned and elegant Fifth. The area I am describing, which, in today's gang parlance, would be called "the turf," is bounded by Lenox Avenue on the west, the Harlem River on the east, 135th Street on the north, and 130th Street on the south. We never lived beyond these boundaries; this is where we grew up. Walking along 145th Street—for example—familiar as it is, and similar, does not have the same impact because I did not know any of the people on the block. But when I turn east on 131st Street and Lenox Avenue, there is first a soda-pop joint, then a shoeshine "parlor," then a grocery store, then a dry cleaners', then the houses. All along the street there are people who watched me grow up, people who grew up with me, people I watched grow up along with my brothers and sisters; and, sometimes in my arms, sometimes underfoot, sometimes at my shoulder—or on it—their children, a riot, a forest of children, who include my nieces and nephews.

When we reach the end of this long block, we find ourselves on wide, filthy, hostile Fifth Avenue, facing that project which hangs over the avenue like a monument to the folly, and the cowardice, of good intentions. All along the block, for anyone who knows it, are immense human gaps, like craters. These gaps are not created merely by those who have moved away, inevitably into some other ghetto; or by those who have risen, almost always into a greater capacity for self-loathing and self-delusion; or yet by those who, by whatever means—War II, the Korean war, a policeman's gun or billy, a gang war, a brawl, madness, an overdose of heroin, or, simply, unnatural exhaustion—are dead. I am talking about those who are left, and I am talking principally about the young. What are they doing? Well, some, a minority, are fanatical churchgoers, members of the more extreme of the Holy Roller sects. Many, many more are "moslems," by affiliation or sympathy, that is to say that they are united by nothing more—and nothing less—than a hatred of the white world and all its works. They are present, for example, at every Buy Black street-corner meeting—meetings in which the speaker urges his hearers to cease trading with white men and establish a separate economy. Neither the speaker nor his hearers can possibly do this, of course, since Negroes do not own General Motors or RCA or the A & P, nor, indeed, do they own more than a wholly insufficient fraction of anything else in Harlem (those who *do* own anything are more interested in their profits than in their fellows). But these meetings nevertheless keep alive in the participators a certain pride of bitterness without which, however futile this bitterness may be, they could scarcely remain alive at all. Many have given up. They stay home and watch the TV screen, living on the earnings of their parents, cousins, brothers, or uncles, and only leave the house to go to the movies or to the nearest bar. "How're you making it?" one may ask, running into them along the block, or in the bar. "Oh, I'm TVing it"; with the saddest, sweetest, most shame-faced of smiles, and from a great distance. This distance one is compelled to respect; anyone who has traveled so far will not easily be dragged again into the world. There are further retreats, of course, than the TV screen or the bar. There are those who are simply sitting on their stoops, "stoned," animated for a moment only, and hideously, by the approach of someone who may lend them the money for a "fix." Or by the approach of someone from whom they can purchase it, one of the shrewd ones, on the way to prison or just coming out.

And the others, who have avoided all of these deaths, get up in   5 the morning and go downtown to meet "the man." They work in the white man's world all day and come home in the evening to this fetid block. They struggle to instill in their children some private sense of honor or dignity which will help the child survive. This means, of course, that they must struggle, stolidly, incessantly, to keep this sense alive in themselves, in spite of the insults, the indifference, and the cruelty they are certain to encounter in their working day. They patiently browbeat the landlord into fixing the heat, the plaster, the plumbing; this demands prodigious patience; nor is patience usually enough. In trying to make their hovels habitable, they are perpetually throwing good money after bad. Such frustration, so long endured, is driving many strong, admirable men and women whose only crime is color to the very gates of paranoia.

One remembers them from another time—playing handball in the playground, going to church, wondering if they were going to be promoted at school. One remembers them going off to war—gladly, to escape this block. One remembers their return. Perhaps one remembers their wedding day. And one sees where the girl is now— vainly looking for salvation from some other embittered, trussed, and struggling boy—and sees the all-but-abandoned children in the streets.

Now I am perfectly aware that there are other slums in which white men are fighting for their lives, and mainly losing. I know that blood is also flowing through those streets and that the human damage there is incalculable. People are continually pointing out to me the wretchedness of white people in order to console me for the wretchedness of blacks. But an itemized account of the American failure does not console me and it should not console anyone else.

That hundreds of thousands of white people are living, in effect, no better than the "niggers" is not a fact to be regarded with complacency. The social and moral bankruptcy suggested by this fact is of the bitterest, most terrifying kind.

The people, however, who believe that this democratic anguish has some consoling value are always pointing out that So-and-So, white, and So-and-So, black, rose from the slums into the big time. The existence—the public existence—of, say, Frank Sinatra and Sammy Davis, Jr. proves to them that America is still the land of opportunity and that inequalities vanish before the determined will. It proves nothing of the sort. The determined will is rare—at the moment, in this country, it is unspeakably rare—and the inequalities suffered by the many are in no way justified by the rise of a few. A few have always risen—in every country, every era, and in the teeth of regimes which can by no stretch of the imagination be thought of as free. Not all of these people, it is worth remembering, left the world better than they found it. The determined will is rare, but it is not invariably benevolent. Furthermore, the American equation of success with the big times reveals an awful disrespect for human life and human achievement. This equation has placed our cities among the most dangerous in the world and has placed our youth among the most empty and most bewildered. The situation of our youth is not mysterious. Children have never been very good at listening to their elders, but they have never failed to imitate them. They must, they have no other models. That is exactly what our children are doing. They are imitating our immorality, our disrespect for the pain of others.

All other slum dwellers, when the bank account permits it, can move out of the slum and vanish altogether from the eye of persecution. No Negro in this country has ever made that much money and it will be a long time before any Negro does. The Negroes in Harlem, who have no money, spend what they have on such gimcracks as they are sold. These include "wider" TV screens, more "faithful" hi-fi sets, more "powerful" cars, all of which, of course, are obsolete long before they are paid for. Anyone who has ever struggled with poverty knows how extremely expensive it is to be poor; and if one is a member of a captive population, economically speaking, one's feet have simply been placed on the treadmill forever. One is victimized, economically, in a thousand ways—rent, for example, or car insurance. Go shopping one day in Harlem—for anything—and compare Harlem prices and quality with those downtown.

10   The people who have managed to get off this block have only got as far as a more respectable ghetto. This respectable ghetto does

not even have the advantages of the disreputable one—friends, neighbors, a familiar church, and friendly tradesmen; and it is not, moreover, in the nature of any ghetto to remain respectable long. Every Sunday, people who have left the block take the lonely ride back, dragging their increasingly discontented children with them. They spend the day talking, not always with words, about the trouble they've seen and the trouble—one must watch their eyes as they watch their children—they are only too likely to see. For children do not like ghettos. It takes them nearly no time to discover exactly why they are there.

The projects in Harlem are hated. They are hated almost as much as policemen, and this is saying a great deal. And they are hated for the same reason: both reveal, unbearably, the real attitude of the white world, no matter how many liberal speeches are made, no matter how many lofty editorials are written, no matter how many civil-rights commissions are set up.

The projects are hideous, of course, there being a law, apparently respected throughout the world, that popular housing shall be as cheerless as a prison. They are lumped all over Harlem, colorless, bleak, high, and revolting. The wide windows look out on Harlem's invincible and indescribable squalor: the Park Avenue railroad tracks, around which, about forty years ago, the present dark community began; the unrehabilitated houses, bowed down, it would seem, under the great weight of frustration and bitterness they contain; the dark, the ominous schoolhouses from which the child may emerge maimed, blinded, hooked, or enraged for life; and the churches, churches, block upon block of churches, niched in the walls like cannon in the walls of a fortress. Even if the administration of the projects were not so insanely humiliating (for example: one must report raises in salary to the management, which will then eat up the profit by raising one's rent; the management has the right to know who is staying in your apartment; the management can ask you to leave, at their discretion), the projects would still be hated because they are an insult to the meanest intelligence.

Harlem got its first private project, Riverton[1]—which is now,

---

[1] The inhabitants of Riverton were much embittered by this description; they have, apparently, forgotten how their project came into being; and have repeatedly informed me that I cannot possibly be referring to Riverton, but to another housing project which is directly across the street. It is quite clear, I think, that I have no interest in accusing any individuals or families of the depredations herein described: but neither can I deny the evidence of my own eyes. Nor do I blame anyone in Harlem for making the best of a dreadful bargain. But anyone who lives in Harlem and imagines that he has *not* struck this bargain, or that what he takes to be his status (in whose eyes?) protects him against the common pain, demoralization, and danger, is simply self-deluded. [author's note]

naturally, a slum—about twelve years ago because at that time Negroes were not allowed to live in Stuyvesant Town. Harlem watched
Riverton go up, therefore, in the most violent bitterness of spirit,
and hated it long before the builders arrived. They began hating it at
about the time people began moving out of their condemned houses
to make room for this additional proof of how thoroughly the white
world despised them. And they had scarcely moved in, naturally,
before they began smashing windows, defacing walls, urinating in
the elevators, and fornicating in the playgrounds. Liberals, both
white and black, were appalled at the spectacle. I was appalled by
the liberal innocence—or cynicism, which comes out in practice as
much the same thing. Other people were delighted to be able to
point to proof positive that nothing could be done to better the lot
of the colored people. They were, and are, right in one respect: that
nothing can be done as long as they are treated like colored people.
The people in Harlem know they are living there because white people do not think they are good enough to live anywhere else. No
amount of "improvement" can sweeten this fact. Whatever money
is now being earmarked to improve this, or any other ghetto, might
as well be burnt. A ghetto can be improved in one way only: out of
existence.

Similarly, the only way to police a ghetto is to be oppressive.
None of the Police Commissioner's men, even with the best will in
the world, have any way of understanding the lives led by the people
they swagger about in twos and threes controlling. Their very presence is an insult, and it would be, even if they spent their entire day
feeding gumdrops to children. They represent the force of the white
world, and the world's real intentions are, simply, for the world's
criminal profit and ease, to keep the black man corralled up here, in
his place. The badge, the gun in the holster, and the swinging club
make vivid what will happen should his rebellion become overt.
Rare, indeed, is the Harlem citizen, from the most circumspect
church member to the most shiftless adolescent, who does not have
a long tale to tell of police incompetence, injustice, or brutality. I
myself have witnessed and endured it more than once. The businessmen and racketeers also have a story. And so do the prostitutes.
(And this is not, perhaps, the place to discuss Harlem's very complex attitude toward black policemen, nor the reasons, according to
Harlem, that they are nearly all downtown.)

15   It is hard, on the other hand, to blame the policeman, blank,
good-natured, thoughtless, and insuperably innocent, for being such
a perfect representative of the people he serves. He, too, believes in
good intentions and is astounded and offended when they are not
taken for the deed. He has never, himself, done anything for which

to be hated—which of us has?—and yet he is facing, daily and nightly, people who would gladly see him dead, and he knows it. There is no way for him not to know it: there are few things under heaven more unnerving than the silent, accumulating contempt and hatred of a people. He moves through Harlem, therefore, like an occupying soldier in a bitterly hostile country; which is precisely what, and where, he is, and is the reason he walks in twos and threes. And he is not the only one who knows why he is always in company: the people who are watching him know why, too. Any street meeting, sacred or secular, which he and his colleagues uneasily cover has as its explicit or implicit burden the cruelty and injustice of the white domination. And these days, of course, in terms increasingly vivid and jubilant, it speaks of the end of that domination. The white policeman standing on a Harlem street corner finds himself at the very center of the revolution now occurring in the world. He is not prepared for it—naturally, nobody is—and, what is possibly much more to the point, he is exposed, as few white people are, to the anguish of the black people around him. Even if he is gifted with the merest mustard grain of imagination, something must seep in. He cannot avoid observing that some of the children, in spite of their color, remind him of children he has known and loved, perhaps even of his own children. He knows that he certainly does not want *his* children living this way. He can retreat from his uneasiness in only one direction: into a callousness which very shortly becomes second nature. He becomes more callous, the population becomes more hostile, the situation grows more tense, and the police force is increased. One day, to everyone's astonishment, someone drops a match in the powder keg and everything blows up. Before the dust has settled or the blood congealed, editorials, speeches, and civil-rights commissions are loud in the land, demanding to know what happened. What happened is that Negroes want to be treated like men.

Negroes want to be treated like men: a perfectly straightforward statement, containing only seven words. People who have mastered Kant, Hegel, Shakespeare, Marx, Freud, and the Bible find this statement utterly impenetrable. The idea seems to threaten profound, barely conscious assumptions. A kind of panic paralyzes their features, as though they found themselves trapped on the edge of a steep place. I once tried to describe to a very well-known American intellectual the conditions among Negroes in the South. My recital disturbed him and made him indignant; and he asked me in perfect innocence, "Why don't all the Negroes in the South move North?" I tried to explain what *has* happened, unfailingly, whenever a significant body of Negroes move North. They do not escape Jim Crow:

they merely encounter another, not-less-deadly variety. They do not move to Chicago, they move to the South Side; they do not move to New York, they move to Harlem. The pressure within the ghetto causes the ghetto walls to expand, and this expansion is always violent. White people hold the line as long as they can, and in as many ways as they can, from verbal intimidation to physical violence. But inevitably the border which has divided the ghetto from the rest of the world falls into the hands of the ghetto. The white people fall back bitterly before the black horde; the landlords make a tidy profit by raising the rent, chopping up the rooms, and all but dispensing with the upkeep; and what has once been a neighborhood turns into a "turf." This is precisely what happened when the Puerto Ricans arrived in their thousands—and the bitterness thus caused is, as I write, being fought out all up and down those streets.

Northerners indulge in an extremely dangerous luxury. They seem to feel that because they fought on the right side during the Civil War, and won, they have earned the right merely to deplore what is going on in the South, without taking any responsibility for it; and that they can ignore what is happening in Northern cities because what is happening in Little Rock or Birmingham is worse. Well, in the first place, it is not possible for anyone who has not endured both to know which is "worse." I know Negroes who prefer the South and white Southerners, because "At least there, you haven't got to play any guessing games!" The guessing games referred to have driven more than one Negro into the narcotics ward, the madhouse, or the river. I know another Negro, a man very dear to me, who says with conviction and with truth, "The spirit of the South is the spirit of America." He was born in the North and did his military training in the South. He did not, as far as I can gather, find the South "worse"; he found it, if anything, all too familiar. In the second place, though, even if Birmingham *is* worse, no doubt Johannesburg, South Africa, beats it by several miles, and Buchenwald was one of the worst things that ever happened in the entire history of the world. The world has never lacked for horrifying examples; but I do not believe that these examples are meant to be used as justification for our own crimes. This perpetual justification empties the heart of all human feeling. The emptier our hearts become, the greater will be our crimes. Thirdly, the South is not merely an embarrassingly backward region, but a part of this country, and what happens there concerns every one of us.

As far as the color problem is concerned, there is but one difference between the Southern white and the Northerner: the Southerner remembers, historically and in his own psyche, a kind of Eden in which he loved black people and they loved him. Historically, the flaming sword laid across this Eden is the Civil War. Personally, it is the Southerner's sexual coming of age, when, without any warning, unbreakable taboos are set up between himself and his past. Everything, thereafter, is permitted him except the love he remembers and has never ceased to need. The resulting, indescribable torment affects every Southern mind and is the basis of the Southern hysteria.

None of this is true for the Northerner. Negroes represent nothing to him personally, except, perhaps, the dangers of carnality. He never sees Negroes. Southerners see them all the time. Northerners never think about them whereas Southerners are never really thinking of anything else. Negroes are, therefore, ignored in the North and are under surveillance in the South, and suffer hideously in both places. Neither the Southerner nor the Northerner is able to look on the Negro simply as a man. It seems to be indispensable to the national self-esteem that the Negro be considered either as a kind of ward (in which case we are told how many Negroes, comparatively, bought Cadillacs last year and how few, comparatively, were lynched), or as a victim (in which case we are promised that he will never vote in our assemblies or go to school with our kids). They are two sides of the same coin and the South will not change— *cannot* change—until the North changes. The country will not change until it re-examines itself and discovers what it really means by freedom. In the meantime, generations keep being born, bitterness is increased by incompetence, pride, and folly, and the world shrinks around us.

It is a terrible, an inexorable, law that one cannot deny the   20
humanity of another without diminishing one's own: in the face of one's victim, one sees oneself. Walk through the streets of Harlem and see what we, this nation, have become.

Response

1. Explain Baldwin's metaphor in the second paragraph: "the fish-hooks, the barbed wire, of this avenue." How do the next four paragraphs develop and support the point?

2. What is meant by Baldwin's ironic term, "democratic anguish" (paragraph 8)? How does he use the notion to dismiss attempts to rationalize the dehumanizing conditions of slums?

3. From the liberal point of view, public housing is intended to benefit the residents, as is the presence of well-meaning police officers. But, says Baldwin in paragraph 11, "The projects in

Harlem are hated. They are hated almost as much as police-men . . . for the same reason." In his view, why do tenants of the projects deface the buildings, and why do they regard police with contempt and hatred? What does he see as the solution?

4. In his conclusion Baldwin warns: "The country will not change until it re-examines itself and discovers what it really means by freedom. . . . One cannot deny the humanity of another without diminishing one's own: in the face of one's victim, one sees oneself." How much do you think the country has changed? Can we consider Baldwin's essay "dated" yet?

5. Baldwin's essay is structured in the rhetorical form of an argu-ment: He presents the issue (the ugliness and frustration of life in the projects); he considers and refutes "counterarguments" to his point of view; he further develops his argument that the projects are hated and hideous; he concludes by proposing his solution to the problem, and his central point, or thesis. Ana-lyze the essay to identify these different sections of the argu-ment.

6. Baldwin explains that for African Americans, the North offers no escape from conditions in the South. Compare Baldwin's comments about the North and the South with Richard Wright's account of moving north in *American Hunger* (Sec-tion V).

7. Note how Baldwin explains "the situation of our youth" in paragraphs 8–10. How does this essay anticipate the viewpoint expressed in his later essay, "A Talk to Teachers" (Section V)? How does his advice in that essay derive from the point he makes in this one?

On Native Ground

Jim Barnes

In this essay from I Tell You Now: Autobiographical
Essays by Native American Writers *(1987) Jim Barnes
writes about the area of eastern Oklahoma where he
grew up. In the early 1800s the Choctaws were forced
to give up their ancestral lands in what is now
Mississippi, Alabama, and Louisiana; under the
Removal Act of 1830, they were moved west to the
"Indian Territory" in Oklahoma, along with several
other southeastern tribes. Barnes interweaves social
history with changes in the natural environment.*

I was five years old the last time I heard the mountain lion scream.
That was in Oklahoma, 1938, when times were hard and life
was good—and sacred. But a year later the WPA had done its work:
roads were cut, burial mounds were dug, small concrete dams were
blocking nearly every stream. The Government was caring for its
people. Many were the make-work jobs. A man could eat again,
while all about him the land suffered. The annual spring migration
of that lone panther was no more. The riverbanks that had been his
roads and way stations bore the scars of the times, the scars of loss.

Jim Barnes, "On Native Ground," in *I Tell You Now: Autobiographical Essays
by Native American Writers*, edited by Brian Swann and Arnold Krupat. Lincoln,
Nebraska: University of Nebraska Press, 1987. Copyright © 1987 by the University
of Nebraska Press. Reprinted by permission of University of Nebraska Press.

In my mind the rivers must always run free. But in truth today I do not recognize them. They are alien bodies on a flattening land where everything has been made safe, civilized into near extinction. Sounds of speedboats drown out the call of the remaining jays and crows. The din of highway traffic carries for miles now that the timber has fallen to chainsaw or chemical rot. Green silence in the heavy heat of summer afternoons is no more.

The Fourche Maline River and Holson Creek flow through much of what I have written. I suspect they were always there, even back in the mid-1950s when I wrote my first bad short story and my first bad verse. My sense of place is inexorably linked to these two streams and to the prairies and woods between them.

5   I was born within spitting distance of the Fourche Maline, on a meadow in a house that no longer stands. A lone clump of gnarled sassafras and oak rises out of the meadow a short mile northeast of Summerfield, in the hill country of eastern Oklahoma, where the land was once heavy with wood and game. Nobody knows why the clump of trees was not cut down when the land was first cleared for the plow. Once there was a house a few feet east of the trees. The broken tile of a well long since filled still rises a few inches above the earth. But you have to look long, for the tall grass hides it like the night. I cannot remember a time when the house stood there. My mother says that, as a child, she lived there for a short while at the turn of the century when her parents first moved up from Texas. But she does not recall the house, nor why it ceased to be.

Maybe the maker of the house knew why the trees were left in the middle of the field. At any rate, the trees are still there and are not threatened. Local legend has it that they once guarded a rich burial mound, but now no mound rises among the trees. Instead, a musky sink in the middle of the clump shows the scars of many a shovel and many a firelit night. The story of one night in particular sticks in my mind, though I was much too young at the time to know of the night at all. But like bedtime ghost stories, some things told again and again when you are young and lying with your brothers and sisters on a pallet before the hearth of the fireplace later illuminate the dim, unremembered years. It is the story of how my brother outran a horse.

Before I could stand alone, we lived on the lane that borders the east edge of the field where the trees still stand. My brother was nearing manhood and owned a horse and was a night rider. He learned that three men, neighbors and good-for-nothings, planned to dig in the trees. He asked to join them. He longed to prove himself a man. They had visions of gold and told him there was money buried there.

So when the October moon was dark, they gathered in the clump of trees and hung a lantern over the chosen spot. There was frost on the limbs of the sassafras and oaks. My brother broke first ground, and a hushed moan moved through the still trees. He dropped the shovel; later, strange pieces of bone-red matter began to show up in the dirt at the edge of the pit. While all were gathered about, another moan, much louder than the first, moved through the night—and my brother leaped out of the dark pit. But the good-for-nothings held him fast and howled with laughter as one of their cronies strode into the circle of the lantern's light, drunk on erupting mirth and bootleg whiskey. Everyone had a good laugh at my brother's expense. And he laughed too.

But the laughter was short-lived. A deep, low moan—ghostly but unmistakably human—rolled up from the bowels of the black earth. There was for a moment, my brother recalls, a stillness like doom upon all of them. Then everybody was running, running: the good-for-nothings were running, the original moaner was running, my brother was running, and all the beasts of the field. A great shadow passed beside my brother. It was a horse. The moan persisted, even over the sound of thumping boots and racing hoofs. Now my brother passed the horse, and burst through the barbed wire fence at the edge of the field with one wild bound. He flung himself down the lane and plunged through the doorway of our house and hugged himself close to the dying coals in the fireplace. An hour passed before he began to cry.

Several days later my father filled in the pit and brought home   10
the lantern, dry of kerosene, the wick burned to a crisp.

The clump of trees in the middle of the field was the hub of the universe of my childhood and my adolescence. We always lived within sight of the field. And after the field became a great meadow, I found several days of bone-breaking work each summer helping a cousin bale the tall and fragrant lespedeza that had been urged to grow there. But never did I seek the shade of those trees for my noonday rest. For me, they were too ghostly, foreboding, sacred. In my mind's eye I could see beyond all doubt that here was the final resting place of the broken bones of some great Choctaw chief. He had made it just this far west. He had come within sight of the blue Kiamichi range to the south, which was to become the last home for his dispossessed people, and had fallen dead on the spot from a homesickness of the soul. Among the sassafras and the oaks he had been buried with all the pomp and honor that was left to his migrating children. For me, the spot was inviolate.

And thus it has remained. Only recently have I had the courage, and the reverence, to penetrate the gnarled clump of trees in the middle of the meadow. I went there in midafternoon and sat as motionless as I could while the sun dropped well below a long, low line of trees far to the west. Sitting there, I tried to grasp something I could not name, something I knew was gone forever. I could not invoke it. I did not know its name. Once, just as the sun went down, I heard a hawk cry out high above the clump of leafless trees. Perhaps there was a moan. But I did not hear it.

Named by the French who early explored eastern Oklahoma, the Fourche Maline is by literal definition and observation a dirty stream, though one which once teemed with all the life that water could possibly bear. It was home to some of the world's largest catfish. I have seen mudcat and shovelbill taken from the river, on bankhooks or trotlines, huge fish that ran to more than a hundred pounds each, their hides so scarred and tough you had to skin them with wire pliers or Vise-Grips. Bullfrogs loud enough to drown a rebel yell, turtles big as washtubs, and cottonmouths all called it home, dared you to enter their domain. I can remember bear tracks on the shoals, mussel shells bitten in half.

The Fourche Maline was always a sluggish river, at least for the last twenty-five miles of its course. Though its head is in the western end of the Sans Bois mountain range, where ridges are still thick with government-protected scrub pine and savannah sandstone, and the water begins pure and clear, it is soon fed by farms and ranches with runoff from cornfields and feedlots and by worked-out coal mines as it snakes its way eastward to join Holson Creek. I can recall a time when the Fourche Maline cleared in early summer even as far as its mouth, and the water of the deep pools tasted of springs. Now the river runs ever more slowly, if at all. Its life grows stagnant out of season.

15   Conversely, Holson Creek—named for Holson Valley, from which it heads northward—was in the past a clear, fast-running stream. It flowed through the pines of Winding Stair and Blue mountains, through pastureland thick with native grasses, among stones that seem still today old as the sky. When I remember Holson Creek as it was in my youth, I can smell the odor of water willows, sharp in the summer, and hear the sounds of barking squirrels, of rapids and small falls, the banks rich with a treasure of arrowheads.

But now both rivers are slow, dammed. Where they meet, mouth to mouth, a lake begins. And for miles back up both streams it is difficult for the eye to discern movement of water, except in flood time, and then there is no guarantee which way they may run.

The land and streams are changing. Even what is protected pollutes: in the wildlife refuge, near the confluence of the Fourche Maline and the Holson, there are so many deer now that tick fever has thinned even the equalizing coyotes and has put salt fear into the veins of poachers, who once knew—who once were, right along with the coyotes—the true balancing force in nature.

Though fishing is sometimes fair, gone are the days of the scream of the mountain lion, the days of the big catfish. No one has seen a bear track in forty years. I doubt you could get snakebitten if you wanted to. But I am a child of the past. I live it in my waking dreams. The white clay banks along the Fourche Maline still hold their lure and the lore I assigned to them. I dug caves there. I danced the old songs. I attacked wagon trains or, on the other side, killed Indians. And once in a rare sundown, I realized that here in the bottomland stood the only native holly tree I knew of anywhere in the great wooded valleys between the Sans Bois mountains to the north and the blue Kiamichi to the south. The holly tree is gone, victim of the backwater of the Corps of Engineers. When backwater rises, is held like a cesspool for weeks on end, all flora and fauna rooted to place die. Even a simple child knows this.

What's more, and the hell of it all: I see but little hope, rather mainly dissolution of river, of land, and thus of spirit. You can see it plain on the faces of those who have witnessed, have lived, these civilizing years. Their faces are not lined without cause; there is something in the blood that needs rivers free, forests and prairies green with promise. Maybe lack of fuel and the death of automobiles will help, but I doubt it: I know people who will hike ten miles or more carrying a six-pack just to be able to throw the cans into a stream to see how long they will stay afloat while they are pumped full of lead.

We have been called a nation of tourists. But I suspect, deep   20
down, some of us somehow know where home is—and what it has become.

Response

1. Barnes recalls the year 1938, "when times were hard and life was good—and sacred." He ties destruction of the natural environment to the construction projects intended to pull the country out of the depression. From 1939 to 1943, the federal Work Projects Administration (WPA) built roads, bridges, and buildings to provide work for the unemployed. The irony in this, in Barnes' view, is that "a man could eat again, while all about him the land suffered" (paragraph 2). What situations today present the country with a similar dilemma?

2. Barnes ties his sense of place to the streams, wooded hills, and prairies of eastern Oklahoma where he grew up. Compare this to the way Rolando Hinojosa discusses "The Sense of Place" in his essay by that title, later in this section.

3. How does Barnes' story about the clump of trees (in paragraphs 5–12) underscore the message of his essay? How does it reflect his view of the relationship between human history and natural history?

4. Barnes details the changes brought by "these civilizing years." What is his outlook for the future? What do you think of his view?

The House on Mango Street

Sandra Cisneros

These selections are representative of the short stories that make up the book The House on Mango Street, *first published in 1984. They portray life in the Chicago neighborhood where Cisneros grew up, as seen through a child's eyes. Cisneros has said that she intended the stories in her book to be "a cross between poetry and fiction," stories "hovering in that grey area between two genres."*

No Speak English

Mamacita is the big mama of the man across the street, third-floor front. Rachel says her name ought to be *Mamasota*, but I think that's mean.

The man saved his money to bring her here. He saved and saved because she was alone with the baby boy in that country. He worked two jobs. He came home late and he left early. Every day.

Then one day Mamacita and the baby boy arrived in a yellow taxi. The taxi door opened like a waiter's arm. Out stepped a tiny pink shoe, a foot soft as a rabbit's ear, then the thick ankle, a flut-

Sandra Cisneros, from *The House on Mango Street*. Houston: Arte Publico Press, 1983. Copyright © 1989 by Sandra Cisneros, published in the United States by Vintage Books, a division of Random House, Inc., New York and distributed in Canada by Random House of Canada by Random House of Canada Limited, Toronto, 1991. Originally published in somewhat different form by Arte Publico Press, Houston in 1984, revised in 1988. Reprinted by permission Susan Bergholz Literary Services, New York.

tering of hips, fuchsia roses and green perfume. The man had to pull her, the taxicab driver had to push. Push, pull. Push, pull. Poof!

All at once she bloomed. Huge, enormous, beautiful to look at, from the salmon-pink feather on the tip of her hat down to the little rosebuds of her toes. I couldn't take my eyes off her tiny shoes.

5 Up, up, up the stairs she went with the baby boy in a blue blanket, the man carrying her suitcases, her lavender hatboxes, a dozen boxes of satin high heels. Then we didn't see her.

Somebody said because she's too fat, somebody because of the three flights of stairs, but I believe she doesn't come out because she is afraid to speak English, and maybe this is so since she only knows eight words. She knows to say: *He not here* for when the landlord comes, *No speak English* if anybody else comes, and *holy smokes*. I don't know where she learned this, but I heard her say it one time and it surprised me.

My father says when he came to this country he ate ham and eggs for three months. Breakfast, lunch and dinner. Ham and eggs. Those were the only words he knew. He doesn't eat ham and eggs anymore.

Whatever her reasons, whether she is fat or can't climb the stairs or is afraid of English, she won't come down. She sits all day by the window and plays the Spanish radio show and sings all the homesick songs about her country in a voice that sounds like a seagull.

Home. Home. Home is a house in a photograph, a pink house, pink as hollyhocks with lots of startled light. The man paints the walls of the apartment pink, but it's not the same you know. She still sighs for her pink house, and then I think she cries. I would.

10 Sometimes the man gets disgusted. He starts screaming and you can hear it all the way down the street.

Ay, she says, she is sad.

Oh, he says, not again.

¿Cuándo, cuándo, cuándo? she asks.

Ay, Caray! We *are* home. This *is* home. Here I am and here I stay. Speak English. Speak English. Christ!

15 Ay! Mamacita, who does not belong, every once in a while lets out a cry, hysterical, high, as if he had torn the only skinny thread that kept her alive, the only road out to that country.

And then to break her heart forever, the baby boy who has begun to talk, starts to sing the Pepsi commercial he heard on T.V.

No speak English, she says to the child who is singing in the language that sounds like tin. No speak English, no speak English, and bubbles into tears. No, no, no as if she can't believe her ears.

Geraldo No Last Name

She met him at a dance. Pretty too, and young. Said he worked in a restaurant, but she can't remember which one. Geraldo. That's all. Green pants and Saturday shirt. Geraldo. That's what he told her.

And how was she to know she'd be the last one to see him alive. An accident, don't you know. Hit and run. Marin, she goes to all those dances. Uptown. Logan. Embassy. Palmer. Aragon. Fontana. The Manor. She likes to dance. She knows how to do cumbias and salsas and rancheras even. And he was just someone she danced with. Somebody she met that night. That's right.

That's the story. That's what she said again and again. Once to the hospital people and twice to the police. No address. No name. Nothing in his pockets. Ain't it a shame.

Only Marin can't explain why it mattered, the hours and hours, for somebody she didn't even know. The hospital emergency room. Nobody but an intern working all alone. And maybe if the surgeon would've come, maybe if he hadn't lost so much blood, if the surgeon had only come, they would know who to notify and where.

But what difference does it make? He wasn't anything to her. He wasn't her boyfriend or anything like that. Just another *brazer* who didn't speak English. Just another wetback. You know the kind. The ones who always look ashamed. And what was she doing out at three a.m. anyway? Marin who was sent home with her coat and some aspirin. How does she explain it? 5

She met him at a dance. Geraldo in his shiny shirt and green pants. Geraldo going to a dance.

What does it matter?

They never saw the kitchenettes. They never knew about the two-room flats and sleeping rooms he rented, the weekly money orders sent home, the currency exchange. How could they?

His name was Geraldo. And his home is in another country. The ones he left behind are far away. They will wonder. Shrug. Remember. Geraldo. He went north . . . we never heard from him again.

Those Who Don't

Those who don't know any better come into our neighborhood scared. They think we're dangerous. They think we will attack them with shiny knives. They are stupid people who are lost and got here by mistake.

But we aren't afraid. We know the guy with the crooked eye is Davey the Baby's brother, and the tall one next to him in the straw brim, that's Rosa's Eddie V. and the big one that looks like a dumb grown man, he's Fat Boy, though he's not fat anymore nor a boy.

All brown all around, we are safe. But watch us drive into a neighborhood of another color and our knees go shakity-shake and our car windows get rolled up tight and our eyes look straight. Yeah. That is how it goes and goes.

Response

1. By writing from a child's point of view, Cisneros leaves the reader to interpret Mamacita's story: "Whatever her reasons . . . she won't come down." Why is it so heartbreaking to the woman when her baby begins to sing in English?

2. In "Geraldo No Last Name," about an anonymous undocumented worker, what values do the characters reveal, and what insight does the story give into the life of the community? In what different ways does the story provide answers to the ironic question, "What does it matter?"

3. Cisneros conveys a sense of place through glimpses into the lives of people who live there. What do we know about Cisneros' neighborhood from these three stories? What is the implied comment about her neighborhood (or any other) in "Those Who Don't"?

4. Of *The House on Mango Street*, Cisneros has said, "I wanted stories like poems, compact and lyrical and ending with a reverberation." In what ways do these stories exhibit those properties? What emotions do you find the stories convey? Do you find this writing style effective?

5. In her essays "Ghosts and Voices: Writing from Obsession" (Section I) and "Notes to a Young(er) Writer" (Section V) Cisneros discusses her motivations for writing. In what ways do these stories from *The House on Mango Street* carry out her purposes?

Notes from a Native Daughter

Joan Didion

This essay is part of the collection in Slouching
Towards Bethlehem *(1968). Didion took the title of
that book from a poem by William Butler Yeats,
which contains the line "Things fall apart; the center
cannot hold." In her preface to the book Didion says
she wrote her essays with Yeats's words
reverberating in her mind. This essay conveys the
sense of loss that pervades much of Didion's writing.*

It is very easy to sit at a bar in, say, La Scala in Beverly Hills,
or Ernie's in San Francisco, and to share in the pervasive delusion
that California is only five hours from New York by air. The truth
is that La Scala and Ernie's are only five hours from New York by
air. California is somewhere else.

Many people in the East (or "back East," as they say in California, although not in La Scala or Ernie's) do not believe this. They
have been to Los Angeles or to San Francisco, have driven through a
giant redwood and have seen the Pacific glazed by the afternoon sun
off Big Sur, and they naturally tend to believe that they have in fact
been to California. They have not been, and they probably never will
be, for it is a longer and in many ways a more difficult trip than they

Joan Didion, "Notes from a Native Daughter," in *Slouching Towards Bethlehem*. New York: Washington Square Press, 1968. Copyright © 1965, 1968 by Joan
Didion. Reprinted by permission of Farrar, Straus & Giroux, Inc.

might want to undertake, one of those trips on which the destination flickers chimercally on the horizon, ever receding, ever diminishing. I happen to know about that trip because I come from California, come from a family, or a congeries of families, that has always been in the Sacramento Valley.

You might protest that no family has been in the Sacramento Valley for anything approaching "always." But it is characteristic of Californians to speak grandly of the past as if it had simultaneously begun, *tabula rasa*, and reached a happy ending on the day the wagons started west. *Eureka*—"I Have Found It"—as the state motto has it. Such a view of history casts a certain melancholia over those who participate in it; my own childhood was suffused with the conviction that we had long outlived our finest hour. In fact that is what I want to tell you about: what it is like to come from a place like Sacramento. If I could make you understand that, I could make you understand California and perhaps something else besides, for Sacramento *is* California, and California is a place in which a boom mentality and a sense of Chekhovian loss meet in uneasy suspension; in which the mind is troubled by some buried but ineradicable suspicion that things had better work here, because here, beneath that immense bleached sky, is where we run out of continent.

In 1847 Sacramento was no more than an adobe enclosure, Sutter's Fort, standing alone on the prairie; cut off from San Francisco and the sea by the Coast Range and from the rest of the continent by the Sierra Nevada, the Sacramento Valley was then a true sea of grass, grass so high a man riding into it could tie it across his saddle. A year later gold was discovered in the Sierra foothills, and abruptly Sacramento was a town, a town any moviegoer could map tonight in his dreams—a dusty collage of assay offices and wagonmakers and saloons. Call that Phase Two. Then the settlers came—the farmers, the people who for two hundred years had been moving west on the frontier, the peculiar flawed strain who had cleared Virginia, Kentucky, Missouri; they made Sacramento a farm town. Because the land was rich, Sacramento became eventually a rich farm town, which meant houses in town, Cadillac dealers, a country club. In that gentle sleep Sacramento dreamed until perhaps 1950, when something happened. What happened was that Sacramento woke to the fact that the outside world was moving in, fast and hard. At the moment of its waking Sacramento lost, for better or for worse, its character, and that is part of what I want to tell you about.

5   But the change is not what I remember first. First I remember running a boxer dog of my brother's over the same flat fields that our great-great-grandfather had found virgin and had planted; I re-

member swimming (albeit nervously, for I was a nervous child, afraid of sinkholes and afraid of snakes, and perhaps that was the beginning of my error) the same rivers we had swum for a century: the Sacramento, so rich with silt that we could barely see our hands a few inches beneath the surface; the American, running clean and fast with melted Sierra snow until July, when it would slow down, and rattlesnakes would sun themselves on its newly exposed rocks. The Sacramento, the American, sometimes the Cosumnes, occasionally the Feather. Incautious children died every day in those rivers; we read about it in the paper, how they had miscalculated a current or stepped into a hole down where the American runs into the Sacramento, how the Berry Brothers had been called in from Yolo County to drag the river but how the bodies remained unrecovered. "They were from away," my grandmother would extrapolate from the newspaper stories. "Their parents had no *business* letting them in the river. They were visitors from Omaha." It was not a bad lesson, although a less than reliable one; children we knew died in the rivers too.

When summer ended—when the State Fair closed and the heat broke, when the last green hop vines had been torn down along the H Street road and the tule fog began rising off the low ground at night—we would go back to memorizing the Products of Our Latin American Neighbors and to visiting the great-aunts on Sunday, dozens of great-aunts, year after year of Sundays. When I think now of those winters I think of yellow elm leaves wadded in the gutters outside the Trinity Episcopal Pro-Cathedral on M Street. There are actually people in Sacramento now who call M Street Capitol Avenue, and Trinity has one of those featureless new buildings, but perhaps children still learn the same things there on Sunday mornings:

Q. *In what way does the Holy Land resemble the Sacramento Valley?*
A. *In the type and diversity of its agricultural products.*

And I think of the rivers rising, of listening to the radio to hear at what height they would crest and wondering if and when and where the levees would go. We did not have as many dams in those years. The bypasses would be full, and men would sandbag all night. Sometimes a levee would go in the night, somewhere upriver; in the morning the rumor would spread that the Army Engineers had dynamited it to relieve the pressure on the city.

After the rains came spring, for ten days or so; the drenched fields would dissolve into a brilliant ephemeral green (it would be yellow and dry as fire in two or three weeks) and the real-estate business would pick up. It was the time of year when people's grandmothers went to Carmel; it was the time of year when girls who could not even get into Stephens or Arizona or Oregon, let alone Stanford or Berkeley, would be sent to Honolulu, on the *Lurline*. I have no recollection of anyone going to New York, with the exception of a cousin who visited there (I cannot imagine why) and reported that the shoe salesmen at Lord & Taylor were "intolerably rude." What happened in New York and Washington and abroad seemed to impinge not at all upon the Sacramento mind. I remember being taken to call upon a very old woman, a rancher's widow, who was reminiscing (the favored conversational mode in Sacramento) about the son of some contemporaries of hers. "That Johnston boy never did amount to much," she said. Desultorily, my mother protested: Alva Johnston, she said, had won the Pulitzer Prize, when he was working for *The New York Times*. Our hostess looked at us impassively. "He never amounted to anything in Sacramento," she said.

Hers was the true Sacramento voice, and, although I did not realize it then, one not long to be heard, for the war was over and the boom was on and the voice of the aerospace engineer would be heard in the land. VETS NO DOWN! EXECUTIVE LIVING ON LOW FHA!

Later, when I was living in New York, I would make the trip back to Sacramento four and five times a year (the more comfortable the flight, the more obscurely miserable I would be, for it weighs heavily upon my mind that we could perhaps not make it by wagon), trying to prove that I had not meant to leave at all, because in at least one respect California—the California we are talking about— resembles Eden: it is assumed that those who absent themselves from its blessings have been banished, exiled by some perversity of heart. Did not the Donner-Reed Party, after all, eat its own dead to reach Sacramento?

10   I have said that the trip back is difficult, and it is—difficult in a way that magnifies the ordinary ambiguities of sentimental journeys. Going back to California is not like going back to Vermont, or Chicago; Vermont and Chicago are relative constants, against which one measures one's own change. All that is constant about the California of my childhood is the rate at which it disappears. An instance: on Saint Patrick's Day of 1948 I was taken to see the legislature "in action," a dismal experience; a handful of florid assemblymen, wearing green hats, were reading Pat-and-Mike jokes into the record. I still think of the legislators that way—wearing green hats, or sitting around on the veranda of the Senator Hotel fanning themselves and being entertained by Artie Samish's emissaries. (Samish was the lobbyist who said, "Earl Warren may be the governor of the state, but I'm the governor of the legislature.") In

fact there is no longer a veranda at the Senator Hotel—it was turned into an airline ticket office, if you want to embroider the point—and in any case the legislature has largely deserted the Senator for the flashy motels north of town, where the tiki torches flame and the steam rises off the heated swimming pools in the cold Valley night.

It is hard to *find* California now, unsettling to wonder how much of it was merely imagined or improvised; melancholy to realize how much of anyone's memory is no true memory at all but only the traces of someone else's memory, stories handed down on the family network. I have an indelibly vivid "memory," for example, of how Prohibition affected the hop growers around Sacramento: the sister of a grower my family knew brought home a mink coat from San Francisco, and was told to take it back, and sat on the floor of the parlor cradling that coat and crying. Although I was not born until a year after Repeal, that scene is more "real" to me than many I have played myself.

I remember one trip home, when I sat alone on a night jet from New York and read over and over some lines from a W. S. Merwin poem I had come across in a magazine, a poem about a man who had been a long time in another country and knew that he must go home:

> . . . But it should be
> Soon. Already I defend hotly
> Certain of our indefensible faults,
> Resent being reminded; already in my mind
> Our language becomes freighted with a richness
> No common tongue could offer, while the mountains
> Are like nowhere on earth, and the wide rivers.

You see the point. I want to tell you the truth, and already I have told you about the wide rivers.

It should be clear by now that the truth about the place is elusive, and must be tracked with caution. You might go to Sacramento tomorrow and someone (although no one I know) might take you out to Aerojet-General, which has, in the Sacramento phrase, "something to do with rockets." Fifteen thousand people work for Aerojet, almost all of them imported; a Sacramento lawyer's wife told me, as evidence of how Sacramento was opening up, that she believed she had met one of them, at an open house two Decembers ago. ("Couldn't have been nicer, actually," she added enthusiastically. "I think he and his wife bought the house next *door* to Mary and Al, something like that, which of course was how *they* met him.") So you might go to Aerojet and stand in the big vendor's lobby where a couple of thousand components salesmen try every week to sell their wares and you might look up at the electrical wallboard that lists Aerojet personnel, their projects and their location at any given time, and you might wonder if I have been in Sacramento lately. MINUTEMAN, POLARIS, TITAN, the lights flash, and all the coffee tables are littered with airline schedules, very now, very much in touch.

But I could take you a few miles from there into towns where the banks still bear names like The Bank of Alex Brown, into towns where the one hotel still has an octagonal-tile floor in the dining room and dusty potted palms and big ceiling fans; into towns where everything—the seed business, the Harvester franchise, the hotel, the department store and the main street—carries a single name, the name of the man who built the town. A few Sundays ago I was in a town like that, a town smaller than that, really, no hotel, no Harvester franchise, the bank burned out, a river town. It was the golden anniversary of some of my relatives and it was 110° and the guests of honor sat on straight-backed chairs in front of a sheaf of gladioluses in the Rebekah Hall. I mentioned visiting Aerojet-General to a cousin I saw there, who listened to me with interested disbelief. Which is the true California? That is what we all wonder.

15   Let us try out a few irrefutable statements, on subjects not open to interpretation. Although Sacramento is in many ways the least typical of the Valley towns, it *is* a Valley town, and must be viewed in that context. When you say "the Valley" in Los Angeles, most people assume that you mean the San Fernando Valley (some people in fact assume that you mean Warner Brothers), but make no mistake: we are talking not about the valley of the sound stages and the ranchettes but about the real Valley, the Central Valley, the fifty thousand square miles drained by the Sacramento and the San Joaquin Rivers and further irrigated by a complex network of sloughs, cutoffs, ditches, and the Delta-Mendota and Friant-Kern Canals.

A hundred miles north of Los Angeles, at the moment when you drop from the Tehachapi Mountains into the outskirts of Bakersfield, you leave Southern California and enter the Valley. "You look up the highway and it is straight for miles, coming at you, with the black line down the center coming at you and at you . . . and the heat dazzles up from the white slab so that only the black line is clear, coming at you with the whine of the tires, and if you don't quit staring at that line and don't take a few deep breaths and slap yourself hard on the back of the neck you'll hypnotize yourself."

Robert Penn Warren wrote that about another road, but he might have been writing about the Valley road, U.S. 99, three hundred miles from Bakersfield to Sacramento, a highway so straight that when one flies on the most direct pattern from Los Angeles to Sacramento one never loses sight of U.S. 99. The landscape it runs through never, to the untrained eye, varies. The Valley eye can discern the point where miles of cotton seedlings fade into miles of tomato seedlings, or where the great corporation ranches—Kern County Land, what is left of DiGiorgio—give way to private operations (somewhere on the horizon, if the place is private, one sees a house and a stand of scrub oaks), but such distinctions are in the long view irrelevant. All day long, all that moves is the sun, and the big Rainbird sprinklers.

Every so often along 99 between Bakersfield and Sacramento there is a town: Delano, Tulare, Fresno, Madera, Merced, Modesto, Stockton. Some of these towns are pretty big now, but they are all the same at heart, one- and two- and three-story buildings artlessly arranged, so that what appears to be the good dress shop stands beside a W. T. Grant store, so that the big Bank of America faces a Mexican movie house. *Dos Peliculas, Bingo Bingo Bingo.* Beyond the downtown (pronounced *down*town, with the Okie accent that now pervades Valley speech patterns) lie blocks of old frame houses—paint peeling, sidewalks cracking, their occasional leaded amber windows overlooking a Foster's Freeze or a five-minute car wash or a State Farm Insurance office; beyond those spread the shopping centers and the miles of tract houses, pastel with redwood siding, the unmistakable signs of cheap building already blossoming on those houses which have survived the first rain. To a stranger driving 99 in an air-conditioned car (he would be on business, I suppose, any stranger driving 99, for 99 would never get a tourist to Big Sur or San Simeon, never get him to the California he came to see), these towns must seem so flat, so impoverished, as to drain the imagination. They hint at evenings spent hanging around gas stations, and suicide pacts sealed in drive-ins.

But remember:

Q. In what way does the Holy Land resemble the Sacramento Valley?
A. In the type and diversity of its agricultural products..

U.S. 99 in fact passes through the richest and most intensely 20 cultivated agricultural region in the world, a giant outdoor hothouse with a billion-dollar crop. It is when you remember the Valley's wealth that the monochromatic flatness of its towns takes on a curious meaning, suggests a habit of mind some would consider perverse. There is something in the Valley mind that reflects a real indifference to the stranger in his air-conditioned car, a failure to perceive even his presence, let alone his thoughts or wants. An implacable insularity is the seal of these towns. I once met a woman in Dallas, a most charming and attractive woman accustomed to the hospitality and social hypersensitivity of Texas, who told me that during the four war years her husband had been stationed in Modesto, she had never once been invited inside anyone's house. No one in Sacramento would find this story remarkable ("She probably had no *rel*atives there," said someone to whom I told it), for the Valley towns understand one another, share a peculiar spirit. They think alike and they look alike. *I* can tell Modesto from Merced, but I have visited there, gone to dances there; besides, there is over the main street of Modesto an arched sign which reads:

Water—Wealth
Contentment—Health

There is no such sign in Merced.

I said that Sacramento was the least typical of the Valley towns, and it is—but only because it is bigger and more diverse, only because it has had the rivers and the legislature; its true character remains the Valley character, its virtues the Valley virtues, its sadness the Valley sadness. It is just as hot in the summertime, so hot that the air shimmers and the grass bleaches white and the blinds stay drawn all day, so hot that August comes on not like a month but like an affliction; it is just as flat, so flat that a ranch of my family's with a slight rise on it, perhaps a foot, was known for the hundred-some years which preceded this year as "the hill ranch." (It is known this year as a subdivision in the making, but that is another part of the story.) Above all, in spite of its infusions from outside, Sacramento retains the Valley insularity.

To sense that insularity a visitor need do no more than pick up a copy of either of the two newspapers, the morning *Union* or the afternoon *Bee*. The *Union* happens to be Republican and impoverished and the *Bee* Democratic and powerful ("THE VALLEY OF THE BEES!" as the McClatchys, who own the Fresno, Modesto and Sacramento *Bees*, used to headline their advertisement in the trade press. "ISOLATED FROM ALL OTHER MEDIA INFLUENCE!"), but they read a good deal alike, and the tone of their chief editorial concerns is strange and wonderful and instructive. The *Union*, in a county heavily and reliably Democratic, frets mainly about the possibility of a local takeover by the John Birch Society; the *Bee*, faithful to the letter of its founder's will, carries on overwrought crusades against phantoms it still calls "the power trusts." Shades of Hiram Johnson, whom the *Bee* helped elect governor in 1910. Shades of Robert La Follette, to whom the *Bee* delivered the Valley in 1924.

There is something about the Sacramento papers that does not quite connect with the way Sacramento lives now, something pronouncedly beside the point. The aerospace engineers, one learns, read the San Francisco *Chronicle*.

The Sacramento papers, however, simply mirror the Sacramento peculiarity, the Valley fate, which is to be paralyzed by a past no longer relevant. Sacramento is a town which grew up on farming and discovered to its shock that land has more profitable uses. (The chamber of commerce will give you crop figures, but pay them no mind—what matters is the feeling, the knowledge that where the green hops once grew is now Larchmont Riviera, that what used to be the Whitney ranch is now Sunset City, thirty-three thousand houses and a country-club complex.) It is a town in which defense industry and its absentee owners are suddenly the most important facts; a town which has never had more people or more money, but has lost its *raison d'etre*. It is a town many of whose most solid citizens sense about themselves a kind of functional obsolescence. The old families still see only one another, but they do not see even one another as much as they once did; they are closing ranks, preparing for the long night, selling their rights-of-way and living on the proceeds. Their children still marry one another, still play bridge and go into the real-estate business together. (There is no other business in Sacramento, no reality other than land—even I, when I was living and working in New York, felt impelled to take a University of California correspondence course in Urban Land Economics.) But late at night when the ice has melted there is always somebody now, some Julian English, whose heart is not quite in it. For out there on the outskirts of town are marshaled the legions of aerospace engineers, who talk their peculiar condescending language and tend their dichondra and plan to stay in the promised land; who are raising a new generation of native Sacramentans and who do not care, really do not care, that they are not asked to join the Sutter Club. It makes one wonder, late at night when the ice is gone; introduces some air into the womb, suggests that the Sutter Club is perhaps not, after all, the Pacific Union or the Bohemian; that Sacramento is not *the city*. In just such self-doubts do small towns lose their character.

I want to tell you a Sacramento story. A few miles out of town   25 is a place, six or seven thousand acres, which belonged in the beginning to a rancher with one daughter. That daughter went abroad and married a title, and when she brought the title home to live on the ranch, her father built them a vast house—music rooms, conservatories, a ballroom. They needed a ballroom because they entertained: people from abroad, people from San Francisco, house parties that lasted weeks and involved special trains. They are long dead, of course, but their only son, aging and unmarried, still lives on the place. He does not live in the house, for the house is no longer there. Over the years it burned, room by room, wing by wing. Only the chimneys of the great house are still standing, and its heir lives in their shadow, lives by himself on the charred site, in a house trailer.

That is a story my generation knows; I doubt that the next will know it, the children of the aerospace engineers. Who would tell it to them? Their grandmothers live in Scarsdale, and they have never met a great-aunt. "Old" Sacramento to them will be something colorful, something they read about in *Sunset*. They will probably think that the Redevelopment has always been there, that the Embarcadero, down along the river, with its amusing places to shop and its picturesque fire houses turned into bars, has about it the true flavor of the way it was. There will be no reason for them to know that in homelier days it was called Front Street (the town was not, after all, settled by the Spanish) and was a place of derelicts and missions and itinerant pickers in town for a Saturday-night drunk: VICTORIOUS LIFE MISSION, JESUS SAVES, BEDS 25¢ A NIGHT, CROP INFORMATION HERE. They will have lost the real past and gained a manufactured one, and there will be no way for them to know, no way at all, why a house trailer should stand alone on seven thousand acres outside town.

But perhaps it is presumptuous of me to assume that they will be missing something. Perhaps in retrospect this has been a story not about Sacramento at all, but about the things we lose and the promises we break as we grow older; perhaps I have been playing out unawares the Margaret in the poem:

> Margaret, are you grieving
> Over Goldengrove unleaving? . . .
> It is the blight man was born for,
> It is Margaret you mourn for.

Response

1. Didion wants to tell the reader "what it is like to come from a place like Sacramento," to make the reader understand California, "for Sacramento *is* California" (paragraph 3). Do you accept her premise? What "view of history" does she establish at the outset? How is that view essential to the message of the essay?

2. How do Didion's recollections of childhood (in paragraphs 5–8) underscore the distinction between people who belonged to old Sacramento, and outsiders? How did the rancher's widow

in paragraph 8 reflect "the true Sacramento voice," and how did it contrast with "the voice of the aerospace engineer"? Notice the details and imagery Didion uses throughout the essay to refer to the newcomers and new parts of town. What underlying attitude does her portrayal suggest?

3. Explain what Didion means when she says, in paragraph 12, "I want to tell you the truth, and already I have told you about the wide rivers." How does that prove her point that "the truth about the place is elusive, and must be tracked with caution" (paragraph 13)? Didion contrasts the Sacramento that is "very now, very much in touch" with the more stable and familiar town of her childhood. How could one answer the question "Which is the true California" (paragraph 14)?

4. What qualities does Sacramento share with "the Valley"? How does Didion illustrate the city's and the Valley's "implacable insularity"? In what sense are both "paralyzed by a past no longer relevant" (paragraph 24)?

5. Didion suggests that land ownership and farming are at the heart of the old way of life in Sacramento. In what ways has the incursion of the defense industry essentially altered that aspect of the place?

6. Didion speculates about what "the children of the aerospace engineers" will grow up knowing about Sacramento. "They will have lost the real past and gained a manufactured one," she says in paragraph 26. Do you find her contrast valid? Do you think those children, growing up in Sacramento after the 1950s, would share her view? How might they describe "what it is like to come from a place like Sacramento"?

7. In the end Didion acknowledges that this essay is not so much about Sacramento as it is about change and her own sense of loss. In that respect a story like this could be told about other places as well. Is the place you come from more like the old Sacramento Didion misses or the Sacramento that has changed and grown since the war? What changes have you observed in the place? How have these changes affected the quality of life there?

The Sense of Place

Rolando Hinojosa

In this essay from The Rolando Hinojosa Reader *(1985) Hinojosa considers what contributes to his sense of the place he comes from, the Rio Grande Valley of Texas on the Mexican border near the Gulf coast. Hinojosa recognizes that "fidelity to history is the first step to fixing a sense of place," wherever the place may be.*

I begin with a quote from a man imprisoned for his participation in the Texas-Santa Fe Expedition of 1841; while in his cell in Mexico City, he spurned Santa Anna's offer of freedom in exchange for renouncing the Republic of Texas. Those words of 1842 were said by a man who had signed the Texas Declaration of Independence and who had served in the Congress of the Republic. Later on, he was to cast a delegate vote for annexation and contributed to the writing of the first state constitution. He would win election to the state legislature and still later he would support secession.

And this is what he said: "I have sworn to be a good Texan; and that I will not forswear. I will die for that which I firmly believe, for I know it is just and right. One life is a small price for a cause so

Rolando Hinojosa, "The Sense of Place," in *The Rolando Hinojosa Reader*, edited by Jose David Saldivar. Houston: Arte Publico Press/University of Houston, 1985. Reprinted with permission from the publisher.

great. As I fought, so shall I be willing to die. I will never forsake Texas and her cause. I am her son."

The words were written by José Antonio Navarro. A Texas historian named James Wilson once wrote that Navarro's name is virtually unknown to Texas school children and, for the most part, unknown to their teachers as well. A lifetime of living in my native land leads me to believe that Professor Wilson is correct in his assessment of the lack of knowledge of this place in which we were born and in which some of us still live.

The year 1983 marks the one hundredth anniversary of the birth of my father, Manuel Guzmán Hinojosa, in the Campacuás Ranch, some three miles north of Mercedes, down in the Valley; his father was born on that ranch as was his father's father. On the maternal side, my mother arrived in the Valley at the age of six-weeks in the year 1887 along with one of the first Anglo-American settlers enticed to the mid-Valley by Jim Wells, one of the early developers on the northern bank. As you may already know, it's no accident that Jim Wells County in South Texas is named for him.

One of the earliest stories I heard about Grandfather Smith was   5
a supposed conversation he held with Lawyer Wells. You are being asked to imagine the month of July in the Valley with no air conditioning in 1887; Wells was extolling the Valley and he said that all it needed was a little water and a few good people. My grandfather replied, "Well, that's all Hell needs, too." The story is apocryphal; it has to be. But living in the Valley, and hearing that type of story laid the foundation for what I later learned was to give me a sense of place. By that I do not mean that I had a feel for the place; no, not at all. I had a sense of it, and by that I mean that I was not learning about the culture of the Valley, but living it, forming part of it, and thus, contributing to it.

But a place is merely that until it is populated, and once populated, the histories of the place and its people begin. For me and mine, history began in 1749 when the first colonists began moving into the southern and northern banks of the Río Grande. That river was not yet a jurisdictional barrier and was not to be until almost one hundred years later; but, by then, the border had its own history, its own culture, and its own sense of place: it was Nuevo Santander, named for old Santander in the Spanish Peninsula.

The last names were similar up and down on both banks of the river, and as second and third cousins were allowed to marry, this further promulgated and propagated blood relationships and that sense of belonging that led the Borderers to label their fellow Mexicans who came from the interior, as *fuereños*, or outsiders; and later, when the people from the North started coming to the Border, these were labeled *gringos*, a word for foreigner, and nothing else, until the *gringo* himself, from all evidence, took the term as a pejorative label.

For me, then, part of a sense of the Border came from sharing: the sharing of names, of places, of a common history, and of belonging to the place; one attended funerals, was taken to cemeteries, and one saw names that corresponded to one's own or to one's friends and neighbors, and relatives.

When I first started to write, and being what we call "empapado," which translates as drenched, imbibed, soaked, or drunk with the place, I had to eschew the romanticism and the sentimentalism that tend to blind the unwary, that get in the way of truth. It's no great revelation when I say that romanticism and sentimentalism tend to corrupt clear thinking as well. The Border wasn't paradise, and it didn't have to be; but it was more than paradise, it was home (and as Frost once wrote, home, when you have to go there, is the place where they have to take you in).

10   And the Border was home; and it was also the home of the petty officeholder elected by an uninformed citizenry; a home for bossism, and for old-time smuggling as a way of life for some. But, it also maintained the remains of a social democracy that cried out for independence, for a desire to be left alone, and for the continuance of a sense of community.

The history one learned there was an oral one and somewhat akin to the oral religion brought by the original colonials. Many of my generation were raised with the music written and composed by Valley people, and we learned the ballads of the Border little knowing that it was a true native art form. And one was also raised and steeped in the stories and exploits of Juan Nepomuceno Cortina, in the nineteenth century, and with stories of the Texas Rangers in that century and of other Ranger stories in this century and then, as always, names, familiar patronymics: Jacinto Treviño, Aniceto Pizaña, the Seditionists of 1915 who had camped in Mercedes, and where my father would take me and show and mark for me the spot where the Seditionists had camped and barbecued their meat half a generation before. These were men of flesh and bone who lived and died there in Mercedes, in the Valley. And then there were the stories of the Revolution of 1910, and of the participation in it for the next ten years off and on by Valley *mexicanos* who fought alongside their south bank relatives, and the stories told to me and to those of my generation by exiles, men and women from Mexico, who earned a living by teaching us school on the northern bank while they bided their time to return to Mexico.

But we didn't return to Mexico; we didn't have to; we were

Borderers with a living and unifying culture born of conflict with another culture and this, too, helped to cement further still the knowing exactly where one came from and from whom one was descended.

The language, too, was a unifier and as strong an element as there is in fixing one's sense of place; the language of the Border is a derivative of the Spanish language of Northern Mexico, a language wherein some nouns and other grammatical complements were no longer used in the Spanish Peninsula, but which persisted there; and the more the linguistically uninformed went out of their way to denigrate the language, the stiffer the resistance to maintain it and to nurture it on the northern bank. And the uninformed failed, of course, for theirs was a momentary diversion while one was committed to its preservation; the price that many Texas Mexicans paid for keeping the language and the sense of place has been exorbitant.

As Borderers, the northbank Border Mexican couldn't, to repeat a popular phrase, "go back to where you came from." The Borderer was there and had been before the interlopers; but what of the indigenous population prior to the 1749 settlement? Since Nuevo Santander was never under the presidio system and since its citizens did not build missions that trapped and stultified the indigenous people, they remained there and, in time, settled down or were absorbed by the colonial population and thus the phrase hurled at the Border Mexican "go back to where you came from" was, to use another popular term, "inoperative." And this, too, fostered that sense of place.

For the writer—this writer—a sense of place was not a matter of importance; it became essential. And so much so that my stories are not held together by the *peripeteia* or the plot as much as by *what* the people who populate the stories say and *how* they say it, how they look at the world out and the world in; and the works, then, become studies of perceptions and values and decisions reached by them because of those perceptions and values which in turn were fashioned and forged by the place and its history.   15

What I am saying here is not to be taken to mean that it is impossible for a writer to write about a place, its history, and its people, if the writer is not from that particular place; it can be done, and it has been done. What I *am* saying is that I needed a sense of place, and that this helped me no end in the way that, I would say, Américo Paredes in *With His Pistol in His Hand*, McMurtry in *Horseman, Pass By* and Gipson in *Hound Dog Man*, and Owens in that fine, strong *This Stubborn Soil*, and Tomás Rivera in . . . *and the earth did not part* were all helped by a sense of place. And I say this, because to me, these writers and others impart a sense of place and a sense of truth about the place and about the values of that place. It isn't a studied attitude, but rather one of a certain love, to use that phrase, and an understanding for the place that they captured in print for themselves; something that was, for themselves, then, at that time and there. A sense of place, as Newark, New Jersey, is for Phillip Roth, and thus we see him surprised at himself when he tells us he dates a *schicksa*, and then, the wonderful storyteller that he is, he tells us of his Jewish traditions and conflicts, and we note that it becomes a pattern in some of his writings whenever he writes of relationships, which, after all, is what writers usually write about: relationships.

I am not making a medieval pitch for the shoemaker to stick to his last here, but if the writer places a lifetime of living in a work, the writer sometimes finds it difficult to remove the place of provenance from the writings, irrespective of where he situates his stories. That's a strong statement and one which may elicit comment or disagreement, but what spine one has is formed early in life, and it is formed at a specific place; later on when one grows up, one may mythicize, adopt a persona, become an actor, restructure family history, but the original facts of one's formation remain as facts always do.

It's clear, then, that I am not speaking of the formula novel, nor is it my intent to denigrate it or its practitioners; far from it. I consider the formula novel as a fine art, if done well, and many of us know that they do exist. I speak of something else—neither nobler nor better, no—merely different from that genre. It's a personal thing, because I found that after many years of hesitancy, and fits and spurts, and false starts, that despite what education I had acquired, I was still limited in many ways; that whatever I attempted to write, came out false and frail. Now, I know I wanted to write, had to write, was burning to write and all of those things that some writers say to some garden clubs, but the truth and heart of the matter was that I did not know where to begin; and there it was again, that adverb of place, the *where*; and then I got lucky: I decided to write whatever it was I had, in Spanish, and I decided to set it on the border, in the Valley. As reduced as that space was, it too was Texas with all of its contradictions and its often repeated one-sided telling of Texas history. When the characters stayed in the Spanish-speaking milieu or society, the Spanish language worked well, and then it was in the natural order of things that English made its entrance when the characters strayed or found themselves in Anglo institutions; in cases where both cultures would come into contact, both languages were used, and I would employ both, and where one and only one would do, I would follow that as well; what dominated, then, was the place, at first. Later on I discovered that generational and class differences also dictated not only usage but which language as well. From this came the *how* they said *what* they said. As the census rolls filled up in the works, so did some distinguishing features, characteristics, viewpoints, values, decisions, and thus I used the Valley and the Border, and the history and the people. The freedom to do this also led me to use the folklore and the anthropology of the Valley and to use whatever literary form I desired and saw fit to use to tell my stories: dialogs, duologs, monologs, imaginary newspaper clippings, and whatever else I felt would be of use. And it *was* the Valley, but it remained forever Texas. At the same time, I could see this Valley, this border, and I drew a map, and this, too, was another key, and this led to more work and to more characters in that place.

It was a matter of luck in some ways, as I said, but mostly it was the proper historical moment; it came along, and I took what had been there for some time, but which I had not been able to see, since I had not fully developed a sense of place; I had left the Valley for the service, for formal university training, and for a series of very odd jobs, only to return to it in my writing.

I have mentioned values and decisions; as I see them, these are matters inculcated by one's elders first, by one's acquaintances later on, and usually under the influence of one's society which is another way of saying one's place of origin. Genetic structure may enter into holding to certain values and perhaps in the manner of reaching decisions, for all I know. Ortega y Gasset, among others, I suspect, wrote that man makes dozens of decisions every day, and that the process helps man to make and to reach more serious, deliberate, and even important decisions when the time presents itself. A preparatory stage, as it were. The point of this is that my decision to write what I write and where I choose to situate the writing is not based on anything else other than to write about what I know, the place I know, the language used, the values held. When someone mentions universality, I say that what happens to my characters happens to other peoples of the world at given times, and I've no doubt on that score. What has helped me to write has also been a certain amount of questionable self-education, a long and fairly misspent youth in the eyes of some, an acceptance of certain facts and some misrepresentations of the past which I could not change, but which led to a rejection not of those unalterable facts but of hypocrisy and the smugness of the self-satisfied. For this and other personal reasons, humor creeps into my writing once in a while, because it was the use of irony, as many of us know, that allowed the Borderer to survive and to maintain a certain measure of dignity.

20

Serious writing is deliberate as well as a consequence of an arrived-to decision; what one does with it may be of value or not, but I believe that one's fidelity to history is the first step in fixing a sense of place, whether that place is a worldwide arena or a corner of it, as is mine.

Response

1. Hinojosa gained his sense of place—his sense of the history and culture of the Valley—by "living it, forming part of it, and thus, contributing to it" (paragraph 5). In what ways did he do this? What elements does he enumerate as contributing to the sense of place?

2. According to Hinojosa, why is it "inoperative" to tell a Borderer "go back to where you came from" (paragraph 14)?

3. Hinojosa observes that a writer's place of origin inevitably tends to influence his writing. He generalizes this point (in paragraph 17), saying "what spine one has is formed early in life, and it is formed at a specific place . . . the original facts of one's formation remain as facts always do." Examine his statement; do you agree? Does your own experience bear it out?

4. Consider Hinojosa's analysis of where a person's values come from (in paragraph 20). Do his observations apply in your own case? How generalizable do you think his views are?

5. "One's fidelity to history is the first step in fixing a sense of place," Hinojosa says in conclusion. The lower Rio Grande Valley was settled by the Spanish in the seventeenth century and by the English 150 years later. The independent Republic of Texas was proclaimed in 1836, and in 1845 Texas was annexed by the United States as the twenty-eighth state. What history does Hinojosa have in mind? Accepting his statement, do you think different Texans would share the same sense of place?

6. Find points of comparison between Hinojosa's essay, Joan Didion's "Notes from a Native Daughter," and James Baldwin's "Autobiographical Notes" (Section I). Do Hinojosa's views echo those of any other writers in this collection?

Zami:
A New Spelling of My Name
Audre Lorde

*This passage from Lorde's 1982 "biomythography"
recalls a trip Lorde made to Washington, D.C., in
1947 with her sister and her parents, who were
immigrants from Grenada. In it she recounts an
experience of racial segregation that marked a
turning point in her own developing social
awareness.*

The first time I went to Washington, D.C. was on the edge of
the summer when I was supposed to stop being a child. At least
that's what they said to us all at graduation from the eighth grade.
My sister Phyllis graduated at the same time from high school. I
don't know what she was supposed to stop being. But as graduation
presents for us both, the whole family took a Fourth of July trip to
Washington, D.C., the fabled and famous capital of our country.

It was the first time I'd ever been on a railroad train during the
day. When I was little, and we used to go to the Connecticut shore,
we always went at night on the milk train, because it was cheaper.

Preparations were in the air around our house before school
was even over. We packed for a week. There were two very large
suitcases that my father carried, and a box filled with food. In fact,

my first trip to Washington was a mobile feast; I started eating as
soon as we were comfortably ensconced in our seats, and did not
stop until somewhere after Philadelphia. I remember it was Philadelphia because I was disappointed not to have passed by the Liberty
Bell.

My mother had roasted two chickens and cut them up into
dainty bite-size pieces. She packed slices of brown bread and butter
and green pepper and carrot sticks. There were little violently yellow iced cakes with scalloped edges called "marigolds," that came
from Cushman's Bakery. There was a spice bun and rock-cakes from
Newton's, the West Indian bakery across Lenox Avenue from St.
Mark's School, and iced tea in a wrapped mayonnaise jar. There were
sweet pickles for us and dill pickles for my father, and peaches with
the fuzz still on them, individually wrapped to keep them from
bruising. And, for neatness, there were piles of napkins and a little
tin box with a washcloth dampened with rosewater and glycerine
for wiping sticky mouths.

5   I wanted to eat in the dining car because I had read all about
them, but my mother reminded me for the umpteenth time that
dining car food always cost too much money and besides, you never
could tell whose hands had been playing all over that food, nor where
those same hands had been just before. My mother never mentioned
that Black people were not allowed into railroad dining cars headed
south in 1947. As usual, whatever my mother did not like and could
not change, she ignored. Perhaps it would go away, deprived of her
attention.

I learned later that Phyllis's high school senior class trip had
been to Washington, but the nuns had given her back her deposit in
private, explaining to her that the class, all of whom were white,
except Phyllis, would be staying in a hotel where Phyllis "would
not be happy," meaning, Daddy explained to her, also in private,
that they did not rent rooms to Negroes. "We will take among-you
to Washington, ourselves," my father had avowed, "and not just for
an overnight in some measly fleabag hotel."

American racism was a new and crushing reality that my parents had to deal with every day of their lives once they came to this
country. They handled it as a private woe. My mother and father
believed that they could best protect their children from the realities of race in America and the fact of American racism by never
giving them name, much less discussing their nature. We were told
we must never trust white people, but *why* was never explained,
nor the nature of their ill will. Like so many other vital pieces of
information in my childhood, I was supposed to know without being
told. It always seemed like a very strange injunction coming from

my mother, who looked so much like one of those people we were never supposed to trust. But something always warned me not to ask my mother why she wasn't white, and why Auntie Lillah and Auntie Etta weren't, even though they were all that same problematic color so different from my father and me, even from my sisters, who were somewhere in-between.

In Washington, D.C. we had one large room with two double beds and an extra cot for me. It was a back-street hotel that belonged to a friend of my father's who was in real estate, and I spent the whole next day after Mass squinting up at the Lincoln Memorial where Marian Anderson had sung after the D.A.R. refused to allow her to sing in their auditorium because she was Black. Or because she was "Colored," my father said as he told us the story. Except that what he probably said was "Negro," because for his times, my father was quite progressive.

I was squinting because I was in that silent agony that characterized all of my childhood summers, from the time school let out in June to the end of July, brought about by my dilated and vulnerable eyes exposed to the summer brightness.

I viewed Julys through an agonizing corolla of dazzling white-   10
ness and I always hated the Fourth of July, even before I came to realize the travesty such a celebration was for Black people in this country.

My parents did not approve of sunglasses, nor of their expense.

I spent the afternoon squinting up at monuments to freedom and past presidencies and democracy, and wondering why the light and heat were both so much stronger in Washington, D.C. than back home in New York City. Even the pavement on the streets was a shade lighter in color than back home.

Late that Washington afternoon my family and I walked back down Pennsylvania Avenue. We were a proper caravan, mother bright and father brown, the three of us girls step-standards in-between. Moved by our historical surroundings and the heat of the early evening, my father decreed yet another treat. He had a great sense of history, a flair for the quietly dramatic and the sense of specialness of an occasion and a trip.

"Shall we stop and have a little something to cool off, Lin?"

Two blocks away from our hotel, the family stopped for a dish   15
of vanilla ice cream at a Breyer's ice cream and soda fountain. Indoors, the soda fountain was dim and fan-cooled, deliciously relieving to my scorched eyes.

Corded and crisp and pinafored, the five of us seated ourselves one by one at the counter. There was I between my mother and father, and my two sisters on the other side of my mother. We settled ourselves along the white mottled marble counter, and when the waitress spoke at first no one understood what she was saying, and so the five of us just sat there.

The waitress moved along the line of us closer to my father and spoke again. "I said I kin give you to take out, but you can't eat here. Sorry." Then she dropped her eyes looking very embarrassed, and suddenly we heard what it was she was saying all at the same time, loud and clear.

Straight-backed and indignant, one by one, my family and I got down from the counter stools and turned around and marched out of the store, quiet and outraged, as if we had never been Black before. No one would answer my emphatic questions with anything other than a guilty silence. "But we hadn't done anything!" This wasn't right or fair! Hadn't I written poems about Bataan and freedom and democracy for all?

My parents wouldn't speak of this injustice, not because they had contributed to it, but because they felt they should have anticipated it and avoided it. This made me even angrier. My fury was not going to be acknowledged by a like fury. Even my two sisters copied my parents' pretense that nothing unusual and anti-American had occurred. I was left to write my angry letter to the president of the United States all by myself, although my father did promise I could type it out on the office typewriter next week, after I showed it to him in my copybook diary.

20   The waitress was white, and the counter was white, and the ice cream I never ate in Washington, D.C. that summer I left childhood was white, and the white heat and the white pavement and the white stone monuments of my first Washington summer made me sick to my stomach for the whole rest of that trip and it wasn't much of a graduation present after all.

Response

1. Why do you think Lorde goes into such detail in describing the elegant picnic her mother packed for the train? What is the effect of her description of the family as "corded and crisp and pinafored" (paragraph 16)?

2. Lorde says that her mother and father, Grenadian immigrants treated racism in this country as "a private woe." How is that attitude illustrated by their behavior? How is their response to the soda fountain incident consistent with that attitude? Why does Lorde use the term "guilty silence" in paragraph 18?

3. How would you characterize or explain the behavior and attitudes of the Catholic school nuns? The waitress in Washington, D.C.?

4. Lorde had severely impaired sight, and she saw Washington, D.C., through extremely light-sensitive eyes. How does she use this literal fact to create an ironic vision of the city? Notice other ways in which she examines the question of color through the eyes of a child trying to make sense of the world. How was her mother's and aunts' color "problematic"? What is the significance of the term used, by her father or herself, to refer to Marian Anderson's color?

5. How does Lorde's reaction to the incident in Washington, D.C., stand in contrast to that of her parents? How does this anecdote foreshadow Lorde's later essay, "The Transformation of Silence into Language and Action" (Section V)?

A Drugstore in Winter

Cynthia Ozick

This essay appeared first in The New York Times
Book Review *in 1982 and was included in Ozick's
first collection of essays,* Art and Ardor *(1983). It is a
memoir of a happy time and place in Ozick's youth
and a philosophical comment about life and writing.*

This is about reading; a drugstore in winter; the gold leaf on
the dome of the Boston State House; also loss, panic, and dread.

First, the gold leaf. (This part is a little like a turn-of-the-cen-
tury pulp tale, though only a little. The ending is a surprise, but
there is no plot.) Thirty years ago I burrowed in the Boston Public
Library one whole afternoon, to find out—not out of curiosity—how
the State House got its gold roof. The answer, like the answer to
most Bostonian questions, was Paul Revere. So I put Paul Revere's
gold dome into an "article," and took it (though I was just as scared
by recklessness then as I am now) to the *Boston Globe*, on Washington Street. The Features Editor had a bare severe head, a closed par-
enthesis mouth, and silver Dickensian spectacles. He made me wait,
standing, at the side of his desk while he read; there was no bone in
me that did not rattle. Then he opened a drawer and handed me
fifteen dollars. Ah, joy of Homer, joy of Milton! Grub Street bliss!

The very next Sunday, Paul Revere's gold dome saw print. Appetite for more led me to a top-floor chamber in Filene's department store: Window Dressing. But no one was in the least bit dressed—it was a dŭmbstruck nudist colony up there, a mob of naked frozen enigmatic manikins, tall enameled skinny ladies with bald breasts and skulls, and legs and wrists and necks that horribly unscrewed. Paul Revere's dome paled beside this gold mine! A sight—mute numb Walpurgisnacht—easily worth another fifteen dollars. I had a Master's degree (thesis topic: "Parable in the Later Novels of Henry James") and a job as an advertising copywriter (9 a.m. to 6 p.m. six days a week, forty dollars per week; if you were male and had no degree at all, sixty dollars). Filene's Sale Days—Crib Bolsters! Lulla-Buys! Jonnie-Mops! Maternity Skirts with Expanding Invisible Trick Waist! And a company show; gold watches to mark the retirement of elderly Irish salesladies; for me the chance to write song lyrics (to the tune of "On Top of Old Smoky") honoring our Store. But "Mute Numb Walpurgisnacht in Secret Downtown Chamber" never reached the *Globe*. Melancholy and meaning business, the Advertising Director forbade it. Grub Street was bad form, and I had to promise never again to sink to another article. Thus ended my life in journalism.

Next: reading, and certain drugstore winter dusks. These come together. It is an aeon before Filene's, years and years before the Later Novels of Henry James. I am scrunched on my knees at a round glass table near a plate glass door on which is inscribed, in gold leaf Paul Revere never put there, letters that must be read backward: | ＰＡＲＫ ＶＩＥＷ ＰＨＡＲＭＡＣＹ | There is an evening smell of late coffee from the fountain, and all the librarians are lined up in a row on the tall stools, sipping and chattering. They have just stepped in from the cold of the Traveling Library, and so have I. The Traveling Library is a big green truck that stops, once every two weeks, on the corner of Continental Avenue, just a little way in from Westchester Avenue, not far from a house that keeps a pig. Other houses fly pigeons from their roofs, other yards have chickens, and down on Mayflower there is even a goat. This is Pelham Bay, the Bronx, in the middle of the Depression, all cattails and weeds, such a lovely place and tender hour! Even though my mother takes me on the subway far, far downtown to buy my winter coat in the frenzy of Klein's on Fourteenth Street, and even though I can recognize the heavy power of a quarter, I don't know it's the Depression. On the trolley on the way to Westchester Square I see the children who live in the boxcar strangely set down in an empty lot some distance from Spy Oak (where a Revolutionary traitor was hanged—served him right for siding with redcoats); the lucky boxcar children dangle their stick-legs from their train-house maw and wave; how I envy them! I envy the orphans of the Gould Foundation, who have their own private swings and seesaws. Sometimes I imagine I am an orphan, and my father is an impostor pretending to be my father.

5   My father writes in his prescription book: *#59330 Dr. O'Flaherty Pow .60/ #59331 Dr. Mulligan Gtt .65/ #59332 Dr. Thron Tab .90.* Ninety cents! A terrifically expensive medicine; someone is really sick. When I deliver a prescription around the corner or down the block, I am offered a nickel tip. I always refuse, out of conscience; I am, after all, the Park View Pharmacy's own daughter, and it wouldn't be seemly. My father grinds and mixes powders, weighs them out in tiny snowy heaps on an apothecary scale, folds them into delicate translucent papers or meticulously drops them into gelatin capsules.

In the big front window of the Park View Pharmacy there is a startling display—goldfish bowls, balanced one on the other in amazing pyramids. A German lady enters, one of my father's cronies—his cronies are both women and men. My quiet father's eyes are water-color blue, he wears his small skeptical quiet smile and receives the neighborhood's life-secrets. My father is discreet and inscrutable. The German lady pokes a punchboard with a pin, pushes up a bit of rolled paper, and cries out—she has just won a goldfish bowl, with two swimming goldfish in it! Mr. Jaffe, the salesman from McKesson & Robbins, arrives, trailing two mists: winter steaminess and the animal fog of his cigar,* which melts into the coffee smell, the tarpaper smell, the eerie honeyed tangled drugstore smell. Mr. Jaffe and my mother and father are intimates by now, but because it is the 1930s, so long ago, and the old manners still survive, they address one another gravely as Mr. Jaffe, Mrs. Ozick, Mr. Ozick. My mother calls my father Mr. O, even at home, as in a Victorian novel. In the street my father tips his hat to ladies. In the winter his hat is a regular fedora; in the summer it is a straw boater with a black ribbon and a jot of blue feather.

What am I doing at this round glass table, both listening and not listening to my mother and father tell Mr. Jaffe about their struggle with "Tessie," the lion-eyed landlady who has just raised, threefold, in the middle of that Depression I have never heard of, the Park View Pharmacy's devouring rent? My mother, not yet forty, wears bandages on her ankles, covering oozing varicose veins; back

---

*Mr. Matthew Bruccoli, another Bronx drugstore child, has written to say that he remembers with certainty that Mr. Jaffe did not smoke. In my memory the cigar is somehow there, so I leave it.

and forth she strides, dashes, runs, climbing cellar stairs or ladders; she unpacks cartons, she toils behind drug counters and fountain counters. Like my father, she is on her feet until one in the morning, the Park View's closing hour. My mother and father are in trouble, and I don't know it. I am too happy. I feel the secret center of eternity, nothing will ever alter, no one will ever die. Through the window, past the lit goldfish, the gray oval sky deepens over our neighborhood wood, where all the dirt paths lead down to seagull-specked water. I am familiar with every frog-haunted monument: Pelham Bay Park is thronged with WPA art—statuary, fountains, immense rococo staircases cascading down a hillside, Bacchus-faced stelae— stone Roman glories afterward mysteriously razed by an avenging Robert Moses. One year—how distant it seems now, as if even the climate is past returning—the bay froze so hard that whole families, mine among them, crossed back and forth to City Island, strangers saluting and calling out in the ecstasy of the bright trudge over such a sudden wilderness of ice.

In the Park View Pharmacy, in the winter dusk, the heart in my body is revolving like the goldfish fleet-finned in their clear bowls. The librarians are still warming up over their coffee. They do not recognize me, though only half an hour ago I was scrabbling in the mud around the two heavy boxes from the Traveling Library— oafish crates tossed with a thump to the ground. One box contains magazines—*Boy's Life*, *The American Girl*, *Popular Mechanix*. But the other, the other! The other transforms me. It is tumbled with storybooks, with clandestine intimations and transfigurations. In school I am a luckless goosegirl, friendless and forlorn. In P.S. 71 I carry, weighty as a cloak, the ineradicable knowledge of my scandal—I am cross-eyed, dumb, an imbecile at arithmetic; in P.S. 71 I am publicly shamed in Assembly because I am caught not singing Christmas carols; in P.S. 71 I am repeatedly accused of deicide. But in the Park View Pharmacy, in the winter dusk, branches blackening in the park across the road, I am driving in rapture through the Violet Fairy Book and the Yellow Fairy Book, insubstantial chariots snatched from the box in the mud. I have never been *inside* the Traveling Library; only grownups are allowed. The boxes are for the children. No more than two books may be borrowed, so I have picked the fattest ones, to last. All the same, the Violet and the Yellow are melting away. Their pages dwindle. I sit at the round glass table, dreaming, dreaming. Mr. Jaffe is murmuring advice. He tells a joke about Wrong-Way Corrigan. The librarians are buttoning up their coats. A princess, captive of an ogre, receives a letter from her swain and hides it in her bosom. I can visualize her bosom exactly—she clutches it against her chest. It is a tall and shapely vase, with a hand-painted flower on it, like the vase on the secondhand piano at home.

I am incognito. No one knows who I truly am. The teachers in P.S. 71 don't know. Rabbi Meskin, my *cheder* teacher, doesn't know. Tessie the lion-eyed landlady doesn't know. Even Hymie the fountain clerk can't know—though he understands other things better than anyone: how to tighten roller skates with a skatekey, for instance, and how to ride a horse. On Friday afternoons, when the new issue is out, Hymie and my brother fight hard over who gets to see *Life* magazine first. My brother is older than I am, and doesn't like me; he builds radios in his bedroom, he is already W2LOM, and operates his transmitter (*da-di-da-dit , da-da-di-da*) so penetratingly on Sunday mornings that Mrs. Eva Brady, across the way, complains. Mrs. Eva Brady has a subscription to *The Writer;* I fill a closet with her old copies. How to Find a Plot. Narrative and Character, the Writer's Tools. Because my brother has his ham license, I say, "I have a license too." "What kind of license?" my brother asks, falling into the trap. "Poetic license," I reply; my brother hates me, but anyhow his birthday presents are transporting: one year *Alice in Wonderland*, *Pinocchio* the next, then *Tom Sawyer*. I go after Mark Twain, and find *Joan of Arc* and my first satire, *Christian Science*. My mother surprises me with *Pollyanna*, the admiration of her Lower East Side childhood, along with *The Lady of the Lake*. Mrs. Eva Brady's daughter Jeannie has outgrown her Nancy Drews and Judy Boltons, so on rainy afternoons I cross the street and borrow them, trying not to march away with too many—the child of immigrants, I worry that the Bradys, true and virtuous Americans, will judge me greedy or careless. I wrap the Nancy Drews in paper covers to protect them. Old Mrs. Brady, Jeannie's grandmother, invites me back for more. I am so timid I can hardly speak a word, but I love her dark parlor; I love its black bookcases. Old Mrs. Brady sees me off, embracing books under an umbrella; perhaps she divines who I truly am. My brother doesn't care. My father doesn't notice. I think my mother knows. My mother reads the *Saturday Evening Post* and the *Woman's Home Companion;* sometimes the *Ladies' Home Journal*, but never *Good Housekeeping*. I read all my mother's magazines. My father reads *Drug Topics* and *Der Tog*, the Yiddish daily. In Louie Davidowitz's house (waiting our turn for the rabbi's lesson, he teaches me chess in *cheder*) there is a piece of furniture I am in awe of: a shining circular table that is also a revolving bookshelf holding a complete set of Charles Dickens. I borrow *Oliver Twist*. My cousins turn up with *Gulliver's Travels*, *Just So Stories*, *Don Quixote*, Oscar Wilde's *Fairy Tales*, uncannily different from the usual kind. Blindfolded, I reach into a Thanksgiving grabbag and pull out *Mrs. Leicester's School*, Mary Lamb's desolate stories of rejected children. Books spill out of rumor, exchange, miracle. In the Park View Pharmacy's lending library I discover, among the nurse romances, a browning, brittle miracle: *Jane Eyre*. Uncle Morris comes to visit (*his* drugstore is on the other side of the Bronx) and leaves behind, just like that, a three-volume Shakespeare. Peggy and Betty Provan, Scottish sisters around the corner, lend me their *Swiss Family Robinson*. Norma Foti, a whole year older, transmits a rumor about Louisa May Alcott; afterward I read *Little Women* a thousand times. Ten thousand! I am no longer incognito, not even to myself. I am Jo in her "vortex"; not Jo exactly, but some Jo-of-the-future. I am under an enchantment: who I truly am must be deferred, waited for and waited for. My father, silently filling capsules, is grieving over his mother in Moscow. I write letters in Yiddish to my Moscow grandmother, whom I will never know. I will never know my Russian aunts, uncles, cousins. In Moscow there is suffering, deprivation, poverty. My mother, threadbare, goes without a new winter coat so that packages can be sent to Moscow. Her fiery justice-eyes are semaphores I cannot decipher.

Some day, when I am free of P.S. 71, I will write stories; mean- 10
while, in winter dusk, in the Park View, in the secret bliss of the Violet Fairy Book, I both see and do not see how these grains of life will stay forever, papa and mama will live forever, Hymie will always turn my skatekey.

Hymie, after Italy, after the Battle of the Bulge, comes back from the war with a present: *From Here to Eternity*. Then he dies, young. Mama reads *Pride and Prejudice* and every single word of Willa Cather. Papa reads, in Yiddish, all of Sholem Aleichem and Peretz. He reads Malamud's *The Assistant* when I ask him to.

Papa and mama, in Staten Island, are under the ground. Some other family sits transfixed in the sun parlor where I read *Jane Eyre* and *Little Women* and, long afterward, *Middlemarch*. The Park View Pharmacy is dismantled, turned into a Hallmark card shop. It doesn't matter! I close my eyes, or else only stare, and everything is in its place again, and everyone.

A writer is dreamed and transfigured into being by spells, wishes, goldfish, silhouettes of trees, boxes of fairy tales dropped in the mud, uncles' and cousins' books, tablets and capsules and powders, papa's Moscow ache, his drugstore jacket with his special fountain pen in the pocket, his beautiful Hebrew paragraphs, his Talmudist's rationalism, his Russian-Gymnasium Latin and German, mama's furnace-heart, her masses of memoirs, her paintings of autumn walks down to the sunny water, her braveries, her reveries, her old, old school hurts.

A writer is buffeted into being by school hurts—Orwell, Forster, Mann!—but after a while other ambushes begin: sorrows, deaths, disappointments, subtle diseases, delays, guilts, the spite of the private haters of the poetry side of life, the snubs of the glamorous, the bitterness of those for whom resentment is a daily gruel, and so on and so on; and then one day you find yourself leaning here, writing at that selfsame round glass table salvaged from the Park View Pharmacy—writing this, an impossibility, a summary of how you came to be where you are now, and where, God knows, is that? Your hair is whitening, you are a well of tears, what you meant to do (beauty and justice) you have not done, papa and mama are under the earth, you live in panic and dread, the future shrinks and darkens, stories are only vapor, your inmost craving is for nothing but an old scarred pen, and what, God knows, is that?

Response

1. What values and conditions of the time are reflected in Ozick's opening anecdote about her brief life in journalism? What connection does this anecdote bear to the rest of her essay?

2. Ozick tells her journalism anecdote in the past tense, but switches to present tense to tell about the drugstore. Why? What is the effect of this tense shift?

3. What do we know about Ozick's family? What circumstances does Ozick suggest in her recollections of "school hurts" at P.S. 71, in paragraph 8?

4. Recalling her former self, Ozick says, "I am incognito. No one knows who I truly am" (paragraph 9), except perhaps old Mrs. Brady and her mother. What did they recognize?

5. Ozick has recreated a picture of contentment and certainty in the midst of the Depression. Recalling how she felt, she says, "My mother and father are in trouble, and I don't know it. I am too happy. I feel the secret center of eternity, nothing will ever alter, no one will ever die" (paragraph 7). What gave her that security? Now, looking back, she says, "I close my eyes, or else only stare, and everything is in its place again, and everyone" (paragraph 12). Ozick could have ended her essay there; how would it be different if she had?

6. Ozick tells us that this is an essay about "loss, panic, and dread." In the poignant ending, it also becomes an essay about becoming a writer. What motivates writing, for her? What does she long for?

American Fish

R. A. Sasaki

This story is included in The Loom and Other Stories
*(1991). As two women chat casually in a market,
they reveal a common experience of living in their
particular time and place.*

Mrs. Hayashi was inspecting a daikon radish in the American
Fish Market in Japantown when she recognized a woman who was
heading toward the burdock roots.

I know her, she thought. What was her name? Suzuki? Kato?
She decided to pretend not to see the woman, and see if the woman
recognized her. She put down the radish and picked up another.

"Oh . . . hello," said the woman, who was now standing next
to her.

Mrs. Hayashi looked up and smiled enthusiastically. "Oh, hi!"
she said. "Long time no see." Immediately she regretted the remark.
What if it was someone she had just seen yesterday?

"How've you been?" the woman asked.   5

"Fine, just fine," Mrs. Hayashi said. I should ask her about her
husband, she thought. Did she have a husband?

"How's your husband?" the woman asked.

Mrs. Hayashi's husband had died ten years before. Obviously,
the woman was someone she had not seen in quite some time.

Thank goodness, she thought. Then it had been appropriate to say "long time no see."

"He passed away several years ago," Mrs. Hayashi said.

10   "Oh, so sorry to hear that," the woman said.

I should ask her about her children, Mrs. Hayashi thought. But since she still did not know if the woman had a husband or not, she couldn't very well assume that she had children. Wouldn't it be awful if I asked her about her children and it turned out she wasn't even married! And even if she was married, and did have children, what if they had died, or committed crimes? After all, everyone couldn't have a son in law school, and Mrs. Hayashi did not like to appear to be boasting. No, she'd better avoid the subject of children.

"How are your kids?" the woman asked.

"Oh, Bill is just fine," Mrs. Hayashi replied. She couldn't stand it. "He'll be graduating from law school next spring," she added, consoling herself with the thought that at least she had refrained from mentioning that her son was at the top of his class.

"That's nice," said the woman. "And what about your daughter?"

15   "I don't have a daughter," Mrs. Hayashi said stiffly. "Just a son." She was beginning to think that the woman wasn't anyone she knew very well.

"Stupid me," said the woman. "I was thinking of someone else."

"How are *your* children?" Mrs. Hayashi asked, throwing caution to the wind.

"Fine," the woman said. "Emily and her husband live in San Jose and have two little girls."

"How nice," Mrs. Hayashi said.

20   There was a pause. Mrs. Hayashi did not know anyone named Emily. Who was this woman?

It occurred to her that the woman might be someone she didn't like. How aggravating, she thought, not to be able to remember whether to be pleasant to someone or not.

"I'm so sorry," the woman said, "But I have a real bad memory for names. It was Suzuki-san, wasn't it?"

"Hayashi," Mrs. Hayashi said, peeved. "Grace Hayashi."

"Of course," said the woman, somewhat vaguely. "Hayashi . . ."

25   "And . . . forgive me," said Mrs. Hayashi, seizing the opportunity, "but you're . . .?"

"Nakamura," the woman said. "Toshi Nakamura."

The name did not even ring a bell.

"Is that the family that runs the bakery on Fillmore?" Mrs. Hayashi asked.

"No," the woman said, "not that Nakamura."

"Then you must be related to Frank Nakamura." 30

"No."

"How odd," Mrs. Hayashi said without thinking, and was embarrassed when she realized she had spoken aloud.

"My maiden name was Fujii," Mrs. Nakamura said.

"Fujii . . ." Mrs. Hayashi said, thinking hard.

"Maybe you know my sister Eiko." 35

"Eiko Fujii . . ." Mrs. Hayashi said, frowning.

Then a horrible thought occurred to Mrs. Hayashi. Perhaps she did not know this woman at all; perhaps Mrs. Nakamura just looked like someone she knew, or someone she should know—a Japanese-American lady in her late fifties, the same age as Mrs. Hayashi, wearing a somewhat faded but sensible raincoat even though it was not raining outside. But then, Mrs. Nakamura had recognized her, too.

"Did I know you in Topaz?" Mrs. Hayashi asked.

"Oh, no," Mrs. Nakamura said. Mrs. Hayashi waited, but the other woman said nothing further.

"You weren't in Topaz?" Mrs. Hayashi continued. 40

"No."

"Where were you—Manzanar?" Mrs. Hayashi asked pleasantly.

"No."

"Oh, well," Mrs. Hayashi said, becoming flustered. "Perhaps you weren't in camp during the war. I don't mean to pry."

"I was in Tule Lake," Mrs. Nakamura said, turning to pick 45 through the burdock roots. She rejected a shriveled bunch of roots and put a fresh bunch in her cart.

"Oh," Mrs. Hayashi said. She felt her face go hot. Tule Lake was where all those branded "disloyal" had been imprisoned during the war. "I see," Mrs. Hayashi said, searching for a way to change the topic.

"Do you?"

Mrs. Hayashi was startled. "I'm sorry," she said. "I don't know what you mean."

"And I don't know what you see," Mrs. Nakamura said.

"Nothing," Mrs. Hayashi said. "I just meant—oh." 50

"Oh," Mrs. Nakamura said.

Mrs. Hayashi by this time was extremely uncomfortable and groped for a way to redeem the situation.

"I knew some people who were in Tule Lake," she said. "The Satos. From Watsonville. Did you know them?"

"No," Mrs. Nakamura said.

55   "It was the silliest thing, really," Mrs. Hayashi went on. "Mr. Sato was a Buddhist priest, and after Pearl Harbor, his name got on some list, and the FBI picked him up. Imagine that."

Mrs. Nakamura was silent.

"As if being Buddhist was a crime," Mrs. Hayashi added, trying to make clear where her sympathies lay. She was not a Buddhist herself, but she thought Mrs. Nakamura might be one.

"My father said he wanted to go back to Japan," Mrs. Nakamura said suddenly. "That's why we were in Tule Lake."

"Oh," Mrs. Hayashi said.

60   "They took his boat away after Pearl Harbor," Mrs. Nakamura continued."He was a fisherman down in Terminal Island. Without a boat, he couldn't make a living. He thought the only thing to do was to go back to Japan."

"I know," Mrs. Hayashi said. "My father was forced to sell his store to the first person who offered to buy. A lifetime of hard work, just thrown away!"

"It made my father mad," Mrs. Nakamura went on. "He said why stay in a country that doesn't want us?"

"That's perfectly logical," Mrs. Hayashi reassured. "Why indeed?"

"Why did *your* parents want to stay?" Mrs. Nakamura asked.

65   "Well," Mrs. Hayashi said, startled. "I don't know." She thought for a moment, then said, "I guess they knew that we, I mean my brothers and sisters and I, would never want to go to Japan. I mean, we were born here. We belonged here. And they wanted the family to stay together."

"That's how my mother and I felt," Mrs. Nakamura said. "That's why we said we wanted to go back to Japan, too—so we'd be all together. Except in those days, that made you disloyal."

"Well, it was ridiculous," Mrs. Hayashi said firmly. "And it caused so much grief."

There was a silence.

"Where did you go back to, in Japan?" Mrs. Hayashi asked gently.

70   "Oh, we didn't go back," Mrs. Nakamura replied cheerfully. "My father changed his mind when he remembered that they didn't have central heating in Japan."

Both women burst out laughing.

Mrs. Hayashi, still laughing, threw a bunch of burdock roots into her cart.

"Well, I should be getting along," Mrs. Nakamura said. "I'm so glad I bumped into you . . ." She stopped, embarrassed.

"Hayashi."

". . . Hayashi-san," she finished. "Now if I could just remember   75
who you are."

They laughed again.

"I'm sure it'll come back to us," Mrs. Hayashi said. "Everything does."

"Do you go to the Buddhist church?" Mrs. Nakamura asked. "Maybe I've seen you there."

"I doubt it," Mrs. Hayashi replied. "I'm Methodist. But I've been to funerals at the Buddhist church, so maybe."

"That must be it—we must have met at someone's funeral,"   80
Mrs. Nakamura agreed. "I'm sure it'll come to me as soon as I walk out of here with my groceries. Isn't it always like that?"

"It can't be that mysterious," Mrs. Hayashi said. "I mean, our lives aren't so terribly complicated. If we didn't know each other in camp, then we knew each other before the war, or after the war. I'm sure I won't be able to sleep until I remember which it was," she added cheerfully. "I hate to forget things. That is, unless they're the sort of things you'd rather not remember."

Mrs. Nakamura looked at her watch.

"My goodness," she said. "I have to run. I have to be at work in an hour."

"Work?" Mrs. Hayashi said.

"Yes; I work at Macy's," Mrs. Nakamura said. "I'm in . . ."   85

"Gift wrap!" Mrs. Hayashi said, remembering.

The two women stared incredulously at each other for an instant, then broke into raucous laughter. Then they bowed slightly, and continued on their separate ways.

Response _____

1. At what point do the women realize that neither knows who the other one is? Why do they keep trying to figure it out?

2. The two women search through the important events of their generation looking for their connection, only to discover it in a mundane, impersonal circumstance of everyday life. In the process, they get to know each other. What experiences and values do they have in common?

3. What is the significance of the story's title? With a light touch, the story makes an ironic comment about the experience of

these women's generation. How do their reminiscences bring this out?

4. Look at how small details work together to portray the character of Mrs. Hayashi. How does she bring to mind the mother in "The Loom," also by R. A. Sasaki (Section III)? Do the two fictional characters seem to derive from a common source in the author's experience?

Looking for Work
Gary Soto ⎯⎯⎯⎯⎯⎯⎯⎯⎯⎯⎯⎯⎯⎯⎯

This essay, from Soto's book Living Up the Street
*(1985), is a reminiscence of life in the Fresno,
California, neighborhood where he grew up. He
recalls a time in his childhood when he was
becoming aware of differences in social class and
their impact on daily life.*

One July, while killing ants on the kitchen sink with a rolled
newspaper, I had a nine-year-old's vision of wealth that would save
us from ourselves. For weeks I had drunk Kool-Aid and watched
morning reruns of *Father Knows Best*, whose family was so uncom-
plicated in its routine that I very much wanted to imitate it. The
first step was to get my brother and sister to wear shoes at dinner.

"Come on, Rick—come on, Deb," I whined. But Rick mimicked me and the same day that I asked him to wear shoes he came
to the dinner table in only his swim trunks. My mother didn't notice, nor did my sister, as we sat to eat our beans and tortillas in the
stifling heat of our kitchen. We all gleamed like cellophane, wiping
the sweat from our brows with the backs of our hands as we talked
about the day: Frankie our neighbor was beat up by Faustino; the
swimming pool at the playground would be closed for a day because
the pump was broken.

Such was our life. So that morning, while doing-in the train of ants which arrived each day, I decided to become wealthy, and right away! After downing a bowl of cereal, I took a rake from the garage and started up the block to look for work.

We lived on an ordinary block of mostly working class people: warehousemen, egg candlers, welders, mechanics, and a union plumber. And there were many retired people who kept their lawns green and the gutters uncluttered of the chewing gum wrappers we dropped as we rode by on our bikes. They bent down to gather our litter, muttering at our evilness.

5   At the corner house I rapped the screen door and a very large woman in a muu-muu answered. She sized me up and then asked what I could do.

"Rake leaves," I answered, smiling.

"It's summer, and there ain't no leaves," she countered. Her face was pinched with lines; fat jiggled under her chin. She pointed to the lawn, then the flower bed, and said: "You see any leaves there—or there?" I followed her pointing arm, stupidly. But she had a job for me and that was to get her a Coke at the liquor store. She gave me twenty cents, and after ditching my rake in a bush, off I ran. I returned with an unbagged Pepsi, for which she thanked me and gave me a nickel from her apron.

I skipped off her porch, fetched my rake, and crossed the street to the next block where Mrs. Moore, mother of Earl the retarded man, let me weed a flower bed. She handed me a trowel and for a good part of the morning my fingers dipped into the moist dirt, ripping up runners of Bermuda grass. Worms surfaced in my search for deep roots, and I cut them in halves, tossing them to Mrs. Moore's cat who pawed them playfully as they dried in the sun. I made out Earl whose face was pressed to the back window of the house, and although he was calling to me I couldn't understand what he was trying to say. Embarrassed, I worked without looking up, but I imagined his contorted mouth and the ring of keys attached to his belt—keys that jingled with each palsied step. He scared me and I worked quickly to finish the flower bed. When I did finish Mrs. Moore gave me a quarter and two peaches from her tree, which I washed there but ate in the alley behind my house.

I was sucking on the second one, a bit of juice staining the front of my T-shirt, when Little John, my best friend, came walking down the alley with a baseball bat over his shoulder, knocking over trash cans as he made his way toward me.

10   Little John and I went to St. John's Catholic School, where we sat among the "stupids." Miss Marino, our teacher, alternated the rows of good students with the bad, hoping that by sitting side-by-

side with the bright students the stupids might become more intelligent, as though intelligence were contagious. But we didn't progress as she had hoped. She grew frustrated when one day, while dismissing class for recess, Little John couldn't get up because his arms were stuck in the slats of the chair's backrest. She scolded us with a shaking finger when we knocked over the globe, denting the already troubled Africa. She muttered curses when Leroy White, a real stupid but a great softball player with the gift to hit to all fields, openly chewed his host when he made his First Communion; his hands swung at his sides as he returned to the pew looking around with a big smile.

Little John asked what I was doing, and I told him that I was taking a break from work, as I sat comfortably among high weeds. He wanted to join me, but I reminded him that the last time he'd gone door-to-door asking for work his mother had whipped him. I was with him when his mother, a New Jersey Italian who could rise up in anger one moment and love the next, told me in a polite but matter-of-fact voice that I had to leave because she was going to beat her son. She gave me a homemade popsicle, ushered me to the door, and said that I could see Little John the next day. But it was sooner than that. I went around to his bedroom window to suck my popsicle and watch Little John dodge his mother's blows, a few hitting their mark but many whirring air.

It was midday when Little John and I converged in the alley, the sun blazing in the high nineties, and he suggested that we go to Roosevelt High School to swim. He needed five cents to make fifteen, the cost of admission, and I lent him a nickel. We ran home for my bike and when my sister found out that we were going swimming, she started to cry because she didn't have the fifteen cents but only an empty Coke bottle. I waved for her to come and three of us mounted the bike—Debra on the cross bar, Little John on the handle bars and holding the Coke bottle which we would cash for a nickel and make up the difference that would allow all of us to get in, and me pumping up the crooked streets, dodging cars and pot holes. We spent the day swimming under the afternoon sun, so that when we got home our mom asked us what was darker, the floor or us? She feigned a stern posture, her hands on her hips and her mouth puckered. We played along. Looking down, Debbie and I said in unison, "Us."

That evening at dinner we all sat down in our bathing suits to eat our beans, laughing and chewing loudly. Our mom was in a good mood, so I took a risk and asked her if sometime we could have turtle soup. A few days before I had watched a television program in which a Polynesian tribe killed a large turtle, gutted it, and then stewed it over an open fire. The turtle, basted in a sugary sauce, looked delicious as I ate an afternoon bowl of cereal, but my sister, who was watching the program with a glass of Kool-Aid between her knees, said, "Caca."

My mother looked at me in bewilderment. "Boy, are you a crazy Mexican. Where did you get the idea that people eat turtles?"

15   "On television," I said, explaining the program. Then I took it a step further. "Mom, do you think we could get dressed up for dinner one of these days? David King does."

"*Ay, Dios,*" my mother laughed. She started collecting the dinner plates, but my brother wouldn't let go of his. He was still drawing a picture in the bean sauce. Giggling, he said it was me, but I didn't want to listen because I wanted an answer from Mom. This was the summer when I spent the mornings in front of the television that showed the comfortable lives of white kids. There were no beatings, no rifts in the family. They wore bright clothes; toys tumbled from their closets. They hopped into bed with kisses and woke to glasses of fresh orange juice, and to a father sitting before his morning coffee while the mother buttered his toast. They hurried through the day making friends and gobs of money, returning home to a warmly lit living room, and then dinner. *Leave It To Beaver* was the program I replayed in my mind:

"May I have the mashed potatoes?" asks Beaver with a smile.

"Sure, Beav," replies Wally as he taps the corners of his mouth with a starched napkin.

The father looks on in his suit. The mother, decked out in earrings and a pearl necklace, cuts into her steak and blushes. Their conversation is politely clipped.

20   "Swell," says Beaver, his cheeks puffed with food.

Our own talk at dinner was loud with belly laughs and marked by our pointing forks at one another. The subjects were commonplace.

"Gary, let's go to the ditch tomorrow," my brother suggests. He explains that he has made a life preserver out of four empty detergent bottles strung together with twine and that he will make me one if I can find more bottles. "No way are we going to drown."

"Yeah, then we could have a dirt clod fight," I reply, so happy to be alive.

Whereas the Beaver's family enjoyed dessert in dishes at the table, our mom sent us outside, and more often than not I went into the alley to peek over the neighbor's fences and spy out fruit, apricot or peaches.

25   I had asked my mom and again she laughed that I was a crazy

chavalo as she stood in front of the sink, her arms rising and falling with suds, face glistening from the heat. She sent me outside where my brother and sister were sitting in the shade that the fence threw out like a blanket. They were talking about me when I plopped down next to them. They looked at one another and then Debbie, my eight-year-old sister, started in.

"What's this crap about getting dressed up?"

She had entered her profanity stage. A year later she would give up such words and slip into her Catholic uniform, and into squealing on my brother and me when we "cussed this" and "cussed that."

I tried to convince them that if we improved the way we looked we might get along better in life. White people would like us more. They might invite us to places, like their homes or front yards. They might not hate us so much.

My sister called me a "craphead," and got up to leave with a stalk of grass dangling from her mouth. "They'll never like us."

My brother's mood lightened as he talked about the ditch—the white water, the broken pieces of glass, and the rusted car fenders that awaited our knees. There would be toads, and rocks to smash them. 30

David King, the only person we knew who resembled the middle class, called from over the fence. David was Catholic, of Armenian and French descent, and his closet was filled with toys. A bear-shaped cookie jar, like the ones on television, sat on the kitchen counter. His mother was remarkably kind while she put up with the racket we made on the street. Evenings, she often watered the front yard and it must have upset her to see us—my brother and I and others—jump from trees laughing, the unkillable kids of the very poor, who got up unshaken, brushed off, and climbed into another one to try again.

David called again. Rick got up and slapped grass from his pants. When I asked if I could come along he said no. David said no. They were two years older so their affairs were different from mine. They greeted one another with foul names and took off down the alley to look for trouble.

I went inside the house, turned on the television, and was about to sit down with a glass of Kool-Aid when Mom shooed me outside.

"It's still light," she said. "Later you'll bug me to let you stay out longer. So go on."

I downed my Kool-Aid and went outside to the front yard. No one was around. The day had cooled and a breeze rustled the trees. Mr. Jackson, the plumber, was watering his lawn and when he saw me he turned away to wash off his front steps. There was more than 35 an hour of light left, so I took advantage of it and decided to look for work. I felt suddenly alive as I skipped down the block in search of an overgrown flower bed and the dime that would end the day right.

Response

1. "Such was our life," observes Soto, after creating a picture of his childhood home life in just two opening paragraphs. Analyze how the details in those two paragraphs work to tell you about his family life, both literally and through the inferences they invite.

2. In this essay Soto portrays himself at an age when he was particularly vulnerable to the messages of TV. To Soto at the age of nine, what was the effect of the television shows? Look at the various references in the story to the middle-class life-style that Soto was noticing. What was his attitude (as a boy) toward the contrast between that and his own family's way of life?

3. This story spans a day in Soto's nine-year-old life. Do you think his feelings about life changed from the beginning to the end of the day? The story is a comment on the part of Soto the adult author about the way of life in his family and boyhood neighborhood; he portrays it in contrast to the middle-class ideal in order to make a point. What is his point of view—and how can we as readers recognize it?

4. Writing about his work, Gary Soto once explained that his poems and stories recreate common events of life in such a way that "particulars stand out as totems of a lusher experience." In other words, the details in a story evoke images and emotions beyond what they say. "Writing makes the ordinary stand out," he says, and allows the writer to suggest that ordinary details have some larger significance. How do you see Soto putting these ideas to work in this story?

5. Compare the perceptions of race and class differences in Soto the boy in this story, Soto the young man portrayed in "One Last Time" (Section V) and "Like Mexicans" (Section II), and Soto the adult writer of all three stories.

V
WRITING
AND SOCIAL CHANGE

Speaking in Tongues: A Letter to Third World Women Writers

Gloria Anzaldua

In this "letter," written in 1980, Anzaldua exhorts women of color to write, in the face of all obstacles. Despite its personal form, the letter's message speaks in one way or another to any reader. This passage is excerpted from a longer version that appeared in This Bridge Called My Back: Writings by Radical Women of Color *(1983).*

21 mayo 80

Dear mujeres de color, companions in writing—

I sit here naked in the sun, typewriter against my knee trying to visualize you. Black woman huddles over a desk in the fifth floor of some New York tenement. Sitting on a porch in south Texas, a Chicana fanning away mosquitos and the hot air, trying to arouse the smoldering embers of writing. Indian woman walking to school or work lamenting the lack of time to weave writing into your life. Asian American, lesbian, single mother, tugged in all directions by children, lover or ex-husband, and the writing.

It is not easy writing this letter. It began as a poem, a long poem. I tried to turn it into an essay but the result was wooden, cold. I have not yet unlearned the esoteric bullshit and pseudo-intellectualizing that school brainwashed into my writing.

How to begin again. How to approximate the intimacy and immediacy I want. What form? A letter, of course.

My dear *hermanas*, the dangers we face as women writers of color are not the same as those of white women though we have many in common. We don't have as much to lose—we never had any privileges. I wanted to call the dangers "obstacles" but that would be a kind of lying. We can't *transcend* the dangers, can't rise above them. We must go through them and hope we won't have to repeat the performance.

5   Unlikely to be friends of people in high literary places, the beginning woman of color is invisible both in the white male mainstream world and in the white women's feminist world, though in the latter this is gradually changing. The *lesbian* of color is not only invisible, she doesn't even exist. Our speech, too, is inaudible. We speak in tongues like the outcast and the insane.

Because white eyes do not want to know us, they do not bother to learn our language, the language which reflects us, our culture, our spirit. The schools we attended or didn't attend did not give us the skills for writing nor the confidence that we were correct in using our class and ethnic languages. I, for one, became adept at, and majored in English to spite, to show up, the arrogant racist teachers who thought all Chicano children were dumb and dirty. And Spanish was not taught in grade school. And Spanish was not required in High School. And though now I write my poems in Spanish as well as English I feel the rip-off of my native tongue.

. . .

Who gave us permission to perform the act of writing? Why does writing seem so unnatural for me? I'll do anything to postpone it—empty the trash, answer the telephone. The voice recurs in me: *Who am I, a poor Chicanita from the sticks, to think I could write?* How dare I even considered becoming a writer as I stooped over the tomato fields bending, bending under the hot sun, hands broadened and calloused, not fit to hold the quill, numbed into an animal stupor by the heat.

How hard it is for us to *think* we can choose to become writers, much less *feel* and *believe* that we can. What have we to contribute, to give? Our own expectations condition us. Does not our class, our culture as well as the white man tell us writing is not for women such as us?

. . .

I think, yes, perhaps if we go to the university. Perhaps if we become male-women or as middleclass as we can. Perhaps if we give up loving women, we will be worthy of having something to say worth saying. They convince us that we must cultivate art for art's sake. Bow down to the sacred bull, form. Put frames and metaframes around the writing. Achieve distance in order to win the coveted title "literary writer" or "professional writer." Above all do not be simple, direct, nor immediate.

. . .

I can write this and yet I realize that many of us women of color who have strung degrees, credentials and published books around our necks like pearls that we hang onto for dear life are in danger of contributing to the invisibility of our sister-writers. "La Vendida," the sell-out.

The danger of selling out one's own ideologies. For the Third World woman, who has, at best, one foot in the feminist literary world, the temptation is great to adopt the current feeling-fads and theory fads, the latest half truths in political thought, the half-digested new age psychological axioms that are preached by the white feminist establishment. Its followers are notorious for "adopting" women of color as their "cause" while still expecting us to adapt to *their* expectations and *their* language.

How dare we get out of our colored faces. How dare we reveal the human flesh underneath and bleed red blood like the white folks. It takes tremendous energy and courage not to acquiesce, not to capitulate to a definition of feminism that still renders most of us invisible.

. . .

Why am I compelled to write? Because the writing saves me from this complacency I fear. Because I have no choice. Because I must keep the spirit of my revolt and myself alive. Because the world I create in the writing compensates for what the real world does not give me. By writing I put order in the world, give it a handle so I can grasp it. I write because life does not appease my appetites and hunger. I write to record what others erase when I speak, to rewrite the stories others have miswritten about me, about you. To become more intimate with myself and you. To discover myself, to preserve myself, to make myself, to achieve self-autonomy. To dispel the myths that I am a mad prophet or a poor suffering soul. To convince myself that I am worthy and that what I have to say is not a pile of shit. To show that I *can* and that I *will* write, never mind their admonitions to the contrary. And I will write about the unmentionables, never mind the outraged gasp of the censor and the audience. Finally I write because I'm scared of writing but I'm more scared of not writing.

Why should I try to justify why I write? Do I need to justify

*being Chicana, being woman! You might as well ask me to try to
justify why I'm alive.*

15   The act of writing is the act of making soul, alchemy. It is the
quest for the self, for the center of the self, which we women of color
have come to think as "other"—the dark, the feminine. Didn't we
start writing to reconcile this other within us? We knew we were
different, set apart, exiled from what is considered "normal," white-
right. And as we internalized this exile, we came to see the alien
within us and too often, as a result, we split apart from ourselves
and each other. Forever after we have been in search of that self, that
"other" and each other. And we return, in widening spirals and never
to the same childhood place where it happened, first in our families,
with our mothers, with our fathers. The writing is a tool for piercing
that mystery but it also shields us, gives a margin of distance, helps
us survive. And those that don't survive? The waste of ourselves: so
much meat thrown at the feet of madness or fate or the state.

24 mayo 80

It is dark and damp and has been raining all day. I love days
like this. As I lie in bed I am able to delve inward. Perhaps today I
will write from that deep core. As I grope for words and a voice to
speak of writing, I stare at my brown hand clenching the pen and
think of you thousands of miles away clutching your pen. You are
not alone.

> *Pen, I feel right at home in your ink doing a pirouette, stirring the
> cobwebs, leaving my signature on the window panes. Pen, how could
> I ever have feared you. You're quite house-broken but it's your wild-
> ness I am in love with. I'll have to get rid of you when you start being
> predictable, when you stop chasing dustdevils. The more you outwit
> me the more I love you. It's when I'm tired or have had too much
> caffeine or wine that you get past my defenses and you say more than
> what I had intended. You surprise me, shock me into knowing some
> part of me I'd kept secret even from myself.*   —*Journal entry.*

In the kitchen Maria and Cherríe's voices falling on these pages.
I can see Cherríe going about in her terry cloth wrap, barefoot washing the dishes, shaking out the tablecloth, vacuuming. Deriving a
certain pleasure watching her perform those simple tasks, I am
thinking *they lied, there is no separation between life and writing.*

The danger in writing is not fusing our personal experience and
world view with the social reality we live in, with our inner life, our
history, our economics, and our vision. What validates us as human
beings validates us as writers. What matters to us is the relationships that are important to us whether with our self or others. We
must use what is important to us to get to the writing. *No topic is*

too trivial. The danger is in being too universal and humanitarian and invoking the eternal to the sacrifice of the particular and the feminine and the specific historical moment.

The problem is to focus, to concentrate. The body distracts, sabotages with a hundred ruses, a cup of coffee, pencils to sharpen. The solution is to anchor the body to a cigarette or some other ritual. And who has time or energy to write after nurturing husband or lover, children, and often an outside job? The problems seem insurmountable and they are, but they cease being insurmountable once we make up our mind that whether married or childrened or working outside jobs we are going to make time for the writing.

Forget the room of one's own—write in the kitchen, lock yourself up in the bathroom. Write on the bus or the welfare line, on the job or during meals, between sleeping or waking. I write while sitting on the john. No long stretches at the typewriter unless you're wealthy or have a patron—you may not even own a typewriter. While you wash the floor or clothes listen to the words chanting in your body. When you're depressed, angry, hurt, when compassion and love possess you. When you cannot help but write.   20

Distractions all—that I spring on myself when I'm so deep into the writing when I'm almost at that place, that dark cellar where some "thing" is liable to jump up and pounce on me. The ways I subvert the writing are many. The way I don't tap the well nor learn how to make the windmill turn.

Eating is my main distraction. Getting up to eat an apple danish. That I've been off sugar for three years is not a deterrent nor that I have to put on a coat, find the keys and go out into the San Francisco fog to get it. Getting up to light incense, to put a record on, to go for a walk—anything just to put off the writing.

Returning after I've stuffed myself. Writing paragraphs on pieces of paper, adding to the puzzle on the floor, to the confusion on my desk making completion far away and perfection impossible.

26 mayo 80

Dear mujeres de color, I feel heavy and tired and there is a buzz in my head—too many beers last night. But I must finish this letter. My bribe: to take myself out to pizza.

So I cut and paste and line the floor with my bits of paper. My   25 life strewn on the floor in bits and pieces and I try to make some order out of it working against time, psyching myself up with decaffeinated coffee, trying to fill in the gaps.

Leslie, my housemate, comes in, gets on hands and knees to read my fragments on the floor and says, "It's good, Gloria." And I think: *I don't have to go back to Texas, to my family of land, mesquites, cactus, rattlesnakes and roadrunners. My family, this com-*

munity of writers. How could I have lived and survived so long without it. And I remember the isolation, re-live the pain again.

"To assess the damage is a dangerous act," writes Cherríe Moraga. To stop there is even more dangerous.

It's too easy, blaming it all on the white man or white feminists or society or on our parents. What we say and what we do ultimately comes back to us, so let us own our responsibility, place it in our own hands and carry it with dignity and strength. No one's going to do my shitwork, I pick up after myself.

It makes perfect sense to me now how I resisted the act of writing, the commitment to writing. To write is to confront one's demons, look them in the face and live to write about them. Fear acts like a magnet; it draws the demons out of the closet and into the ink in our pens.

30   The tiger riding our backs (writing) never lets us alone. *Why aren't you riding, writing, writing!* It asks constantly till we begin to feel we're vampires sucking the blood out of too fresh an experience; that we are sucking life's blood to feed the pen. Writing is the most daring thing I have ever done and the most dangerous. Nellie Wong calls writing "the three-eyed demon shrieking the truth."

Writing is dangerous because we are afraid of what the writing reveals: the fears, the angers, the strengths of a woman under a triple or quadruple oppression. Yet in that very act lies our survival because a woman who writes has power. And a woman with power is feared.

. . .

I say mujer magica, empty yourself. Shock yourself into new ways of perceiving the world, shock your readers into the same. Stop the chatter inside their heads.

Your skin must be sensitive enough for the lightest kiss and thick enough to ward off the sneers. If you are going to spit in the eye of the world, make sure your back is to the wind. Write of what most links us with life, the sensation of the body, the images seen by the eye, the expansion of the psyche in tranquility: moments of high intensity, its movement, sounds, thoughts. *Even though we go hungry we are not impoverished of experiences.*

. . .

There is no need for words to fester in our minds. They germinate in the open mouth of the barefoot child in the midst of restive crowds. They wither in ivory towers and in college classrooms.

35   Throw away abstraction and the academic learning, the rules, the map and compass. Feel your way without blinders. To touch

more people, the personal realities and the social must be evoked—not through rhetoric but through blood and pus and sweat.

Write with your eyes like painters, with your ears like musicians, with your feet like dancers. You are the truthsayer with quill and torch. Write with your tongues of fire. Don't let the pen banish you from yourself. Don't let the ink coagulate in your pens. Don't let the censor snuff out the spark, nor the gags muffle your voice. Put your shit on the paper.

We are not reconciled to the oppressors who whet their howl on our grief. We are not reconciled.

Find the muse within you. The voice that lies buried under you, dig it up. Do not fake it, try to sell it for a handclap or your name in print.

Love,
Gloria

Response

1. What motivates Anzaldua to write? What does she advocate to other would-be writers, and what dangers does she warn against?

2. Rather than a poem or a "wooden, cold" essay, Anzaldua conveys her ideas in the form of a letter. How does this affect the way the passage communicates her message? To what extent does her message apply to readers other than the third-world women writers to whom her letter is addressed?

3. Anzaldua describes her academic experience as largely negative. How does her experience with writing instruction compare with yours? What does she value in terms of writing style and content? How do her views compare with those of other writers and with your own?

4. In paragraph 21 Anzaldua mentions distractions: "The ways I subvert the writing are many. The way I don't tap the well nor learn how to make the windmill turn." What are some of your ways?

5. To what extent do you find a similar message in Anzaldua's "letter" and Sandra Cisneros's "Ghosts and Voices: Writing from Obsession" (Section I)? The two passages are quite different in tone and manner of writing. How do you think these differences affect the way the writing communicates each author's message?

A Talk to Teachers

James Baldwin

This essay is based on a talk Baldwin gave to a group of teachers in 1963. As in his "Autobiographical Notes" and "Fifth Avenue, Uptown: A Letter from Harlem," he deals with themes of identity and human dignity in the broad context of U.S. society. This essay is included in the collection of Baldwin's nonfiction, The Price of the Ticket, *published in 1985.*

Let's begin by saying that we are living through a very dangerous time. Everyone in this room is in one way or another aware of that. We are in a revolutionary situation, no matter how unpopular that word has become in this country. The society in which we live is desperately menaced, not by Khrushchev, but from within. So any citizen of this country who figures himself as responsible—and particularly those of you who deal with the minds and hearts of young people—must be prepared to "go for broke." Or to put it another way, you must understand that in the attempt to correct so many generations of bad faith and cruelty, when it is operating not only in the classroom but in society, you will meet the most fantastic, the most brutal, and the most determined resistance. There is no point in pretending that this won't happen.

Since I am talking to schoolteachers and I am not a teacher myself, and in some ways am fairly easily intimidated, I beg you to let me leave that and go back to what I think to be the entire purpose of education in the first place. It would seem to me that when a child is born, if I'm the child's parent, it is my obligation and my high duty to civilize that child. Man is a social animal. He cannot exist without a society. A society, in turn, depends on certain things which everyone within that society takes for granted. Now, the crucial paradox which confronts us here is that the whole process of education occurs within a social framework and is designed to perpetuate the aims of society. Thus, for example, the boys and girls who were born during the era of the Third Reich, when educated to the purposes of the Third Reich, became barbarians. The paradox of education is precisely this—that as one begins to become conscious one begins to examine the society in which he is being educated. The purpose of education, finally, is to create in a person the ability to look at the world for himself, to make his own decisions, to say to himself this is black or this is white, to decide for himself whether there is a God in heaven or not. To ask questions of the universe, and then learn to live with those questions, is the way he achieves his own identity. But no society is really anxious to have that kind of person around. What societies really, ideally, want is a citizenry which will simply obey the rules of society. If a society succeeds in this, that society is about to perish. The obligation of anyone who thinks of himself as responsible is to examine society and try to change it and to fight it—at no matter what risk. This is the only hope society has. This is the only way societies change.

Now, if what I have tried to sketch has any validity, it becomes thoroughly clear, at least to me, that any Negro who is born in this country and undergoes the American educational system runs the risk of becoming schizophrenic. On the one hand he is born in the shadow of the stars and stripes and he is assured it represents a nation which has never lost a war. He pledges allegiance to that flag which guarantees "liberty and justice for all." He is part of a country in which anyone can become president, and so forth. But on the other hand he is also assured by his country and his countrymen that he has never contributed anything to civilization—that his past is nothing more than a record of humiliations gladly endured. He is assumed by the republic that he, his father, his mother, and his ancestors were happy, shiftless, watermelon-eating darkies who loved Mr. Charlie and Miss Ann, that the value he has as a black man is proven by one thing only—his devotion to white people. If you think I am exaggerating, examine the myths which proliferate in this country about Negroes.

All this enters the child's consciousness much sooner than we as adults would like to think it does. As adults, we are easily fooled because we are so anxious to be fooled. But children are very different. Children, not yet aware that it is dangerous to look too deeply at anything, look at everything, look at each other, and draw their own conclusions. They don't have the vocabulary to express what they see, and we, their elders, know how to intimidate them very easily and very soon. But a black child, looking at the world around him, though he cannot know quite what to make of it, is aware that there is a reason why his mother works so hard, why his father is always on edge. He is aware that there is some reason why, if he sits down in the front of the bus, his father or mother slaps him and drags him to the back of the bus. He is aware that there is some terrible weight on his parents' shoulders which menaces him. And it isn't long—in fact it begins when he is in school—before he discovers the shape of his oppression.

5   Let us say that the child is seven years old and I am his father, and I decide to take him to the zoo, or to Madison Square Garden, or to the U.N. Building, or to any of the tremendous monuments we find all over New York. We get into a bus and we go from where I live on 131st Street and Seventh Avenue downtown through the park and we get into New York City, which is not Harlem. Now, where the boy lives—even if it is a housing project—is in an undesirable neighborhood. If he lives in one of those housing projects of which everyone in New York is so proud, he has at the front door, if not closer, the pimps, the whores, the junkies—in a word, the danger of life in the ghetto. And the child knows this, though he doesn't know why.

I still remember my first sight of New York. It was really another city when I was born—where I was born. We looked down over the Park Avenue streetcar tracks. It was Park Avenue, but I didn't know what Park Avenue meant *downtown*. The Park Avenue I grew up on, which is still standing, is dark and dirty. No one would dream of opening a Tiffany's on that Park Avenue, and when you go downtown you discover that you are literally in the white world. It is rich—or at least it looks rich. It is clean—because they collect garbage downtown. There are doormen. People walk about as though they owned where they are—and indeed they do. And it's a great shock. It's very hard to relate yourself to this. You don't know what it means. You know—you know instinctively—that none of this is for you. You know this before you are told. And who is it for and who is paying for it? And why isn't it for you?

Later on when you become a grocery boy or messenger and you try to enter one of those buildings a man says, "Go to the back door." Still later, if you happen by some odd chance to have a friend in one of those buildings, the man says, "Where's your package?" Now this by no means is the core of the matter. What I'm trying to get at is that by this time the Negro child has had, effectively, almost all the doors of opportunity slammed in his face, and there are very few things he can do about it. He can more or less accept it with an absolutely inarticulate and dangerous rage inside—all the more dangerous because it is never expressed. It is precisely those silent people whom white people see every day of their lives—I mean your porter and your maid, who never say anything more than "Yes, Sir" and "No, Ma'am." They will tell you it's raining if that is what you want to hear, and they will tell you the sun is shining if *that* is what you want to hear. They really hate you—really hate you because in their eyes (and they're right) you stand between them and life. I want to come back to that in a moment. It is the most sinister of the facts, I think, which we now face.

There is something else the Negro child can do, too. Every street boy—and I was a street boy, so I know—looking at the society which has produced him, looking at the standards of that society which are not honored by anybody, looking at your churches and the government and the politicians, understands that this structure is operated for someone else's benefit—not for his. And there's no reason in it for him. If he is really cunning, really ruthless, really strong—and many of us are—he becomes a kind of criminal. He becomes a kind of criminal because that's the only way he can live. Harlem and every ghetto in this city—every ghetto in this country—is full of people who live outside the law. They wouldn't dream of calling a policeman. They wouldn't, for a moment, listen to any of those professions of which we are so proud on the Fourth of July. They have turned away from this country forever and totally. They live by their wits and really long to see the day when the entire structure comes down.

The point of all this is that black men were brought here as a source of cheap labor. They were indispensable to the economy. In order to justify the fact that men were treated as though they were animals, the white republic had to brainwash itself into believing that they were, indeed, animals and *deserved* to be treated like animals. Therefore it is almost impossible for any Negro child to discover anything about his actual history. The reason is that this "animal," once he suspects his own worth, once he starts believing that he is a man, has begun to attack the entire power structure. This is why America has spent such a long time keeping the Negro in his place. What I am trying to suggest to you is that it was not an accident, it was not an act of God, it was not done by well-meaning people muddling into something which they didn't understand. It was a deliberate policy hammered into place in order to make money from black flesh. And now, in 1963, because we have never faced this fact, we are in intolerable trouble.

10   The Reconstruction, as I read the evidence, was a bargain between the North and South to this effect: "We've liberated them from the land—and delivered them to the bosses." When we left Mississippi to come North we did not come to freedom. We came to the bottom of the labor market, and we are still there. Even the Depression of the 1930s failed to make a dent in Negroes' relationship to white workers in the labor unions. Even today, so brainwashed is this republic that people seriously ask in what they suppose to be good faith, "What does the Negro want?" I've heard a great many asinine questions in my life, but that is perhaps the most asinine and perhaps the most insulting. But the point here is that people who ask that question, thinking that they ask it in good faith, are really the victims of this conspiracy to make Negroes believe they are less than human.

In order for me to live, I decided very early that some mistake had been made somewhere. I was not a "nigger" even though you called me one. But if I was a "nigger" in your eyes, there was something about *you*—there was something *you* needed. I had to realize when I was very young that I was none of those things I was told I was. I was not, for example, happy. I never touched a watermelon for all kinds of reasons that had been invented by white people, and I knew enough about life by this time to understand that whatever you invent, whatever you project, is you! So where we are now is that a whole country of people believe I'm a "nigger," and I *don't*, and the battle's on! Because if I am not what I've been told I am, then it means that *you're* not what you thought *you* were *either*! And that is the crisis.

It is not really a "Negro revolution" that is upsetting the country. What is upsetting the country is a sense of its own identity. If, for example, one managed to change the curriculum in all the schools so that Negroes learned more about themselves and their real contributions to this culture, you would be liberating not only Negroes, you'd be liberating white people who know nothing about their own history. And the reason is that if you are compelled to lie about one aspect of anybody's history, you must lie about it all. If you have to lie about my real role here, if you have to pretend that I hoed all that cotton just because I loved you, then you have done something to yourself. You are mad.

Now let's go back a minute. I talked earlier about those silent people—the porter and the maid—who, as I said, don't look up at the sky if you ask them if it is raining, but look into your face. My ancestors and I were very well trained. We understood very early that this was not a Christian nation. It didn't matter what you said or how often you went to church. My father and my mother and my grandfather and my grandmother knew that Christians didn't act this way. It was as simple as that. And if that was so there was no point in dealing with white people in terms of their own moral professions, for they were not going to honor them. What one did was to turn away, smiling all the time, and tell white people what they wanted to hear. But people always accuse you of reckless talk when you say this.

All this means that there are in this country tremendous reservoirs of bitterness which have never been able to find an outlet, but may find an outlet soon. It means that well-meaning white liberals place themselves in great danger when they try to deal with Negroes as though they were missionaries. It means, in brief, that a great price is demanded to liberate all those silent people so that they can breathe for the first time and *tell* you what they think of you. And a price is demanded to liberate all those white children—some of them near forty—who have never grown up, and who never will grow up, because they have no sense of their identity.

What passes for identity in America is a series of myths about one's 15 heroic ancestors. It's astounding to me, for example, that so many people really appear to believe that the country was founded by a band of heroes who wanted to be free. That happens not to be true. What happened was that some people left Europe because they couldn't stay there any longer and had to go someplace else to make it. That's all. They were hungry, they were poor, they were convicts. Those who were making it in England, for example, did not get on the *Mayflower*. That's how the country was settled. Not by Gary Cooper. Yet we have a whole race of people, a whole republic, who believe the myths to the point where even today they select political representatives, as far as I can tell, by how closely they resemble Gary Cooper. Now this is dangerously infantile, and it shows in every level of national life. When I was living in Europe, for example, one of the worst revelations to me was the way Americans walked around Europe buying this and buying that and insulting everybody—not even out of malice, just because they didn't know any better. Well, that is the way they have always treated me. They weren't cruel, they just didn't know you were alive. They didn't know you had any feelings.

What I am trying to suggest here is that in the doing of all this for 100 years or more, it is the American white man who has long since lost his grip on reality. In some peculiar way, having created this myth about Negroes, and the myth about his own history, he created myths about the world so that, for example, he was astounded that some people could prefer Castro, astounded that there are people in the world who don't go into hiding when they hear the word "Communism," astounded that Communism is one of the realities of the twentieth century which we will not overcome by pretending that it does not exist. The political level in this country now, on the part of people who should know better, is abysmal.

The Bible says somewhere that where there is no vision the people perish. I don't think anyone can doubt that in this country today we are menaced—intolerably menaced—by a lack of vision.

It is inconceivable that a sovereign people should continue, as we do so abjectly, to say, "I can't do anything about it. It's the government." The government is the creation of the people. It is responsible to the people. And the people are responsible for it. No American has the right to allow the present government to say, when Negro children are being bombed and hosed and shot and beaten all over the Deep South, that there is nothing we can do about it. There must have been a day in this country's life when the bombing of the children in Sunday School would have created a public uproar and endangered the life of a Governor Wallace. It happened here and there was no public uproar.

I began by saying that one of the paradoxes of education was that precisely at the point when you begin to develop a conscience, you must find yourself at war with your society. It is your responsibility to change society if you think of yourself as an educated person. And on the basis of the evidence—the moral and political evidence—one is compelled to say that this is a backward society. Now if I were a teacher in this school, or any Negro school, and I was dealing with Negro children, who were in my care only a few hours of every day and would then return to their homes and to the streets, children who have an apprehension of their future which with every hour grows grimmer and darker, I would try to teach them—I would try to make them know—that those streets, those houses, those dangers, those agonies by which they are surrounded, are criminal. I would try to make each child know that these things are the result of a criminal conspiracy to destroy him. I would teach him that if he intends to get to be a man, he must at once decide that he is stronger than this conspiracy and that he must never make his peace with it. And that one of his weapons for refusing to make his peace with it and for destroying it depends on what he decides he is worth. I would teach him that there are currently very few standards in this country which are worth a man's respect. That it is up to him to begin to change these standards for the sake of the life and the health of the country. I would suggest to him that the popular culture—as represented, for example, on television and in comic books and in movies—is based on fantasies created by very ill people, and he must be aware that these are fantasies that have nothing to do with reality. I would teach him that the press he reads is not as free as it says it is—and that he can do something about that, too. I would try to make him know that just as American history is longer, larger, more various, more beautiful, and more terrible than anything anyone has ever said about it, so is the world larger, more daring, more beautiful and more terrible, but principally larger—and that it belongs to him. I would teach him that he doesn't have to be bound by the expediencies of any given administration, any given policy, any given morality; that he has the right and the necessity to examine everything. I would try to show him that one has not learned anything about Castro when one says, "He is a Communist." This is a way of his learning something about Castro, something about Cuba, something, in time, about the world. I would suggest to him that he is living, at the moment, in an enormous province. America is not the world and if America is going to become a nation, she must find a way— and this child must help her to find a way to use the tremendous potential and tremendous energy which this child represents. If this country does not find a way to use that energy, it will be destroyed by that energy.

Response _____

1. "We are living through a very dangerous time," says Baldwin in opening. "The society in which we live is desperately menaced . . . from within." What danger is Baldwin referring to?

2. Explain the crucial paradox of education, as Baldwin sees it. What is the responsibility of an educated person? Do you accept his view?

3. Baldwin presents his ideas in terms of the African-American male experience. Do you think he intended to limit his point in this way? Do you think that what he says might be said as well on behalf of other groups?

4. Who does Baldwin take to be his audience in this "Talk"? How do you know? The audience denoted by "you" seems to shift as the essay progresses. How does the tone and content of the essay reflect Baldwin's shifting concept of his audience?

5. Why, in Baldwin's view, is it "almost impossible for any Negro child to discover anything about his actual history" (paragraph 9)? When he says that "because we have never faced this fact, we are in intolerable trouble," whom does he include in "we"? Who suffers from the ignorance of history, and why?

6. Baldwin's "Talk" contains a warning and advice, not just for teachers but for all of us. In his conclusion he echoes his opening sentence; what is the danger this society faces? What needs to be done? If Baldwin were delivering this talk today, do you think he would change it? Why or why not?

The Lesson
Toni Cade Bambara

This story from Gorilla, My Love *(1972) takes place in New York, where Bambara grew up. In "A Sort of Preface" in that book, she humorously denies that she writes about her own life or people she knows, lest she offend someone; she says, "I deal in straight-up fiction myself, cause I value my family and friends, and mostly cause I lie a lot anyway"— leaving the reader to judge.*

Back in the days when everyone was old and stupid or young and foolish and me and Sugar were the only ones just right, this lady moved on our block with nappy hair and proper speech and no makeup. And quite naturally we laughed at her, laughed the way we did at the junk man who went about his business like he was some big-time president and his sorry-ass horse his secretary. And we kinda hated her too, hated the way we did the winos who cluttered up our parks and pissed on our handball walls and stank up our hall-ways and stairs so you couldn't halfway play hide-and-seek without a goddamn gas mask. Miss Moore was her name. The only woman on the block with no first name. And she was black as hell, cept for her feet, which were fish-white and spooky. And she was always planning these boring-ass things for us to do, us being my cousin, mostly, who lived on the block cause we all moved North the same time and to the same apartment then spread out gradual to breathe. And our parents would yank our heads into some kinda shape and crisp up our clothes so we'd be presentable for travel with Miss Moore, who always looked like she was going to church, though she never did. Which is just one of things the grownups talked about when they talked behind her back like a dog. But when she came calling with some sachet she'd sewed up or some gingerbread she'd made or some book, why then they'd all be too embarrassed to turn her down and we'd get handed over all spruced up. She'd been to college and said it was only right that she should take responsibility for the young ones' education, and she not even related by marriage or blood. So they'd go for it. Specially Aunt Gretchen. She was the main gofer in the family. You got some ole dumb shit foolishness you want somebody to go for, you send for Aunt Gretchen. She been screwed into the go-along for so long, it's a blood-deep natural thing with her. Which is how she got saddled with me and Sugar and Junior in the first place while our mothers were in a la-de-da apartment up the block having a good ole time.

So this one day Miss Moore rounds us all up at the mailbox and it's puredee hot and she's knockin herself out about arithmetic. And school suppose to let up in summer I heard, but she don't never let up. And the starch in my pinafore scratching the shit outta me and I'm really hating this nappy-head bitch and her goddamn college degree. I'd much rather go to the pool or to the show where it's cool. So me and Sugar leaning on the mailbox being surly, which is a Miss Moore word. And Flyboy checking out what everybody brought for lunch. And Fat Butt already wasting his peanut-butter-and-jelly sandwich like the pig he is. And Junebug punchin on Q.T.'s arm for potato chips. And Rosie Giraffe shifting from one hip to the other waiting for somebody to step on her foot or ask her if she from Georgia so she can kick ass, preferably Mercedes'. And Miss Moore asking us do we know what money is, like we a bunch of retards. I mean real money, she say, like it's only poker chips or monopoly papers we lay on the grocer. So right away I'm tired of this and say so. And would much rather snatch Sugar and go to the Sunset and terrorize the West Indian kids and take their hair ribbons and their money too. And Miss Moore files that remark away for next week's lesson on brotherhood, I can tell. And finally I say we oughta get to the subway cause it's cooler and besides we might meet some cute boys. Sugar done swiped her mama's lipstick, so we ready.

So we heading down the street and she's boring us silly about what things cost and what our parents make and how much goes for rent and how money ain't divided up right in this country. And then she gets to the part about we all poor and live in the slums, which I don't feature. And I'm ready to speak on that, but she steps out in the street and hails two cabs just like that. Then she hustles half the crew in with her and hands me a five-dollar bill and tells me to calculate 10 percent tip for the driver. And we're off. Me and Sugar and Junebug and Flyboy hangin out the window and hollering to everybody, putting lipstick on each other cause Flyboy a faggot anyway, and making farts with our sweaty armpits. But I'm mostly trying to figure how to spend this money. But they all fascinated with the meter ticking and Junebug starts laying bets as to how much it'll read when Flyboy can't hold his breath no more. Then Sugar lays bets as to how much it'll be when we get there. So I'm stuck. Don't nobody want to go for my plan, which is to jump out at the next light and run off to the first bar-b-que we can find. Then the driver tells us to get the hell out cause we there already. And the meter reads eighty-five cents. And I'm stalling to figure out the tip and Sugar say give him a dime. And I decide he don't need it bad as I do, so later for him. But then he tries to take off with Junebug foot still in the door so we talk about his mama something ferocious. Then we check out that we on Fifth Avenue and everybody dressed up in stockings. One lady in a fur coat, hot as it is. White folks crazy.

"This is the place," Miss Moore say, presenting it to us in the voice she uses at the museum. "Let's look in the windows before we go in."

"Can we steal?" Sugar asks very serious like she's getting the 5 ground rules squared away before she plays. "I beg your pardon," say Miss Moore, and we fall out. So she leads us around the windows of the toy store and me and Sugar screamin, "This is mine, that's mine, I gotta have that, that was made for me, I was born for that," till Big Butt drowns us out.

"Hey, I'm goin to buy that there."

"That there? You don't even know what it is, stupid."

"I do so," he say punchin on Rosie Giraffe. "It's a microscope."

"Whatcha gonna do with a microscope, fool?"

"Look at things." 10

"Like what, Ronald?" ask Miss Moore. And Big Butt ain't got the first notion. So here go Miss Moore gabbing about the thousands of bacteria in a drop of water and the somethinorother in a speck of blood and the million and one living things in the air around us is invisible to the naked eye. And what she say that for? Junebug go to town on that "naked" and we rolling. Then Miss Moore ask what it cost. So we all jam into the window smudgin it up and the price tag say $300. So then she ask how long'd take for Big Butt and Junebug to save up their allowances. "Too long," I say. "Yeh," adds Sugar, "outgrown it by that time." And Miss Moore say no, you never outgrow learning instruments. "Why, even medical students and interns and," blah, blah, blah. And we ready to choke Big Butt for bringing it up in the first damn place.

"This here costs four hundred eighty dollars," say Rosie Giraffe. So we pile up all over her to see what she pointin out. My eyes tell me it's a chunk of glass cracked with something heavy, and different-color inks dripped into the splits, then the whole thing put into a oven or something. But for $480 it don't make sense.

"That's a paperweight made of semi-precious stones fused together under tremendous pressure," she explains slowly, with her hands doing the mining and all the factory work.

"So what's a paperweight?" asks Rosie Giraffe.

15   "To weigh paper with, dumbbell," say Flyboy, the wise man from the East.

"Not exactly," say Miss Moore, which is what she say when you warm or way off too. "It's to weigh paper down so it won't scatter and make your desk untidy." So right away me and Sugar curtsy to each other and then to Mercedes who is more the tidy type.

"We don't keep paper on top of the desk in my class," say Junebug, figuring Miss Moore crazy or lying one.

"At home, then," she say. "Don't you have a calendar and a pencil case and a blotter and a letter-opener on your desk at home where you do your homework?" And she know damn well what our homes look like cause she nosys around in them every chance she gets.

"I don't even have a desk," say Junebug. "Do we?"

20   "No. And I don't get no homework neither," say Big Butt.

"And I don't even have a home," say Flyboy like he do at school to keep the white folks off his back and sorry for him. Send this poor kid to camp posters, is his specialty.

"I do," says Mercedes. "I have a box of stationery on my desk and a picture of my cat. My godmother bought the stationery and the desk. There's a big rose on each sheet and the envelopes smell like roses."

"Who wants to know about your smelly-ass stationery," say Rosie Giraffe fore I can get my two cents in.

"It's important to have a work area all your own so that . . ."

25   "Will you look at this sailboat, please," say Flyboy, cuttin her off and pointin to the thing like it was his. So once again we tumble all over each other to gaze at this magnificent thing in the toy store which is just big enough to maybe sail two kittens across the pond if you strap them to the posts tight. We all start reciting the price

tag like we in assembly. "Handcrafted sailboat of fiberglass at one thousand one hundred ninety-five dollars."

"Unbelievable," I hear myself say and am really stunned. I read it again for myself just in case the group recitation put me in a trance. Same thing. For some reason this pisses me off. We look at Miss Moore and she lookin at us, waiting for I dunno what.

Who'd pay all that when you can buy a sailboat set for a quarter at Pop's, a tube of glue for a dime, and a ball of string for eight cents? "It must have a motor and a whole lot else besides," I say. "My sailboat cost me about fifty cents."

"But will it take water?" say Mercedes with her smart ass.

"Took mine to Alley Pond Park once," say Flyboy. "String broke. Lost it. Pity."

"Sailed mine in Central Park and it keeled over and sank. Had   30
to ask my father for another dollar."

"And you got the strap," laugh Big Butt. "The jerk didn't even have a string on it. My old man wailed on his behind."

Little Q.T. was staring hard at the sailboat and you could see he wanted it bad. But he too little and somebody'd just take it from him. So what the hell. "This boat for kids, Miss Moore?"

"Parents silly to buy something like that just to get all broke up," say Rosie Giraffe.

"That much money it should last forever," I figure.

"My father'd buy it for me if I wanted it."   35

"Your father, my ass," say Rosie Giraffe getting a chance to finally push Mercedes.

"Must be rich people shop here," say Q.T.

"You are a very bright boy," say Flyboy. "What was your first clue?" And he rap him on the head with the back of his knuckles, since Q.T. the only one he could get away with. Though Q.T. liable to come up behind you years later and get his licks in when you half expect it.

"What I want to know is," I says to Miss Moore though I never talk to her, I wouldn't give the bitch that satisfaction, "is how much a real boat costs? I figure a thousand'd get you a yacht any day."

"Why don't you check that out," she says, "and report back to   40
the group?" Which really pains my ass. If you gonna mess up a perfectly good swim day least you could do is have some answers. "Let's go in," she say like she got something up her sleeve. Only she don't lead the way. So me and Sugar turn the corner to where the entrance is, but when we get there I kinda hang back. Not that I'm scared, what's there to be afraid of, just a toy store. But I feel funny, shame. But what I got to be shamed about? Got as much right to go in as anybody. But somehow I can't seem to get hold of the door, so I step

away for Sugar to lead. But she hangs back too. And I look at her and she looks at me and this is ridiculous. I mean, damn, I have never ever been shy about doing nothing or going nowhere. But then Mercedes steps up and then Rosie Giraffe and Big Butt crowd in behind and shove, and next thing we all stuffed into the doorway with only Mercedes squeezing past us, smoothing out her jumper and walking right down the aisle. Then the rest of us tumble in like a glued-together jigsaw done all wrong. And people lookin at us. And it's like the time me and Sugar crashed into the Catholic church on a dare. But once we got in there and everything so hushed and holy and the candles and the bowin and the handkerchiefs on all the drooping heads, I just couldn't go through with the plan. Which was for me to run up to the altar and do a tap dance while Sugar played the nose flute and messed around in the holy water. And Sugar kept givin me the elbow. Then later teased me so bad I tied her up in the shower and turned it on and locked her in. And she'd be there till this day if Aunt Gretchen hadn't finally figured I was lying about the boarder takin a shower.

Same thing in the store. We all walkin on tiptoe and hardly touchin the games and puzzles and things. And I watched Miss Moore who is steady watchin us like she waitin for a sign. Like Mama Drewery watches the sky and sniffs the air and takes note of just how much slant is in the bird formation. Then me and Sugar bump smack into each other, so busy gazing at the toys, 'specially the sailboat. But we don't laugh and go into our fat-lady bump-stomach routine. We just stare at that price tag. Then Sugar run a finger over the whole boat. And I'm jealous and want to hit her. Maybe not her, but I sure want to punch somebody in the mouth.

"Watcha bring us here for, Miss Moore?"

"You sound angry, Sylvia. Are you mad about something?" Givin me one of them grins like she tellin a grown-up joke that never turns out to be funny. And she's lookin very closely at me like maybe she plannin to do my portrait from memory. I'm mad, but I won't give her that satisfaction. So I slouch around the store bein very bored and say, "Let's go."

Me and Sugar at the back of the train watchin the tracks whizzin by large then small then gettin gobbled up in the dark. I'm thinkin about this tricky toy I saw in the store. A clown that somersaults on a bar then does chin-ups just cause you yank lightly at his leg. Cost $35. I could see me askin my mother for a $35 birthday clown. "You wanna who that costs what?" she'd say, cocking her head to the side to get a better view of the hole in my head. Thirty-five dollars could buy new bunk beds for Junior and Gretchen's boy. Thirty-five dollars and the whole household could go visit Granddaddy Nelson in the country. Thirty-five dollars would pay for the rent and the piano bill too. Who are these people that spend that much for performing clowns and $1,000 for toy sailboats? What kinda work they do and how they live and how come we ain't in on it? Where we are is who we are, Miss Moore always pointin out. But it don't necessarily have to be that way, she always adds then waits for somebody to say that poor people have to wake up and demand their share of the pie and don't none of us know what kind of pie she talkin about in the first damn place. But she ain't so smart cause I still got her four dollars from the taxi and she sure ain't gettin it. Messin up my day with this shit. Sugar nudges me in my pocket and winks.

Miss Moore lines us up in front of the mailbox where we started   45
from, seem like years ago, and I got a headache for thinkin so hard. And we lean all over each other so we can hold up under the draggy-ass lecture she always finishes us off with at the end before we thank her for borin us to tears. But she just looks at us like she readin tea leaves. Finally she say, "Well, what did you think of F.A.O. Schwartz?"

Rosie Giraffe mumbles, "White folks crazy."

"I'd like to go there again when I get my birthday money," says Mercedes, and we shove her out the pack so she has to lean on the mailbox by herself.

"I'd like a shower. Tiring day," say Flyboy.

Then Sugar surprises me by sayin, "You know, Miss Moore, I don't think all of us here put together eat in a year what that sailboat costs." And Miss Moore lights up like somebody goosed her. "And?" she say, urging Sugar on. Only I'm standin on her foot so she don't continue.

"Imagine for a minute what kind of society it is in which some   50
people can spend on a toy what it would cost to feed a family of six or seven. What do you think?"

"I think," say Sugar pushing me off her feet like she never done before, cause I whip her ass in a minute, "that this is not much of a democracy if you ask me. Equal chance to pursue happiness means an equal crack at the dough, don't it?" Miss Moore is besides herself and I am disgusted with Sugar's treachery. So I stand on her foot one more time to see if she'll shove me. She shuts up, and Miss Moore looks at me, sorrowfully I'm thinkin. And somethin weird is goin on, I can feel it in my chest.

"Anybody else learn anything today?" lookin dead at me. I walk away and Sugar has to run to catch up and don't even seem to notice when I shrug her arm off my shoulder.

"Well, we got four dollars anyway," she says.

"Uh hunh."

55   "We could go to Hascombs and get half a chocolate layer and then go to the Sunset and still have plenty money for potato chips and ice-cream sodas."

"Uh hunh."

"Race you to Hascombs," she say.

We start down the block and she gets ahead which is O.K. by me cause I'm goin to the West End and then over to the Drive to think this day through. She can run if she want to and even run faster. But ain't nobody gonna beat me at nuthin.

Response

1. How does the narrator, Sylvia, portray herself at the beginning of the story? How do we know she has changed by the time she tells the story?

2. Why did the children and adults in the neighborhood respond to Miss Moore as they did?

3. What was "the lesson" in the story? Did Miss Moore accomplish what she intended on this occasion?

4. What indications does the story give of Miss Moore's influence on Sylvia? How do the day's events affect Sylvia? What is her frame of mind at the end of the story?

5. How is Miss Moore's view of education like that of James Baldwin as expressed in "A Talk to Teachers"?

The Plum Plum Pickers

Raymond Barrio ⎯⎯⎯⎯⎯⎯⎯⎯⎯⎯⎯⎯⎯

This passage is a chapter from Barrio's 1969 novel about the lives of Chicano migrant workers. In his book Barrio uses the relentless ripening and regeneration of the fruit as a symbol of the workers' political maturing: they gradually become aware of their common bond and the possibility of action to form a new, more humane society. This chapter shows the character Manuel awakening to the circumstances under which he labors.

Dawn.

Outside, the coolest night.

Outside, the soft, plush, lingering sheen of nightlight.

Within his breezy air-conditioned shack Manuel lay half asleep in the middle of the biggest apricot orchard in the world, nothing but apricot trees all around, in one of a long double row of splintered boards nailed together and called a shack. A migrant's shack. He struggled to come awake. Everything seemed to be plugged up. A distant roar closed in steadily. He awoke in a cold sweat. He sat up abruptly in the cold darkness.

The roar grew louder and louder. He leaned forward, hunched 5 in his worn, torn covers, and peered through the grimy window. A huge black monster was butting through trees, moving and pitching about, its headlights piercing the armor of night, then swinging away again as the roaring lessened. Manuel smiled. The roar of a tractor. He rubbed the sleep from his eyes. He stretched his aching arms and shoulders. He thought of Lupe and the kids back in Drawbridge.

On the very brink of the full onslaught of summer's punishing heat, with the plums and pears and apricots fattening madly on every vine, branch, bush, and limb in every section of every county in the country, pickers were needed right now immediately on every farm and orchard everywhere and all at once. The frantic demand for pickers increased rapidly as the hot days mounted. That sure looked good out there. What a cool job that was. Driving a tractor at night. Maybe he could get Ramiro to teach him to drive one.

Manuel well knew what his physical energy was.

His physical energy was his total worldly wealth.

No matter how anxious he was to work, he did have his limit. He had to rest his body. The finger joint he'd injured still hurt. He missed Lupe's chatter. He'd signed up with that shrewd contractor, Roberto Morales, that shrewd, fat, energetic contratista, manipulator of migrating farmworkers, that smiling middleman who promised to deliver so many hands to the moon at such and such a time at such and such an orchard at such and such a price, for such a small commission. A tiny percentage. Such a little slice. Silvery slavery—modernized.

10   Roberto Morales, an organization man, was a built-in toll gate. A parasite. A collector of drops of human sweat. An efficiency expert. Had he not been Mexican, he would have made a fantastic capitalist, like Turner. He was Turner upside down. Sucking blood from his own people. With the help and convenient connivance of Turner's insatiable greed.

The agricultural combine's imperative need to have its capital personally plucked when ripe so as to materialize its honest return on its critical investment in order to keep its executives relaxed in blue splendor in far-off desert pools was coupled to the migrant workers' inexorable and uncompromising need to earn pennies to fend off stark starvation.

Good money.

Good dough.

Good hard work.

15   Pick fast.

Penny a bucket.

Check off.

Get the count right.

Cotsplumsprunespeachesbeanspeas.

Pods.   20
The seed of life.
And:—don't complain . . .
Manuel lay back in the blackness. As the darkness receded and
the light of day started creeping imperiously across its own land, he
thought that these powerful orchard land owners were awfully generous to give him such a beautiful hostel to stop in overnight. The
skylight hotel. There the land stood. A heaving, sleeping mother
earth. A marvelous land. Ripening her fruit once again. Once more.
Ripening it fatly and pregnantly for the thousandth time. It must be
plucked said the wise man. For it cannot hang around on limbs a
minute extra. At no man's convenience. As soon as the baby's ready.
Lush and full of plump juices. Hugging its new seed around its own
ripeness. The plum and the cot and the peach and the pear must
plummet again to earth. Carrying the seed of its own delicate rebirth
and redestruction back home to earth again. A clever mother earth
who in her all-but-unbelievable generosity was capable of giving man
fivefold, tenfold the quantity of fruit he could himself eat, five times
fifty, and yet the pickers were never paid enough to satisfy their
hunger beyond their actual working hours. And yet it was called a
moral world. An ethical world. A good world. A happy world. A
world full of golden opportunities. Manuel simply couldn't figure it
out.
What was wrong with the figures?
Why was mother earth so generous? And men so greedy?   25
You got twenty-five cents a basket for tomatoes. A dollar a crate
for some fruit. You had to work fast. That was the whole thing. A
frantic lunatic to make your barely living wage. If you had no rent
to pay, it was OK. You were ahead, amigo. Pay rent, however, stay
in one place, and you couldn't migrate after other easy pickings. The
joy of working was looking over your dreams locked to hunger.
Manuel studied the whorls in the woodwork whirling slowly,
revealed in the faint crepuscular light penetrating his shack. His cot
was a slab of half-inch plywood board twenty-two inches wide and
eight feet long, the width of the shack, supported by two two-by-
four beams butted up against the wall at both ends beneath the side
window. The shack itself was eight by twelve by seven feet high. Its
roof had a slight pitch. The rain stains in the ceiling planks revealed
the ease with which the rain penetrated. Except for two small panes
of glass exposed near the top, most of the window at the opposite
end was boarded up. A single, old, paint-encrusted door was the only
entry. No curtains. No interior paneling. Just a shack. A shack of
misery. He found he was able to admire and appreciate the simplicity and the strength of the construction. He counted the upright

studs, level, two feet apart, the double joists across the top supporting the roof. Cracks and knotholes aplenty, in the wall siding, let in
bright chinks of light during the day and welcome wisps of clear
fresh air at night. The rough planking of the siding was stained dark.
The floor was only partly covered with odd sections of plywood.
Some of the rough planking below was exposed, revealing cracks
leading down to the cool black earth beneath. A small thick table
was firmly studded to a portion of the wall opposite the door. A few
small pieces of clear lumber stood bunched together, unsung, un-
used, unhurried, in the far corner. An overhead shelf, supported from
the ceiling by a small extending perpendicular arm, containing some
boxes of left-over chemicals and fertilizers, completed the furnish-
ings in his temporary abode.

It was habitable.

He could raise his family in it.

30   If they were rabbits.

The first rays of a brute new day clinked in through the small
rectangle of panes. The ray hovered, then peaked, then rested on the
covers pushed up by his knees. He recalled his mountain trips with
his uncle to the great forbidding barrancas near Durango in Central
Mexico, and stopping to rest in the middle of the wild woods, and
coming unexpectedly upon a crumbling, splintered hulk of a shack
that was all falling apart. It barely gave them shelter from the sudden pelting storm they were trying to escape, he as a young frightened boy, but shelter it was—and how beautiful that experience was,
then, for they were free, daring, adventurers, out there in that wilderness, alone and daring, with nothing between them and God's
own overpowering nature, alone. They belonged to nothing. To no
one. But themselves. They were dignity purified. No one forced them
to go or stay there. They were delighted and grateful to the shack.
For the protection it afforded them. Though it was hardly more than
a ratty pile of splinters. Far worse than this one he was now occupying . . . but also somehow far more beautiful in his memory.

And now. Here he was. Shut up in this miserable shack. So
sturdily built. Thinking how it sickened him inside because it was
more a jail cell than a shelter. He didn't care how comfortable and
convenient the growers made the shacks for him. They were huts of
slavery. What he wanted was an outlet for his pride. A sudden fierce
wave of anger made him want to cross the shack with his fists. There
had to be some way to cross the ungulfable bridge. Why was necessity always the bride of hunger? To be free . . . ah, and also to be able
to eat all one wanted. My heart, mi corazón, why did work always
have to blend with such misery? The welcome warmth of the sun's
early rays, penetrating more, warmed his frame. But it was a false,
false hope. He knew it. The work that lay ahead of him that day

would drain and stupefy and fatigue him once again to the point of senseless torpor, ready to fall over long before the work day was done. And that fatigue wasn't nearly so bad to bear as the deadly repetitious monotony of never changing, never resting, doing the same plucking over and over and over again. But he had to do it. He had no choice. It was all he could do. It had to be done if he wanted the money. And he had to have the money, if he wanted to feed his family. The brain in his arms was his only capital. Not very much, true, but it was the only sacrifice he could offer the money gods, the only heart he could offer on the pyramid of gold.

His life. La gran vida.

Wide awake now, fully refreshed, his whole body lithe and toned, Manuel was ashamed to find himself eager to start in work, knowing that he would do well, but ashamed because he could think of nothing he would rather do more. The final step.

The final the final the final the final the final the final step.   35

To want to work oneself to death. A la muerte. It wasn't the work itself that bothered him. It was the total immersion, the endless, ceaseless, total use of all his energies and spirit and mind and being that tore him apart within. He didn't know what else he was good for or could do with his life. But there had to be something else. He had to be something more than a miserable plucking animal. Pluck pluck pluck. Feed feed feed. Glug glug glug. Dressing quickly, rolling up his blanket roll and stuffing it into a corner to use again that night, Manuel stepped coolly out into the morning sweetness and breathed the honeyscented humidity rinsing air rising from the honied soil, and joined the thickening throng of his fellow pluckers milling about the large open barn serving as a cookout. Feeding all the pickers was another of the fat man's unholy prerogatives, for he cheated and overpriced on meals too. Roberto Morales, the fat man, the shrewd contratista, was a bully man, busily darting his blob about, exhorting his priceless pickers to hurry, answering questions, giving advice, in the cool half-light, impatiently, pushing, giving orders. Manuel, in order to avoid having to greet him, scowled at his toes when Roberto came trouncing by, saying, "Apúrense, compañeros, hurry, hurry, hurry, amigos." Sure. Amigos. Sí. Sí. Frens. They all gulped their food down hurriedly, standing. Just like home. Paper plates, plastic cups. Wooden spoons. And bits of garbage flying into large canisters. Then in the still cool nightlike morning air, like a flood of disturbed birds, they all picked up their pails and filed into the orchard.

The apricots were plump.

Smooth.

A golden syrupy orange.

Manuel popped two into his mouth, enjoying their cool natural   40 sweetness after the bitter coffee. He knew he could not eat too many. His stomach muscles would cramp. Other pickers started pulling rapidly away from him. Let them. Calmly he calculated the struggle. Start the press sure, slow, and keep it going steady. Piecework. Fill the bucket, fill another, and still another. The competition was among a set of savages, as savage for money as himself, savages with machetes, hacking their way through the thickets of modern civilization back to the good old Aztec days, waiting to see who'd be first in line to wrench his heart out. Savage beasts, eager to fill as many buckets as possible in as short a time as possible, cleaning out an entire orchard, picking everything in sight clean, tons of fruit, delivering every bit of ripe fruit to the accountants in their cool air-conditioned orifices.

The competition was not between pickers and growers.

It was between pickers—Jorge and Guillermo.

Between the poor and the hungry, the desperate, and the hunted, the slave and the slave, slob against slob, the depraved and himself. You were your own terrible boss. That was the cleverest part of the whole thing. The picker his own bone picker, his own willing built-in slave driver. God, that was good! That was where they reached into your scrotum and screwed you royally and drained your brain and directed your sinews and nerves and muscles with invisible fingers. To fatten their coffers. And drive you to your coffin. That sure was smart. Meant to be smart. Bookkeepers aren't dumb. You worked hard because you wanted to do that hard work above everything else. Pick fast pick hard pick furious pick pick pick. They didn't need straw bosses studying your neck to see if you kept bobbing up and down to keep your picking pace up. Like the barn-stupid chicken, you drove yourself to do it. You were your own money monkey foreman, monkey on top of your own back.

You over-charged yourself.

45   With your own frenzy.

Neat.

You pushed your gut and your tired aching arms and your twitching legs pumping adrenalin until your tongue tasted like coarse sandpaper.

You didn't even stop to take a drink, let alone a piss, for fear you'd get fined, fired, or bawled out.

And then, after all that effort, you got your miserable pay.

50   Would the bobbing boss's sons stoop to that?

His fingers were loose and dexterous now. The plump orange balls plopped pitter patter like heavy drops of golden rain into his swaying, sweaty canvas bucket. His earnings depended entirely on how quickly he worked and how well he kept the pressure up. The morning sun was high. The sweet shade was fragrant and refreshing and comfortable under the leafy branches. The soil too was still cool and humid. It was going to be another hot one.

There.

Another row ended.

He swung around the end of the row and for a moment he was all alone, all by himself. He looked out far across the neighboring alfalfa field, dark green and rich and ripe. Then he looked at the long low Diablo Range close by, rising up into the misty pale blue air kept cool by the unseen bay nearby. This was all his. For a flowing, deceptive minute, all this rich, enormous terrain was all his. All this warm balmy baby air. All this healthful sunny breeze. All those hills, this rich fertile valley, these orchards, these tiled huertas, these magnificent farms, all, all his . . . for his eyes to feast upon. It was a moment he wished he could capture forever and etch permanently on his memory, making it a part of living life for his heart to feast joyously on, forever. Why couldn't he stop? Why? Why couldn't he just put the bucket down and open his arms and walk into the hills and merge himself with the hills and just wander invisibly in the blue?

What Manuel couldn't really know was that he was complet- 55
ing yet another arc in the unending circle that had been started by one of his Mexican forebears exactly two hundred years before—for even the memory of history was also robbed from him—when Gaspar de Portolá, hugging the coastline, nearing present-day San Francisco, climbed what is now Sweeney Ridge, and looked down upon San Francisco's magnificent landlocked Bay, overlooking what is now the International Airport.

Both don Gaspar and don Manuel were landlords and landless at precisely the same instant of viewing all this heady beauty. And both were equally dispossessed. Both were also possessed of a keen sense of pride and natural absorption with the ritual and mystery of all life. The living that looked mighty good in a flash to Manuel lasted a good deal longer for don Gaspar whose stumbling accident swept him into the honored and indelible pages of glorious history.

Manuel was now a mere straw among the enormous sludge of humanity flowing past, a creature of limb and his own driving appetites, a creature of heed and need. Swinging around another end run he placed his ladder on the next heavy limb of the next pregnant tree. He reached up. He plucked bunches of small golden fruit with both hands. He worked like a frenzied windmill in slow motion. He cleared away an arc as far as the circumference of his plucking fingers permitted. A living model for da Vinci's outstretched man. Adam heeding God's moving finger. He moved higher. He repeated another circle. Then down and around again to another side of the tree, until he cleared it, cleared it of all visible, viable, delectable, succulent fruit. It was sweet work. The biggest difference between him and the honey-gathering ant was that the ant had a home.

Several pickers were halfway down the next row, well in advance of him. He was satisfied he was pacing himself well. Most of the band was still behind him. The moving sun, vaulting the sky dome's crackling earth parting with its bronzing rays, pounded its fierce heat into every dead and living crevice. Perspiration poured down his sideburns, down his forehead, down his cheek, down his neck, into his ears, off his chin. He tasted its saltiness with the tip of his dry tongue. He wished he'd brought some salt tablets. Roberto Morales wasn't about to worry about the pickers, and Manuel wasn't worried either. Despite the heat, he felt some protection from the ocean and bay. It had been much, much worse in Texas, and much hotter in Delano in the San Joaquín Valley and worst of all in Satan's own land, the Imperial Valley.

No matter which way he turned, he was trapped in an endless maze of apricot trees, as though forever, neat rows of them, neatly planted, row after row, just like the blackest bars on the jails of hell. There had to be an end. There had to be. There—trapped. There had to be a way out. Locked. There had to be a respite. Animal. The buckets and the crates kept piling up higher. Brute. He felt alone. Though surrounded by other pickers. Beast. Though he was perspiring heavily, his shirt was powder dry. Savage. The hot dry air. The hot dry air sucking every drop of living moisture from his brute body. Wreck. He stopped and walked to the farthest end of the first row for some water, raised the dented dipper from the brute tank, drank the holy water in great brute gulps so he wouldn't have to savor its tastelessness, letting it spill down his torn shirt to cool his exhausted body, to replenish his brute cells and animal pores and stinking follicles and pig gristle, a truly refined wreck of an animal, pleased to meetcha. Predator.

60   Lunch.

Almost too exhausted to eat, he munched his cheese with tortillas, smoked on ashes, then lay back on the cool ground for half an hour. That short rest in the hot shade replenished some of his humor and resolve. He felt his spirit swell out again like a thirsty sponge in water. Then up again. The trees. The branches again. The briarly branches. The scratching leaves. The twigs tearing at his shirt sleeves. The ladder. The rough bark. The endlessly unending piling up of bucket upon box upon crate upon stack upon rack upon mound upon mountain. He picked a mountain of cots automatically. An automator. A beast. A ray of enemy sun penetrated the tree that was hiding him and split his forehead open. His mind whirred. He blacked out. Luckily he'd been leaning against a heavy branch. His feet hooked to the ladder's rung. His half-filled bucket slipped from his grasp and fell in slow motion, splattering the fruit he'd so laboriously picked. To the ground. Robert happened by and shook his head. "Whatsamatter, can't you see straight, pendejo." Manuel was too tired even to curse. He should have had some salt pills.

Midafternoon.

The summer's fierce zenith passed overhead. It passed. Then dropped. It started to light the ocean behind him, back of the hills. Sandy dreams. Cool nights. Cold drinks. Soft guitar music with Lupe sitting beside him. All wafting through his feverish moments. Tiredness drained his spirit of will. Exhaustion drained his mind. His fingers burned. His arms flailed the innocent trees. He was slowing down. He could hardly fill his last bucket. Suddenly the whistle blew. The day's work was at last ended.

Ended!

The contratista Roberto Morales stood there.   65

His feet straddled. Mexican style. A real robber. A Mexican general. A gentlemanly, friendly, polite, grinning, vicious, thieving brute. The worst kind. To his own people. Despite his being a fellow Mexican, despite his torn, old clothing, everyone knew what kind of clever criminal he was. Despite his crude, ignorant manner, showing that he was one of them, that he'd started with them, that he grew up with them, that he'd suffered all the sordid deprivations with them, he was actually the shrewdest, smartest, richest cannibal in forty counties around. They sure couldn't blame the güeros for this miscarriage. He was a crew chief. How could anyone know what he did to his own people? And what did the güeros care? So the anglo growers and güero executives, smiling in their cool filtered offices, puffing their elegant thin cigars, washed their clean blond bloodless dirtless hands of the whole matter. All they did was hire Roberto Morales. Firm, fair, and square. For an agreed-upon price. Good. How he got his people down to the pickings was no concern of theirs. They were honest, those güeros. They could sleep at night. They fulfilled their end of the bargain, and cheated no one. Their only crime, their only soul grime indeed was that they just didn't give a shit how that migratory scum lived. It was no concern of theirs. Their religion said it was no concern of theirs. Their wives said it was no concern of theirs. Their aldermen said it was no concern of theirs. Their—

Whenever Roberto Morales spoke, Manuel had to force himself not to answer. He had to keep his temper from flaring.

"Now," announced Morales at last, in his friendliest tone.

"Now. I must take two cents from every bucket. I am sorry. There was a miscalculation. Everybody understands. Everybody?" He slid his eyes around, smiling, palms up.

The tired, exhausted pickers gasped as one.

70   Yes. Everyone understood. Freezing in place. After all that hard work.

"Any questions, men?"

Still grinning, knowing, everyone realizing that he had the upper hand, that that would mean a loss of two or three dollars out of each picker's pay that day, a huge windfall for Morales.

"You promised to take nothing!" Manuel heard himself saying. Everyone turned in astonishment to stare at Manuel.

"I said two cents, hombre. You got a problem or what?"

75   "You promised."

The two men, centered in a huge ring of red-ringed eyes, glared at each other. Reaching for each other's jugular. The other exhausted animals studied the tableau through widening eyes. It was so unequal. Morales remained calm, confident, studying Manuel. As though memorizing his features. He had the whole advantage. Then, with his last remaining energy, Manuel lifted his foot and clumsily tipped over his own last bucket of cots. They rolled away in all directions around everyone's feet.

Roberto Morales' eyes blazed. His fists clenched. "You pick them up, Gutiérrez."

So. He knew his name. After all. For answer, Manuel kicked over another bucket, and again the fruit rolled away in all directions.

Then an astonishing thing happened.

80   All the other pickers moved toward their own buckets still standing beside them on the ground awaiting the truck gatherer, and took an ominous position over them, straddling their feet over them. Without looking around, without taking his eyes off Manuel, Roberto Morales said sharply, "All right. All right, men. I shall take nothing this time."

Manuel felt a thrill of power course through his nerves.

He had never won anything before. He would have to pay for this, for his defiance, somehow, again, later. But he had shown defiance. He had salvaged his money savagely and he had earned respect from his fellow slaves. The gringo hijos de la chingada would never know of this little incident, and would probably be surprised, and perhaps even a little mortified, for a few minutes. But they wouldn't give a damn. It was bread, pan y tortillas out of his children's mouths. But they still wouldn't give a single damn. Manuel had wrenched Morales' greedy fingers away and removed a fat slug of a purse from his sticky grasp. And in his slow way, in his stupid, accidental, dangerous way, Manuel had made an extravagant discovery, as don Gaspar had also made two centuries before, in almost exactly the same spot. And that was—that a man counted for something. For men, Manuel dimly suspected, are built for something more important and less trifling than the mere gathering of prunes and apricots, hour upon hour, decade upon decade, insensibly, mechanically, antlike. Men are built to experience a certain sense of honor and pride.

Or else they are dead before they die.

Response

1. Notice how throughout the passage descriptions of the natural environment and of the crops are filled with imagery of "mother earth," fertile and generous. What is the intended irony in this?

2. Manuel compares his present shack with the one he and his uncle once occupied in the mountains of Mexico. How do the shacks compare, physically and functionally? What is Manuel's image of himself in each shack? In each case, what is his view of nature and his relationship to it?

3. In three segments in this passage Manuel reflects on the character and role of Roberto Morales, the ironically named labor contractor. What is Morales' function? How does he relate to the laborers and to his gringo employers? Why does he back off in the final incident?

4. Manuel is in constant struggle between the image of himself as a beast in servitude and himself as a man of pride and dignity. Look through the passage to find recurrent language to support each image.

5. Manuel moves from anger at his entrapment, to recognition of how the economic system oppresses the workers including himself, to taking the first defiant action that leads to understanding and change. Trace his development through these stages.

6. Barrio compares Manuel to Gaspar de Portolá, a heroic eighteenth-century Spanish explorer, in paragraphs 55–56. What is the point of the comparison? In what sense are don Gaspar and Manuel both "landlords and landless . . . equally dispossessed," as Manuel gazes at the beautiful landscape? How are they both great discoverers? Manuel is unaware of this historical antecedent, "for even the memory of history was also robbed from him," says Barrio. What difference do you think it would make if he knew this history?

Notes to a Young(er) Writer

Sandra Cisneros

This essay was originally a lecture Cisneros gave to a public school audience in Santa Barbara, California, in 1986. In it she indicates that she has not just a personal, but a political motive for writing.

When I was young(er), I wanted to die young, about 30—a suicide preferably—because I couldn't think of a more romantic way for a writer to die than young. And a suicide.

Now that I am *30*, any and all suicidal thoughts that ever entered my goofy head have permanently fled. I want more than anything to live—long enough to learn what I'm doing with my art, long enough so that I can rightfully say I am a writer.

The great Japanese artist Hokusai admitted that at the age of 78 he had learned a little about the structure of nature, but at 80 he would have still more progress, at 90 penetrate the mystery of things, and finally at 100 arrive at a marvelous stage.

I've only been writing since 1974, more or less, since I enrolled in my first writing class taught by a professional writer in my junior year in college. It's true I did write all the four years I was in high school, enough so that everyone knew me as the "poet," fanatically so that, ultimately, I became the literary magazine editor. And yes,

Sandra Cisneros, "Notes to a Young(er) Writer," in *The Americas Review* (6:1), 1979. University of Houston, Arte Publico Press. Reprinted with permission from the publisher.

I've mentioned in other papers my interviews that I used to write when I was in grade school, mostly things I kept to myself in a spiral notebook—never anything I showed to anyone. When did I talk to anyone and when did anyone ever talk to me?

But those years before that first college writing class, I was   5
more a reader than a writer—an important first step to *becoming* a writer. I was getting myself ready to *be* a writer with the books I borrowed from the Chicago Public Library, the books I read instead of doing my household chores, instead of learning how to cook or taking care of my little brothers, instead of talking to the best friend I didn't have or the boys who never noticed me. I was reading and reading, nurturing myself with books like vitamins, only I didn't know it then.

What if that first creative writing class had never come around? What if I didn't go to college? Where would I be now? Maybe and most probably I'd still be scribbling my poems and stories in spiral notebooks, not showing them to anybody.

When I was growing up in Chicago, and going to college in Chicago, and not travelling anywhere except on CTA buses and sub-way trains but desperately wanting to break loose, I liked to think of my favorite American poet, Emily Dickinson, who lived during the last century in a little town called Amherst and hardly travelled beyond. I liked to think of that extraordinary woman who in her later life never even strayed beyond the house and its gardens, but who wrote in her lifetime 1,775 poems. No one knew she was a poet until after she died, and then, when they discovered those poems handwritten on sheets of paper folded and stitched together, the world rang like a bell.

I used to think of her and she gave me inspiration and hope all the years in high school and the first two in college when I was too busy being in love to write. Inside, some part of me secretly clung to the dream of becoming a writer. But for many years what I didn't realize about Emily Dickinson was that she had a few essentials going for her: 1) an education, 2) a room of her own in a house of her own that she shared with her sister Lavinia, and 3) money inherited along with the house after her father died. She even had a maid, an Irish housekeeper who did, I suspect, most of the household chores. It's true Emily Dickinson baked and sewed for her sister Lavinia and her beloved brother Austin, but she baked and sewed because she wanted to, not because she *had* to. I wonder if Emily Dickinson's Irish housekeeper wrote poetry or if she ever had the secret desire to study and be anything besides a housekeeper.

Maybe she was a woman like my mama who could sing a Puccini opera, cook a dinner for nine with only five dollars, who could

draw and tell stories and who probably would've enjoyed a college
education but whose only taste of college was reading the books her
children brought home from the university. Maybe Emily Dickinson's Irish housekeeper had to sacrifice her life so that Emily could
live hers locked upstairs in the corner bedroom writing her 1,775
poems. That's what I'm thinking.

10   So I'm pretty lucky to be here today. I'm here because my
mother let me stay in my room reading and studying, perhaps because she didn't want me to inherit her sadness and her rolling pin.

        And I'm here because I didn't marry my first boyfriend, that
pest who never gave me any time alone, something crucial to every
writer—"aloneness" breeds art—and who couldn't understand why
I didn't want what he wanted: marriage and a house in the suburbs.
(Always knew I was smarter than him.) He never understood my
desire to be a writer, my need to do something for my people. But of
course, he wasn't Mexican, didn't grow up poor, and had no ambition to be/do anything in his life other than buy that house, put his
feet up and sigh.

        In some ways, when I looked at everybody else around me in
college—the kids whose daddies were paying for their tuition, their
little red sportscar and their designer clothes—I envied them. How
nice to think of nothing other than getting a job and making as much
money as possible. How nice to think of no one but yourself. They
didn't have any responsibilities. They didn't feel guilty and sad when
they looked out the window of their sportscar and passed the poor
tenement apartments of Uptown. What were the poor to them but a
burden on their taxes? They had never had pancakes and peanut
butter for dinner. What did they know of need?

        When I think those kids are now the people changing history,
the ones in government and business, altering and making our laws,
it makes me sad. It makes me sad because they never feel compelled
to change the world for anyone but themselves. No understanding
of how hard it is to rise above harsh circumstances. Nothing. Like
speaking another language.

        But in many ways I feel luckier than them. I can write of worlds
they never dreamed of, of things they never could learn from a college textbook. I am the first woman in my family to pick up a pen
and record what I see around me, a woman who has the power to
speak and is privileged enough to be heard. That *is* a responsibility.

15   I don't know when I first said to myself I am going to be a
writer. Perhaps that first day my mother took me to the public library when I was five, or perhaps again when I was in high school
and my English teacher forced me to read a poem outloud and I became entranced with the sounds, or perhaps when I enrolled in that

creative writing class in college, not knowing it would lead to other creative writing workshops and graduate school. Perhaps.

I've been writing a little over ten years now, and, if there's anything I've learned, it's how much more I need to learn. I don't want to die young. I don't want to drive fast, or get on airplanes, or sit with my back to the door when I'm in a bar. For the sake of my writing I want a long life. There are so few of us writing about the powerless, and that world, the world of thousands of silent women, women like my mama and Emily Dickinson's housekeeper, needs to be, must be recorded so that their stories can finally be heard. I want a long life to learn my art well, so that at 73 I too, like Hokusai, can admit, "If God should let me live five years longer, *then* I might call myself an artist."

Response

1. Cisneros tells how she abandoned her romantic image of a writer as she came to understand more about the role social class plays in people's ability to achieve their goals. What did she figure out about Emily Dickinson, and what did it have to do with her own aspirations? To what circumstances does she attribute her success in becoming a writer?

2. Cisneros describes feelings she had as a college student toward some of her peers. If you were her fellow student, how would you feel about her attitude?

3. Cisneros says she is "a woman who has the power to speak and is privileged enough to be heard. That *is* a responsibility" (paragraph 14). What does she take to be her responsibility as a writer? How does this echo her message in "Ghosts and Voices: Writing from Obsession" (Section I)? In this essay, what does she suggest is her purpose in writing?

4. Consider the title, "Notes to a Young(er) Writer." What advice for young(er) writers can we infer from the passage? How does Cisneros' message compare to that of Gloria Anzaldua in "Speaking in Tongues: Letter to Third World Women Writers"?

The Transformation of Silence into Language and Action

Audre Lorde

This essay is derived from a speech Lorde gave in 1977 to an audience of scholars. She explains that when she was told she might have cancer, she suddenly recognized the urgency of speaking out on issues she considered important; that is the message of this essay, which appears in Sister Outsider *(1984).*

I have come to believe over and over again that what is most important to me must be spoken, made verbal and shared, even at the risk of having it bruised or misunderstood. That the speaking profits me, beyond any other effect. I am standing here as a Black lesbian poet, and the meaning of all that waits upon the fact that I am still alive, and might not have been. Less than two months ago I was told by two doctors, one female and one male, that I would have to have breast surgery, and that there was a 60 to 80 percent chance that the tumor was malignant. Between that telling and the actual surgery, there was a three-week period of the agony of an involuntary reorganization of my entire life. The surgery was completed, and the growth was benign.

But within those three weeks, I was forced to look upon myself and my living with a harsh and urgent clarity that has left me still shaken but much stronger. This is a situation faced by many women, by some of you here today. Some of what I experienced during that time has helped elucidate for me much of what I feel concerning the transformation of silence into language and action.

In becoming forcibly and essentially aware of my mortality, and of what I wished and wanted for my life, however short it might be, priorities and omissions became strongly etched in a merciless light, and what I most regretted were my silences. Of what had I *ever* been afraid? To question or to speak as I believed could have meant pain, or death. But we all hurt in so many different ways, all the time, and pain will either change or end. Death, on the other hand, is the final silence. And that might be coming quickly, now, without regard for whether I had ever spoken what needed to be said, or had only betrayed myself into small silences,while I planned someday to speak, or waited for someone else's words. And I began to recognize a source of power within myself that comes from the knowledge that while it is most desirable not to be afraid, learning to put fear into a perspective gave me great strength.

I was going to die, if not sooner then later, whether or not I had ever spoken myself. My silences had not protected me. Your silence will not protect you. But for every real word spoken, for every attempt I had ever made to speak those truths for which I am still seeking, I had made contact with other women while we examined the words to fit a world in which we all believed, bridging our differences. And it was the concern and caring of all those women which gave me strength and enabled me to scrutinize the essentials of my living.

The women who sustained me through that period were Black   5
and white, old and young, lesbian, bisexual, and heterosexual, and we all shared a war against the tyrannies of silence. They all gave me a strength and concern without which I could not have survived intact. Within those weeks of acute fear came the knowledge— within the war we are all waging with the forces of death, subtle and otherwise, conscious or not—I am not only a casualty, I am also a warrior.

What are the words you do not yet have? What do you need to say? What are the tyrannies you swallow day by day and attempt to make your own, until you will sicken and die of them, still in silence? Perhaps for some of you here today, I am the face of one of your fears. Because I am woman, because I am Black, because I am lesbian, because I am myself—a Black woman warrior poet doing my work—come to ask you, are you doing yours?

And of course I am afraid, because the transformation of silence into language and action is an act of self-revelation, and that always seems fraught with danger. But my daughter, when I told her of our topic and my difficulty with it, said, "Tell them about how you're never really a whole person if you remain silent, because there's always that one little piece inside you that wants to be spoken out, and if you keep ignoring it, it gets madder and madder and hotter and hotter, and if you don't speak it out one day it will just up and punch you in the mouth from the inside."

In the cause of silence, each of us draws the face of her own fear—fear of contempt, of censure, or some judgment, or recognition, of challenge, of annihilation. But most of all, I think, we fear the visibility without which we cannot truly live. Within this country where racial difference creates a constant, if unspoken, distortion of vision, Black women have on one hand always been highly visible, and so, on the other hand, have been rendered invisible through the depersonalization of racism. Even within the women's movement, we have had to fight, and still do, for that very visibility which also renders us most vulnerable, our Blackness. For to survive in the mouth of this dragon we call america, we have had to learn this first and most vital lesson—that we were never meant to survive. Not as human beings. And neither were most of you here today, Black or not. And that visibility which makes us most vulnerable is that which also is the source of our greatest strength. Because the machine will try to grind you into dust anyway, whether or not we speak. We can sit in our corners mute forever while our sisters and our selves are wasted, while our children are distorted and destroyed, while our earth is poisoned; we can sit in our safe corners mute as bottles, and we will still be no less afraid.

In my house this year we are celebrating the feast of Kwanza, the African-american festival of harvest which begins the day after Christmas and lasts for seven days. There are seven principles of Kwanza, one for each day. The first principle is Umoja, which means unity, the decision to strive for and maintain unity in self and community. The principle for yesterday, the second day, was Kujichagulia—self-determination—the decision to define ourselves, name ourselves, and speak for ourselves, instead of being defined and spoken for by others. Today is the third day of Kwanza, and the principle for today is Ujima—collective work and responsibility—the decision to build and maintain ourselves and our communities together and to recognize and solve our problems together.

10   Each of us is here now because in one way or another we share a commitment to language and to the power of language, and to the reclaiming of that language which has been made to work against us. In the transformation of silence into language and action, it is vitally necessary for each one of us to establish or examine her function in that transformation and to recognize her role as vital within that transformation.

For those of us who write, it is necessary to scrutinize not only the truth of what we speak, but the truth of that language by which we speak it. For others, it is to share and spread also those words that are meaningful to us. But primarily for us all, it is necessary to teach by living and speaking those truths which we believe and know beyond understanding. Because in this way alone we can survive, by taking part in a process of life that is creative and continuing, that is growth.

And it is never without fear—of visibility, of the harsh light of scrutiny and perhaps judgment, of pain, of death. But we have lived through all of those already, in silence, except death. And I remind myself all the time now that if I were to have been born mute, or had maintained an oath of silence my whole life long for safety, I would still have suffered, and I would still die. It is very good for establishing perspective.

And where the words of women are crying to be heard, we must each of us recognize our responsibility to seek those words out, to read them and share them and examine them in their pertinence to our lives. That we not hide behind the mockeries of separations that have been imposed upon us and which so often we accept as our own. For instance, "I can't possibly teach Black women's writing—their experience is so different from mine." Yet how many years have you spent teaching Plato and Shakespeare and Proust? Or another, "She's a white woman and what could she possibly have to say to me?" Or, "She's a lesbian, what would my husband say, or my chairman?" Or again, "This woman writes of her sons and I have no children." And all the other endless ways in which we rob ourselves of ourselves and each other.

We can learn to work and speak when we are afraid in the same way we have learned to work and speak when we are tired. For we have been socialized to respect fear more than our own needs for language and definition, and while we wait in silence for that final luxury of fearlessness, the weight of that silence will choke us.

The fact that we are here and that I speak these words is an   15
attempt to break that silence and bridge some of those differences between us, for it is not difference which immobilizes us, but silence. And there are so many silences to be broken.

Response

1. Lorde speaks of the danger of self-revelation and of fear. For what reasons might people fear the visibility that comes with speaking out?
2. African-American women, Lorde observes, "have been ren-

dered invisible through the depersonalization of racism" (paragraph 8). Explain how racism can deprive an individual of personal identity.

3. Lorde addressed the spoken version of this essay to an audience of scholars concerned with lesbians and literature. In the essay, she addresses her readers directly several times. Who do you think is her intended audience? What indications does she give?

4. Explain the "separations that have been imposed upon us and which so often we accept as our own" (paragraph 13). In what ways do we "rob ourselves of ourselves and each other"?

5. Evaluate Lorde's observation that "we have been socialized to respect fear more than our own needs for language and definition" (paragraph 14). How might this observation apply to daily life?

6. Lorde claims in her conclusion that speaking out, as she is doing in this essay, offers a way for people to bridge their differences, "for it is not difference which immobilizes us, but silence." What do you think of this statement? Do you share her view?

7. To what extent does Lorde suggest the same causes for silence that bell hooks recognized in "Talking Back" (Section I)? How does her message in this essay compare with that of Gloria Anzaldua in "Speaking in Tongues: A Letter to Third World Women Writers"?

Tomorrow Is Coming, Children
Toshio Mori

Mori wrote this story while he was an internee in Topaz Relocation Center. It was first published in 1943 in the Topaz Camp magazine, Trek, *and later became the opening story in Mori's book* Yokohama, California *(1949). In the story an issei grandmother, in a relocation camp, explains some personal history to her grandchildren. The grandmother exhibits the dignity and tenacity of spirit typical of characters in Mori's stories.*

Long ago, children, I lived in a country called Japan. Your grandpa was already in California earning money for my boat ticket. The village people rarely went out of Japan and were shocked when they heard I was following your grandpa as soon as the money came.

"America!" they cried. "America is on the other side of the world! You will be in a strange country. You cannot read or write their language. What will you do?" I smiled, and in my dreams I saw the San Francisco your grandpa wrote about: San Francisco, the city with strange enticing food; the city with gold coins; the city with many strange faces and music; the city with great buildings and ships.

One day his letter came with the money. "Come at once," he

Toshio Mori, "Tomorrow Is Coming, Children," in *Yokohama, California.* (1985) University of Washington Press, Seattle. Originally published Caldwell, Idaho, The Caxton Printers, Ltd., 1949. Printed with permission.

wrote. "Don't delay." The neighbors rushed excitedly to the house. "Don't go! Live among us," they cried. "There will be war between America and Japan. You will be caught in mid-Pacific. You will never reach America." But I was determined. They painted the lonely lives of immigrants in a strange land. They cried on my shoulders and embraced me. "I have bought my ticket and my things are packed. I am going," I said.

For thirty days and nights the village people invited me to their houses, and I was dined and feted. It was hard not to change my mind and put off the trip. They came to see me off at the station. They waved their hands cheerfully though their eyes were sad. But my spirits were not dampened. I was looking ahead, thinking of your grandpa and San Francisco.

5   My brother went with me to Kobe, and not until the boat was pulling away from the pier did I feel a pain in my breast. Yes, I cried. The first night I could not sleep. I kept hearing my friends' words: "Hurry back. We will be waiting. Remember us. . . . Best of health to you." The boat began to toss and we could not go up on deck. I grew seasick. What kind of a boat? Tiny, though at that time we thought it was big. The liners of today are three and four times as large. . . . Yes, your grandma is old. She is of the first generation. You children are of the third. . . .

The sea was rough and I was sick almost all the way. There were others in the room just as ill. I couldn't touch the food. I began to have crazy thoughts. Why was I going to America? Why had I been foolish enough to leave my village? For days I could not lift my head. Turn back? Did the ship turn back for me? No, child. A steamer never turns back for an individual. Not for death or birth or storm. No more does life.

Now your grandma is old. She will die some day just like your grandpa. Yes, child, I know, you love me. But when I pass away and the days roll by, you will find life goes on. How do I know? Just this morning Annabelle lost a quarter somewhere on the street. Her mama told her not to hold it in her hands but put it in her purse. No, she wanted her way and lost it. That is experience, child. That is how I know. I lost Grandpa. I lost my boy. I lost my mother and father. Long ago I lost my friends in Japan. . . . Here, I am rambling. . . .

When the boat finally passed the Golden Gate, I had my first glimpse of San Francisco. I was on deck for hours, waiting for the golden city of dreams. I stood there with the other immigrants, chatting nervously and excitedly. First we saw only a thin shoreline. "America! America! We're in America!" someone cried. Others took up the cry, and presently the deck was full of eager faces. Finally we began to see the dirty brown hills and the houses that jutted out of the ground. This was different from what I had dreamed, and I was speechless. I had expected to see the green hills of Japan and the low sloping houses duplicated here. No, child, it wasn't disappointment exactly, but I had a lump in my throat. "This is San Francisco. My San Francisco," I murmured to myself.

What was I wearing, Annabelle? My best kimono, a beautiful thing. But do you know what your grandpa did when he saw me come off the boat? He looked at it and shook his head. He hauled me around as if he were ashamed of me. I could not understand.

"Never wear this thing again," he told me that night.   10

"Why?" I demanded. "It is a beautiful kimono."

"You look like a foreigner," he said. "You must dress like an American. You belong here."

He gave me a dress, a coat, a hat, stockings, and shoes, my first American clothes. I stopped dozens of times in front of the mirror to see how I looked. Yes, I remember the big hats they used to wear then, and the long skirts that dusted the dirt off the streets. Some day I shall go up to the attic of our Oakland home and bring down the album and show you the pictures of those old days.

I cannot find the street now where your grandpa and I lived that first year but it is somewhere in San Francisco. We had a small empty house and no money. We spread our blankets on the floor and slept. We used big boxes for tables and small ones for chairs. The city of my dreams began to frighten me. Rocks were thrown at the house and the windows smashed to bits. Loud cries and laughter followed each attack, and I cowered in the corner waiting for the end.

"Oh, why did I come? Whatever did we come for?" I asked your   15
grandpa.

He only looked at me. "Just a little more time. . . . a little more time," his eyes seemed to say.

I could not refuse. But we moved out of San Francisco. We came across the Bay, and after much saving your grandpa bought a bath-house in Oakland. And that was where your daddy was born. We lived in the rear, and for four years it was our home. Ah, the year your daddy was born! That was when for the first time I began to feel at home.

It was on account of a little neighbor, the white American wife of a Japanese acrobat. They were touring the country as headliners but had settled down in Oakland for some reason. They lived next door with their adopted Japanese children. "Mich-chan, Taka-chan! Come home! Mich-chan, Taka-chan!" Her cries used to ring across the yard like a caress.

The Japanese acrobat came often. "Please come and talk with my American wife. She is lonely and has no friend here," he told me.

20   I shook my head ashamedly. "I am lonely, too, but I cannot speak English. When your American wife starts talking, I am in trouble," I explained.

Then he would laugh and scold me. "Talk? You don't have to talk. My wife will understand. Please do not be afraid."

One day the American lady came, and we had tea. We drank silently and smiled. All the time I was hoping she would not begin talking. She liked my tea and cakes, I could tell. She talked of simple things so that I would grasp a little of it. She would pick up her teacup and ask, "Satsuma? Satsuma, Japan?"

I would nod eagerly. "Yes, Satsuma."

She came often. Every time we sat silently, sipped tea, and smiled. Every once in awhile her Japanese husband came and thanked me. "She is happy. She has a friend."

25   "I do not speak to her. I cannot express myself," I told him.

"No, no. She understands. You do not have to talk."

Ah, I can never forget her. She knitted baby clothes for your daddy. "I think it will be a girl," she said. But it was your daddy. I cried when she had to go away again. Yes, it was long ago. All your uncles and aunts came afterwards: Mamoru, Yuri, Willie, Mary Ann, Yoshio and Betty.

Yes, time is your friend in America, children. See, my face and hands are wrinkled, my hair gray. My teeth are gone, my figure bent. These are of America. I still cannot speak English too well, but I live among all kinds of people and come and go like the seasons, the bees, and the flowers. Ah, San Francisco, my dream city. My San Francisco is everywhere. I like the dirty brown hills, the black soil and the sandy beaches. I like the tall buildings, the bridges, the parks and the roar of city traffic. They are of me and I feel like humming.

You don't understand, Johnny? Ah, you are young. You will. Your grandma wants to be buried here in America. Yes, little ones. Once I had a brother and a sister in Japan. Long ago they wrote me a letter. Come back, sister, they said. We want to see you again. Hurry. Oh, it was long before you were born. But I did not return. I never saw them again. Now they are dead. I stayed in America; I belong here.

30   Now I do not ask myself: why did I come? The fog has lifted. Yes, Annabelle and Johnny, we are at war. I do not forget the fact. How can I ever forget? My mother country and my adopted land at war! Incredulous! After all these years when men of peace got along

together. Your grandma sometimes cries in the night when her eyes open. No, not for herself. She is thinking of your Uncle Mamoru in the U.S. Infantry "somewhere" overseas and his comrades, and the people going through hardships and sufferings. In time of war, weak men fall and the strong triumph.

You will learn, little ones, that life is harsh at times. War is painful. If there were no war we would not be in a relocation center. We would be back in our house on Market Street, hanging out our wash on the clothesline and watering our flower garden. You would be attending school with your neighborhood friends. Ah, war is terrifying. It upsets personal life and hopes. But war has its good points too.

In what way, Johnny? Well, you learn your lessons quickly during wartimes. You become positive. You cannot sit on the fence, you must choose sides. War has given your grandmother an opportunity to find where her heart lay. To her surprise her choice had been made long ago, and no war will sway her a bit. For grandma the sky is clear. The sun is shining.

But I am old. This is where you come in. Children, you must grow big and useful. This is your world. . . .

Now run along to bed like a good boy and girl. Sleep and rise early. Tomorrow is coming, children.

Response ———————————————————————

1. Telling the children that "life goes on" (paragraph 7), the grandmother recounts her experience of loss after loss. Do you think she means it when she says in paragraph 28, "time is your friend in America"? In what paradoxical sense could this be true for her?

2. To answer Johnny's skepticism about the "good points" of war, the grandmother explains that it forces one to choose sides, to clarify "where her heart lay" (paragraph 32)—but she doesn't elaborate on her decision. What do you think she has in mind?

3. Mori has been criticized for apparent tolerance of injustice in stories such as this one; his critics take the grandmother to be advocating acceptance and endurance of the internment experience when she says "tomorrow is coming, children." But in his introduction to the 1985 edition of *Yokohama, California* the writer Lawson Inada takes a different view. He reminds us that in Topaz in 1943 this story had to be acceptable to a camp

audience that included the authorities; he suggests that the story is filled with irony. In his view the grandmother, quietly resisting her experience, is exhorting the children to remember the injustice, teaching "survival tactics, strategy—in the guise of a bedtime story." Which interpretation do you find most plausible? How does the language of the story support your view?

The Panther Waits
Simon J. Ortiz

*This story opens with a quote from Tecumseh, a
Shawnee chief in what is now Ohio, during the time
of the westward expansion by white settlers. With
his twin brother, a visionary religious leader,
Tecumseh worked to unite the different tribes in a
confederation to resist the European encroachment.
His brother was killed at Tippecanoe in 1811;
Tecumseh himself died in battle in 1813. Ortiz
weaves this history into a modern-day story. It
appears in the anthology* Words in the Blood *(1984).*

*"That people will continue longest in the enjoyment of peace who
timely prepare to vindicate themselves and manifest a determination
to protect themselves whenever they are wronged."*
Tecumseh, 1811

Tahlequah is cold in November, and Sam, Billy, and Jay sat underneath a lusterless sun. They had been drinking all afternoon. Beer.
Wine. They were talking, trying not to feel the cold.

Maybe we need another vision, Billy.

Ah shoot, vision. I had one last night and it was pretty awful—
got run over by a train and somebody stole my wife.

He he he. Have another beer, Billy.

Simon J. Ortiz, "The Panther Waits," in *Words in the Blood*, edited by Jamake
Highwater. Markham, Ontario: Meridian, 1984. Permission given by the author.

5   Maybe, though, you know. It might work.

Forget it, huh. Cold beer vision, that's what I like.

No, Sam, I mean I've been thinking about that old man that used to be drunk all the time.

Your old man, he he he, he was drunk all the time.

Yeah, but not him. He was just a plain old drunk. I mean Harry Brown, that guy that sat out by the courthouse a lot. He used to have this paper with him.

10   Harry J. Brown, you mean? He was a kook, a real kookie kook, that one?

Yeah. Well, one time me and my brother, Taft, before he died in that car wreck down by Sulphur, well, me and him we asked Harry to buy us some beer at Sophie's Grill, you know, and he did. And then he wanted a can and sure, we said, but we had to go down by the bridge before we would give him one. We did and sat down by the bushes there and gave him a beer.

Yeah, we used to, too. He'd do anything for a beer, old Harry J. Brown. And your brother, he was a hell of a drinker, too, he he he.

We sat and drank beer for a while, just sitting, talking a bit about fishing or something, getting up once in a while to pee, and just bullshitting around. And then we finished all the beer and was wishing we had more, but we had no money, and we said to Harry, Harry, we gotta go now.

He was kind of fallen asleep, you know, just laid his head on his shoulder like he did sometimes on the cement courthouse steps. We shook his shoulder.

15   Uh, uh yeah, he said. And then he sort of shook his head and sort of like cleared his eyes with his hand, you know, like he was seeing kind of far and almost like we were strangers to him, like he didn't know us, although we'd been together all afternoon.

We said we was leaving, and he looked straight up into Taft's eyes and then over to me and then back to Taft. And then he rubbed his old brown hand over his eyes again and said, Get this. He said, Yes, kinda slow in his voice and careful, Yes, it's true, and it will come true.

I just realized, Harry Brown said slowly but clearly then, not like later on when you'd hardly understand what he was saying at the courthouse.

Realized, he repeated, you're the two. Looking straight into Taft's and my eyes. And then he kind of smiled and made a small laugh and then he shook and started to cry.

Harry, Taft said, you old fool, what the hell you talking about. C'mon, get a hold of yourself, shape up, old buddy. Taft always liked to talk to old guys. Sometimes nobody else would talk to them or make fun of them, remember? But Taft was always buddies with them.

Yeah, they gave him wine, that wino, Sam giggled. He knew   20
how to hit them up.

Anyway, Harry sat up then and didn't look at us no more, but he said, Sit down, I want to show you something. And then he pulled out this paper.

It was just a old piece of paper, sort of browned and folded, soft-looking, like he'd carried it a long time. Listen, he said, and then he didn't say anything. And we said again, We gotta go soon, Harry.

Wait. Wait, he said, you just wait. It's time to wait. And so we kept sitting there, wondering what in the world he was up to. The way Harry Brown was, his eyes sort of closed and thinking, made us interested.

Finally, he cleared his throat and spit some beer foam out and then he said, I just remembered something I thought I forgot. It's not from a long time ago, I don't think but longer than a man's age, anyway. I'm maybe seventy years along and that's not too long and what I remembered is longer than that. I carry this with me all the time. Once I thought I lost it, but then it had got thrown in the washing machine by Amy, my daughter, and she pulled it out of my pants, and you can't tell what it says clearly, but it's there, and it will always be there. I can still see it.

And then Harry opened up the paper. There was nothing on it,   25
just a brown piece of wrinkled paper. There's nothing there, Harry, I said, nothing but a piece of paper.

There's something there, he said, serious and solemn. There's something there. It's clear in my mind.

I looked over at Taft, who was on his knees staring at the paper and he caught my eye. I kind of shrugged, but Taft didn't say anything. I knew old Harry Brown's mind probably wasn't all that clear anymore with his old age and all the wine he drank all the time. But you know, he spoke clearly, and the way he was talking was serious and sure.

He said, They traveled all over. They went south, west, north, east, all those states now that you learn about in books. Even Florida, even Mississippi, even Missouri, all over they did.

Who did? Taft asked. I was wondering myself.

The two brothers. Look, you can see their marks and their   30
roads. He was pointing with his shaky old scarred finger. That old man had thick fingers. I've seen him lift a beer cap off the old kind of beer bottle with his thumb. The scar was from when the state police slammed his hand some years ago.

Taft was looking at the paper with a curious look on his face. I mean curious and serious, too. I still couldn't see anything. Nothing. I thought maybe there was a faint picture of something, but there didn't seem to be anything—just paper.

Taft looked over at me then and made a motion with his chin, and I looked at the paper again and listened.

They tried to tell all the people. They said, You Indians—they meant all the Indians wherever they went and even us now I'm sure—you Indians must be together and be one people. You are all together on this land. This land is your home and you must see yourself as all together. You people, you gotta understand this. There is no other way we're gonna be able to save our land and our people unless we decide to be all together.

The brothers traveled all over. Alabama, Canada, Kentucky, Georgia, all those states now on the map. Some places people said to them, We don't want to be together. We're always fighting with those other people. They don't like us and we don't like them. They steal and they're not trustworthy.

35   But the brothers insisted, We are all different people, that's for sure, but we are all human people, all humankind, all sisters and brothers, and this is all our land. We have to settle with each other. No more fighting, no more arguing, because it is the land and our home we have to fight for. That is what we have come to convince you about.

The brothers said, We will all have to fight before it's too late. They are coming. They keep coming and they want to take our land and our people. We have told them, No, we cannot sell our mother earth, we cannot sell the ocean, we cannot sell the air, we cannot give our lives away. We will have to defend them, and we must do it all together. We must do it, the brothers said. Listen.

Taft just kept looking at the paper and the brown finger of Harry Brown moving over the paper, and I kept looking, too. I still didn't see anything except the wrinkles and folds of the paper, but what Harry was saying with his serious-story voice put something there I think, and I looked over at Taft again. He was nodding his head like he understood perfectly what the old man was saying.

They were talking about the Americans coming and they wanted the Indians to be all together so they could help each other fight them off. So they could save their land and their families. That's what I remembered just awhile ago. I thought I'd forgotten, but I don't think I'll ever forget. It's as close to me as you two are.

Harry paused and then he went on. They were two brothers like you are. One of them, the older, was called Tecumtha. I've heard it means *the panther in waiting*. And the other was one who had old drunk problems like me, but he saved himself and helped his people. Maybe the vision they said he had came from his sickness of drinking, but it happened and they tried to do something about it. That's what is on here, look.

And Taft and I looked again, but I still couldn't see anything.   40
But I didn't say so, and Taft said, Yeah, Harry, I see.

And then we had to go. We was supposed to pick up some bailing wire from Stokes' Store and take it back to our old man. Before we left, Harry looked up at us again, straight into our faces. His eyes had cleared, you know, and he said, They were two brothers.

Taft and I talked some about it and then later on somebody— you know Ron and Jimmy, the two brothers from up by Pryor?

Yeah, Jimmy the all-state fullback? Boy, was he something. Yeah, I know them.

Yeah. Well, Ron told me old Harry Brown told them that same story, too, but they couldn't see nothing on the paper, either. They said it was kind of blue not brownish like I'd seen. I told Taft and he said, Well those two guys are too dumb and ignorant to see anything if it was right in front of their nose.

Jimmy got a scholarship to college and works for an oil com-   45
pany down in Houston, and Ron, I think, he's at the tribal office, desk job and all that, doing pretty good. I said to Taft, You didn't see anything, either. And he looked at me kind of pissed and said, Maybe not, but I know what Harry meant.

Geesus, that Taft could drink. He coulda been something, too, but he sure could drink like a hurricane, he he he. Tell us again what happened, Jay.

No, Sam, it was just a car wreck.

Maybe we need another vision, Billy said.

Response ———————————————————————

1. In this story Ortiz dispenses with the usual conventions of written dialogue, such as quotation marks and saying who is speaking. Why do you think he does this? What is the effect of this style?

2. Harry Brown, in the traditional role of the elder, told his story to the brothers Jay and Taft, introducing it with the words, "Yes, it's true, and it will come true." The story he told has been passed down orally, but he pointed to an old piece of paper as if the story was on it. What is the message in the story? What is the role of the paper? Why did Taft say he saw what was on it, but later the brothers Ron and Jimmy couldn't see anything?

3. Alcohol use plays a prominent role in the story. Look for the different ways it is mentioned. What do you think is Ortiz's point of view about this?

4. Look for the different senses in which the term "vision" is used in the story—alcoholic, spiritual, social, political. From this story, what do you think is the author's vision for Native American people?

5. In another one of his stories, entitled "What Indians Do," Ortiz talks about the storytelling tradition. The storyteller does more than relate events; he or she participates with the listeners in the story, and they all become part of it: "The story includes them in. You see, it's more like an event, the story telling. The story is not just a story then—it's occurring, coming into being." How does "The Panther Waits" illustrate Ortiz's point? After reading the story, how do you interpret the title?

One Last Time

Gary Soto _____

*In this story Soto looks back on working in the fields
outside Fresno, California, as a youth, picking grapes
and cutting cotton. This experience planted in him
the seeds of determination to escape that way of life.
This story appears in the autobiographical collection*
Living Up the Street *(1985).*

Yesterday I saw the movie *Gandhi* and recognized a few of the
people—not in the theater but in the film. I saw my relatives, dusty
and thin as sparrows, returning from the fields with hoes balanced
on their shoulders. The workers were squinting, eyes small and
veined, and were using their hands to say what there was to say to
those in the audience with popcorn and Cokes. I didn't have anything, though. I sat thinking of my family and their years in the
fields, beginning with Grandmother who came to the United States
after the Mexican revolution to settle in Fresno where she met her
husband and bore children, many of them. She worked in the fields
around Fresno, picking grapes, oranges, plums, peaches, and cotton,
dragging a large white sack like a sled. She worked in the packing
houses, Bonner and Sun-Maid Raisin, where she stood at a conveyor
belt passing her hand over streams of raisins to pluck out leaves and

pebbles. For over twenty years she worked at a machine that boxed raisins until she retired at sixty-five.

Grandfather worked in the fields, as did his children. Mother also found herself out there when she separated from Father for three weeks. I remember her coming home, dusty and so tired that she had to rest on the porch before she trudged inside to wash and start dinner. I didn't understand the complaints about her ankles or the small of her back, even though I had been in the grape fields watching her work. With my brother and sister I ran in and out of the rows; we enjoyed ourselves and pretended not to hear Mother scolding us to sit down and behave ourselves. A few years later, however, I caught on when I went to pick grapes rather than play in the rows.

Mother and I got up before dawn and ate quick bowls of cereal. She drove in silence while I rambled on how everything was now solved, how I was going to make enough money to end our misery and even buy her a beautiful copper tea pot, the one I had shown her in Long's Drugs. When we arrived I was frisky and ready to go, self-consciously aware of my grape knife dangling at my wrist. I almost ran to the row the foreman had pointed out, but I returned to help Mother with the grape pans and jug of water. She told me to settle down and reminded me not to lose my knife. I walked at her side and listened to her explain how to cut grapes; bent down, hands on knees, I watched her demonstrate by cutting a few bunches into my pan. She stood over me as I tried it myself, tugging at a bunch of grapes that pulled loose like beads from a necklace. "Cut the stem all the way," she told me as last advice before she walked away, her shoes sinking in the loose dirt, to begin work on her own row.

I cut another bunch, then another, fighting the snap and whip of vines. After ten minutes of groping for grapes, my first pan brimmed with bunches. I poured them on the paper tray, which was bordered by a wooden frame that kept the grapes from rolling off, and they spilled like jewels from a pirate's chest. The tray was only half filled, so I hurried to jump under the vines and begin groping, cutting, and tugging at the grapes again. I emptied the pan, raked the grapes with my hands to make them look like they filled the tray, and jumped back under the vine on my knees. I tried to cut faster because Mother, in the next row, was slowly moving ahead. I peeked into her row and saw five trays gleaming in the early morning. I cut, pulled hard, and stopped to gather the grapes that missed the pan; already bored, I spat on a few to wash them before tossing them like popcorn into my mouth.

5   So it went. Two pans equaled one tray—or six cents. By lunchtime I had a trail of thirty-seven trays behind me while mother had sixty or more. We met about halfway from our last trays, and I sat

down with a grunt, knees wet from kneeling on dropped grapes. I washed my hands with the water from the jug, drying them on the inside of my shirt sleeve before I opened the paper bag for the first sandwich, which I gave to Mother. I dipped my hand in again to unwrap a sandwich without looking at it. I took a first bite and chewed it slowly for the tang of mustard. Eating in silence I looked straight ahead at the vines, and only when we were finished with cookies did we talk.

"Are you tired?" she asked.

"No, but I got a sliver from the frame," I told her. I showed her the web of skin between my thumb and index finger. She wrinkled her forehead but said it was nothing.

"How many trays did you do?"

I looked straight ahead, not answering at first. I recounted in my mind the whole morning of bend, cut, pour again and again, before answering a feeble "thirty-seven." No elaboration, no detail. Without looking at me she told me how she had done field work in Texas and Michigan as a child. But I had a difficult time listening to her stories. I played with my grape knife, stabbing it into the ground, but stopped when Mother reminded me that I had better not lose it. I left the knife sticking up like a small, leafless plant. She then talked about school, the junior high I would be going to that fall, and then about Rick and Debra, how sorry they would be that they hadn't come out to pick grapes because they'd have no new clothes for the school year. She stopped talking when she peeked at her watch, a bandless one she kept in her pocket. She got up with an *"Ay, Dios,"* and told me that we'd work until three, leaving me cutting figures in the sand with my knife and dreading the return to work.

Finally I rose and walked slowly back to where I had left off, again kneeling under the vine and fixing the pan under bunches of grapes. By that time, 11:30, the sun was over my shoulder and made me squint and think of the pool at the Y.M.C.A. where I was a summer member. I saw myself diving face first into the water and loving it. I saw myself gleaming like something new, at the edge of the pool. I had to daydream and keep my mind busy because boredom was a terror almost as awful as the work itself. My mind went dumb with stupid things, and I had to keep it moving with dreams of baseball and would-be girlfriends. I even sang, however softly, to keep my mind moving, my hands moving.

I worked less hurriedly and with less vision. I no longer saw that copper pot sitting squat on our stove or Mother waiting for it to whistle. The wardrobe that I imagined, crisp and bright in the closet, numbered only one pair of jeans and two shirts because, in half a day, six cents times thirty-seven trays was two dollars and

10

twenty-two cents. It became clear to me. If I worked eight hours, I might make four dollars. I'd take this, even gladly, and walk downtown to look into store windows on the mall and long for the bright madras shirts from Walter Smith or Coffee's, but settling for two imitation ones from Penney's.

That first day I laid down seventy-three trays while Mother had a hundred and twenty behind her. On the back of an old envelope, she wrote out our numbers and hours. We washed at the pump behind the farm house and walked slowly to our car for the drive back to town in the afternoon heat. That evening after dinner I sat in a lawn chair listening to music from a transistor radio while Rick and David King played catch. I joined them in a game of pickle, but there was little joy in trying to avoid their tags because I couldn't get the fields out of my mind: I saw myself dropping on my knees under a vine to tug at a branch that wouldn't come off. In bed, when I closed my eyes, I saw the fields, yellow with kicked up dust, and a crooked trail of trays rotting behind me.

The next day I woke tired and started picking tired. The grapes rained into the pan, slowly filling like a belly, until I had my first tray and started my second. So it went all day, and the next, and all through the following week, so that by the end of thirteen days the foreman counted out, in tens mostly, my pay of fifty-three dollars. Mother earned one hundred and forty-eight dollars. She wrote this on her envelope, with a message I didn't bother to ask her about.

The next day I walked with my friend Scott to the downtown mall where we drooled over the clothes behind fancy windows, bought popcorn, and sat at a tier of outdoor fountains to talk about girls. Finally we went into Penney's for more popcorn, which we ate walking around, before we returned home without buying anything. It wasn't until a few days before school that I let my fifty-three dollars slip quietly from my hands, buying a pair of pants, two shirts, and a maroon T-shirt, the kind that was in style. At home I tried them on while Rick looked on enviously; later, the day before school started, I tried them on again wondering not so much if they were worth it as who would see me first in those clothes.

15   Along with my brother and sister I picked grapes until I was fifteen, before giving up and saying that I'd rather wear old clothes than stoop like a Mexican. Mother thought I was being stuck-up, even stupid, because there would be no clothes for me in the fall. I told her I didn't care, but when Rick and Debra rose at five in the morning, I lay awake in bed feeling that perhaps I had made a mistake but unwilling to change my mind. That fall Mother bought me two pairs of socks, a packet of colored T-shirts, and underwear. The T-shirts would help, I thought, but who would see that I had new underwear and socks? I wore a new T-shirt on the first day of school,

then an old shirt on Tuesday, then another T-shirt on Wednesday, and on Thursday an old Nehru shirt that was embarrassingly out of style. On Friday I changed into the corduroy pants my brother had handed down to me and slipped into my last new T-shirt. I worked like a magician, blinding my classmates, who were all clothes conscious and small-time social climbers, by arranging my wardrobe to make it seem larger than it really was. But by spring I had to do something—my blue jeans were almost silver and my shoes had lost their form, puddling like black ice around my feet. That spring of my sixteenth year, Rick and I decided to take a labor bus to chop cotton. In his old Volkswagen, which was more noise than power, we drove on a Saturday morning to West Fresno—or Chinatown as some call it—parked, walked slowly toward a bus, and stood gawking at the winos, toothy blacks, Okies, *Tejanos* with gold teeth, whores, Mexican families, and labor contractors shouting "Cotton" or "Beets," the work of spring.

We boarded the "Cotton" bus without looking at the contractor who stood almost blocking the entrance because he didn't want winos. We boarded scared and then were more scared because two blacks in the rear were drunk and arguing loudly about what was better, a two-barrel or four-barrel Ford carburetor. We sat far from them, looking straight ahead, and only glanced briefly at the others who boarded, almost all of them broken and poorly dressed in loudly mismatched clothes. Finally when the contractor banged his palm against the side of the bus, the young man at the wheel, smiling and talking in Spanish, started the engine, idled it for a moment while he adjusted the mirrors, and started off in slow chugs. Except for the windshield there was no glass in the windows, so as soon as we were on the rural roads outside Fresno, the dust and sand began to be sucked into the bus, whipping about like irate wasps as the gravel ticked about us. We closed our eyes, clotted up our mouths that wanted to open with embarrassed laughter because we couldn't believe we were on that bus with those people and the dust attacking us for no reason.

When we arrived at a field we followed the others to a pickup where we each took a hoe and marched to stand before a row. Rick and I, self-conscious and unsure, looked around at the others who leaned on their hoes or squatted in front of the rows, almost all talking in Spanish, joking, lighting cigarettes—all waiting for the foreman's whistle to begin work. Mother had explained how to chop cotton by showing us with a broom in the backyard.

"Like this," she said, her broom swishing down weeds. "Leave one plant and cut four—and cut them! Don't leave them standing or the foreman will get mad."

The foreman whistled and we started up the row stealing

glances at other workers to see if we were doing it right. But after awhile we worked like we knew what we were doing, neither of us hurrying or falling behind. But slowly the clot of men, women, and kids began to spread and loosen. Even Rick pulled away. I didn't hurry, though. I cut smoothly and cleanly as I walked at a slow pace, in a sort of funeral march. My eyes measured each space of cotton plants before I cut. If I missed the plants, I swished again. I worked intently, seldom looking up, so when I did I was amazed to see the sun, like a broken orange coin, in the east. It looked blurry, unbelievable, like something not of this world. I looked around in amazement, scanning the eastern horizon that was a taut line jutted with an occasional mountain. The horizon was beautiful, like a snapshot of the moon, in the early light of morning, in the quiet of no cars and few people.

20   The foreman trudged in boots in my direction, stepping awkwardly over the plants, to inspect the work. No one around me looked up. We all worked steadily while we waited for him to leave. When he did leave, with a feeble complaint addressed to no one in particular, we looked up smiling under straw hats and bandanas.

By 11:00, our lunch time, my ankles were hurting from walking on clods the size of hardballs. My arms ached and my face was dusted by a wind that was perpetual, always busy whipping about. But the work was not bad, I thought. It was better, so much better, than picking grapes, especially with the hourly wage of a dollar twenty-five instead of piece work. Rick and I walked sorely toward the bus where we washed and drank water. Instead of eating in the bus or in the shade of the bus, we kept to ourselves by walking down to the irrigation canal that ran the length of the field, to open our lunch of sandwiches and crackers. We laughed at the crackers, which seemed like a cruel joke from our Mother, because we were working under the sun and the last thing we wanted was a salty dessert. We ate them anyway and drank more water before we returned to the field, both of us limping in exaggeration. Working side by side, we talked and laughed at our predicament because our Mother had warned us year after year that if we didn't get on track in school we'd have to work in the fields and then we would see. We mimicked Mother's whining voice and smirked at her smoky view of the future in which we'd be trapped by marriage and screaming kids. We'd eat beans and then we'd see.

Rick pulled slowly away to the rhythm of his hoe falling faster and smoother. It was better that way, to work alone. I could hum made-up songs or songs from the radio and think to myself about school and friends. At the time I was doing badly in my classes, mainly because of a difficult stepfather, but also because I didn't care anymore. All through junior high and into my first year of high school there were those who said I would never do anything, be anyone. They said I'd work like a donkey and marry the first Mexican girl that came along. I was reminded so often, verbally and in the way I was treated at home, that I began to believe that chopping cotton might be a lifetime job for me. If not chopping cotton, then I might get lucky and find myself in a car wash or restaurant or junkyard. But it was clear; I'd work, and work hard.

I cleared my mind by humming and looking about. The sun was directly above with a few soft blades of clouds against a sky that seemed bluer and more beautiful than our sky in the city. Occasionally the breeze flurried and picked up dust so that I had to cover my eyes and screw up my face. The workers were hunched, brown as the clods under our feet, and spread across the field that ran without end—fields that were owned by corporations, not families.

I hoed trying to keep my mind busy with scenes from school and pretend girlfriends until finally my brain turned off and my thinking went fuzzy with boredom. I looked about, no longer mesmerized by the beauty of the landscape, no longer wondering if the winos in the fields could hold out for eight hours, no longer dreaming of the clothes I'd buy with my pay. My eyes followed my chopping as the plants, thin as their shadows, fell with each strike. I worked slowly with ankles and arms hurting, neck stiff, and eyes stinging from the dust and the sun that glanced off the field like a mirror.

By quitting time, 3:00, there was such an excruciating pain in   25
my ankles that I walked as if I were wearing snowshoes. Rick laughed at me and I laughed too, embarrassed that most of the men were walking normally and I was among the first timers who had to get used to this work. "And what about you, wino," I came back at Rick. His eyes were meshed red and his long hippie hair was flecked with dust and gnats and bits of leaves. We placed our hoes in the back of a pickup and stood in line for our pay, which was twelve fifty. I was amazed at the pay, which was the most I had ever earned in one day, and thought that I'd come back the next day, Sunday. This was too good.

Instead of joining the others in the labor bus, we jumped in the back of a pickup when the driver said we'd get to town sooner and were welcome to join him. We scrambled into the truck bed to be joined by a heavy-set and laughing *Tejano* whose head was shaped like an egg, particularly so because the bandana he wore ended in a point on the top of his head. He laughed almost demonically as the pickup roared up the dirt path, a gray cape of dust rising behind us. On the highway, with the wind in our faces, we squinted at the fields as if we were looking for someone. The *Tejano* had quit laughing but was smiling broadly, occasionally chortling tunes he never finished. I was scared of him, though Rick, two years older and five inches taller, wasn't. If the *Tejano* looked at him, Rick stared back for a second or two before he looked away to the fields.

I felt like a soldier coming home from war when we rattled into Chinatown. People leaning against car hoods stared, their necks following us, owl-like; prostitutes chewed gum more ferociously and showed us their teeth; Chinese grocers stopped brooming their storefronts to raise their cadaverous faces at us. We stopped in front of the Chi Chi Club where Mexican music blared from the juke box and cue balls cracked like dull ice. The *Tejano*, who was dirty as we were, stepped awkwardly over the side rail, dusted himself off with his bandana, and sauntered into the club.

Rick and I jumped from the back, thanked the driver who said *de nada* and popped his clutch, so that the pickup jerked and coughed blue smoke. We returned smiling to our car, happy with the money we had made and pleased that we had, in a small way, proved ourselves to be tough; that we worked as well as other men and earned the same pay.

We returned the next day and the next week until the season was over and there was nothing to do. I told myself that I wouldn't pick grapes that summer, saying all through June and July that it was for Mexicans, not me. When August came around and I still had not found a summer job, I ate my words, sharpened my knife, and joined Mother, Rick, and Debra for one last time.

Response

1. On each of the jobs he describes, Soto learned something; his attitude toward the work and toward himself shifted. In each case, how did the experience change him?

2. Soto's relationship with his mother forms a backdrop for the story. What can we infer about her life and about what she wanted her son to learn? How does the story indicate this?

3. Soto had conflicting feelings about agricultural labor and the people who did it; when he went to work in the fields, his experience produced mixed feelings about himself. Find indications of his ambivalence in the story. Why did he say of picking grapes, "it was for Mexicans, not me"? How did working in the fields affect his sense of his own identity? Judging from this story, what attitude toward field work and laborers does the adult Soto have, as a writer looking back on that period in his life?

4. Chronologically, this story fits midway between "Looking for Work" (Section IV), when Soto was younger, and "Like Mexicans" (Section II), when he was about to get married. In all three stories, Soto is concerned with the interaction of social class and ethnicity; how does his understanding of this issue develop and change over time?

5. In Soto's, as in many people's experience, education separated him from his past. Do Soto's stories show him "keeping close to home," in the sense that bell hooks discussed in her essay by that title (Section II)?

6. How does the picture of agricultural labor in this story compare with that presented in the passage from Raymond Barrio's *The Plum Plum Pickers*? How do the two authors' intents differ? How do you respond as a reader to their different treatments of the topic?

All-Around Man

Piri Thomas

In this story from Savior, Savior, Hold My Hand
*(1972) Thomas looks back at the time immediately
after his release from prison in 1956. His story reveals
something of what ex-convicts face in trying to start
a new life.*

Gotta get me a job. Gotta get me a job. Like any job. I fell flat
asleep with that chant running thru my mind. Mingled with my
chant was that of my parole officer: "Did you get a job yet . . . did
you get a job yet? You gotta have a job. You're on parole . . . you're
on parole . . . you're on parole."

When I woke up the next morning and as I dressed quietly, the
chant was still ringing in my ears. I looked at the clock. It was smiling a 7:30 A.M. I made a strong cup of Cafe Bustelo. I sipped it, made
a face on account it was too hot and I had forgotten to brush my
teeth. While the coffee cooled, I brushed my teeth with care, digging
myself in the mirror.

I did all kinds of numbers, like gargling, letting the gargle go
down as far into my throat as I dared without throwing up. I stopped
being a daredevil when I began to gag. I looked at myself in the mirror and smiled as tears forced out of my eyes on account of my stupid gargle game.

Piri Thomas, "All-Around Man," in *Savior, Savior, Hold My Hand*. New York:
Doubleday and Co., 1972. Used with permission.

I walked out into the kitchen and swallowed my good-o Bustelo coffee and then gargled again, but this time without living dangerously.

I hit the candy store and bought the New York *Times* and *El   5 Diario*. Went back to my stoop and like many other mornings since I had gotten out of prison, I turned to the want ads and looked immediately under CONSTRUCTION. Like my eyes were looking for one of the ads to say: BRICK MASONS WANTED, but most of it read, *Construction Engineers Wanted* . . .

ELECTRICIANS	UNION
PLUMBERS	UNION
CARPENTERS	UNION

My eyes caught a *Brick Mason Wanted, Tall-Build Construction Co Union.*

"Aw shit," I said out loud. "Hey, here's something. *Construction Work Overseas.*" Fat chance, I thought. Like I gotta almost get permission to cross the street.

People were coming out of the building on their way to work. I scrunched my behind to the corner of the stoop.

"Ah, buenos dias, Piri."

I looked up. It was Mrs. Lopez, middle-aged, short, chubby, and,   10 like always, very cheerful. She taught Sunday School at Tia's church. As I watched her eyeing me, I braced myself for a short sermon on how come I wasn't visiting the church.

"Er, Piri," she started in her good-natured way. But I cut her off mucho fast in self-defense.

"Como esta, Señora Lopez? Going to work?"

"Si. You don't haf job yet, Piri?"

"Uh-hu," I shook my head.

"Lessen, where I work, they are looking for a . . . how you   15 say . . . all-around man."

"All-around, Mrs. Lopez?" I smiled.

"Si. You know. Delivery, giving out material to the sewing machine operadoras, cleaning, going out for lunches and coffee."

"I don't know, Mrs. Lopez. I'm trying to find work as a bricklayer."

"Bricklayer?" She didn't understand.

"Albañil," I said, helping her out in Spanish.   20

"Oh si, oye. That is good monee . . . Bueno. Bueno suerte. I have to go now. Give my love to your Tia. Oh," she smiled, "when you coming to visit church?"

"Pronto, Señora Lopez. Hasta luego." I smiled.

I watched her slowly making her way towards Lexington Avenue, and I mulled over her words, All-Around Man . . . All-Around Man. My mind was quick thinking about the mucho past mornings of getting up, buying the New York *Times*, going to construction sites, asking for a job as a brickmason or as a brickmason's helper or a brickmason's apprentice. Hell, even brickmason's water boy. I had even gotten close a few times to copping a job.

I remembered the closest.

25   A construction company was putting up low-income projects right in my Barrio. I had walked up to an Italian-looking heavyset guy.

"Say," I smiled. "You the foreman?"

"Yeah." He looked straight at me.

"I'm looking for a job."

"Doing what?"

30   "Bricklaying."

"Got any experience?"

I went for broke.

"Lemme show you." Before he had a chance to say anything, I picked up a trowel and laid six bricks without touching the line, cut the mortar off as pretty as a Madison Avenue barber, jointed with a conductor's stroke, and smiled at the foreman . . .

"Didn't even smear the bricks." I laid the level on the side and then let it lay on the top, the bubble was dead on level.

35   "Not bad, kid . . . Union?"

The tight look around my mouth told him.

"Not in. You trying?"

My head nodded up and down. You better believe it.

"Try for apprentice?"

40   "Yeah, Mac." I spread my hands out to him. "You must know how it is with the union."

"Yeah, I know, but there's ways of getting around that. I might be able to help, but you probably hafta start off like an apprentice. But you shouldn't have no trouble. You lay bricks like an old-timer. Where did'cha work before? There ain't much non-union bricklaying going on, not if the union can help it."

"Around. I worked different places."

"Where? Cause they'll wanna know, you know, like for reference."

"Uh, upstate, near Syracuse."

45   "Non-union?"

"Yeah," I smiled, "non-union."

"You work on different construction gangs?"

"Naw, just one." I was trying hard not to lie to this hombre, like I had a really chevere feeling he wanted to help me.

"How long?"

"Does it make a difference?" My eyes looked at the trowel and   50
at the bricks and mortar and they seemed to be getting further and further away.

"Hell, yes, son, the more time you've put in bricklaying, the better it is, specially when it was steady with one construction company. It shows you're steady and dependable when they keep you on, and like especially if they're non-union."

I wanted to laugh. Like this was a not-for-real scene. My mind thought up mucho fictitious construction companies, so that I could shoot out a lie.

I looked at the bricks. I stole a couple of seconds lighting up a smoke, took a deep breath, and let it out Gung Ho, with some kind of intermingled thoughts of, "AND THE TRUTH SHALL MAKE YOU FREE." I looked him dead in his Italian eyes and, trying not to feel ashamed of it or proud either, I told him soft—but clear like, "Look, I'm not gonna con you. I worked with bricks for about four years or so. Like steady. But it wasn't with no construction company. I learned brickmasonry at Comstock State Prison during a six years outta fifteen year bit. I gotta certificate of Brickmasonry with thousands of hours of practical and theory experience. In fact, I became a bricklayer instructor. I can do damn near any type of construction, brickwork and . . ."

The foreman's head nodded and like his mouth started to say something but I cut in . . .

"And I got about eight more years to do on parole. And like if I   55
could get in, even as an apprentice, my parole officer could vouch for me as well as other people that know me and . . ."

"What were you in for?"

I laid it out natural-like.

"Armed Robbery, Attempted Armed Robbery. Felonious Assault with intent to kill . . ."

"Jesus Christ, kid." His eyes were looking dead into mine. "The union is tough to get into. I won't go into the crap involved. It was gonna be hard to get you in, being straight, but having been in the can, that blows it, kid. There's guys trying to get in that could be priests and aren't making it and . . ."

"Damn, damn, damn." I could feel crushing disappointment   60
spreading over my face. I pulled a grin from out of my guts and gave the foreman a half-salute in a way of saying, thanks anyway, and started to walk away.

"Hey, kid," he called.

I looked back at him, casually checking out his heavily lined face. He stood stiffly, almost rigid as a board. He seemed strangely ill at ease, a bit out of place standing there in his cement-plastered coveralls.

"Why doncha try something else? There's udder things. You can make it. I'm sorry, I don't wanna fool ya, but you got as much chance as a snowball in hell. Someday things'll change." He rubbed his nose with a hand that had a hundred pounds of calluses on it.

"Thanks anyway, mister. I appreciate you're being straight with me."

65   "Hey, kid, like I got experience with jails. I don't mean I was in but my brother-in-law did time."

"OK, mister." I smiled. "I know ya understand."

I walked off the construction site and looked back at all the building going on. I barely heard the foreman yelling at me.

"Hey, kid, keep batting."

I waved back and walked off thinking, *I will, paisan*, but like I got a baddo feeling my bat got mucho holes in it.

70   I came back to now time and dug Mrs. Lopez making the right turn at the corner heading for the Lexington Avenue IRT. I jumped off the stoop, stuffed the New York *Times* into the garbage can, shoved *El Diario* into my back pocket and ran like hell after Mrs. Lopez, laughing and thinking, "Look out, mundo, here comes the all-around man."

I caught up with Mrs. Lopez.

"Señora, oye, señora." I puffed my way up to her.

"Que pasa, Piri?" She looked a little alarmed.

"Is it all right if I go with you for that all-around job?" I asked. "Think it's taken?"

75   "I don't theenk so, Piri. They don't stay too long on that job."

Holy Mother of the Lord, I thought. Must be some kind of work in some kind of salt mines.

We got to a raunchy-looking ten-story building and a tired, jerking elevator jerked us up floor by floor to number ten. The elevator man, as on every floor, missed his stop, like stopping two feet below or two feet above the floor.

"Cat really needs a level," I said, but the elevator man had a chevere sense of humor. I remembered his Puerto Rican accent as he stopped on every floor . . .

Theese is Ponce. . . .
  next floor

Theese is San Juan. . . .
  next floor
Theese is Mayagüez. . . .
  next floor
Theese is Fajardo. . . .
  next floor
Theese is Aguadilla. . . .
  next floor
Theese is Carolina. . . .
  next floor
Theese is Jayuya. . . .
  next floor
Theese is Caguas. . . .
  next floor
Theese is Santurce. . . .
  next floor
Theese is San Germán.

We got off at San Germán and I smiled at him and said, "Oye,
how come you didn't mention Bayamón. Like that's where my people are from?"

He smiled and said, "Don't worree, thas the next floor."   80

"Caramba, man, like that's el rufo . . ."

The elevator man grinned. "Si, don't complain, Bayamón is
close to heaven."

"Chevere." I tapped his shoulder with love.

Mrs. Lopez led me through the most chaotic scrambled-up
skirt-making factory I had ever dug. All the women, about fifty of
them, were roaring away at their sewing machines like their lives
depended on it and, como, like it did. Cause I found out they were
doing piece work and that's like if you don't produce, you get no
juice. I felt my face put on a disgusted look, like legalized slavery.
The pay for each skirt was so low the operators had to tear the heart
out of their sewing machine motors to come out an inch above defeat. Memories came back to me of mucho, but mucho times when
I saw Mommie coming home bent and weary after long hours of
hassling packed subways and roaring heartless sewing machines.

I noticed one thing though. The women, most of whom were   85
Puertorriquenos, damn near drowned out the deafening noises of the
motors with their yakking. Caramba, it was a joy (almost) to listen
to about fifty women trade gossip like it was going out of style. Talk
about put-ups and put-downs. Their tongues were mucho sharp, and
dirty linen was being pulled out of all kinds of closets. Yet it was
friendly talk and I had the feeling they yakked to take their minds
off aching backs and fingers that had been run through by mucho
sewing machine needles, not to mention the screaming yelling
boss-o, who I dug was making his way toward Mrs. Lopez and me.

He was digging his watch and como like his eyes fastened on pobre Mrs. Lopez with a . . . you are late again and ought to be shot at dawn.

Mrs. Lopez smiled at him and offered me as a sacrificial sign of peace.

"Mr. Greenstein, I breeng you an all-around man."

I had been feeling so damn angry and frustrated that I was determined not to lose my sense of humor, so I smiled an all-around smile at Mr. Greenstein, who was built like a tough, little ornery bull and had practically not a hair on his cabeza. In the meantime he looked me up and down and grunted, "You is speaking English?"

90   "Yes, sir, Mr. Greenstein. I am quite proficient in its usage."

My mind did a quick flash back into prison time, when all my English was mixed in with street talk and when the first big words I had learned had come from a college kid who was doing time for murder. He and his girl had killed her mother and put her in a bathtub with a cover of plaster of paris. I mouthed the words over in my brain, *manifestation and conglomeration*, and how I had walked around the prison yard socking my newfound knowledge by telling my prison amigos, "Hey, diggit, I am a conglomeration of a manifestation of myself."

"And you can maybe talk Spanish also?"

"Pure Spanish no, but I can handle Puerto Rican."

God, but my face was straight. I wanted to burst out laughing.

95   "You are not being afraid of hard vork?"

"No, I'm not, Mr. Greenstein. If the pay is fair."

Mr. Greenstein must have had eyes in the back of his head cause he turned around like greased lightning and his roaring voice grabbed two women by the throat who had stopped sewing and were involved in something important, like a little friendly yakking session.

"Vot am I goink to do?" he yelled to them. "Maybe I should pay you joust to speak." The two women dove for their machines and roared away in a dead heat and Mr. Greenstein's voice unwrapped itself from around their throats.

"The pay is forty dollars a week. You vork forty hours. Time and a half for doing overtime. You ever vork as all-around man?"

100   Probably have, I thought, just ain't recognized it.

"Sur have. What do I have to do?"

"You vanting job?"

"Yes, sir, Mr. Greenstein."

Mr. Greenstein was about to say something to me when suddenly he stopped, his eye dead fixed on Mrs. Lopez. All this time she had been standing beside us like one of the gang, smiling and nodding in agreement at everything said. Mr. Greenstein's eyes looked like they couldn't believe that they were looking at fat little Mrs. Lopez, who was feeling that she was in like Flynn with Mr. Greenstein for having brought him an all-around man.

"Mein Gott, since ven you becomink mine partner? You vorking here yet or maybe you got plans for retirement?" 105

Mrs. Lopez's bubble of democratic comradeship blew up and she moved away so fast that by the time Mr. Greenstein gave me his warm attention again, she had socked six skirts through the sewing machine.

Mr. Greenstein nodded warmly and with mucho approval. Then in a very friendly manner, he told me, "She is von of our best vorkers. I am loving them all, but got to keep on top or no producing. Hokay, you start now."

I nodded a "Si, señor. What do I do?"

"Goot, this is nice place to vork in. You vork, nobody bodder you. You sweep place out at closing time. That's a half hour or maybe one hour overtime if you're slow."

My eyebrow did a pick up at the warning sound of "one hour 110 overtime if you're slow."

"In the morning," he continued, "you put the garbage out, store material, and you keep the goils busy with bundles. You learn sizes. You hang skirts. You make delivery. You get lunch for anybody who vants. You know anything about sewing machine motors?"

"Er, not too much," I answered, unsure whether or not he would hold my ignorance of machine motors against me.

"Don't vorry, I'll teach you."

God, I thought, I'm gonna be a machine mechanic, too.

"And you help my partner to stretch cloth for cutting. That's 115 him."

My eyes followed his pointed finger to a cutting table, where a thin man with a beard and a skullcap on his head was sadly stretching cloth by himself.

"He's my partner. He also is a rabbi and my brother-in-law."

God, I thought, *you sure got this cat sewed up.*

"Go and tell him you is helping him."

I spent the rest of the day running around and stretching cloth. 120 El Bosso, Mr. Greenstein, spared no one, not even the partner-rabbi and brother-in-law combination, the blessing of his roaring mouth. But it was always in his own language. The partner must have gotten bawled out a couple hundred times. Towards the end of the day he was completely insult-whipped.

I stood on the other side of the table smoothing my side of the cloth while he took care of his with a quiet, patient-like dignity,

when all of a sudden he caught a blast in his ears from Mr. Greenstein about having laid out a layer of green material instead of blue.

The poor combination in front of me took it like a champ.
When Mr. Greenstein cut out, I looked up from the cloth at the way-
out sound of a pent-up expelling sigh. It was the combination. He
murmured, sad-like, "Sveare tsuzien a Yid."

"What does that mean?" I asked muy friendly.

He nodded his head sadly and with a dying smile answered,
"It's hard to be a Jew."

125   I let out a deep sigh and smiling compassionately said, "Sveare
tsuzien a Puerto Rican too."

The combination laughed.

There was some kind of strong instantaneous friendship established between us for a moment. Perhaps it was because we both
knew the feeling of insults. I checked myself out at getting to like
him. Man, he was making mucho dinero while getting insulted,
while the rest of us workers were getting mucho exploited. I stopped
laughing and he turned off likewise. I stared at his intense, thinly
bearded face. He adjusted his skullcap and grunted.

"Vell, let's get to vorking. Much to do . . . much to do."

"Yeah!! Ain't there?" I thought and went on spreading red cloth
on top of different colored cloths.

130   Caramba! Mrs. Lopez wasn't kidding when she said all-around
man. I think it would have been more chevere for her to have said,
all-around superman.

My parole officer was pleased I was taking care of business with
my newfound slavery. He even nodded approval when I told him I
was thinking of getting a part-time job three nights a week at Macy's, cause like after taxes, social security, living benefit, death ben-
efits, subway, lunch, my share to Tia, the forty-eight bucks (with
overtime) got so chewed up, I kept feeling I owed somebody money.
So the months rolled by and at the night job I was spotless, dressed
up like a general, pushing an elevator up and down and shouting out
things like:

First Floor	*Women's Underthings*
Second Floor	*Men's Underthings*
Third Floor	*Anything at all*

As a matter of fact, I felt a little superior every time I stepped
in the elevator at Mr. Greenstein's factory.

"Hey, Panchito."

"Si, Hermano." The Puerto Rican elevator man would smile.

135   "My elevator at Macy's is like a Cadillac compared to your
Ford-thing-go," I would say.

"Perhaps," he would grin, "but mine goes all over Puerto Rico, where does yours go?"

"Mine goes to women's underthings . . . men's underthings . . . and anything at all."

We played the game mucho times, but like it wasn't a funny thing inside. At least not for me. The factory and the elevator job both kept me dead tired, and I could hardly save up any bread.

Wow, Mr. Combination Partner-Rabbi and Brother-in-Law, sveare tsuzien . . . dammit to hell, why can't I lay bricks?

Anybody can hang up a skirt or push an elevator, but not every-   140
body can lay down a leveled brick.

How about that for an all-around man?

Response

1. Thomas had several strikes against him when it came to getting a union job. What stood in his way?

2. Consider how Thomas acted with the foreman on the bricklaying job, and with Mr. Greenstein; how does his behavior reflect the attitudes he developed in prison, as portrayed in *Seven Long Times* (Section I)? Judging from this story, do you think he kept writing for the same reasons he expressed while he was in prison?

3. At the cutting table, Thomas and the "combination" man found a common bond for a moment. Why did they both abruptly stop laughing at the same time?

4. At the end, Thomas reveals the anger and frustration under the humor. What is the irony in the final question, echoing the title of the story?

5. Do you find Thomas's language use and writing style effective for purposes of this story? If you don't already know, guess at the meaning of the slang term *chevere* from the way the word is used in the story. Do you find you need to speak Spanish to understand the story?

Black Boy

Richard Wright _____

This is a chapter from Wright's autobiographical account of life under Jim Crow, the traditional and legal system of racial discrimination that prevailed in the American South through the first half of this century. This portion of Wright's autobiography, covering his years in the South, was published as Black Boy *in 1945. At the time of this story Wright was eighteen years old and had recently moved to Memphis, Tennessee, from his home in Mississippi. He was working as an errand-boy for a business, earning ten dollars a week and saving his money to go north.*

One morning I arrived early at work and went into the bank lobby where the Negro porter was mopping. I stood at a counter and picked up the Memphis *Commercial Appeal* and began my free reading of the press. I came finally to the editorial page and saw an article dealing with one H. L. Mencken. I knew by hearsay that he was the editor of the *American Mercury,* but aside from that I knew nothing about him. The article was a furious denunciation of

Richard Wright, from *Black Boy.* New York: Harper and Row, 1945. Copyright © 1937, 1942, 1944, 1945 by Richard Wright. Reprinted by permission of Harper Collins Publishers.

Mencken, concluding with one, hot, short sentence: Mencken is a fool.

I wondered what on earth this Mencken had done to call down upon him the scorn of the South. The only people I had ever heard denounced in the South were Negroes, and this man was not a Negro. Then what ideas did Mencken hold that made a newspaper like the *Commercial Appeal* castigate him publicly? Undoubtedly he must be advocating ideas that the South did not like. Were there, then, people other than Negroes who criticized the South? I knew that during the Civil War the South had hated northern whites, but I had not encountered such hate during my life. Knowing no more of Mencken than I did at that moment, I felt a vague sympathy for him. Had not the South, which had assigned me the role of a non-man, cast at him its hardest words?

Now, how could I find out about this Mencken? There was a huge library near the riverfront, but I knew that Negroes were not allowed to patronize its shelves any more than they were the parks and playgrounds of the city. I had gone into the library several times to get books for the white men on the job. Which of them would now help me to get books? And how could I read them without causing concern to the white men with whom I worked? I had so far been successful in hiding my thoughts and feelings from them, but I knew that I would create hostility if I went about this business of reading in a clumsy way.

I weighed the personalities of the men on the job. There was Don, a Jew; but I distrusted him. His position was not much better than mine and I knew that he was uneasy and insecure; he had always treated me in an offhand, bantering way that barely concealed his contempt. I was afraid to ask him to help me to get books; his frantic desire to demonstrate a racial solidarity with the whites against Negroes might make him betray me.

Then how about the boss? No, he was a Baptist and I had the 5 suspicion that he would not be quite able to comprehend why a black boy would want to read Mencken. There were other white men on the job whose attitudes showed clearly that they were Kluxers or sympathizers, and they were out of the question.

There remained only one man whose attitude did not fit into an anti-Negro category, for I had heard the white men refer to him as a "Pope lover." He was an Irish Catholic and was hated by the white Southerners. I knew that he read books, because I had got him volumes from the library several times. Since he, too, was an object of hatred, I felt that he might refuse me but would hardly betray me. I hesitated, weighing and balancing the imponderable realities.

One morning I paused before the Catholic fellow's desk.

"I want to ask you a favor," I whispered to him.

"What is it?"

10   "I want to read. I can't get books from the library. I wonder if you'd let me use your card?"

He looked at me suspiciously.

"My card is full most of the time," he said.

"I see," I said and waited, posing my question silently.

"You're not trying to get me into trouble, are you, boy?" he asked, staring at me.

15   "Oh, no, sir."

"What book do you want?"

"A book by H. L. Mencken."

"Which one?"

"I don't know. Has he written more than one?"

20   "He has written several."

"I didn't know that."

"What makes you want to read Mencken?"

"Oh, I just saw his name in the newspaper," I said.

"It's good of you to want to read," he said. "But you ought to read the right things."

25   I said nothing. Would he want to supervise my reading?

"Let me think," he said. "I'll figure out something."

I turned from him and he called me back. He stared at me quizzically.

"Richard, don't mention this to the other white men," he said.

"I understand," I said. "I won't say a word."

30   A few days later he called me to him.

"I've got a card in my wife's name," he said. "Here's mine."

"Thank you, sir."

"Do you think you can manage it?"

"I'll manage fine," I said.

35   "If they suspect you, you'll get in trouble," he said.

"I'll write the same kind of notes to the library that you wrote when you sent me for books," I told him. "I'll sign your name."

He laughed.

"Go ahead. Let me see what you get," he said.

That afternoon I addressed myself to forging a note. Now, what were the names of books written by H. L. Mencken? I did not know any of them. I finally wrote what I thought would be a foolproof note: *Dear Madam: Will you please let this nigger boy*—I used the word "nigger" to make the librarian feel that I could not possibly be the author of the note—*have some books by H. L. Mencken?* I forged the white man's name.

40   I entered the library as I had always done when on errands for

whites, but I felt that I would somehow slip up and betray myself. I doffed my hat, stood a respectful distance from the desk, looked as unbookish as possible, and waited for the white patrons to be taken care of. When the desk was clear of people, I still waited. The white librarian looked at me.

"What do you want, boy?"

As though I did not possess the power of speech, I stepped forward and simply handed her the forged note, not parting my lips.

"What books by Mencken does he want?" she asked.

"I don't know, ma'am," I said, avoiding her eyes.

"Who gave you this card?"   45

"Mr. Falk," I said.

"Where is he?"

"He's at work, at the M_____ Optical Company," I said. "I've been in here for him before."

"I remember," the woman said. "But he never wrote notes like this."

Oh, God, she's suspicious. Perhaps she would not let me have   50
the books? If she had turned her back at that moment, I would have ducked out the door and never gone back. Then I thought of a bold idea.

"You can call him up, ma'am," I said, my heart pounding.

"You're not using these books, are you?" she asked pointedly.

"Oh, no, ma'am. I can't read."

"I don't know what he wants by Mencken," she said under her breath.

I knew now that I had won; she was thinking of other things   55
and the race question had gone out of her mind. She went to the shelves. Once or twice she looked over her shoulder at me, as though she was still doubtful. Finally she came forward with two books in her hand.

"I'm sending him two books," she said. "But tell Mr. Falk to come in next time, or send me the names of the books he wants. I don't know what he wants to read."

I said nothing. She stamped the card and handed me the books. Not daring to glance at them, I went out of the library, fearing that the woman would call me back for further questioning. A block away from the library I opened one of the books and read a title: *A Book of Prefaces*. I was nearing my nineteenth birthday and I did not know how to pronounce the word "preface." I thumbed the pages and saw strange words and strange names. I shook my head, disappointed. I looked at the other book; it was called *Prejudices*. I knew what that word meant; I had heard it all my life. And right off I was on guard against Mencken's books. Why would a man want to call a book

Prejudices? The word was so stained with all my memories of racial hate that I could not conceive of anybody using it for a title. Perhaps I had made a mistake about Mencken? A man who had prejudices must be wrong.

When I showed the books to Mr. Falk, he looked at me and frowned.

"That librarian might telephone you," I warned him.

60 "That's all right," he said. "But when you're through reading those books, I want you to tell me what you get out of them."

That night in my rented room, while letting the hot water run over my can of pork and beans in the sink, I opened *A Book of Prefaces* and began to read. I was jarred and shocked by the style, the clear, clean, sweeping sentences. Why did he write like that? And how did one write like that? I pictured the man as a raging demon, slashing with his pen, consumed with hate, denouncing everything American, extolling everything European or German, laughing at the weaknesses of people, mocking God, authority. What was this? I stood up, trying to realize what reality lay behind the meaning of the words . . . Yes, this man was fighting, fighting with words. He was using words as a weapon, using them as one would use a club. Could words be weapons? Well, yes, for here they were. Then, maybe, perhaps, I could use them as a weapon? No. It frightened me. I read on and what amazed me was not what he said, but how on earth anybody had the courage to say it.

Occasionally I glanced up to reassure myself that I was alone in the room. Who were these men about whom Mencken was talking so passionately? Who was Anatole France? Joseph Conrad? Sinclair Lewis, Sherwood Anderson, Dostoevski, George Moore, Gustave Flaubert, Maupassant, Tolstoy, Frank Harris, Mark Twain, Thomas Hardy, Arnold Bennett, Stephen Crane, Zola, Norris, Gorky, Bergson, Ibsen, Balzac, Bernard Shaw, Dumas, Poe, Thomas Mann, O. Henry, Dreiser, H. G. Wells, Gogol, T. S. Eliot, Gide, Baudelaire, Edgar Lee Masters, Stendhal, Turgenev, Huneker, Nietzsche, and scores of others? Were these men real? Did they exist or had they existed? And how did one pronounce their names?

I ran across many words whose meanings I did not know, and I either looked them up in a dictionary or, before I had a chance to do that, encountered the word in a context that made its meaning clear. But what strange world was this? I concluded the book with the conviction that I had somehow overlooked something terribly important in life. I had once tried to write, had once reveled in feeling, had let my crude imagination roam, but the impulse to dream had been slowly beaten out of me by experience. Now it surged up again and I hungered for books, new ways of looking and seeing. It

was not a matter of believing or disbelieving what I read, but of
feeling something new, of being affected by something that made
the look of the world different.

As dawn broke I ate my pork and beans, feeling dopey, sleepy.
I went to work, but the mood of the book would not die; it lingered,
coloring everything I saw, heard, did. I now felt that I knew what
the white men were feeling. Merely because I had read a book that
had spoken of how they lived and thought, I identified myself with
that book. I felt vaguely guilty. Would I, filled with bookish notions,
act in a manner that would make the whites dislike me?

I forged more notes and my trips to the library became fre-   65
quent. Reading grew into a passion. My first serious novel was Sinclair Lewis's *Main Street*. It made me see my boss, Mr. Gerald, and
identify him as an American type. I would smile when I saw him
lugging his golf bags into the office. I had always felt a vast distance
separating me from the boss, and now I felt closer to him, though
still distant. I felt now that I knew him, that I could feel the very
limits of his narrow life. And this had happened because I had read
a novel about a mythical man called George F. Babbitt.

The plots and stories in the novels did not interest me so much
as the point of view revealed. I gave myself over to each novel without reserve, without trying to criticize it; it was enough for me to
see and feel something different. And for me, everything was something different. Reading was like a drug, a dope. The novels created
moods in which I lived for days. But I could not conquer my sense
of guilt, my feeling that the white men around me knew that I was
changing, that I had begun to regard them differently.

Whenever I brought a book to the job, I wrapped it in newspaper—a habit that was to persist for years in other cities and under
other circumstances. But some of the white men pried into my packages when I was absent and they questioned me.

"Boy, what are you reading those books for?"

"Oh, I don't know, sir."

"That's deep stuff you're reading, boy."   70

"I'm just killing time, sir."

"You'll addle your brains if you don't watch out."

I read Dreiser's *Jennie Gerhardt* and *Sister Carrie* and they re-
vived in me a vivid sense of my mother's suffering; I was overwhelmed. I grew silent, wondering about the life around me. It would
have been impossible for me to have told anyone what I derived
from these novels, for it was nothing less than a sense of life itself.
All my life had shaped me for the realism, the naturalism of the
modern novel, and I could not read enough of them.

Steeped in new moods and ideas, I bought a ream of paper and tried to write; but nothing would come, or what did come was flat beyond telling. I discovered that more than desire and feeling were necessary to write and I dropped the idea. Yet I still wondered how it was possible to know people sufficiently to write about them? Could I ever learn about life and people? To me, with my vast ignorance, my Jim Crow station in life, it seemed a task impossible of achievement. I now knew what being a Negro meant. I could endure the hunger. I had learned to live with hate. But to feel that there were feelings denied me, that the very breath of life itself was beyond my reach, that more than anything else hurt, wounded me. I had a new hunger.

75   In buoying me up, reading also cast me down, made me see what was possible, what I had missed. My tension returned, new, terrible, bitter, surging, almost too great to be contained. I no longer *felt* that the world about me was hostile, killing; I *knew* it. A million times I asked myself what I could do to save myself, and there were no answers. I seemed forever condemned, ringed by walls.

I did not discuss my reading with Mr. Falk, who had lent me his library card; it would have meant talking about myself and that would have been too painful. I smiled each day, fighting desperately to maintain my old behavior, to keep my disposition seemingly sunny. But some of the white men discerned that I had begun to brood.

"Wake up there, boy!" Mr. Olin said one day.

"Sir!" I answered for the lack of a better word.

"You act like you've stolen something," he said.

80   I laughed in the way I knew he expected me to laugh, but I resolved to be more conscious of myself, to watch my every act, to guard and hide the new knowledge that was dawning within me.

If I went north, would it be possible for me to build a new life then? But how could a man build a life upon vague, unformed yearnings? I wanted to write and I did not even know the English language. I bought English grammars and found them dull. I felt that I was getting a better sense of the language from novels than from grammars. I read hard, discarding a writer as soon as I felt that I had grasped his point of view. At night the printed page stood before my eyes in sleep.

Mrs. Moss, my landlady, asked me one Sunday morning:

"Son, what is this you keep on reading?"

"Oh, nothing. Just novels."

85   "What you get out of 'em?"

"I'm just killing time," I said.

"I hope you know your own mind," she said in a tone which implied that she doubted if I had a mind.

I knew of no Negroes who read the books I liked and I wondered if any Negroes ever thought of them. I knew that there were Negro doctors, lawyers, newspapermen, but I never saw any of them. When I read a Negro newspaper I never caught the faintest echo of my preoccupation in its pages. I felt trapped and occasionally, for a few days, I would stop reading. But a vague hunger would come over me for books, books that opened up new avenues of feeling and seeing, and again I would forge another note to the white librarian. Again I would read and wonder as only the naïve and unlettered can read and wonder, feeling that I carried a secret, criminal burden about with me each day.

That winter my mother and brother came and we set up housekeeping, buying furniture on the installment plan, being cheated and yet knowing no way to avoid it. I began to eat warm food and to my surprise found that regular meals enabled me to read faster. I may have lived through many illnesses and survived them, never suspecting that I was ill. My brother obtained a job and we began to save toward the trip north, plotting our time, setting tentative dates for departure. I told none of the white men on the job that I was planning to go north; I knew that the moment they felt I was thinking of the North they would change toward me. It would have made them feel that I did not like the life I was living, and because my life was completely conditioned by what they said or did, it would have been tantamount to challenging them.

I could calculate my chances for life in the South as a Negro   90 fairly clearly now.

I could fight the southern whites by organizing with other Negroes, as my grandfather had done. But I knew that I could never win that way; there were many whites and there were but few blacks. They were strong and we were weak. Outright black rebellion could never win. If I fought openly I would die and I did not want to die. News of lynchings were frequent.

I could submit and live the life of a genial slave, but that was impossible. All of my life had shaped me to live by my own feelings and thoughts. I could make up to Bess and marry her and inherit the house. But that, too, would be the life of a slave; if I did that, I would crush to death something within me, and I would hate myself as much as I knew the whites already hated those who had submitted. Neither could I ever willingly present myself to be kicked, as Shorty had done. I would rather have died than do that.

I could drain off my restlessness by fighting with Shorty and Harrison. I had seen many Negroes solve the problem of being black by transferring their hatred of themselves to others with a black skin and fighting them. I would have to be cold to do that, and I was not cold and I could never be.

I could, of course, forget what I had read, thrust the whites out of my mind, forget them; and find release from anxiety and longing in sex and alcohol. But the memory of how my father had conducted himself made that course repugnant. If I did not want others to violate my life, how could I voluntarily violate it myself?

95   I had no hope whatever of being a professional man. Not only had I been so conditioned that I did not desire it, but the fulfillment of such an ambition was beyond my capabilities. Well-to-do Negroes lived in a world that was almost as alien to me as the world inhabited by whites.

What, then, was there? I held my life in my mind, in my consciousness each day, feeling at times that I would stumble and drop it, spill it forever. My reading had created a vast sense of distance between me and the world in which I lived and tried to make a living, and that sense of distance was increasing each day. My days and nights were one long, quiet, continuously contained dream of terror, tension, and anxiety. I wondered how long I could bear it.

Response

1. Wright's appetite for reading was stimulated by the discovery of H. L. Mencken (1880–1956), an author, editor, and critic. What was the special appeal of Mencken for Wright?

2. Wright had an eighth-grade education, all that was available to him in a segregated school system. Why were African Americans denied access to the library? Why did the librarian pointedly question Wright's motives, and why did Wright tell her "I can't read"?

3. Reading reawakened in Wright "the impulse to dream" and gave him "a sense of life itself" (paragraph 73). How did he respond to novels? What new feelings did his reading inspire? "In buoying me up," he says in paragraph 75, "reading also cast me down." What was the "new hunger" he felt? What was the cost of his new awareness?

4. Why did Wright feel guilty about his reading, as if he "carried a secret, criminal burden" (paragraph 88)? How do you interpret his feelings?

5. In considering his "chances for life in the South as a Negro" Wright offers a brief social commentary on responses to oppression (paragraphs 90–95). What avenues of behavior did he recognize as options, and how did he evaluate each? If he had lived twenty years later, how might his list have been different?

American Hunger

Richard Wright

This passage begins the second part of Wright's autobiography, a continuation of the story begun in Black Boy *(1945). Originally written as a single work, the autobiography was divided into separate parts for publication. This portion was published in scattered segments during the 1940s and did not appear as a book until it was published in 1977 as* American Hunger—*which had been Wright's original title for the whole work. It begins with Wright's arrival in Chicago, which he had anticipated with optimism at the end of* Black Boy.

My first glimpse of the flat black stretches of Chicago depressed and dismayed me, mocked all my fantasies. Chicago seemed an unreal city whose mythical houses were built of slabs of black coal wreathed in palls of gray smoke, houses whose foundations were sinking slowly into the dank prairie. Flashes of steam showed intermittently on the wise horizon, gleaming translucently in the winter sun. The din of the city entered my consciousness, entered to remain for years to come. The year was 1927.

What would happen to me here? Would I survive? My expectations were modest. I wanted only a job. Hunger had long been my daily companion. Diversion and recreation, with the exception of reading, were unknown. In all my life—though surrounded by many people—I had not had a single satisfying, sustained relationship with another human being and, not having had any, I did not miss it. I made no demands whatever upon others.

The train rolled into the depot. Aunt Maggie and I got off and walked slowly through the crowds into the station. I looked about to see if there were signs saying: FOR WHITE—FOR COLORED. I saw none. Black people and white people moved about, each seemingly intent upon his private mission. There was no racial fear. Indeed, each person acted as though no one existed but himself. It was strange to pause before a crowded newsstand and buy a newspaper without having to wait until a white man was served. And yet, because everything was so new, I began to grow tense again, although it was a different sort of tension than I had known before. I knew that this machine-city was governed by strange laws and I wondered if I would ever learn them.

As we waited for a streetcar to take us to Aunt Cleo's home for temporary lodging, I looked northward at towering buildings of steel and stone. There were no curves here, no trees; only angles, lines, squares, bricks and copper wires. Occasionally the ground beneath my feet shook from some faraway pounding and I felt that this world, despite its massiveness, was somehow dangerously fragile. Streetcars screeched past over steel tracks. Cars honked their horns. Clipped speech sounded about me. As I stood in the icy wind, I wanted to talk to Aunt Maggie, to ask her questions, but her tight face made me hold my tongue. I was learning already from the frantic light in her eyes the strain that the city imposed upon its people. I was seized by doubt. Should I have come here? But going back was impossible. I had fled a known terror, and perhaps I could cope with this unknown terror that lay ahead.

5   The streetcar came. Aunt Maggie motioned for me to get on and pushed me toward a seat in which a white man sat looking blankly out the window. I sat down beside the man and looked straight ahead of me. After a moment I stole a glance at the white man out of the corners of my eyes; he was still staring out the window, his mind fastened upon some inward thought. I did not exist for him; I was as far from his mind as the stone buildings that swept past in the street. It would have been illegal for me to sit beside him in the part of the South that I had come from.

The car swept past soot-blackened buildings, stopping at each block, jerking again into motion. The conductor called street names in a tone that I could not understand. People got on and off the car, but they never glanced at one another. Each person seemed to regard the other as a part of the city landscape. The white man who sat beside me rose and I turned my knees aside to let him pass, and another white man sat beside me and buried his face in a newspaper. How could that possibly be? Was he conscious of my blackness?

We went to Aunt Cleo's address and found that she was living in a rented room. I had imagined that she lived in an apartment and I was disappointed. I rented a room from Aunt Cleo's landlady and decided to keep it until I got a job. I was baffled. Everything seemed makeshift, temporary. I caught an abiding sense of insecurity in the personalities of the people around me. I found Aunt Cleo aged beyond her years. Her husband, a product of a southern plantation, had, like my father, gone off and left her. Why had he left? My aunt could not answer. She was beaten by the life of the city, just as my mother had been beaten. Wherever my eyes turned they saw stricken, frightened black faces trying vainly to cope with a civilization that they did not understand. I felt lonely. I had fled one insecurity and had embraced another.

When I rose the next morning the temperature had dropped below zero. The house was as cold to me as the southern streets had been in winter. I dressed, doubling my clothing. I ate in a restaurant, caught a streetcar and rode south, rode until I could see no more black faces on the sidewalks. I had now crossed the boundary line of the Black Belt and had entered that territory where jobs were perhaps to be had from white folks. I walked the streets and looked into shop windows until I saw a sign in a delicatessen: PORTER WANTED.

I went in and a stout white woman came to me.

"Vat do you vant?" she asked.   10

The voice jarred me. She's Jewish, I thought, remembering with shame the obscenities I used to shout at Jewish storekeepers in Arkansas.

"I thought maybe you needed a porter," I said.

"Meester 'Offman, he eesn't here yet," she said. "Vill you vait?"

"Yes, ma'am."

"Seet down."   15

"No, ma'am. I'll wait outside."

"But eet's cold out zhere," she said.

"That's all right," I said.

She shrugged. I went to the sidewalk. I waited for half an hour in the bitter cold, regretting that I had not remained in the warm store, but unable to go back inside. A bald, stoutish white man went into the store and pulled off his coat. Yes, he was the boss man . . . I went in.

"Zo you vant a job?" he asked.   20

"Yes, sir," I answered, guessing at the meaning of his words.

"Vhere you vork before?"

"In Memphis, Tennessee."

"My brudder-in-law vorked in Tennessee vonce," he said.

25   I was hired. The work was easy, but I found to my dismay that I could not understand a third of what was said to me. My slow southern ears were baffled by their clouded, thick accents. One morning Mrs. Hoffman asked me to go to a neighboring store—it was owned by a cousin of hers—and get a can of chicken à la king. I had never heard the phrase before and I asked her to repeat it.

"Don't you know nosing?" she demanded of me.

"If you would write it down for me, I'd know what to get," I ventured timidly.

"I can't vite!" she shouted in a sudden fury. "Vat kinda boy ees you?"

I memorized the separate sounds that she had uttered and went to the neighboring store.

30   "Mrs. Hoffman wants a can of Cheek Keeng Awr Lar Keeng," I said slowly, hoping that he would not think I was being offensive.

"All vite," he said, after staring at me a moment.

He put a can into a paper bag and gave it to me; outside in the street I opened the bag and read the label: Chicken à La King. I cursed, disgusted with myself. I knew those words. It had been her thick accent that had thrown me off. Yet I was not angry with her for speaking broken English; my English, too, was broken. But why could she not have taken more patience? Only one answer came to my mind. I was black and she did not care. Or so I thought . . . I was persisting in reading my present environment in the light of my old one. I reasoned thus: Though English was my native tongue and America my native land, she, an alien, could operate a store and earn a living in a neighborhood where I could not even live. I reasoned further that she was aware of this and was trying to protect her position against me.

[It was not until I had left the delicatessen job that I saw how grossly I had misread the motives and attitudes of Mr. Hoffman and his wife. I had not yet learned anything that would have helped me to thread my way through these perplexing racial relations. Accepting my environment at its face value, trapped by my own emotions, I kept asking myself what had black people done to bring this crazy world upon them?

[The fact of the separation of white and black was clear to me; it was its effect upon the personalities of people that stumped and dismayed me. I did not feel that I was a threat to anybody; yet, as soon as I had grown old enough to think I had learned that my entire personality, my aspirations had long ago been discounted; that, in a measure, the very meaning of the words I spoke could not be fully understood.

(And when I contemplated the area of No Man's Land into 35 which the Negro mind in America had been shunted I wondered if there had ever existed in all human history a more corroding and devastating attack upon the personalities of men than the idea of racial discrimination. In order to escape the racial attack that went to the roots of my life, I would have gladly accepted any way of life but the one in which I found myself. I would have agreed to live under a system of feudal oppression, not because I preferred feudalism but because I felt that feudalism made use of a limited part of a man, defined him, his rank, his function in society. I would have consented to live under the most rigid type of dictatorship, for I felt that dictatorships, too, defined the use of men, however degrading that use might be.

(While working in Memphis I had stood aghast as Shorty had offered himself to be kicked by the white men; but now, while working in Chicago, I was learning that perhaps even a kick was better than uncertainty . . . I had elected, in my fevered search for honorable adjustment to the American scene, not to submit and in doing so I had embraced the daily horror of anxiety, of tension, of eternal disquiet. I could now sympathize with—though I could never bring myself to approve—those tortured blacks who had given up and had gone to their white tormentors and had said: "Kick me, if that's all there is for me; kick me and let me feel at home, let me have peace!"

(Color hate defined the place of black life as below that of white life; and the black man, responding to the same dreams as the white man, strove to bury within his heart his awareness of this difference because it made him lonely and afraid. Hated by whites and being an organic part of the culture that hated him, the black man grew in turn to hate in himself that which others hated in him. But pride would make him hide his self-hate, for he would not want whites to know that he was so thoroughly conquered by them that his total life was conditioned by their attitude; but in the act of hiding his self-hate, he could not help but hate those who evoked his self-hate in him. So each part of his day would be consumed in a war with himself, a good part of his energy would be spent in keeping control of his unruly emotions, emotions which he had not wished to have, but could not help having. Held at bay by the hate of others, preoccupied with his own feelings, he was continuously at war with reality. He became inefficient, less able to see and judge the objective world. And when he reached that state, the white people looked at him and laughed and said:

("Look, didn't I tell you niggers were that way?"

(To solve this tangle of balked emotion, I loaded the empty part of the ship of my personality with fantasies of ambition to keep it from toppling over into the sea of senselessness. Like any other American, I dreamed of going into business and making money; I dreamed of working for a firm that would allow me to advance until I reached an important position; I even dreamed of organizing secret groups of blacks to fight all whites. . . . And if the blacks would not agree to organize, then they would have to be fought. I would end up again with self-hate, but it was now a self-hate that was projected outward upon other blacks. Yet I knew—with that part of my mind that the whites had given me—that none of my dreams was possible. Then I would hate myself for allowing my mind to dwell upon the unattainable. Thus the circle would complete itself.

40   (Slowly I began to forge in the depths of my mind a mechanism that repressed all the dreams and desires that the Chicago streets, the newspapers, the movies were evoking in me. I was going through a second childhood; a new sense of the limit of the possible was being born in me. What could I dream of that had the barest possibility of coming true? I could think of nothing. And, slowly, it was upon exactly that nothingness that my mind began to dwell, that constant sense of wanting without having, of being hated without reason. A dim notion of what life meant to a Negro in America was coming to consciousness in me, not in terms of external events, lynchings, Jim Crowism, and the endless brutalities, but in terms of crossed-up feeling, of psyche pain. I sensed that Negro life was a sprawling land of unconscious suffering, and there were but few Negroes who knew the meaning of their lives, who could tell their story.)

Word reached me that an examination for postal clerk was impending and at once I filed an application and waited. As the date for the examination drew near, I was faced with another problem. How could I get a free day without losing my job? In the South it would have been an unwise policy for a Negro to have gone to his white boss and asked for time to take an examination for another job. It would have implied that the Negro did not like to work for the white boss, that he felt he was not receiving just consideration and, inasmuch as most jobs that Negroes held in the South involved a personal, paternalistic relationship, he would have been risking an argument that might have led to violence.

I now began to speculate about what kind of man Mr. Hoffman was, and I found that I did not know him; that is, I did not know his basic attitude toward Negroes. If I asked him, would he be sympathetic enough to allow me time off with pay? I needed the money. Perhaps he would say: "Go home and stay home if you don't like this job"? I was not sure of him. I decided, therefore, that I had better not risk it. I would forfeit the money and stay away without telling him.

The examination was scheduled to take place on a Monday; I had been working steadily and I would be too tired to do my best if I took the examination without the benefit of rest. I decided to stay away from the shop Saturday, Sunday, and Monday. But what could I tell Mr. Hoffman? Yes, I would tell him that I had been ill. No, that was too thin. I would tell him that my mother had died in Memphis and that I had gone down to bury her. That lie might work.

I took the examination and when I came to the store on Tuesday Mr. Hoffman was astonished, of course.

"I didn't sink you vould ever come back," he said.   45

"I'm awfully sorry, Mr. Hoffman."

"Vat happened?"

"My mother died in Memphis and I had to go down and bury her," I lied.

He looked at me, then shook his head.

"Rich, you lie," he said.   50

"I'm not lying," I lied stoutly.

"You vanted to do somesink, zo you zayed ervay," he said, shrugging.

"No, sir. I'm telling you the truth." I piled another lie upon the first one.

"No. You lie. You disappoint me," he said.

"Well, all I can do is tell you the truth," I lied indignantly.   55

"Vy didn't you use the phone?"

"I didn't think of it." I told a fresh lie.

"Rich, if your mudder die, you vould tell me," he said.

"I didn't have time. Had to catch the train." I lied yet again.

"Vhere did you get the money?"   60

"My aunt gave it to me," I said, disgusted that I had to lie and lie again.

"I don't vant a boy vat tells lies," he said.

"I don't lie," I lied passionately to protect my lies.

Mrs. Hoffman joined in and both of them hammered at me.

"Ve know. You come from ze Zouth. You feel you can't tell us   65
ze truth. But ve don't bother you. Ve don't feel like people in ze Zouth. Ve treat you nice, don't ve?" they asked.

"Yes, ma'am," I mumbled.

"Zen vy lie?"

"I'm not lying," I lied with all my strength.

I became angry because I knew that they knew that I was lying. I had lied to protect myself, and then I had to lie to protect my lie. I had met so many white faces that would have violently disapproved of my taking the examination that I could not have risked telling Mr. Hoffman the truth. But how could I now tell him that I had lied because I was so unsure of myself? Lying was bad, but revealing my own sense of insecurity would have been worse. It would have been shameful, and I did not like to feel ashamed.

70   Their attitudes had proved utterly amazing. They were taking time out from their duties in the store to talk to me, and I had never encountered anything like that from whites before. A southern white man would have said: "Get to hell out of here!" or "All right, nigger. Get to work." But no white people had ever stood their ground and probed at me, questioned me at such length. It dawned upon me that they were trying to treat me as an equal, which made it even more impossible for me ever to tell them that I had lied, why I had lied. I felt that if I confessed I would give them a moral advantage over me that would be unbearable.

"All vight, zay and vork," Mr. Hoffman said. "I know you're lying, but I don't care, Rich."

I wanted to quit. He had insulted me. But I liked him in spite of myself. Yes, I had done wrong, but how on earth could I have known the kind of people I was working for? Perhaps Mr. Hoffman would have gladly consented for me to take the examination, but my hopes had been far weaker than my powerful fears.

Working with them from day to day and knowing that they knew I had lied from fear crushed me. I knew that they pitied me and pitied the fear in me. I resolved to quit and risk hunger rather than stay with them. I left the job that following Saturday, not telling them that I would not be back, not possessing the heart to say good-bye. I just wanted to go quickly and have them forget that I had ever worked for them.

After an idle week, I got a job as a dishwasher in a North Side café that had just opened. My boss, a white woman, directed me in unpacking barrels of dishes, setting up new tables, painting, and so on. I had charge of serving breakfast; in the late afternoons I carted trays of food to patrons in the hotel who did not want to come down to eat. My wages were fifteen dollars a week; the hours were long, but I ate my meals on the job.

75   The cook was an elderly Finnish woman with a sharp, bony face. There were several white waitresses. I was the only Negro in the café. The waitresses were a hard, brisk lot and I was keenly aware of how their attitudes contrasted with those of southern white girls. They had not been taught to keep a gulf between me and themselves; they were relatively free of the heritage of racial hate.

One morning as I was making coffee, Cora came forward with a tray loaded with food and squeezed against me to draw a cup of coffee.

"Pardon me, Richard," she said.

"Oh, that's all right," I said in an even tone.

But I was aware that she was a white girl and that her body was pressed closely against mine, an incident that had never happened to me before in my life, an incident charged with the memory of dread. But she was not conscious of my blackness or of what her actions would have meant in the South. And had I not been born in the South, her trivial act would have been as unnoticed by me as it was by her. As she stood close to me, I could not help thinking that if a southern white girl had wanted to draw a cup of coffee, she would have commanded me to step aside so that she might not come in contact with me. The work of the hot and busy kitchen would have had to cease for the moment so that I could have taken my tainted body far enough away to allow the southern white girl a chance to get a cup of coffee. There lay a deep, emotional safety in knowing that the white girl who was now leaning carelessly against me was not thinking of me, had no deep, vague, irrational fright that made her feel that I was a creature to be avoided at all costs.

One summer morning a white girl came late to work and 80 rushed into the pantry where I was busy. She went into the women's room and changed her clothes; I heard the door open and a second later I was surprised to hear her voice:

"Richard, quick! Tie my apron!"

She was standing with her back to me and the strings of her apron dangled loose. There was a moment of indecision on my part, then I took the two loose strings and carried them around her body and brought them again to her back and tied them in a clumsy knot.

"Thanks a million," she said, grasping my hand for a split second, and was gone.

I continued my work, filled with all the possible meanings that that tiny, simple, human event could have meant to any Negro in the South where I had spent most of my hungry days.

I did not feel any admiration for the girls, nor any hate. My 85 attitude was one of abiding and friendly wonder. For the most part I was silent with them, though I knew that I had a firmer grasp of life than most of them. As I worked I listened to their talk and perceived its puzzled, wandering, superficial fumbling with the problems and facts of life. There were many things they wondered about that I could have explained to them, but I never dared.

During my lunch hour, which I spent on a bench in a near-by park, the waitresses would come and sit beside me, talking at ran-

dom, laughing, joking, smoking cigarettes. I learned about their taw-
dry dreams, their simple hopes, their home lives, their fear of feeling
anything deeply, their sex problems, their husbands. They were an
eager, restless, talkative, ignorant bunch, but casually kind and impersonal for all that. They knew nothing of hate and fear, and strove
instinctively to avoid all passion.

I often wondered what they were trying to get out of life, but I
never stumbled upon a clue, and I doubt if they themselves had any
notion. They lived on the surface of their days; their smiles were
surface smiles, and their tears were surface tears. Negroes lived a
truer and deeper life than they, but I wished that Negroes, too, could
live as thoughtlessly, serenely as they. The girls never talked of their
feelings; none of them possessed the insight or the emotional equip-
ment to understand themselves or others. How far apart in culture
we stood! All my life I had done nothing but feel and cultivate my
feelings; all their lives they had done nothing but strive for petty
goals, the trivial material prizes of American life. We shared a common tongue, but my language was a different language from theirs.

It was in the psychological distance that separated the races
that the deepest meaning of the problem of the Negro lay for me.
For these poor, ignorant white girls to have understood my life would
have meant nothing short of a vast revolution in theirs. And I was
convinced that what they needed to make them complete and grown-
up in their living was the inclusion in their personalities of a knowledge of lives such as I lived and suffered containedly.

(As I, in memory, think back now upon those girls and their
lives I feel that for white America to understand the significance of
the problem of the Negro will take a bigger and tougher America
than any we have yet known. I feel that America's past is too shallow, her national character too superficially optimistic, her very morality too suffused with color hate for her to accomplish so vast and
complex a task. Culturally the Negro represents a paradox: Though
he is an organic part of the nation, he is excluded by the entire tide
and direction of American culture. Frankly, it is felt to be right to
exclude him, and it is felt to be wrong to admit him freely. Therefore
if, within the confines of its present culture, the nation ever seeks
to purge itself of its color hate, it will find itself at war with itself,
convulsed by a spasm of emotional and moral confusion. If the nation ever finds itself examining its real relation to the Negro, it will
find itself doing infinitely more than that; for the anti-Negro attitude of whites represents but a tiny part—though a symbolically
significant one—of the moral attitude of the nation. Our too-young
and too-new America, lusty because it is lonely, aggressive because
it is afraid, insists upon seeing the world in terms of good and bad,

the holy and the evil, the high and the low, the white and the black; our America is frightened of fact, of history, of processes, of necessity. It hugs the easy way of damning those whom it cannot understand, of excluding those who look different, and it salves its conscience with a self-draped cloak of righteousness. Am I damning my native land? No; for I, too, share these faults of character! And I really do not think that America, adolescent and cocksure, a stranger to suffering and travail, an enemy of passion and sacrifice, is ready to probe into its most fundamental beliefs.

(I know that not race alone, not color alone, but the daily values that give meaning to life stood between me and those white girls with whom I worked. Their constant outward-looking, their mania for radios, cars, and a thousand other trinkets made them dream and fix their eyes upon the trash of life, made it impossible for them to learn a language which could have taught them to speak of what was in their or others' hearts. The words of their souls were the syllables of popular songs.

(The essence of the irony of the plight of the Negro in America, to me, is that he is doomed to live in isolation while those who condemn him seek the basest goals of any people on the face of the earth. Perhaps it would be possible for the Negro to become reconciled to his plight if he could be made to believe that his sufferings were for some remote, high, sacrificial end; but sharing the culture that condemns him, and seeing that a lust for trash is what blinds the nation to his claims, is what sets storms to rolling in his soul.)

Though I had fled the pressure of the South, my outward conduct had not changed. I had been schooled to present an unalteringly smiling face and I continued to do so despite the fact that my environment allowed more open expression. I hid my feelings and avoided all relationships with whites that might cause me to reveal them.

One afternoon the boss lady entered the kitchen and found me sitting on a box reading a copy of the *American Mercury*.

"What on earth are you reading?" she demanded.

I was at once on guard, though I knew I did not have to be.

"Oh, just a magazine," I said.

"Where did you get it?" she asked.

"Oh, I just found it," I lied; I had bought it.

"Do you understand it?" she asked.

"Yes, ma'am."

"Well," she exclaimed, "the colored dishwasher reads the *American Mercury!*"

She walked away, shaking her head. My feelings were mixed. I was glad that she had learned that I was not completely dumb, yet I felt a little angry because she seemed to think it odd for dishwashers to read magazines. Thereafter I kept my books and magazines wrapped in newspaper so that no one would see them, reading them at home and on the streetcar to and from work.

Tillie, the Finnish cook, was a tall, ageless, red-faced, raw-boned woman with long, snow-white hair which she balled in a knot at the nape of her neck. She cooked expertly and was superbly efficient. One morning as I passed the sizzling stove I thought I heard Tillie cough and spit. I paused and looked carefully to see where her spittle had gone, but I saw nothing; her face, obscured by steam, was bent over a big pot. My senses told me that Tillie had coughed and spat into that pot, but my heart told me that no human being could possibly be so filthy. I decided to watch her. An hour or so later I heard Tillie clear her throat with a grunt, saw her cough, and spit into the boiling soup. I held my breath; I did not want to believe what I had seen.

Should I tell the boss lady? Would she believe me? I watched Tillie for another day to make sure that she was spitting into the food. She was; there was no doubt of it. But who would believe me if I told them what was happening? I was the only black person in the café. Perhaps they would think that I hated the cook? I stopped eating my meals there and bided my time.

105   The business of the café was growing rapidly and a Negro girl was hired to make salads. I went to her at once.

"Look, can I trust you?" I asked.

"What are you talking about?" she asked.

"I want you to say nothing, but watch that cook."

"For what?"

110   "Now, don't get scared. Just watch the cook."

She looked at me as though she thought I was crazy; and, frankly, I felt that perhaps I ought not to say anything to anybody.

"What do you mean?" she demanded.

"All right," I said. "I'll tell you. That cook spits in the food."

"What are you saying?" she asked aloud.

115   "Keep quiet," I said.

"Spitting?" she asked me in a whisper. "Why would she do that?"

"I don't know. But watch her."

She walked away from me with a funny look in her eyes. But half an hour later she came rushing to me, looking ill, sinking into a chair.

"Oh, God, I feel awful!"

120   "Did you see it?"

"She *is* spitting in the food!"

"What ought we do?" I asked.

"Tell the lady," she said.

"She wouldn't believe me," I said.

She widened her eyes as she understood. We were black and   125
the cook was white.

"But I can't work here if she's going to do that," she said.

"Then you tell her," I said.

"She wouldn't believe me either," she said.

She rose and ran to the women's room. When she returned she
stared at me. We were two Negroes and we were silently asking
ourselves if the white boss lady would believe us if we told her that
her expert white cook was spitting in the food all day long as it
cooked upon the stove.

"I don't know," she wailed in a whisper and walked away.   130

I thought of telling the waitresses about the cook, but I could
not get up enough nerve. Many of the girls were friendly with Tillie.
Yet I could not let the cook spit in the food all day. That was wrong
by any human standard of conduct. I washed dishes, thinking, wondering; I served breakfast, thinking, wondering; I served meals in the
apartments of patrons upstairs, thinking, wondering. Each time I
picked up a tray of food I felt like retching. Finally the Negro salad
girl came to me and handed me her purse and hat.

"I'm going to tell her and quit, goddamn," she said.

"I'll quit too, if she doesn't fire her," I said.

"Oh, she won't believe me," she wailed in agony.

"You tell her. You're a woman. She might believe you."   135

Her eyes welled with tears and she sat for a long time; then she
rose and went abruptly into the dining room. I went to the door and
peered. Yes, she was at the desk, talking to the boss lady. She returned to the kitchen and went into the pantry; I followed her.

"Did you tell her?" I asked.

"Yes."

"What did she say?"

"She said I was crazy."   140

"Oh, God!" I said.

"She just looked at me with those gray eyes of hers," the girl
said. "Why would Tillie do that?"

"I don't know," I said.

The boss lady came to the door and called the girl; both of them
went into the dining room. Tillie came over to me; a hard cold look
was in her eyes.

"What's happening here?" she asked.   145

"I don't know," I said, wanting to slap her across the mouth.

She muttered something and went back to the stove, coughed, spat into a bubbling pot. I left the kitchen and went into the back areaway to breathe. The boss lady came out.

"Richard," she said.

Her face was pale, I was smoking a cigarette and I did not look at her.

150 "Is this true?"

"Yes, ma'am."

" It couldn't be. Do you know what you're saying?"

"Just watch her," I said.

"I don't know," she moaned.

155 She looked crushed. She went back into the dining room, but I saw her watching the cook through the doors. I watched both of them, the boss lady and the cook, praying that the cook would spit again. She did. The boss lady came into the kitchen and stared at Tillie, but she did not utter a word. She burst into tears and ran back into the dining room.

"What's happening here?" Tillie demanded.

No one answered. The boss lady came out and tossed Tillie her hat, coat, and money.

"Now, get out of here, you dirty dog!" she said.

Tillie stared, then slowly picked up her hat, coat, and the money; she stood a moment, wiped sweat from her forehead with her hand, then spat, this time on the floor. She left.

160 Nobody was ever able to fathom why Tillie liked to spit into the food.

Brooding over Tillie, I recalled the time when the boss man in Mississippi had come to me and had tossed my wages to me and said:

"Get out, nigger! I don't like your looks."

And I wondered if a Negro who did not smile and grin was as morally loathsome to whites as a cook who spat into the food. . . .

I worked at the café all spring and in June I was called for temporary duty in the post office. My confidence soared; if I obtained an appointment as a regular clerk, I could spend at least five hours a day writing.

165 I reported at the post office and was sworn in as a temporary clerk. I earned seventy cents an hour and I went to bed each night now with a full stomach for the first time in my life. When I worked nights, I wrote during the day; when I worked days, I wrote during the night.

But the happiness of having a job did not keep another worry from rising to plague me. Before I could receive a permanent appointment I would have to take a physical examination. The weight requirement was one hundred and twenty-five pounds and I—with my long years of semistarvation—barely tipped the scales at a hundred and ten. Frantically I turned all of my spare money into food and ate. But my skin and flesh would not respond to the food. Perhaps I was not eating the right diet? Perhaps my chronic anxiety kept my weight down. I drank milk, ate steak, but it did not give me an extra ounce of flesh. I visited a doctor who told me that there was nothing wrong with me except malnutrition, that I must eat and sleep long hours. I did and my weight remained the same. I knew now that my job was temporary and that when the time came for my appointment I would have to resume my job hunting again.

At night I read Stein's *Three Lives*, Crane's *The Red Badge of Courage*, and Dostoevski's *The Possessed*, all of which revealed new realms of feeling. But the most important discoveries came when I veered from fiction proper into the field of psychology and sociology. I ran through volumes that bore upon the causes of my conduct and the conduct of my people. I studied tables of figures relating population density to insanity, relating housing to disease, relating school and recreational opportunities to crime, relating various forms of neurotic behavior to environment, relating racial insecurities to the conflicts between whites and blacks . . .

I still had no friends, casual or intimate, and felt the need for none. I had developed a self-sufficiency that kept me distant from others, emotionally and psychologically. Occasionally I went to house-rent parties, parties given by working-class families to raise money to pay the landlord, the admission to which was a quarter or a half dollar. At these affairs I drank home-brewed beer, ate spaghetti and chitterlings, laughed and talked with black, southern-born girls who worked as domestic servants in white middle-class homes. But with none of them did my relations rest upon my deepest feelings. I discussed what I read with no one, and to none did I confide. Emotionally, I was withdrawn from the objective world; my desires floated loosely within the walls of my consciousness, contained and controlled.

As a protective mechanism, I developed a terse, cynical mode of speech that rebuffed those who sought to get too close to me. Conversation was my way of avoiding expression; my words were reserved for those times when I sat down alone to write. My face was always a deadpan or a mask of general friendliness; no word or event could jar me into a gesture of enthusiasm or despair. A slowly, hesitantly spoken "Yeah" was my general verbal reaction to almost everything I heard. "That's pretty good," said with a slow nod of the head, was my approval. "Aw, naw," muttered with a cold smile, was

my rejection. Even though I reacted deeply, my true feelings raced
along underground, hidden.

170   I did not act in this fashion deliberately; I did not prefer this
kind of relationship with people. I wanted a life in which there was
a constant oneness of feeling with others, in which the basic emotions of life were shared, in which common memory formed a common past, in which collective hope reflected a national future. But I
knew that no such thing was possible in my environment. The only
ways in which I felt that my feelings could go outward without fear
of rude rebuff or searing reprisal was in writing or reading, and to
me they were ways of living.

Aunt Maggie had now rented an apartment in which I shared a
rear room. My mother and brother came and all three of us slept in
that one room; there was no window, just four walls and a door. My
excessive reading puzzled Aunt Maggie; she sensed my fiercely indrawn nature and she did not like it. Being of an open, talkative
disposition, she declared that I was going about the business of living wrongly, that reading books would not help me at all. But nothing she said had any effect. I had long ago hardened myself to criticism.

"Boy, are you reading for law?" my aunt would demand.

"No."

"Then why are you reading all the time?"

175   "I like to."

"But what do you get out of it?"

"I get a great deal out of it."

And I knew that my words sounded wild and foolish in my
environment, where reading was almost unknown, where the high-
est item of value was a dime or a dollar, an apartment or a job; where,
if one aspired at all, it was to be a doctor or a lawyer, a shopkeeper
or a politician. The most valued pleasure of the people I knew was a
car, the most cherished experience a bottle of whisky, the most
sought-after prize somebody else's wife. I had no sense of being in-
ferior or superior to the people about me; I merely felt that they had
had no chance to learn to live differently. I never criticized them or
praised them, yet they felt in my neutrality a deeper rejection of
them than if I had cursed them.

Repeatedly I took stabs at writing, but the results were so poor
that I would tear up the sheets. I was striving for a level of expression that matched those of the novels I read. But I always somehow
failed to get onto the page what I thought and felt. Failing at sustained narrative, I compromised by playing with single sentences
and phrases. Under the influence of Stein's *Three Lives*, I spent hours
and days pounding out disconnected sentences for the sheer love of
words.

I would write: 180
"The soft melting hunk of butter trickled in gold down the stringy grooves of the split yam."
Or:
"The child's clumsy fingers fumbled in sleep, feeling vainly for the wish of its dream."
"The old man huddled in the dark doorway, his bony face lit by the burning yellow in the windows of distant skyscrapers."

My purpose was to capture a physical state or movement that   185
carried a strong subjective impression, an accomplishment which seemed supremely worth struggling for. If I could fasten the mind of the reader upon words so firmly that he would forget words and be conscious only of his response, I felt that I would be in sight of knowing how to write narrative. I strove to master words, to make them disappear, to make them important by making them new, to make them melt into a rising spiral of emotional stimuli, each greater than the other, each feeding and reinforcing the other, and all ending in an emotional climax that would drench the reader with a sense of a new world. That was the single aim of my living.

Autumn came and I was called for my physical examination for the position of regular postal clerk. I had not told my mother or brother or aunt that I knew I would fail. On the morning of the examination I drank two quarts of buttermilk, ate six bananas, but it did not hoist the red arrow of the government scales to the required mark of one hundred and twenty-five pounds. I went home and sat disconsolately in my back room, hating myself, wondering where I could find another job. I had almost got my hands upon a decent job and had lost it, had let it slip through my fingers. Waves of self-doubt rose to haunt me. Was I always to hang on the fringes of life? What I wanted was truly modest, and yet my past, my diet, my hunger, had snatched it from before my eyes. But these self-doubts did not last long; I dulled the sense of loss through reading, reading, writing and more writing.

The loss of my job did not evoke in me any hostility toward the system of rules that had barred my first grasp at the material foundations of American life. I felt that it was unfair that my lack of a few pounds of flesh should deprive me of a chance at a good job, but I had long ago emotionally rejected the world in which I lived and my reaction was: Well, this is the system by which people want the world to run whether it helps them or not. To me, my losing was only another manifestation of that queer, material way of American living that computed everything in terms of the concrete: weight, color, race, fur coats, radios, electric refrigerators, cars, money . . . It seemed that I simply could not fit into a materialistic life.

The living arrangement of my mother, brother, and Aunt Maggie—now that I had no promise of being a postal clerk—quickly deteriorated. In Aunt Maggie's eyes I was a plainly marked failure and she feared that perhaps she would have to feed me. The emotional atmosphere in the cramped quarters became tense, ugly, petty, bickering. Fault was found with my reading and writing; it was claimed that I was swelling the electric bill. Though I had saved almost no money, I decided to rent an apartment. Aunt Cleo was living in a rented room and I invited her to share the apartment with me, my mother, and brother, and she consented. We moved into a tiny, dingy two-room den in whose kitchen a wall bed fitted snugly into a corner near the stove. The place was alive with vermin and the smell of cooking hung in the air day and night.

I asked for my job back at the café and the boss lady allowed me to return; again I served breakfast, washed dishes, carted trays of food up into the apartments. Another postal examination was scheduled for spring and to that end I made eating an obsession. I ate when I did not want to eat, drank milk when it sickened me. Slowly my starved body responded to food and overcame the lean years of Mississippi, Arkansas, and Tennessee, counteracting the flesh-sapping anxiety of fear-filled days.

190   I read Proust's *A Remembrance of Things Past*, admiring the lucid, subtle but strong prose, stupefied by its dazzling magic, awed by the vast, delicate, intricate, and psychological structure of the Frenchman's epic of death and decadence. But it crushed me with hopelessness, for I wanted to write of the people in my environment with an equal thoroughness, and the burning example before my eyes made me feel that I never could.

My ability to endure tension had now grown amazingly. From the accidental pain of southern years, from anxiety that I had sought to avoid, from fear that had been too painful to bear, I had learned to like my unintermittent burden of feeling, had become habituated to acting with all of my being, had learned to seek those areas of life, those situations, where I knew that events would complement my own inner mood. I was conscious of what was happening to me; I knew that my attitude of watchful wonder had usurped all other feelings, had become the meaning of my life, an integral part of my personality; that I was striving to live and measure all things by it. Having no claims upon others, I bent the way the wind blew, rendering unto my environment that which was my environment's, and rendering unto myself that which I felt was mine.

It was a dangerous way to live, far more dangerous than violating laws or ethical codes of conduct; but the danger was for me and me alone. Had I not been conscious of what I was doing, I could have easily lost my way in the fogbound regions of compelling fantasy. Even so, I floundered, staggered; but somehow I always groped my way back to that path where I felt a tinge of warmth from an unseen light.

Hungry for insight into my own life and the lives about me, knowing my fiercely indrawn nature, I sought to fulfill more than my share of all obligations and responsibilities, as though offering libations of forgiveness to my environment. Indeed, the more my emotions claimed my attention, the sharper—as though in ultimate self-defense—became my desire to measure accurately the reality of the objective world so that I might more than meet its demands. At twenty years of age the mold of my life was set, was hardening into a pattern, a pattern that was neither good nor evil, neither right nor wrong.

Response

1. When Wright went to Chicago in 1927, he was part of a large-scale African-American migration to northern cities in the first decades of this century. What were Wright's first perceptions of the physical and social environment of Chicago? In what ways did it teach him that "perhaps even a kick was better than uncertainty" (paragraph 36)?

2. In Chicago, Wright says in paragraph 32, "I was persisting in reading my present environment in the light of my old one." How does his relationship with the Hoffmans demonstrate this? In what ways was Wright "trapped by [his] own emotions" (paragraph 33)?

3. Explain Wright's unorthodox use of parentheses. In the first parenthetical comment of this chapter (paragraphs 33–40) he analyzes the effects of racial discrimination, as a "corroding and devastating attack upon the personalities of men." Why does he see it as worse than life under feudalism or a dictatorship? Paraphrase Wright's explanation of how racism can be internalized, turning into self-hatred and anger at other African Americans. How does Wright indicate the emerging motivation for his writing?

4. What was Wright's perception of the waitresses in his second job? Why did he believe he "had a firmer grasp of life than most of them" (paragraph 85) and that "Negroes lived a truer and deeper life than they" (paragraph 87)?

5. Explain the basic paradox of American society, according to

Wright's parenthetical comment in paragraphs 89–91. Wright saw racial prejudice as just a small part of the "moral attitude" of the nation; he condemned the values and goals of the dominant culture that blinded it to the reality of racism. Explain the bitter irony he saw in this. Do you think Wright would alter his analysis if he were evaluating American society today?

6. Throughout the period of his life described in this passage, Wright was preoccupied with repressed emotions. As his awareness grew, so did his alienation. In his social contacts he increasingly maintained an "attitude of watchful wonder," as he says near the end of the passage. How did his social isolation feed his early attempts at writing? Judging from what he says in this passage and from your reading of his work, what motivated his writing?

7. Among the authors in this anthology, Wright came first: as a writer he preceded the others both chronologically and in terms of his vision of American culture. How do you see his writing as setting a precedent for those who followed?

Topics for Writing

TOPICS for Section I:
On Being a Writer

1. In his "Autobiographical Notes" James Baldwin states that "one writes out of one thing only—one's own experience." Considering his own development as a writer, he observes: "Any writer, looking back . . . finds that the things which hurt him and the things which helped him cannot be divorced from each other; he could be helped in a certain way only because he was hurt in a certain way." Consider whether these observations apply to yourself. Drawing on your reading and your own experience, respond to his point of view.

2. Sandra Cisneros says in "Ghosts and Voices,"

   > If I were asked what it is I write about, I would have to say I write about those ghosts inside that haunt me . . . Perhaps later there will be time to write by inspiration. In the meantime, in my writing as well as in that of other Chicanas and other women, there is the necessary phase of dealing with those ghosts and voices most urgently haunting us, day by day.

   Based on your reading of Cisneros and any of the other writers we've discussed, evaluate her claim about women's writing. To what extent do you find it holds true for other writers? What does it mean to you?

3. In "Boxing on Paper" Ishmael Reed says that "it takes an extraordinary amount of effort to understand someone from a background different from your own, especially when your life

393

doesn't really depend upon it." To what extent does your experience bear out this statement? Evaluate Reed's idea either
from the perspective of understanding other people, or of being
understood yourself.

4. Simon J. Ortiz and Elizabeth Cook-Lynn, coming from different tribes and different regions of the country, both write about
how the oral tradition and ritual affect their writing. Compare
their ideas on this issue, and explain how Native American
history and oral traditions play a special role in their writing.

5. Elizabeth Cook-Lynn quotes the Navajo poet and artist Grey
Cohoe saying, "have confidence in what you know." Other authors in Section I convey a similar message. How is this theme
reiterated by different writers? What different circumstances
can make it difficult for a person to accept and carry out Cohoe's advice? How does it apply to you?

6. In an essay entitled "Writing Autobiography" in her book
Talking Back bell hooks (whose real name is Gloria Watkins)
says,

> To me, telling the story of my growing up years was intimately
> connected with the longing to kill the self I was without really
> having to die. I wanted to kill that self in writing. Once that self
> was gone—out of my life forever—I could more easily become
> the me of me.

Writing her own story turned out to be difficult, she says. Later,
reading her own manuscript was an experience of self-discov-
ery:

> In the end I did not feel as though I had killed the Gloria of my
> childhood. Instead I had rescued her. She was no longer the en-
> emy within, the little girl who had to be annihilated for the
> woman to come into being. In writing about her, I reclaimed
> that part of myself I had long ago rejected, left uncared for, just
> as she had often felt alone and uncared for as a child. Remem-
> bering was part of a cycle of reunion, a joining of fragments, "the
> bits and pieces of my heart" that the narrative made whole again.

Looking back, do you recognize aspects of your former self that
you would like either to be rid of or to be reunited with? How
can writing help you become "the you of you"?

7. In an article in *Harvard Education Review* (58:3, 1988) Lisa
Delpit, an educator in a large urban school system, makes the
following comment:

> To imply to children or adults that it doesn't matter how you
> talk or how you write is to ensure their ultimate failure. I prefer
> to be honest with my students. Tell them that their language
> and cultural style is unique and wonderful but that there is a
> political power game that is also being played, and if they want

to be in on that game there are certain games that they too must play. . . . They must be encouraged to understand the value of the language they already possess; however, they must also understand the power realities in this country. Otherwise they will be unable to work to change these realities.

Consider Delpit's ideas in light of Kurt Vonnegut's essay "How to Write with Style." Vonnegut says:

> The writing style which is most natural for you is bound to echo speech you heard when a child. . . . Many Americans grow up hearing a language other than English, or an English dialect a majority of Americans cannot understand. All these varieties of speech are beautiful, just as the varieties of butterflies are beautiful. No matter what your first language, you should treasure it all your life. If it happens not to be standard English, and if it shows itself when you write standard English, the result is usually delightful, like a very pretty girl with one eye that is green and one that is blue.

And later he adds, "We are members of an egalitarian society, so there is no reason for us to write, in case we are not classically educated aristocrats, as though we were classically educated aristocrats."

To what extent do you see Delpit's and Vonnegut's views as being in conflict or in agreement? As a student writer, respond to their attitudes about language use with your own opinion on the issue.

8. James Baldwin in "Autobiographical Notes," Sandra Cisneros in "Ghosts and Voices: Writing from Obsession," and Joan Didion in "Why I Write" all reveal personal views about why they write and what they intend to accomplish as writers. Their views are shaped in part by their cultural backgrounds, which are very different. Yet for all of them, writing seems to be part of a process of figuring out or affirming their own identity. Compare and contrast the ways these authors seek a sense of identity through writing. How do you respond to their ideas?

9. In the essays in this section a number of writers reveal their different reasons for writing. Compare and contrast two or more of them in terms of their motivations and goals as writers, drawing upon your reading to support your observations. How do you respond as a reader to what these writers say? Let your own point of view about their ideas give your comparison a focus.

10. When we write we reveal something of ourselves; as Vonnegut says in "How to Write with Style,"

> [Writers] reveal a lot about themselves to readers. We call these revelations, accidental and intentional, elements of literary style.

These revelations are fascinating to us as readers. They tell us what sort of person it is with whom we are spending time. Does the writer sound ignorant or informed, crazy or sane, stupid or bright, crooked or honest, humorless or playful—? And on and on.

In the topics we choose to discuss and the points of view we take toward them, we tell the reader about our interests, likes and dislikes, attitudes toward life, hopes, concerns, expectations. We also reveal something about the way we think in how we arrange our ideas, the kinds of details we bring to the reader's attention, the manner in which we present our point of view.

In this section you have been reading work by writers who come from different times, places, and backgrounds. Choose one of these authors to get to know better. Read one or more additional selections by that author in this book. Based on your reading, form some generalizations about what type of person this writer reveals himself or herself to be through his/her writing. Discuss what you have discovered about this writer as a person, supporting your analysis with relevant examples from your reading.

TOPICS for Section II:
Identity and Community _____

1. Put yourself in the context portrayed by Ishmael Reed—the multinational society we live in. You might consider your citizenship, your family's national or cultural heritage, and the culture of everyday life where you live. Who are you? On what experiences do you base what you say? Share a sense of this with your readers by providing concrete details, examples, or anecdotes.

2. In "My Baseball Years" Philip Roth recalls how critical baseball was to his moral and educational development and to his sense of identity. Think about the activities and associations that have played an important role in your own experience. For you, what has come closest to fulfilling the function that baseball did for Roth?

3. In the passage from The Names, N. Scott Momaday is concerned with the way his sense of self derives from his relation to his ancestry. Examine your connection to one or more of

your forebears—a grandmother, grandfather, or other. Like
Momaday, draw upon real experience, stories told, and imagination. Consider the extent to which Momaday's words apply:
"an idea of one's ancestry and posterity is really an idea of the
self."

4. Gloria Anzaldua's story "Lifeline" raises the issue of how gen-
    der and sexual preference play a role in one's sense of identity.
    Her story portrays the painful consequences of denial, ambi-
    guity, or rejection of one's identity, either by oneself or by an-
    other person.

    The issue of gender and identity is raised indirectly by
    James Baldwin in "The Discovery of What It Means to Be an
    American":

    > The American writer, in Europe, is released, first of all, from the
    > necessity of apologizing for himself. It is not until he *is* released
    > from the habit of flexing his muscles and proving that he is just
    > a "regular guy" that he realizes how crippling this habit has
    > been.

    Have you ever, like Baldwin, felt freedom in not conform-
    ing to conventional masculine or feminine expectations of be-
    havior? Or have you ever had to deal with negative conse-
    quences of nonconformity? In your point of view, what role
    should gender identity play in daily life?

5. In "Keeping Close to Home" bell hooks recalls when she first
    left Kentucky to go to Stanford University:

    > My parents had not been delighted that I had been accepted and
    > adamantly opposed my going so far from home. At the time, I
    > did not see their opposition as an expression of their fear that
    > they would lose me forever. Like many working-class folks, they
    > feared what college education might do to their children's minds
    > even as they unenthusiastically acknowledged its importance.

    In fact, education often separates one from one's past, as hooks
    realized. What has been your experience? Do you anticipate
    that this will be an issue for you, and how do you handle it?

6. "Patriotism" is a notion that gets defined differently by indi-
    viduals in different times and circumstances. What is it? Com-
    pare the concepts of patriotism that emerge in the passages by
    Baldwin, Okada, and Roth—and any other readings you choose
    to relate. What is your own perspective?

7. Several writers—Anaya, Baldwin, Okada, and Roth—present
    their varying perspectives on "being American." Survey the
    range of viewpoints and respond with your own point of view;
    which perspective do you most readily relate to, and why?

TOPICS for Section III:
Other Generations and Traditions _____

1. In "The Seam of the Snail" Cynthia Ozick describes her moth-
    er's character in contrast to her own; she uses the differences
    between them to comment upon herself as a person and as a
    writer. Using her essay as a model, write about yourself and
    some other person close to you, focusing on an essential point
    of difference between yourself and that other person. Like
    Ozick, try to show the connection between this person and
    yourself.

2. R. A. Sasaki in "The Loom" tells the story of her mother's life.
    She writes the narrative, which even includes a character rep-
    resenting herself, in the third person. In the end, she wraps the
    story up with an implicit comment about her mother's life that
    reveals her point of view as both author and daughter. Similar
    to the way Sasaki tells this story, write about the life of one of
    your parents or an older person you know. Include a character
    in your story that represents yourself, but tell the story in the
    third person. Make your point of view about this person's life
    give a focus to your story.

3. In *Bless Me, Ultima* Rudolfo Anaya portrays a young boy's re-
    lationship with a very old woman. The story reflects the cus-
    tomary treatment of the aged in Anaya's traditional culture,
    and it shows the special understanding that can link a child
    and a grandparent or other very old person. If you have had
    such a relationship, write about it, showing how it is different
    from your relationship with your parents.

4. Paule Marshall in "From the Poets in the Kitchen" observes
    that talk was "highly functional" for her mother and her
    friends. In Marshall's view, what purposes did the kitchen con-
    versations serve? To what extent does her analysis apply to
    talk in groups that you are familiar with in your everyday life?
    How does conversation serve the same functions for groups
    that you know?

5. In Hisaye Yamamoto's "Seventeen Syllables" and Maxine
    Hong Kingston's "No Name Woman," the mothers tell their
    daughters stories with an "educational" intent. Explain why
    the mothers tell their stories, and tell whether you feel they
    achieve their purpose. Discuss how your own mother or father
    or other adult has used stories for a purpose in your own up-
    bringing. Explain the purpose and whether or not it was
    achieved in your case.

6. Maxine Hong Kingston in "No Name Woman" says, "Those of

us in the first American generations have had to figure out how the invisible world the emigrants built around our childhoods fit in solid America." Later she asks, "Chinese Americans, when you try to understand what things in you are Chinese, how do you separate what is peculiar to childhood, to poverty, insanities, one family, your mother who marked your growing with stories, from what is Chinese?"

Others in this country have also had to reconcile differences between the culture of their parents and that of the larger society. In fact many people—not just Chinese Americans— might ask their own version of Kingston's question. Does a question like this matter to you? How would you ask it, and for your own circumstances, how would you go about answering it?

7. Frank Chin wrote an Afterword to the 1976 edition of John Okada's *No-No Boy*. In it he expressed his concern with rejecting the fake, stereotyped image of his culture that prevailed in the absence of real, honest portrayals. He wrote:

> What if there were no whites in American literary history. There is no Melville, no Mark Twain, no Kay Boyle, no Gertrude Stein, no Tom Robbins, not even a Rod McKuen. A white American writer would feel edgy if all the books ever written in America were by blacks, browns, reds, yellows, and all whites had ever published were cookbooks full of recipes for apple pie and fried chicken. . . . That's what I grew up with.

Chin reiterates this theme in "Railroad Standard Time": he clings to his link with his true heritage, embodied by his grandfather's watch, in the face of the fake versions of that heritage he found in movies and popular novels.

Do you also have to deal with stereotypes of people like yourself in daily life? Where do they come from, and how are they presented? How do you hang on to your true heritage or sense of yourself and assert your identity in the face of the fake images?

TOPICS for Section IV:
A Sense of Time and Place _____

1. Writing about his work, Gary Soto once explained that his poems and stories recreate common events of life in such a way that "particulars stand out as totems of a lusher experience." In other words, the details in a story evoke images and emotions beyond what they say. "Writing makes the ordinary

stand out," he says. Literature "reshapes experience" and "helps define the world for us."

Consider how the above statements apply to Soto's "Looking for Work," which concerns the events of a single day. Analyze this story to see how Soto uses ordinary details to create a larger picture of a way of life. Using his story as a model, try your hand at a style of writing that "makes the ordinary stand out." Confine yourself to the events of an ordinary day, or just an ordinary morning, and pay attention to the small details that will give your writing the quality of real life.

2.   In her little story "Those Who Don't" Sandra Cisneros makes a point about how people feel about "a neighborhood of another color." Do you find her point valid? Do you know a neighborhood that would be perceived one way by those who live there and another way by "those who don't"? Explain the different points of view.

3.   In "Fifth Avenue, Uptown: A Letter from Harlem" James Baldwin portrays the dehumanizing conditions of life in urban slums. His essay was published in 1960. Consider his description from the perspective of life in a present-day city that you know. In your opinion, can we consider Baldwin's essay "dated" yet, in either its particulars or its overall view? Why or why not?

4.   Sandra Cisneros wrote about the Mexican neighborhood she grew up in, in Chicago; James Baldwin wrote about Harlem; R. A. Sasaki wrote about San Francisco's Japantown. Write about an urban area you know where residents share a particular ethnic, national, or cultural identity. Consider its history, the role this community plays in the life of the larger city, and the quality of life for its residents.

5.   In her essay "Notes from a Native Daughter" Joan Didion describes changes in Sacramento since the end of World War II. In the end Didion acknowledges that the essay is not so much about Sacramento as it is about her own sense of loss in the face of change. Her story could, in fact, be told about other places as well. Consider the place you come from or a place you know well. What changes have you observed in the place? How have these changes affected the quality of life there? Write a description of that place that conveys the way you feel about it, choosing descriptive details to get your point across.

6.   In "On Native Ground" Jim Barnes traces the changes he has seen in the hill country of eastern Oklahoma where he grew up—not the social environment, but the land and the rivers.

He says, "The Fourche Maline River and Holson Creek flow through much of what I have written. . . . My sense of place is inexorably linked to these two streams and to the prairies and woods between them." Barnes is concerned with the effects of human progress on the land. Write about a place you know, focusing like Barnes on the natural environment. Find out what the place used to be like, and how and why it has changed in recent years. Like Barnes, use concrete details to convey your sense of the place.

7.   In "The Sense of Place" Rolando Hinojosa says, "One's fidelity to history is the first step to fixing a sense of place, whether that place is a worldwide arena or a corner of it, as is mine." Do you share his point of view? Consider your own sense of a particular place; to what extent does your connection to it depend on your knowledge of its history? Why do you think this is?

TOPICS for Section V:
Writing and Social Change

1.   In "Notes to a Young(er) Writer" Sandra Cisneros recalls the feelings she had toward some of her peers in college, "the kids whose daddies were paying for their tuition." As an adult looking back, she says:

> When I think those kids are now the people changing history, the ones in government and business, altering and making our laws, it makes me sad. It makes me sad because they never feel compelled to change the world for anyone but themselves. No understanding of how hard it is to rise above harsh circumstances.

If you were going to school with Cisneros, how would you respond, as a peer, to the attitudes she expresses? What do you think about her adult viewpoint?

2.   In "One Last Time" Gary Soto recalls driving with his brother to West Fresno to find the labor buses "and labor contractors shouting 'Cotton' or 'Beets,' the work of spring." In *The Plum Plum Pickers*, Barrio depicts the role of a labor contractor in the character of Roberto Morales. Despite the rise of the farm-workers' union in the 1970s, such contractors now dominate the farm labor system in California; large growers generally do not hire farmworkers directly, but hire a contractor to bring them in. Find out something about the conditions of migrant

farm labor today. Compare present circumstances with those portrayed by Soto and Barrio. Let your own point of view give your comparison a focus.

3.   Whether or not you are *una mujer de color* (and even if you are not a woman), you are a "companion in writing"; answer Gloria Anzaldua's letter. Take one thing she says if you want, or several points, or the letter as a whole. Just as she does, say what you think.

4.   In "The Transformation of Silence into Language and Action" Audre Lorde addresses her readers: "What are the words you do not yet have? What do you need to say?" When she says "I am . . . a Black woman warrior poet doing my work—come to ask you, are you doing yours?" take her words as directed to yourself. Consider her questions in the context of the whole essay, and respond—to her questions, her essay, her tone, her theme—from your own experience and point of view.

5.   Writing *American Hunger* in the early 1940s, Richard Wright condemned the materialism he saw in U.S. society. Describing the waitresses he worked with in Chicago, he said,

> I often wondered what they were trying to get out of life. . . . They lived on the surface of their days; their smiles were surface smiles, and their tears were surface tears. . . . All their lives they had done nothing but strive for petty goals, the trivial material prizes of American life. . . . I know that not race alone, not color alone, but the daily values that give meaning to life stood between me and those white girls with whom I worked. Their constant outward-looking, their mania for radios, cars, and a thousand other trinkets made them dream and fix their eyes upon the trash of life, made it impossible for them to learn a language which could have taught them to speak of what was in their or others' hearts. The words of their souls were the syllables of popular songs.

Consider this picture in a present-day context. Think about people you know and the circumstances of daily life as you know it. Do you see the "lust for trash" that caused Wright such anguish? Do you believe that materialism blinds people to their own and others' true feelings? Do people ignore the concerns of others in their striving for "the trivial material prizes of American life"—or have "the daily values that give meaning to life" changed from what Wright observed? Reexamine Wright's analysis, and discuss the extent to which it applies today.

6.   James Baldwin in "A Talk to Teachers" says there is a conflict between the interests of a stable society and the purpose of education. A paradox of education in this country, he says, is

that "precisely at the point when you begin to develop a conscience, you must find yourself at war with your society. It is your responsibility to change society if you think of yourself as an educated person."

Reexamine the way Baldwin presents this argument in his essay. What do you think about his view? Explain his position as you understand it, and respond with your own opinion, drawing on your experience, observation of others, and reading.

7. Several writers in this section express, directly or indirectly, the idea that people faced with injustice should rock the boat—do something to cause change in society. Consider the ways some version of this message is conveyed in any of the following: Gloria Anzaldua's "Speaking in Tongues: A Letter to Third World Women Writers," Toni Cade Bambara's "The Lesson," James Baldwin's "A Talk to Teachers," Raymond Barrio's *The Plum Plum Pickers*, and Audre Lorde's "The Transformation of Silence into Language and Action." The authors have chosen various rhetorical forms: letter, story, essay derived from a lecture. As a reader, what do you find most effective, and why? How did you respond when you read the different selections? What do you think of the authors' messages?

8. Speaking at commencement in 1987 at a major U.S. university, Pulitzer Prize-winning historian Leon Litwack told students,

> History teaches us that it is not the rebels or the dissidents who endanger society but rather the unthinking, the unquestioning, the obedient, the silent, and the indifferent. . . . The time to be alarmed about our students is not when they are exercising their freedom of expression but when they are quiet, when they despair of changing society, of even understanding it.

Gloria Anzaldua in "Speaking in Tongues" expresses a similar viewpoint when she says, "writing saves me from [the] complacency I fear. . . . I'm scared of writing but I'm more scared of not writing."

To what extent are Litwack's and Anzaldua's ideas compatible with your own outlook and that of your fellow students? In what ways do you prefer to exercise your freedom of expression, as both of them advocate? Draw on your reading and experience to develop your response and support your point of view.

9. In his book *The ABC of Reading* (1934) the poet Ezra Pound wrote, "Artists are the antennae of the race." Extending his "biological analogy," he explained:

> Artists are the antennae; an animal that neglects the warnings of its perceptions needs very great powers of resistance if it is to

survive. . . . A nation which neglects the perceptions of its artists declines. After a while it ceases to act, and merely survives.
There is probably no use in telling this to people who can't see
it without being told.

Evaluate Pound's analogy by considering how it applies or does
not apply, in your view, to any one or more of the writers in
this section. Do you agree with his last sentence?

TOPICS ACROSS SECTIONS

1. Sandra Cisneros in "Ghosts and Voices: Writing from Obsession" says, "It's ironic I had to leave home to discover the voice
   I had all along, but isn't that how it always goes." James Baldwin in "The Discovery of What It Means to Be an American"
   and Simon J. Ortiz in "The Language We Know" also talk about
   what one can learn by leaving home. Compare these authors'
   experiences: Why did they go? What did they discover? What
   effect did their experiences have on them?
       What has been your own experience of leaving home? Like
   Cisneros, Baldwin, and Ortiz, have you learned things you
   couldn't have learned without leaving? Why do you think this
   is?

2. Paule Marshall, in "From the Poets in the Kitchen," comments
   on the theory that "the idiom of a people, the way they use
   language, reflects not only the most fundamental views they
   hold of themselves and the world but their very conception of
   reality." In a similar vein, Simon J. Ortiz in "The Language We
   Know" recalls his experience of learning English:

   > It has occurred to me that I learned English simply because I
   > was forced to, as so many other Indian children were. But I know,
   > also, there was another reason, and this was that I loved lan-
   > guage, the sound, meaning, and magic of language. Language
   > opened up vistas of the world around me, and it allowed me to
   > discover knowledge that would not be possible for me to know
   > without the use of language.

   If you know more than one language, does your experience bear out the observations made by Marshall and Ortiz?
   How do you think your knowledge of another language shapes
   your perception of the world?

3. Bell hooks in "Talking Back" and Paule Marshall in "From the
   Poets in the Kitchen" emphasize the power and richness of the
   "world of woman talk." How do the two writers value and respond to their special experience of women's talk? How do they

describe the circumstances that both encourage and proscribe women's speech? How universal or how culture-specific do you think their observations are? Compare your own knowledge or recollections of adult women's talk and analyze its effect on you. Write from the perspective of your own experience and your reading of hooks, Marshall, and any other writers.

4. In "From the Poets in the Kitchen" by Paule Marshall, one of the women gathered in the kitchen says, "In this man world you got to take yuh mouth and make a gun!"

In *Black Boy*, Richard Wright tells how he felt when he first read H. L. Mencken's writing: "This man was fighting, fighting with words. He was using words as a weapon, using them as one would use a club."

In your judgment, do any of the writers in this collection use words as a weapon? If so, are they effective? What do you think about their writing? Explain and support your point of view with reference to your reading.

5. Kurt Vonnegut, Jr., says in "How to Write with Style,"

> Many Americans grow up hearing a language other than English, or an English dialect a majority of Americans cannot understand. All these varieties of speech are beautiful, just as the varieties of butterflies are beautiful. No matter what your first language, you should treasure it all your life.

Other writers discuss the influence of language heard in their childhood: Sandra Cisneros ("Ghosts and Voices: Writing from Obsession"), Simon J. Ortiz ("The Language We Know"), Paule Marshall ("From the Poets in the Kitchen"), and Gloria Anzaldua ("Speaking in Tongues: Letter to Third World Women Writers"). Is your experience like any of theirs? Write about the way English, or a language other than English, was used in your childhood environment. How do you feel about the language of your childhood? How does it influence your language use now?

6. Consider the recollections of childhood in the writing of Sandra Cisneros and Gary Soto. Like many people, these authors consciously compared their own family life with that of the ideal families depicted on television.

Watch some currently popular show that centers on the life of a TV family. What values are communicated in it? What image of family life is portrayed? Based on your own experience and your reading, consider how that image relates to ordinary, real family life as you know it. What do you think of this show and its message(s)?

7. In the writing of bell hooks ("Keeping Close to Home"), Gary Soto ("Like Mexicans" and "One Last Time"), and Sandra Cisneros ("Notes to a Young(er) Writer"), the authors are concerned with the way social class affected their sense of identity as they were becoming educated adults. Compare the attitudes expressed by these writers, and relate your own experience to theirs (even if it is very different). Consider what role social class plays in your own approach to your education, the support you have for it, the value you place on it, and your goals.

8. In "The Sense of Place" Rolando Hinojosa offers what he says he considers a debatable statement: "What spine one has is formed early in life, and it is formed at a specific place; later on when one grows up, one may mythicize, adopt a persona, become an actor, restructure family history, but the original facts of one's formation remain as facts always do."

   James Baldwin expresses a similar sentiment in "The Discovery of What It Means to Be an American" when he says: "Even the most incorrigible maverick has to be born somewhere. He may leave the group that produced him—he may be forced to—but nothing will efface his origins, the marks of which he carries with him everywhere."

   Based on your own experience, and your reading about others', do you accept these statements? Explain and support your point of view.

9. In "Fifth Avenue, Uptown: A Letter from Harlem" James Baldwin describes the dehumanizing conditions of urban ghetto life in the 1950s. Writing in 1960, he warned: "The country will not change until it re-examines itself and discovers what it really means by freedom. . . . One cannot deny the humanity of another without diminishing one's own: in the face of one's victim, one sees oneself."

   In his introduction to the new edition (1984) of *Notes of a Native Son* Baldwin wrote, "The conundrum of color is the inheritance of every American, be he/she legally or actually Black or White." Looking back at race relations in the United States from the perspective of the 1980s, Baldwin observed, "There have been superficial changes, with results at best ambiguous and, at worst, disastrous. Morally, there has been no change at all and a moral change is the only real one."

   Do you agree with Baldwin's judgment? Why or why not? Argue for your own point of view by drawing on your own experience, observations, and reading.

10. Paula Gunn Allen is a Native American writer and literary

critic. In her book *The Sacred Hoop* (1986) she observes that Native Americans tend "to view space as spherical and time as cyclical, whereas the non-Indian tends to view space as linear and time as sequential." Thus, "traditional tribal narratives possess a circular structure, incorporating event within event, piling meaning upon meaning, until the accretion finally results in a story." Discuss how these ideas are reflected in any of the following stories: N. Scott Momaday, from *The Names*; Rudolfo Anaya, from *Bless Me, Ultima*; Elizabeth Cook-Lynn, "The Power of Horses"; Leslie Marmon Silko, "Yellow Woman"; Simon J. Ortiz, "The Panther Waits."

11. Rolando Hinojosa, in an essay entitled "A Voice of One's Own," reflects on the importance of reading in his early years. He says that his love of books derived from "the example set at home by parents who read to themselves and to each other and who—not once—ever ordered us to read something or . . . denigrated the book or the choice of our reading material."

    Paule Marshall ("From the Poets in the Kitchen"), Cynthia Ozick ("A Drugstore in Winter"), and Richard Wright (in *Black Boy*) write about the importance of reading in their development as individuals and as writers, even though they did not all enjoy the encouragement Hinojosa had. You too have been a reader, perhaps in more than one language, for most of your life. Just as Marshall, Ozick, and Wright have done, write about yourself as a reader. Consider the significance of specific kinds of reading in your experience, and what stands out in your recollections.

12. In "From the Poets in the Kitchen" Paule Marshall recalls her discovery, in the Brooklyn Public Library, of the poetry of Paul Laurence Dunbar and of other writers of the Harlem Renaissance. She says, "What I needed, what all the kids—West Indian and native black American alike—with whom I grew up needed, was an equivalent of the Jewish shul, someplace where we could go after school—the schools that were shortchanging us—and read works by those like ourselves and learn about our history."

    Marshall suggests, in other words, that schools failed to expose children like herself to literature and history with which they could identify. Comment, from your knowledge and experience, on this notion that schools "shortchange" some of the students. Do you think it is true? Explain and support your opinion either way, drawing on your own school experience and your reading.

13. In a number of stories in this collection we see women char-
     acters who by virtue of their culture, race, and gender are dis-
     franchised within the larger society. Consider, for example:
     Ichiro's mother in Okada's *No-No Boy*; the mother in R. A.
     Sasaki's "The Loom"; Rosie's mother in Hisaye Yamamoto's
     "Seventeen Syllables"; Marleen's mother in Elizabeth Cook-
     Lynn's "The Power of Horses"; Mamacita in Sandra Cisneros's
     "No Speak English"; and the women in Paule Marshall's "From
     the Poets in the Kitchen." We see each of these women han-
     dling relationships with husbands, children, and work in an
     alien culture. The women exhibit different responses, different
     ways of coping with the circumstances of their lives.
         Analyze and respond to one or more of these characters.
     Explain the circumstances of the woman's life and her re-
     sponse to them. Consider what the author's purpose might be
     in his or her portrayal of this character. Evaluate the character
     from your own point of view and in terms of your response to
     her as a reader. If you choose to discuss two or more characters,
     let your comparison be shaped by your point of view.

14. Describe the fathers in Okada's *No-No Boy* and Yamamoto's
     "Seventeen Syllables." What circumstances is each man cop-
     ing with in his life? Why does each behave as he does? Argue
     why we should or should not regard either man as a sympa-
     thetic character—that is, a character intended to arouse the
     reader's compassion.

15. N. Scott Momaday, Elizabeth Cook-Lynn, Leslie Marmon
     Silko, and Simon J. Ortiz all come from Native American cul-
     tures with a strong oral tradition. All reflect this tradition in
     their writing; stories passed down from older generations play
     a role in their written stories. In Momaday's passage from *The
     Names*, Cook-Lynn's "The Power of Horses," Silko's "Yellow
     Woman," and Ortiz's "The Panther Waits," the protagonists
     hear stories that have come down from older people, but they
     are not all the same; the oral stories within the written stories
     play somewhat different roles. Examine the nature and func-
     tion of stories told in any of these passages. Explain their sig-
     nificance to the central character in the written story.

16. In the mid-1940s Richard Wright and James Baldwin met in
     New York. Wright, who was 16 years older and already a rec-
     ognized author, inspired and encouraged Baldwin to persist in
     his determination to be a writer. Though they came from dif-
     ferent parts of the country and had different backgrounds, the
     two men shared some common perceptions and experiences.
     Both understood the debilitating effects of internalized racism.

Both emphasized the need to understand the social roots of racism; both saw basic contradictions in American society, which they determined to address in their writing.

Based on your reading of Wright's and Baldwin's work, compare the two men's visions of American society, and discuss how their views motivated and influenced their writing.

17. "The past is all that makes the present coherent," says James Baldwin in "Autobiographical Notes." Many writers stress the importance of knowing about history, in different ways and from different points of view. Consider, among others, the following readings:

> James Baldwin, "Autobiographical Notes" and "A Talk to Teachers"
>
> Elizabeth Cook-Lynn, "You May Consider Speaking About Your Art"
>
> Rudolfo Anaya, "The New World Man"
>
> N. Scott Momaday, from *The Names*
>
> Paule Marshall, "From the Poets in the Kitchen"
>
> Joan Didion, "Notes from a Native Daughter"
>
> Rolando Hinojosa, "The Sense of Place"

Examine the views of one or more writers on this topic. What is the significance of past events in the writer's eyes, and how does knowledge of the past affect her or him as an individual and as a writer? Explain your interpretation of the writer's message, and respond with your own opinion based on your experience and reading.

18. In a recent interview, Leslie Marmon Silko rejected such distinctions as "Native American literature," "black literature," or "Jewish literature." She said, "I think what writers, storytellers, and poets have to say necessarily goes beyond such trivial boundaries as origin. There's also the danger of demeaning literature when you label certain books by saying this is black, this is Native American, and then, this is just writing."

In a similar vein, Jim Barnes in "On Native Ground" says,

> I am proud of the Choctaw blood I carry, and I am equally proud of the Welsh blood in my veins. But I object to the term "regional writer" or "ethnic writer" or even "Native American writer," though it may apply to a number of us in a general sense. . . . Whenever the universal grows out of the specific and vision is achieved, you can tell yourself here is art and it should be preserved. . . . There may be works about a place, about a people, by a writer native to the area; but none of this gives anyone the right to catalog or label the works "regional," "Native American," "Black," or whatever.

On the other hand, many writers would probably agree with James Baldwin's observation that "one writes out of one thing only—one's own experience." Do you see these views as compatible? Why, or why not? What would other writers say? As a reader, what is your opinion about this issue? Draw on your reading to support your point of view.

19. In "The Transformation of Silence into Language and Action" Audre Lorde warns against the "separations that have been imposed upon us and which so often we accept as our own." Lorde gives as an example a teacher who says, "I can't possibly teach Black women's writing—their experience is so different from mine." In Lorde's view, we need to beware of the "endless ways in which we rob ourselves of ourselves and each other."

In *Talking Back* bell hooks offers a similar point of view as she recalls a course on Contemporary Black Women Novelists she taught to an all-white class at Yale. Many of the students were uncomfortable that there were no black women in the class. Hooks writes,

> I stressed that the ideal situation for learning is always one where there is diversity and dialogue, where there would be women and men from various groups. But I also insisted that we should all be capable of learning about an ethnic/racial group and studying its literature even if no person from that group is present. I told students that I did not think that I needed to be a white man to understand Hemingway's *The Sun Also Rises* nor did I think I needed to be in a classroom with white men to study this novel. However, I do recognize that as a black woman reading this white male writer I might have insights and interpretations that would be quite different from those of white male readers. . . . I would, however, consider my insights equally valuable.

What do you think of Lorde's and hooks's ideas? How do they relate to your own experience of studying multicultural literature?

20. In an essay called "Translating Literature into Life" (1935) the British writer Arnold Bennett challenged his readers:

> What is the object of reading unless something definite comes of it? . . . I will ask you to take down any book at random from your shelves and conduct in your own mind an honest inquiry as to what has been the effect of that particular book on your actual living. If you can put your hand on any subsequent period, or fractional moment, of your life and say: 'I acted more wisely then, I perceived more clearly then, I felt more deeply then, I saw more beauty then, I was kinder then, I was happier then, than I should have been if I had not read that book'—if you can honestly say this, then your reading of that book has not been utterly futile. But if you cannot say this, then the chances are that you have been studying a manual of carpentry while

continuing to sit on a three-legged chair and to dine off an orange box.

Evaluate your own recent reading according to Bennett's standards. Can you consider any of it worthwhile by his criteria? Why or why not?

21. In an essay called "Why I Write" (1946) the British author George Orwell wrote:

> I think there are four great motives for writing, at any rate for writing prose. They exist in different degrees in every writer, and in any one writer the proportions will vary from time to time, according to the atmosphere in which he is living. They are:
>
> 1. Sheer egoism. Desire to seem clever, to be talked about, to be remembered after death, to get your own back on grownups who snubbed you in childhood, etc. etc. . . .
>
> 2. Aesthetic enthusiasm. Perception of beauty in the external world, or, on the other hand, in words and their right arrangement. Pleasure in the impact of one sound on another, in the firmness of good prose or the rhythm of a good story. Desire to share an experience which one feels is valuable and ought not to be missed. . . .
>
> 3. Historical impulse. Desire to see things as they are, to find out true facts and store them up for the use of posterity.
>
> 4. Political purpose—using the word "political" in the widest possible sense. Desire to push the world in a certain direction, to alter other people's ideas of the kind of society that they should strive after. . . .
>
> It can be seen how these various impulses must war against one another, and how they must fluctuate from person to person and from time to time.

To what extent do you think Orwell's analysis applies to any of the writers in this collection? Explain and support your point of view with specific references to your reading.

22. Imagine that you have been appointed to a committee charged with revising the curriculum for high school English in your community. In this imaginary scenario, students are required to take a course in American (U.S.) literature. The traditional "classics" will be represented, of course. In your role as a committee member, would you additionally recommend including any of the authors you have read in this collection? If so, which would you consider most important for high school students in your community to study? Write your recommendations, and explain your choices.

23. Go to the library, talk to people, and use whatever appropriate resources are available to you, to conduct a small-scale research project: Investigate some aspect of the social, political, or historical context of the writing in this collection. Make your topic specific enough that you can discuss it in detail in a

short paper. Write an essay on the topic that not only presents information but takes a point of view as well.

The following topics are examples suggested by the readings; they are presented as general ideas, not narrowed down or specified. In most cases, these suggested topics are allusions in passages. If you look back over readings that have interested you, you will find additional topics to investigate.

- The Battle of Wounded Knee
  (related writing: Elizabeth Cook-Lynn)
- Indian school system
- Termination policy
- Tecumseh
  (related writing: Simon J. Ortiz)
- Indian territory
- The Removal Act of 1830
  (related writing: Jim Barnes)
- Yellow Woman stories
  (related writing: Leslie Marmon Silko)
- La Virgen de Guadalupe
- Aztlan
- Curanderas
  (related writing: Rudolfo Anaya)
- The Harlem Renaissance of the 1920s
  (related writing: Paule Marshall, Langston Hughes, Richard Wright)
- Life during the Great Depression
  (related writing: Cynthia Ozick, Paule Marshall, Jim Barnes)
- Jim Crow
- Brown vs. Board of Education and public school desegregation
  (related writing: Richard Wright, James Baldwin, Audre Lorde)
- Public housing projects and postwar "urban renewal"
  (related writing: James Baldwin)
- The internment of Japanese-Americans during World War II
- No-no Boys
- The "Reparations Bill" (Civil Liberties Act of 1988)
  (related writing: John Okada, Toshio Mori, R. A. Sasaki)
- Migrant agricultural labor in California

- Undocumented farm workers
  (related writing: Raymond Barrio, Gary Soto)
- Job training and rehabilitation programs in federal or state prisons
  (related writing: Piri Thomas)
- Virginia Woolf's *A Room of One's Own*
  (related writing: Sandra Cisneros, Gloria Anzaldua)
- The Before Columbus Foundation
- Small presses and the U.S. publishing industry
  (related writing: Ishmael Reed and others)

24. Investigate an author's life and viewpoints, to provide a context for your reading of his or her work. Find out what the writer's major concerns and outlooks are or were. Consult such sources as biographies, autobiographies, articles, and interviews.

25. Read a book-length work by one of the authors represented in this anthology. Write a paper based on your reading of this book and possibly some secondary sources as well. Devise your own topic, perhaps adapting one of the following general approaches, as appropriate:

- Consider what the author has said about being a writer, and her or his goals as a writer, in this anthology. Relate the book you read to the ideas of the writer as presented in these shorter works. Present your own point of view about the writer's work.
- Choose a theme, character, or issue from the book that seems significant or thought-provoking to you. Discuss how this theme, character, or issue is treated and developed in the book. Present your own point of view about it.
- Find out about the social, political, or historical context in which the author writes (or wrote). How does this context help you understand this writer's views and purpose for writing? How does it help you understand the book you read?

Whatever topic you choose, your task is to investigate, explain, interpret, and argue: explore and explain ideas based on your reading; interpret what the text means or what the author's intent is; and take a point of view on your topic and support it. Develop and support your discussion with sufficient reference to the book to make your paper both understandable and informative to a reader who hasn't read the book.

Author and Title
Index ⸻